DIPLOMACY OF A TINY STATE

Second Edition

In diplomacy, one may be in the best of terms one day but the next day when the tables are turned, one could be regarded as an enemy for reasons of the state. This is what I would call 'the national feeling'. When two nations were on good terms, their ambassadors behaved cordially, but once the nations quarrelled, the ambassadors found it difficult to maintain the personal friendship.

World Scientific
Singapore • New Jersey • London • Hong Kong

Published by

World Scientific Publishing Co. Pte. Ltd.

P O Box 128, Farrer Road, Singapore 9128

USA office: Suite 1B, 1060 Main Street, River Edge, NJ 07661

UK office: 73 Lynton Mead, Totteridge, London N20 8DH

DIPLOMACY OF A TINY STATE

ISBN 981-02-1219-4

Printed in Singapore.

Foreword

The picture of the diplomat as an elegant if somewhat devious character dedicated to advancing the interests of his country by hook or by crook is an exaggeration which does little justice to a profession whose importance has grown in recent years. Today international developments have as much impact on the affairs of a country as domestic factors. The purpose of diplomacy is to so influence foreign countries as to safeguard and promote trade, cultural interests, protection of nationals and above all national security. The primary function of a diplomat is to furnish his government with facts and analysis about the country in which he is serving and at the same time influence the host country in ways calculated to best promote the interests of the ambassador's country.

A good ambassador is one who can provide his government with information and viewpoints beyond what his government can harvest from gleaning newspaper reports and official reports. He must probe beneath the surface of things and extract truths tucked away in normally inaccessible areas of that country's politics and economics. An outstanding ambassador is one who continues to enjoy the confidence and respect of his hosts even when relations between the two countries concerned do from time to time become dangerously strained.

Since Mr Lee retired as Ambassador mutative changes, requiring new approaches to diplomacy, have taken place in international relations. Not only has nearly half a century of Cold War abruptly ended but Communism, which appeared impregnable since the establishment of the first Communist state in Russia over seventy years ago, has disappeared like mist before the rising sun of the 21st century to pose new and equally threatening problems for the world.

For Japan the passing away of an Emperor who had seen the collapse of a Japanese Empire won by the sword and defeated by the sword has also seen the Phoenix-like rise out of the ashes of defeat a Japan which is now one of the great economic powers.

The other major change today is that the centre of world politics and economics has now shifted to the Pacific Ocean which is fringed not only by the great powers but is also by four of the world's six continents.

These are the significant changes which will determine war and peace for the next century and which will challenge diplomacy.

Lee Khoon Choy, whom I have known for many years, possesses in great measure the qualities necessary to make a good ambassador. As you will be made aware in this book he has the gift of empathising with the people in the country he is accredited to without losing his objectivity. He has an insatiable curiosity about other people — a desire to know why they are the way they are. For example, when he was in Indonesia he set out sympathetically but with detachment to probe into the "dream world" of Indonesian culture.

Certainly while he was ambassador he made my task as Foreign Minister easier by his insightful despatches. He made available to me knowledge and understanding which were absent from books and newspaper reports directed at the public in general. As Singapore's ambassador K. C. Lee assessed problems and developments from the standpoint of Singapore's interest.

What do Singapore ambassadors really do abroad? Do they fill their time attending cocktails and banquets or just going to seed?

Mr Lee's memoirs tell you that there is more to being a diplomat than wining and dining.

S. RAJARATNAM

Acknowledgement

First of all, I would like to thank Mr S Rajaratnam who was Foreign Minister when I was a diplomat, and later became Second Deputy Prime Minister, for his kind words in his foreword for this book. I would also wish to thank Mr S R Nathan who was the Permanent Secretary of the Foreign Ministry during the period of my ambassadorship for having read through the whole script and for his critical and constructive suggestions and comments. Last but not least, I am indebted to Mrs Sharon Siddique for her valuable observations particularly on the chapters on Indonesia.

Thanks also to those leaders, civil servants and people mentioned in the book for their contributions which made it possible for me to write this book. My conversation with them, their frank views and opinions gave me an insight to their thinking, beliefs and ways of life.

Contents

Introduction

Very few people in Singapore knew what diplomacy was when she became independent on 9th August 1965. Mr S. Rajaratnam was appointed the Minister for Foreign Affairs when the Republic was established. He too had no diplomatic experience. The tiny state had to handle its own diplomatic relations with the family of nations.

The scarcity of experienced diplomats and the non-existence of career diplomats made the task rather difficult. The Ministry had to fall back on politicians, senior bureaucrats and prominent businessmen to take on the jobs. The Ministry decided on wealthy businessmen as Ambassadors because the Ministry need not worry about paying them a salary, but expected them to spend on entertainment. Singapore then was financially handicapped. Our industrialization had not taken root and we could not afford to overspend. Prominent businessmen like Ko Teik Kin, a rubber magnate formerly Chairman of the Chinese Chamber of Commerce, and Lien Ying Chow, a prominent banker and hotelier, were appointed as High Commissioners to Kuala Lumpur. Tan Siak Kew and Ho Rih Hwa, two prominent businessmen, were also appointed as Ambassadors to Thailand. Later, another businessman Wee Mong Cheng was appointed as Ambassador to Japan. Zi Awyang, one prominent member of the business world who became Ambassador to Thailand and served in Bangkok for nearly decades, died at his post when he reached 90 years old.

For politicians, the first to become Ambassador was Kenny Byrne, former Minister for Labour, who was appointed High Commissioner to New Zealand and then later to India and Iran. I was the second politician to be appointed as Ambassador to

Egypt, then later Indonesia. Then came Yaacob Mohamed, Minister of State, who went to the Philippines, then later India and Egypt. Yong Nyuk Lin, the former Minister of Education and later Minister of Communication, went to London as High Commissioner for a short period. When I returned from Jakarta, Rahim Ishak, Minister of State took over and then handed over to Othman Wok, Minister of Social Affairs. Other politicians appointed as Ambassadors included Jek Yuen Thong, once Minister for Labour and later Minister for Culture, who was sent to Britain as High Commissioner, and Chiang Hai Sing, who had a sting of Kuala Lumpur, Bonn, then Moscow and now Egypt. J. F. Conceicao, a lecturer in the University, who later became Member of Parliament for Katong was sent to Moscow and later Indonesia and now back to Moscow.

The Ministry also picked professors and university lecturers as Ambassadors. Tommy Koh, Dean of the Faculty of Law, was one of the earliest to be sent to the United Nations as our Permanent Representative. He stayed in New York the longest. He was replaced by the next Dean of the Law Faculty Jayakumar, who later became the Minister of Law. Then Chan Heng Chee, another professor of Political Science, took over the job as Permanent Representative of the United Nations. Another Dean of the Faculty of Chemistry Ang Kok Peng was one of the earlier professor robed in as Ambassador. He was the first Ambassador to Japan. His job was taken over by a lecturer from the Nanyang University Loy Kin Fook, who had previously studied in Japan. Another professional Dr. Lee Yong Leng was appointed as High Commissioner for Britain.

The old timers in the diplomatic game were also from the Academic field. Maurice Baker, who had close relations with the then Prime Minister of Malaysia, Tun Abdul Razak was sent to Malaysia as High Commissioner. They became close friends when they studied together in London and they were the earlier founders of the Malayan Forum which was an organisation established to discuss politics in Malaya and Singapore and how to go about achieving independence. In those days Lee Kuan Yew, Dr Goh Keng Swee and Dr Toh Chin Chye were all leading members of the Forum. Since I was then studying Journalism in London, I also participated in the Forum.

Other old timers included Kumaraswamy, a lecturer of Law,

who held posts as Ambassadors to Australia and then the United States. He is now a Judge at the Judicial bench.

Two members of the opposition in the Parliament were also appointed as Ambassadors. The first was A. P. Rajah, a member of the Progressive Party in early 1950s, a lawyer by profession was appointed Ambassador to India and later Australia. The next was the former Chief Minister of Singapore, David Marshall another lawyer by profession was appointed Ambassador to France and has stayed on for nearly 20 years. At 83, he is still our Ambassador to France.

A leading journalist who was a non-politician, Wee Kim Wee, editor of the Straits Times, was appointed High Commissioner for Malaysia. He stayed there for six years and then went to Japan as Singapore's Ambassador for three and a half years and retired for personal reasons. He is now the President of Singapore.

The Ministry gradually built up a team of career diplomats and today they fill most of the Ambassadors posting around the world.

The immediate task of the tiny state in the early independent days was to repair the strained relations created by the separation of Malaysia and Singapore. There was the unhealthy relations between Indonesia and Singapore as a result of Sukarno's confrontation policy. We had also to iron out the soured relations between Singapore and Malaysia after the separation of the two states. We had to pacify the uneasy feelings of the Arab World because we allowed Israeli military advisers and instructors to train our soldiers. Singapore had decided to train its own troops fast when Malaysian soldiers, who were stationed in Farrer Park camps refused to give way to our growing number of soldiers after independence. We were looking for military instructors from various countries including the United Kingdom, America, India, Egypt and other friendly countries. None of them would come to our help because they were afraid to antagonise the Malaysians. At that time, many were sceptical that Singapore could ever survive because she has no natural resources, nor market for our goods. Then came the Israelis who offered to provide the service and we had no alternative but to let them in.

This had antagonised many Arab countries which were fighting the Israelis. Egypt was then the leading country in the Arab World. She was friendly to Singapore but displeased.

The Minister for Foreign Affairs, Rajaratnam sprang a surprise on me one day soon after the 1968 general elections when he called me to his office. I was then Minister of State for Culture. "What about becoming Ambassador to Cairo?" he said. I was taken aback and said I knew nothing about diplomacy. I gave Rajaratnam various reasons why I could not accept the appointment. I told him that I had from my first deceased wife two sons who were in middle school. During this critical time if I were to leave them behind without a mother and they turned bad, I would never forgive myself for the rest of my life. My youngest daughter from my second wife was only six months old.

The other reasons was that as Minister of State for Culture, I had formed the Singapore Arts Council and had raised $1.2 million with a view to establish an Academy of Arts to promote multi-racial dancing, music and drama. I seriously thought that the people of a new nation needed a strong foundation for the cultivation of their cultural stamina. But at a time when the economic and diplomatic survival of the nation took precedence, culture had to take the back seat. When I left for Cairo, my ideal of an Academy fizzled out.

The reasons I gave did not convince Rajaratnam not to consider me as a candidate for Ambassadorship. The next morning the then Prime Minister Lee Kuan Yew called me up to the Istana. We had a long frank discussion. The premier explained to me the significance of my job and said I was the one found most suitable by the Cabinet. He asked me to think about the matter more seriously. At that time, reasons of family matters did not bother our leaders. They had to give way to the problems of survival of the state.

I went home and discussed the matter with my wife and sons who asked me not to worry about them. The next morning, I told Rajaratnam that I would accept the post.

To be frank, when I accepted the job, I did not know what it was to be an Ambassador. Nobody in Singapore could tell me the nature of an Ambassador's job. I did not even know that I would be addressed as 'Excellency' until I had presented my credentials in Cairo. Before I went, I also consulted Ahmed Ibrahim, who was my precedessor, the first Ambassador to Cairo. He advised me not to accept the job because it would be difficult to deal with the Arabs.

I read up all books available on diplomacy and consulted

friends of the diplomatic corp.

I was given two weeks notice to leave Singapore. It was a frantic two weeks. I had to arrange for my sister-in-law to look after my two sons, make new clothings and pack. There were a number of farewell dinners organised by the Hong Lim Constituency and various organisations to which I was their advisers. At the Hong Lim Constituency dinner, Rajaratnam, had to speak as Minister for Foreign affairs to explain to voters why they had to be deprived of my service for one-and-a-half years (that was the original contract). I was away from my constituents for six-and-a-half years. I spent two years in Cairo and later transferred to Indonesia for another four-and-a-half years. I did not resign from the Parliament and still kept the post as Minister of State for Culture and later changed to Minister of State for Foreign Affairs when I was transferred to Indonesia. Whenever I returned to Singapore for consultation, I would meet the people and get in touch with the leaders.

One Member of Parliament from Bukit Merah, Lim Guan Hoo, the one whom I recommended to join the party and who was later chosen as candidate for the Bukit Merah by-election, was a tremendous help to me during my absence from Hong Lim. I appointed him as Adviser to the Hong Lim Peoples Action Party branch and met the people on my behalf for six-and-a-half years. Lim who was a Parliamentary Secretary passed away on 3rd August 1977 after 172 days in a coma. He collapsed in front of Premier Lee at the National Stadium at the 10th anniversary celebrations of the Vigilante Corps. He was suffering from high blood pressure. He was then 38. It was a great pity for he could contribute so much more to the party and government.

When I was appointed Ambassador to Egypt, least did I expect that I would be accredited to four other countries operating from Cairo. Between 1968 and 1970, I was Ambassador to Egypt, High Commissioner to Pakistan, Ambassador to Yugoslavia, Ethiopia and Lebanon, all at the same time. There was a great deal of travelling, arranging for presentation of credentials and after presentation of credentials, meeting Ministers and the diplomatic corp of these countries. I did all the job with a shoestring of embassy staff. I had one first secretary, one third secretary for administration and one personal assistant.

The first time when I went to Pakistan to present credentials, the Foreign Minister Rajaratnam wrote to me stipulating that I would get extra allowance for my extra work. But owing to the stringent rules of the Singapore treasury, his promise was not carried out. He later wrote to me to say that I should take the matter in 'my usual stride'. I laughed it off and did not take the matter seriously.

Our treasury was known for its 'tight purse' policy, or you may call it 'stinginess' when it came to spending on public funds. When I presented credentials to Pakistan, I suggested that I should bring along my personal assistant with me to Islamabad in order to help me out in arranging for appointments. The Ministry rejected my proposal.

I landed in Rawalpindi and stayed at Hotel Intercontinental in early 1969. Protocol arrangement was made to receive me and to send me off as well as providing transport for the presentation of credentials. Other than that, I had to hire my own car and make my own arrangements. After presentation of credentials, I had to call on the Doyen (Head of the diplomatic corp), Foreign Minister and Cabinet Ministers and the Heads of Missions of some of the countries friendly to Singapore. My time in Rawalpindi was limited, for I had to return to Cairo to do my major task. Whenever I hired a car, I had to be sure that the car had a flag pole. I brought our National flag along and personally hoisted the flag on the car. I could not make my appointments while travelling because there was no hand phone then in Rawalpindi. In any case, it would be improper for an Ambassador to phone to another Ambassador to make an appointment. Such things would better be done by their secretaries. I did not have one. I had to rely on the telephone operation of the hotel where I stayed to act as my 'temporary secretary'. Everything could be done with a tip. Of course, we could not claim back any tips from the treasury. Initially, I had to impersonate as my own secretary to speak to an Ambassador's secretary. When the protocol officer sent me off, he asked where was my secretary and I said he had to stay behind to do some work.

It was a gruesome experience. I decided that such things should not be repeated. I wrote back to Singapore and stated that I would not like to be accredited to any other country without a personal assistant. I told the Ministry of my experience, and they allowed me to bring my personal assistant when I presented credentials to Ethiopia, Yugoslavia and Lebanon. Nobody in the Ministry had any experience in presenting credentials in an accredited country and therefore could not understand the difficulties of their Ambassador. That was why they had rejected my proposal in the first instance.

Just to mention another incident of the 'tight fist' money policy of our treasury. When I presented credentials to Emperor Haile Selasie, a tailcoat, a cock hat and two white gloves were required by the Imperial protocol. These were necessities as presentation of credentials to the Emperor 'the King of Kings' was a highly official occasion. I wrote back to the Ministry asking them for money to make the tailcoat. The answer was that I should hire one. I went round Cairo trying to hire for one but there was no such shops. Even if there were such shops, it would be difficult to find one to suit my size. I decided to spend my own money for the tailcoat. I wore it only once in a lifetime. I do not know the whereabouts of this tailcoat.

These were some of the teething problems of diplomacy which an Ambassador of a small country faced when the Ministry lack experience in handling foreign affairs and when the Ambassador had cover more than one country.

Being a tiny budding state with very limited financial resources, it was not possible for Singapore to establish embassies in all the countries she has diplomatic relations. First of all, there was the shortage of diplomatic staff. It was an expensive affair to set up an embassy. One has to locate a premises (either buy or rent an office), then send diplomatic personnels to man it with expenses for public utilities, telephones, faxes and other expenses. It would be much cheaper to make an Ambassador accredited to the countries from a more permanent centre.

How does an Ambassador in Cairo for instance, cover events of four countries to which he is accredited to? In my case, there were Pakistan, Ethiopia, Yugoslavia and Lebanon. It was impossible for me to gather enough information from these countries, without any assistance, to satisfy the requirements of the Ministry. The Ministry did not expect me to carry out an impossible job. What they required of me was to make my presence felt as far as possible. I would sometimes attend their national day or visit these countries from time to time. When I went to present credentials, Ali Bhuto was making exciting and inflammatory speeches right in front of the Intercontinental Hotel where I was staying. The next day, the streets were littered with the ruins of debris, burnt cars and semblance of the aftermath of riots. In Ethiopia, although Emperor Haile Selasie was still in full control, there was already an undercurrent of uneasiness and restlessness among the population. One could smell that something was wrong somewhere when a large junk of wealth was in the hands of a small minority and the large majority lived in blatant poverty. The situation would not last long, I thought. Emperor Haile Selasie later died miserably in a small flat, put under house arrest by military leaders after a coup.

In Yugoslavia, Tito's 'self-management' type of Socialism was undergoing a period of experiment. The man-in-the-street lived harmoniously under Tito's brand of Socialism, a system very much unlike the Russian type of Socialism. It was more liberal, so liberal that striptease show (completely stripped) was allowed in the hotel where I stayed. Although all was well when I visited Yugoslavia several times, I sensed that something was wrong somewhere when I spoke to the Yugoslavian. In fact, nobody in Yugoslavia called themselves 'Yugoslavians' as Singaporean Chinese, Malays and Indians would call ourselves 'Singaporeans'. I have friends who were Serbians, Crotians, Montinegro, Slovians or belonging to other communities. They would always say 'I am a Serbian', 'I am a Crotian' or 'I am a Slovian'. In the Foreign Ministry, for instance, if the Minister was Serbian, the Permanent Secretary must be either Slovian or Crotian and the power of the different communities was distributed accordingly in the various departments. How could a society last long if there was no sense of common belonging? True enough, the political chaos and threat of civil war today in Yugoslavia finally broke out. I least expected it to be that serious.

Many of Yugoslavia's problems would be simplified if its inhabitants could view themselves as citizens of a country rather than members of different communities.

Tito succeeded in molding the mixed ethnic groups into a nation called Yugoslavia. But he failed to mold the people into a cohesive nation called themselves 'Yugoslavians'. Yugoslavia's explosive ethnic mix mowed meekly under his iron fist. He became Europe's Fiddler on the Roof, a maverick communist paid lavish court by both West and East. Even the strongman Tito cannot rule from the grave, his body now faces eviction from its palatial Belgrade shrine. For 35 years, Tito had ruled Yugoslavia and had given peace to the country until his death at the age of 87. But now Tito's Yugoslavia is no more. The Serbians who comprise the country's largest nationality are beginning to question: How did Tito, a Croat, rule Yugoslavia for so long? Serbia, not Croatia, always dominated Yugoslavia in pre-Tito days when the region was known as the 'Balkans Power Peg', its jigsaw of tribes always warring or striking shortlived backroom deals with one another. Serbian and Croatia were traditional enemies. Tito did all he could to weaken Serbia's strength, even carving two semi-autonomous regions belonging to Serbia. The Serbians hated Tito very much but the hatred did not emerged until Tito's death. The anti-Tito campaign was led by extreme-rightwing Serbian nationalist Vojislay Seselij, better known by his nickname 'The Red Duke'. Leader of an armed Serbian extremistist movement known as the Chetniks, Mr. Seselij even threatened to tear up the tomb of Tito and rid Serbia of the 'ghost of the Croat's death' some months ago. He had wanted Tito's body cut into six pieces and distributed amount the six republics 'as a symbol of the way Tito split up Yugoslavia'. These signs reflect the growing nationalism in Serbia, much of which is manipulated by the propagandistic press. Though there has been no official declaration of war, Serbia is in a de facto state of war with neighbouring Croatia, so it is natural that Tito should be the target.

There was a revival of the old rumour that he was not a Croat at all but a Russian who took on the name and identity of a Croat whose death was covered up. Allegations surfaced that he was a Freemason. Legendary stories about his appetite for women were revived — including an actress 60 years his junior. His wife, Jovanka, a mere three decades younger than him, has had her fair share of malicious gossip. Tito's influence was always more in terms of personal might than communist power anyway — his marble tomb where I visited did not display the red communist star of Yugoslavia. Nor did Tito erected towering statue to commemorate his achievements. He did not encourage the cult of Tito but made certain his grip on power. The system of government that he put in place for after his death — which consists of a collective presidency with representatives from each republic and region — is a weak system without him and has broken down in old Balkans squabbling, helped by the Eastern European wave of democracy that has swept away Communist. I met Tito three times. He was quite charming, had charisma. It is a pity that his image should suffer damage after his death.

The same happened to Lebanon, a country which is like heaven when I presented credentials in 1969. Beirut was the 'paradise' for rich Arab oil tycoons. The lavished Phonecia Hotel was something fabulous. The famous Casino Leban provided the grandest show in the world. To be in Beirut was like entering heaven. Today, it is hell. The tragedy was the same now experienced by the Yugoslavians. In Lebanon, religion has the upperhand over race. The Lebanese were mostly Arabs, the minority were Christians. They believed in different Gods and they killed one another over religion. The tragedy for Lebanon is that it is now probably too late for its people to rediscover the many bonds which could unite them. What compounds the tragedy is that Lebanon's future depends to a great extent on the operation of factors and factions outside its control. It is only strong international pressures exerted on all parties to the dispute which could now bring about any movement towards a negotiated compromise.

I was lucky that when I left my post in Belgrade and Beirut, the two countries were still in good shape. If I have to cover the five countries at this juncture I really would not know what to do: Lebanon's internal war has not completely solved, Yugoslavia started a civil war, Ethiopia a serious famine and Pakistan, long split into two countries — Pakistan and Bangladash has undergone earth shaking chances.

Diplomatic assignments to these countries gave me a rare opportunity to have an insight into the societies and when events occur in these countries, make it easier for me to understand the situation.

But my main task in Cairo in 1968 was to pacify the Arabs in anticipation of Singapore's recognition of Israel. How did I carried out my mission?

I realised that Singapore was a tiny budding state. I had only skeleton staff and my funds were limited. I realised that I had to rely on bigger embassies with wider resources to help me. At that time, the America Embassy was closed because the American leaders had deep misunderstanding with President Nasser. The Americans wanted Nasser to join the Baghdad Pact comprising

Iraq, Turkey and Pakistan to stop the advance of Russian Communism, but Nasser wanted to stear a neutral non-aligned policy. Americans refused to give financial support for the Aswan Dam and Nasser went to the Russians for help. Gradually, Nasser became more and more dependent on the Soviet Union until he lost his mobility. Since there was no American Embassy, I cultivated the friendship of Sir Harold Beeley, British Ambassador, who was an expert in the Arabic language and Arabic affairs. Through him, I managed to tap the vast resources of the British Embassy. I was supplied a copy of the translations of all Arab newspapers and comments daily free of charge. I had a good insight into the Arab mind by talking to Sir Harold. I tried to sound him out on the question of recognition of Israel. According to him, most of the French speaking African countries as well as the English speaking Africa countries had already recognised Israel. Some had actually established diplomatic relations. The United Arab Republic meaning Egypt, he said, did not take much offence in the case of those countries which had recognised Israel previously, particularly before the June war. But he warned that they would be very annoyed and agitated about new recognition because this meant moral support to encourage Israel to continue its aggression and to continue to defy the United Nations resolution.

I also cultivated the friendship of the Indian Ambassador Apa Pant, who was close to President Nasser. We became close friends through our common interest in Yoga. I went to his house every Wednesday to do Yoga and to have Indian 'apong' breakfast. Apa had a good insight of Nasser's thinking.

Nobody could ignore the Russian Ambassador, who was then described as 'the overlord' of Egypt. As Egypt was completely dependent on the Soviet Union, the Russian Ambassador became the most important person in the country. The Ambassador, the short stout looking, square faced with a determined square chin behaved like an 'overlord'. When the Russian Embassy celebrated its National Day, nearly the whole Cabinet turned up. The road leading to the Embassy was choked with cars and it was most difficult to shake his hands because of the long queue. It was important to know what the Russians think of Nasser and of Israel.

One Egyptian bureaucrat in the Foreign Ministry who had

helped me a great deal was En El-Din Ramsy, who was then the newly appointed Director of Asian Desk. Ramsy had just returned from Burma where he was Egypt's Ambassador. He learnt how to play golf in Rangoon and was the only Egyptian Ambassador in Cairo who played golf. He was friendly, frank and helpful. We soon became good friends and could speak out our minds frankly. I got the impression that the Egyptians did not mind at all if Singapore recognised Israel, so long as we make a clear stand towards the Arab cause. In other words, we should not condone Israeli occupation of Arab territories and that we still support the United Nation's resolution No. 22.

I also sounded out the reaction of Arab Ambassador in Cairo as to the reaction to the problem of recognition of Israel.

I reported my impressions to Rajaratnam who took note of my recommendations. When Singapore recognised Israel, nothing happened to our Embassy. In fact, I hosted a dinner for the Minister for Justice in my residence. Singapore had explained in our statement of recognition that 'Singapore remains committed to the belief that no country however big or small should be denied the right to exist, the fruits of conquest should not forcibly be converted into spoils of war'. In other words, Singapore did not condone Israel occupation of Arab territories.

My mission was accomplished. There was fear that our Embassy might be burnt or at least faced demonstration. Nothing of that sort had happened. I was relieved.

Three months after we have recognised Israel, Romania also recognised Israel, but they made a mistake of opening up an Embassy in Jerusalam. The Egyptian Government withdrew her Ambassador from Rumania. The Rumanians too withdrew its Ambassador. All Ambassadors of Arab countries boycotted the Rumanian National Day celebrated on 21st August 1969.

In the game of diplomacy, it is necessary to be conscious of the feelings of the host country. We would have suffered the same fate as the Rumanians if we had not taken into consideration the feelings of the Arabs vis-a-vis the Israeli-occupied territories. We made our stand clear in this respect and escaped the wrath of the Egyptians when we recognised Israel.

Having accomplished my mission, I was getting ready to go home to continue my political career. I was all the time concerned about my constituents which I had neglected for two years.

Suddenly, I received a telex from Rajaratnam, requesting me to go to Indonesia as Ambassador. I was flabbergasted. How could they do a thing like that to me? I would be voted out in the next general elections if I neglected my voters too long, I thought. I wrote to Rajaratnam, explaining the reasons for rejecting his request. In his reply, Rajaratnam told me not to worry about my seat in Parliament, for we were a one-party government and that my voters would understand. When I continue to insist that I should return to Singapore, cable came and said my assignment to Indonesia was a Cabinet decision and that I was 'the only suitable man to be trusted with the post in Jakarta'.

My first reaction to my Indonesian assignment was that I had to go to a country where I had to chase away flies with my own hands and where cockroaches could be found inside the tomato ketchup bottle at meals. I had the experience when I visited Jakarta in 1955 for the Bandung Afro-Asian Conference. My memory of Jakarta was a big village with very little modern sanitation. I would have to suffer, I thought.

But I gave some serious thought to my new assignment: I would be going to the biggest and closest neighbour, the largest country in the South-East Asian region and which can do a great deal of harm to Singapore if relations between the two countries were bad. Very few people in Singapore knew much about Indonesia. It would be an advantage for Singapore and for myself if I could go there to understand the country and people better.

Before I went to Indonesia, most Singaporeans including government Cabinet members had a misconception of the Indonesian people. The general perception was that Indonesia was another Malay and Islamic country. We were very defensive because of that perception. I had to start from the bottom, trying to study the culture and characteristics of the people when I arrived in Jakarta. I made friends with people at the top — generals and ministers — as well as with the man-in-the-street. At the beginning, most generals and ministers appeared hostile to me possibly because I was ethnically Chinese.

Two leading Sumatrans gave me a clue to the Javanese society and encouraged me to make a deeper study of the subject. They were Moctar Lubis, the prominent Indonesian writer and author of many books and who was imprisoned by the Sukarno regime and Adam Malik, the journalist turned politician and was Foreign

Minister when I presented credentials. I knew both of them long before I was Ambassador to Indonesia. Both of them were Bataks. The remarks made by Mocktar stuck in my mind and I pondered over them frequently. He said to me when I paid a courtesy call on him soon after I presented credentials: "As a Sumatran, I find it difficult to understand the Javanese mind. The Javanese generally believe that their rulers are sent from heaven to lead them and that they will never fail. God has given the leader the power. Sukarno had bluffed the people for 17 years and yet the Javanese still worship him after his death. When his power was taken away by force, the Javanese said the God had taken away his power'. It was never a practice in those days for Ambassadors to call on journalists. I thought it would be good to cultivate fellow journalists (being one myself and had worked for several newspapers) who were in closer touch with the various strata of society.

I knew Adam Malik when he was Editor-in-chief of Antara News Agency when I went to Jakarta in 1955 for the Bandung Conference. Adam realised that he too could not understand the Javanese when he tried to arrange for Prime Minister Lee Kuan Yew's visit to Indonesia, during the early period of my assignment. He promised me confidently that he could arrange for the visit when I first met him as Foreign Minister. He said it could be done within six months. After having failed to do so as Foreign Minister, he frankly disclosed to me some of his obstacles and revealed to me the persons I had to cultivate — they were all Javanese. He told me frankly once that even he could not understand the Javanese.

I cultivated three top generals — all Javanese. First, it was Sudjono Humardhani, Personal Assistant to President Suharto on economic affairs. In fact, he was the religious adviser to Suharto. Mocktar had told me that Humardhani had gone to Bali to look for Gadja Mada's mask and had placed it at the Presidential Palace for one thousand days. It was a mystical belief that whoever ruled Indonesia needed three things: first, the Gadja Mada's mask, for Gadja Mada had ruled Indonesia during the Madjapahit Kingdom for many decades; second, the 'Kenghwa' in Chinese, a rare type of flowers which grew in the jungle and which could bring prosperity to the country and third, the Gadja Mada's magic kris (an Indonesian type of national sword) which is a symbolism of authority. It seems that the kris was found missing after Sukarno's death.

I struck a close friendship with Humardhani because of our common interest in mysticism and yoga. I was introduced to him by my schoolmate Lim Eng Huai, better known as Adil Nurimba in Indonesian circles. He was my classmate in Chung Ling High School, having gone to Penang to study from Medan. He was a successful shipping magnate when I arrived in Jakarta. He made an arrangement for me to play golf with Humardhani soon after my arrival for they were close friends. I tried to get the Indonesian Ministry of Foreign Affairs to arrange for me to see Humardhani and it took them three months to do so. When the time came for me to call on Humardhani, I had already played golf with him several times. We laughed when we met officially.

Through the courtesy and effort of Humardhani, I was the only Ambassador in Indonesia who had a clear view of the Gadja Mada's mask. It was secretly stored away inside a small temple in Bali and only the Panglima (Commander-in-Chief) of Bali could give instruction to view the mask. I was brought to the temple and the priest made prayers before opening the box and the mask was wrapped in cloth. It was red in colour and had a long nose. It was the mask worn by Gadja Mada and was known to possess mystical powers. It was rumoured that the military officer who took the mask to the Palace died soon after.

My friendship with Humardhani helped me a great deal in understanding the Javanese mind. We talked about Javanese mysticism. It made me understand the difference between a Javanese and a Malay. In the case of Malays, they are predominantly influenced by Islamic teachings, whereas the Javanese has a deeper cultural background with a longer cultural history covering Buddhism and Hinduism.

I discovered that to be a Javanese is not exactly the same as being a Malay. More that half of the Javanese Muslims are 'Abangan', a term describing muslims who are less orthodox and more liberal in their beliefs. For instance, a muslim is supposed to have faith only in Mohammed and Allah whereas the 'Abangan' believes that spirits dealt in stones, trees, statues, kris and many other objects. I was invited by an ex-Ambassador to Singapore who was a muslim but an 'Abangan'. When we entered his house, there was a Chinese stature of an old man made of ivory. He whispered in my ears: "This is the person I consult whenever I have problems. He always provide me the solutions."

I also discovered that the Javanese muslims are liberal in choosing their life partners. A muslim can marry a Christian or Buddhist without having to convert the partner. Thus, in a family the father may be muslim but the mother a christian and the son a buddhist. Such things are common in Indonesia.

I reported all my observations to Singapore and gradually our perception of Indonesia changed.

I brought Humardhani to see Prime Minister Lee Kuan Yew and he gave a gloring report about our leader to President Suharto. But he did not help me finalised my arrangement for Lee Kuan Yew's visit. I found that I had another hurdle to overcome and that was General Sumitro, then the Deputy Commander of Kopkamtib (the Internal Security Department), who was known to be the most powerful military leader in the Suharto regime. I started to cultivate Sumitro's friendship. Sumitro was fat and short with a square face and a mustache. He had a hot temper but was very friendly when in a good mood. Trained in Germany and spoke good German, he was frank and never hide the fact that he could make all his wives happy. He had four wives. I used to play golf with him. A muslim is allowed to marry four wives so long as he can make all of them happy.

During one golf game, Sumitro told me that he was unhappy that he could not meet Prime Minister Lee Kuan Yew when he visited Singapore. He only spoke to Dr Goh Keng Swee and Wong Lin Ken, the then Minister for Home Affairs. He had the impression that Lee Kuan Yew was arrogant and unapproachable. He said he tried to make arrangement to see Lee Kuan Yew through his Ambassador but failed. I told him that I could arrange for him to see Lee Kuan Yew and assured him that he was not arrogant and unapproachable. I said nobody in the Prime Minister's office knew that he wanted to see Lee Kuan Yew. He was taken by surprise and asked me to arrange for the meeting for he had something which President Suharto wanted to explain to Lee Kuan Yew. I asked him for a date and he fixed a date in early April 1972 and told me not to inform his Ambassador Sunarso.

'Keep it a secret and I will teach that person a lesson', he added. I flew back to Singapore and got a date for Sumitro to see Prime Minister Lee.

The two leaders met and spoke for one hour and fifteen minutes. It was a friendly talk covering the reason for Singapore to hang the two Indonesian marines.

Sumitro was really jubilant and happy after meeting Lee Kuan Yew. He said to me 'I am really very happy. It is nonsense to say that your Prime Minister is arrogant. I appreciate that he has been very frank. I want to thank you very much for having arranged this meeting'. The same night we dined and danced till zero hours in the morning at the Maxim.

Meanwhile, I also cultivated the friendship of another powerful and most feared general in Indonesia who was a leading member of Suharto inner circle — General Ali Murtopo, Personal Assistant to the President in Political Affairs. He was a close ally of Sudjono Humardhani.

Having done my job in cultivating the three most powerful Javanese Generals in Suharto regime, I just sat back to wait for a date for Prime Minister Lee Kuan Yew's visit. Adam Malik was happy that I could help him accomplish the task which was difficult for him to do in his position.

It was an uphill battle in my Jakarta mission. I stayed alone in a big bungalow with many servants but without my family. My wife had to look after the children who had to stay in Singapore for their education. I not only had an uphill battle but had to battle with loneliness. Apart from these, my life was in danger when I crossed the third hurdle and all was set for the visit of the Prime Minister. Sometime in the March of 1973, I received a death threat. Two men brought the letter personally to my residence. The letter alleged that the flow of Chinese capital to Indonesia via Singapore was aimed at dominating the Indonesian economy.

It alleged that Singapore was permitting smugglers to operate unchecked between Singapore and Sumatra and that Singapore was determined to wound the Indonesian nation by openly hanging two Indonesian marines. The letter demanded that as Ambassador of Singapore, I must urge the Singapore Government to 'alter' such politics. The letter warned that 'we are not responsible for the safety of the Ambassador and his Embassy staff in Jakarta, if during the month of April, the Ambassador do not make public alterations in the attitude of his Government'. The letter was signed by the representative of the Association of Anti-Chinese Movements in Jakarta, Sastro Damul.

There had already been many murders, kidnaps and assasinations of Ambassadors in several countries by hostile elements. I had to take the threat seriously. I flew back to Singapore and asked for a bodyguard, but it was refused. I went to Thomson Road Police Training to practice shooting, for I possess a revolver as all Ministers to State were provided with one. I slept with my revolver below my pillow and kept alert. I brought my revolver along whenever I attended a reception. I told the Police Commissioner in Jakarta of my plight and he gave me two names in case I needed help.

That letter turned out to be only a threat. Apparently, some elements in Indonesia were not happy with the progress I have made in arranging for Lee Kuan Yew's visit and wanted to test my nerves. If I had not the nerves I could have resigned and when a new Ambassador takes over, the whole visit might be jeopardized. I did not tell my wife about the threat until after my Jakarta assignment.

That was another aspect of risk which an Ambassador had to take. The Ministry could do nothing to help when I faced the problem of personal risk.

When Lee Kuan Yew's visit was fixed, I was recalled for consultation. The first question he asked me was, "How can I make Suharto happy? How can I befriend him?" I took the opportunity to suggest an idea which I had related to Rajaratnam but Rajaratnam preferred that I raise it to him myself. I asked Prime Minister a frank question: "Do you want to be his real friend or just a cordial friend?" of course, he wanted to be Suharto's real friend. Then I suggested that when he was putting flowers to the graves of national heroes in Kalibata, he should also sprinkle some on the graves of the two Indonesians we had hanged. Sometime in 1967, the Singapore Supreme Court sentenced two Indonesian marines to death sentence for sabotage in Singapore, killing three persons. This appealed to Privy Council without success. We hanged them despite President Suharto's appeal to our government not to hang them. They were treated as heroes by the Indonesian authorities and were buried in Kalibata (the burial ground) reserved for nation heroes. I told the Prime Minister not to get angry with my suggestion in the first instance. He was taken aback by my suggestion and asked me to explain why he should do the things I had suggested. I explained to him the Javanese belief in the existence of soul. I had by then acquired a deeper understanding of the Javanese mind. I said it would be difficult for Suharto to consider him as a good friend if he had not pacified the souls which Singapore had hung. In Java, it was not uncommon for leaders to consult souls in front of their graves for advise. The Prime Minister said he needed time to think it over and would let me know of his decision. He was afraid that the Indonesians might take the gesture as a token of apology and the newspapers would say he had apologized for his misdeeds.

When Lee Kuan Yew sprinkled flowers on the graves of the two Indonesian marines, I saw tears flowing down from the cheeks of Rukmito, Indonesian Ambassador to Singapore. The other Generals present too were moved. The next morning, all Indonesian newspapers praised Lee Kuan Yew for his magnanimity and that he was a 'great leader'.

Lee Kuan Yew's trip to Indonesia was an unprecedented success. He wore batik for the first time following my advice and that took the Indonesian hosts by surprise. He had never worn a batik for a long time since the breakoff with Tengku Abdul Rahman.

I had accomplished my second mission. With the closer personal relations between Lee Kuan Yew and Suharto, the two countries got on very well and as years gone by developed mutual trust, understanding and friendship.

The tie up of friendship between Singapore and Indonesia had strengthen the unity and development of Asean. It was difficult for Asean to make any headway when the two leading countries were not on good terms.

After my mission in Jakarta, it appears that the Ministry had wanted me to carry on despite the fact that I had done four years and that I was a politician. I wrote to Lee Kuan Yew and requested that I be given a break. I returned to Singapore after serving in Indonesia for four and a half years.

It was a satisfying job for me. In fact, when Dr Goh Keng Swee, the then Deputy Minister and Defence Minister found that I was not making headway after two years in Jakarta, he advised me to call it a day. He said "Don't waste your time, the Indonesians are not going to invite Lee Kuan Yew for a visit". I told Dr Goh that it was not my habit to abandon a job half done and that I needed more time to finish my mission. For my contribution towards establishing better relations between Singapore and Indonesia, President Suharto bestowed on me 'Bintang Bakti Utama', the highest service award.

The Ministry's next target was Communist China. In 1974, China was still in the midst of the cultural revolution. In 1975, Rajaratnam and I visited Beijing for the first time. The strain caused by the cultural revolution was still visible. Nobody would speak openly and many of our old friends and former newspaper colleagues and even relatives shunned to see us. I tried to contact one common friend of ours Xiao Chien, a leading journalist who was once a room-mate of Rajaratnam in London. But we were told that they could not find him. Even my own brother who stayed in China for 22 years dared not talk to me openly in a private room in Beijing. I asked him how was life in China, he said while looking at the ceiling: "All is well under the leadership of Chairman Mao Tse-Tung". Later when he left with his wife, she slipped a note into my hands which said "Get us out of this country as quick as possible." I sneaked out one evening from my hotel and went to a small Overseas Chinese hotel where my brother was living and there he broke into tears and told me the sufferings he had endured in China. I managed to get them out of China through the help of the then Foreign Minister Chiao Kuan Hua.

That was the tight situation China was experiencing when we arrived. We met Chou En-Lai and had an hour's discussion with him about the prospect of establishing relations between the two countries. Chou En-Lai was then hospitalised with cancer. He died several months after we left. When we visited China again in 1976 with Prime Minister Lee Kuan Yew, Chou En-Lai had passed away and our top leaders had to see Chairman Mao, another leader who was virtually sinile. We visit many places including Yenan, the Mecca of Chinese Communism. In 1980, I arranged for the second visit of Lee Kuan Yew to China and after that relations between the two countries moved rapidly. Singapore citizens were allowed to visit China without much restrain after Lee Kuan Yew's second visit to China. There was less fear of the Chinese interfering with the internal affairs of Singapore and for that internal affairs of Asean countries after Lee Kuan Yew's second visit. It was felt that it would take China many more years to reach the economic standards of the outside world and that China would need a great deal of help from foreign countries particularly from Chinese abroad.

Although Singapore's relations with China became closer and closer as years went by, she did not establish diplomatic relations with China because Prime Minister Lee Kuan Yew had promised not to do so until after Indonesia has established diplomatic relations. Early this year, when Indonesia established diplomatic relations with China, Singapore followed and now we have an Ambassador in Beijing.

Besides promoting ties with China, I took up various assignments as leader of Singapore's mission to Iran to attend the ruling party's anniversary celebration as well as the non-aligned Ministers Conference in Cuba. Together with Prime Minister Lee Kuan Yew, we also visited Egypt, Yugoslavia and then once again Iran when the Shah of Iran was still powerful.

To be involved in the foreign affairs of a small state, one has to make many journeys. At home, I had the first experience of helping to run a foreign ministry. It meant a lot of reading. We got weekly reports from Ambassadors relating events of each individual countries. They had to keep the Ministry informed of the political, economic, cultural and social events and their changes. It was an interesting experience. Some reports were interesting. They were concise and to the point. Others however were boring and irrelevant. When I come across boring reports, I would cast them aside for the archieves. The good reports were invariably summarised and sent to the Cabinet for their reference. Sometimes, the full report was sent to keep them informed of happenings throughout the world.

When I came back from Jakarta, I thought that was the end of my diplomatic career. I never imagine that I would be sent abroad again as Ambassador. After the middle of 1970, Lee Kuan Yew started to speak up his mind about wanting new blood to take over. The warning became stronger as 1980s approached. Many new blood were already introduced into the party and government. When general elections were around the corner in 1984, I made up my mind to quit politics. I was already 60 and thought it was futile to compete with the younger blood who were more qualified than myself. I announced to my constituents in Braddell Heights where I experienced two walkovers that I had decided to step down. That took them by surprise for I was still physically strong.

The next morning after my announcement, I received a call from Foreign Minister S. Dhanabalan offering me the post of Ambassador to Japan. The post was kept vacant after Wee Kim

Wee had resigned because of personal reasons. The Ministry could not find anyone suitable for the job. Since I had six and half years of experience in diplomacy having served in six countries, he wanted to know whether I would accept the job. I consulted my wife and she agreed to the idea. But we insisted that the children will have to come along to stay in Japan. I did not want to stay alone again as I did in Jakarta. Loneliness was too bitter an experience for me in Jakarta. For that matter, my wife had to bear the complete burden of looking after the family during my absence.

Forty eight years ago, when I came out of my hiding place in Bukit Brapit, off Bukit Mertajam (I was hiding from the Japanese because I was deeply involved in anti-Japanese activities in school), I went for three months intensive course and became a teacher in Japanese. Every morning, I had to bow to Tenno Heika (the Japanese Emperor) in the school playground facing east. How could I foresee that 48 years later, I would be appointed as Ambassador to Japan and present credentials to him. In those days no Japanese were allowed to lift his eyes on the Emperor. When I presented credentials to him on July 10, 1984, I look at the Emperor straight in the eyes, which were so small that they were almost invisible. He was short and frail. This was the man who had once ruled the whole of Asia and South East Asia with a tight fist and who was regarded as 'God' to the Japanese.

Emperor Hirohito has lost all his powers after the Japanese defeat. But by going down to his people, shaking their hands to encourage them to work hard and through the Japanese faith in their 'Tenno Heika', Japan rose from the debris of a devastated country to that of an economic giant - all within 40 years. It was the inspiration and leadership given by the Emperor that gave them strength to rebuild their country.

Had the Americans and the Allied powers carried out the suggestion to do away with Emperor, one would have doubts if the Japanese could revive their economy so quickly.

My assignment to Japan gave me an opportunity to study the reasons behind her rapid economic recovery. These reasons are stated in the chapter 'Myth and Reality Japan'. In this chapter, I also spell out various Japanese racial characteristics that helped to make Japan an economic giant and also explains why the country is rich but the people poor.

Of all the countries that I was assigned to, Japan was the most comfortable and enjoyable. First of all, she was the most advanced economically and scientifically. One could get anything under the sun so long as one has the means. It was a country where I had no specific mission to perform because relations between Singapore and Japan was cordially good. It was only a matter of helping to attract more Japanese capital investment to Singapore and of sizing up the political changes in Japan.

I was in Japan for four years and two months. I saw the once popular and powerful Kakuei Tanaka losing ground and later paralysed after the Lockheed scandal. I witnessed the rise and fall of Nakasone, one of the most popular and dynamic Prime Minister after the war. When I left Japan, Takeshita, one of Tanaka's men was Prime Minister. I watched with great interest the inner-feud that went on between Tanaka and Takeshita and how with the superiority of his political funds, he gained the upper hand over Tanaka's nominee Nikaido. During my term in Japan, I came into contact with three Foreign Ministers - first Shintaro Abe, then Kunanari and then Uno who later became Prime Minister and resigned in disgrace. When Kunanari was Foreign Minister, I had an interesting encounter with him as the Dean of Asean Ambassadors. Japan was about to send her Ex-Foreign Minister Sakurauchi to Hanoi and Phom Penh when Japan had not recognised the Heng Samrin regime of Cambodia. Asean Ambassadors in Tokyo felt that Sukurauchi's visit to Cambodia meant Japan's swift in policy of non recognition of Cambodia. I tried to make an appointment for Asean Ambassadors to see Kunanari on an urgent basis but he was too busy and could not see us until a few days later. When we saw him, he appeared rather impatient and said we could have whispered to the ears of his subordinates. In other words he was hinting that we should not have wasted his time. I was rather annoyed with his arrogance and told him abruptly that we had special mandate from our government to see him urgently over Japan's policy and we were not wasting his time. He was rather startled by my raised voice and began listening to our arguments. The next day, Sakurauchi cancelled his trip to Cambodia. That was an example of how smaller countries like Asean could exert influence on a more powerful country like Japan if we were united in our stand. On several other occasions, we had successfully put pressure on Japan to accommodate our views.

Asean Ambassadors were a privilege group much envied by the diplomatic corp. The Japanese Gaimusho (Ministry of Foreign Affairs) officials gave special attention to Asean Ambassadors because Japan considered Asean to be an important hinterland with vast natural resource and of strategic importance to Japan. In fact, Prime Minister Nakasone, who was excellent in diplomacy, sent a roast turkey to Asean Ambassadors on their birthday. I was told that he did this to only the American Ambassador and Asean Ambassadors.

Being a politician myself, I took a great interest in Japanese politics. I mixed with politicians from the ruling Liberal Democratic Party, the Socialist Party, the Komeito as well as the Communist Party. I studied the Japanese political system as well as Japanese bureaucracy. I also got in touch with leaders in the cultural field — famous Japanese artists, musicians as well as religious leaders. Fundamentally, I wanted to know the Japanese mind. In Japan, I took the opportunity of studying the nature of Japanese thinking which to my mind was important to Singapore. Our leaders have always spoke of learning from Japan without much knowledge of the Japanese mind. I can see the one useful thing we learnt from Japan is quality control and how to increase productivity — in other words, the Japanese way of promoting productivity. In several other matters, Singapore is completely different from the Japanese society. For instance, Japan has never allowed its society to be Aglicized. Japan is the most scientifically and economically advanced country in Asia and for that matter one of the most advanced in the world. The Japanese did not obtained their knowledge of science through English or any other Western language. They did not Anglicized the population in order to achieve scientific and economic advancement. Less than one percent of the population speaks English. The young people learn their first lesson of English when they reach Middle School. In Singapore the entire population has been Anglicized because English has become the first language and the mother tongue becomes a second language. This is where I think we are not learning from Japan. The other problem is Elitism. The Japanese parents do not encourage their offsprings from sticking their necks out to show they are smarter than others. There is a proverb which says 'A nail that sticks out is nailed down'. They taught their offsprings to rely on collective performance and take on collective responsibility. One ups-manship is always discouraged. There are no honours degrees in Japanese universities. Everybody passed out with an ordinary degree. The students are not trained in the university but receive their first training when they join the multi-national or government service.

In Singapore, elitism is encouraged to the extent of starting elite schools. Promotion in the civil service in most multi-national companies as well as politics is based on the academic qualifications of candidates. There is a tendency of the elitist trying to outshine one another, everyone trying to climb over another's head. A candidate is promoted according to his academic qualification and whether he has a helicopter view. Experiences do not count. In politics one high-flyer can be promoted to be a full Cabinet Minister soon after he is elected even for the first time.

Elitism is non-existent in Japanese politics. No single member of Parliament becomes a Cabinet Minister until he has been elected five times. Before a Cabinet is formed, leaders of all factions will present a list of Members of Parliament who have been elected at least five times to the Prime Minister for consideration as a Cabinet Minister.

Singapore and Japan are two completely different world in terms of elitism. The Japanese will always respect the elderly statesmen whereas in Singapore there is a tendency for young leaders to forget elderly statesmen however much they may have done for the nation.

In most countries that I have served, for instance in Egypt, Indonesia and Japan, diplomats especially Ambassadors are given a special reception by the Foreign Ministry with the Foreign Minister personally thanking them for having served the country. In Singapore once an Ambassador has served his term, he is forgotten. The Ministry is quick in demanding for the return of their diplomatic passports including that of their children. When I returned to Singapore after my Japan assignment, the Ministry asked me to return my passport the very next day. The protocal officer was efficient in his duties.

A fellow colleague of mine who had served in Taiwan as Singapore commercial representative, William Cheng, told me of his unhappy experience when he had completed his duties in Taiwan. Upon return to Singapore he went to see the Director of Administration to report the completion of his task. He asked the Director what was expected of a retired diplomat. The director said: 'You don't have to come again.' When he wanted to surrender his diplomat passport, the Director who was in an impatient mood said: 'leave it on the counter'.

William was flabbergasted. Was this the way for the Ministry of Foreign Affairs to treat someone who had served the country conscientiously for nine years. The same treatment was applied to many other of my fellow colleagues who had served abroad as Singapore ambassadors. There was not even a farewell or thank-you handshake from the Minister, nor from the Permanent Secretary, not to mention a golden handshake.

This is the normal Singapore style of 'utilitarian approach' to services done. One is soon forgotten when one leaves the service or position. The Ministry thinks that it is unnecessary to say thank you to the ambassadors when they have fulfilled their tasks. Once you have finished your job, you are non-existence.

I returned in July, near National Day. I was aware of the intensive preparations for that important day. I was expecting an invitation to attend his auspicious day for the nation for which I had helped to build. That invitation never came, I had to watch the National Day celebration from the television. I met Tommy Koh, our Ambassador to the United states who had returned to Singapore for consultation from Washington. He asked me: 'Why didn't you attend the National Day?' I replied: 'I did not receive any invitation.' He exclaimed: 'How can it be, there must be a mistake somewhere.' In 1989, I received an invitation to attend the National Day with special seats just behind existing Members of Parliament. Apparently, it was negligence on the part of the organisers. But till today, I have not received any invitation to attend the National Day reception at the Istana whereas the ordinary members of Citizens Consultative Committees and other grassroot leaders are invited. Not only myself, but all ex-members of Parliament who have served the country for many years have not been invited to such functions. Although I was awarded the Distinguished Service Order (Darjah Utama Bintang Cemerlang) or D.U.B.C. in September 1990, for my contribution to the building of the nation, I was never invited to National Day reception at the Istana after I retired from the Parliament.

I remember the late Minister of State and Ambassador to the Philippines, India and Egypt, Mohammed Yaacob having told me once a Malay Proverb which says that 'clogs once outlived their usefulness are thrown away.' 'Were old guards being treated the same way?' Yaacob asked.

My experience in Japan also dawned on me that those in charge of the Ministry of Foreign Affairs lack experience in handling embassies abroad. On one occasion in Japan, I suddenly received a written instruction from the Ministry that I needed to ask for written permission if I decided to leave the Capital (in my case it was Tokyo). This instruction sounds ridiculous to me. All Singapore Ambassadors around the world received similar instructions. Several of them complained loudly when we met in Singapore, but none dared raised any objections.

When Brigadier General, Lee Hsien Loong, then Minister of Trade and Industry came to Tokyo with the Economic Development Board mission for a seminar in Osaka, he asked me to accompany him. I told him of the restrictions and he could not believe it. He felt that the Ministry should not treat Ambassadors like children. I went with him to Osaka without asking the Ministry for permission. After B. G. Lee Hsien Loong's return to Singapore, the instruction was cancelled. But I was reprimanded by the Permanent Secretary for complaining to a Minister who was not in charge of the Foreign Ministry and warned me that in future, I should make complaints direct to him.

In Japan, the cost of living was highest in the world and the exchange rate of Japanese Yen with the Singapore currency kept soaring. When I arrived, it was one Singapore Dollar for Two Hundred and Fifty Yens. Within one year, one Singapore Dollar was worth only One Hundred and Fifty Yens. I wrote back to Singapore asking to readjust our overseas cost of living allowance, for the staff were finding it difficult to live comfortably. There was no reply and I wrote four times and finally when there was still no reply, I wrote a stinking letter to the Permanent Secretary Chia Chiong Fook complaining that he did not have the interest and welfare of his overseas staff at heart.

I have asked for the revision of the overseas allowance not for myself, for I was receiving my pension and my allowances were adequate. It was for my staff who were suffering badly in terms of their spending power.

At almost the tailend of my assignment, our overseas allowance was raised by about 20 percent, still far short of requirements. It took the Ministry more than two years to make a decision on something vital to the welfare of overseas staff. I was angry because they did not even bother to reply to my letter.

Another matter which the Ministry lacks experience concerns disbursement of entertainment allowance for Ambassadors. At the time when I was in Japan, it would be impossible for an ambassador to entertain anyone in a respectable restaurant for less than S$100.00, for food was really expensive in respectable restaurant. When I started to entertain my guest, the junior staff of the Ministry would query me why I should spend so much money. I was flabbergasted and replied that if they continue to query me, I would stop entertaining guests and the queries stopped.

These are little problems which an Ambassador of a tiny state faced when the Ministry back home lacked experienced staff to deal with overseas matters. An Ambassador needs a lot of patience when dealing with irritating problems on administration.

In my assignment in Japan, I had also to cover the Republic of Korea, a country I would call Confucius dreamland. I visited Seoul once every three months. We had no embassy and no staff. I had to operate from a hotel. I went to the country at a time when rapid changes were taking place. I presented credentials to Choon Do-Hwan, a General who came into power after Park Chung-Hee was assasinated. He did a lot to bring about economic prosperity to the country, but his brother being corrupt spoilt his image. The angry students overthrew him and he self exiled himself to a little hut in Sorak, living like a hermit. When I left I bade farewell to the President Roh Tae-Woo, another general who won the general elections with his quick wit and wise strategy. I arranged for Roh Tae-Woo to meet Lee Kuan Yew in Seoul before he became the President. He wanted to learn a few tricks from Lee Kuan Yew on how to govern a country. President Roh Tae-Woo had great admiration for Lee Kuan Yew's achievements in Singapore.

On the eve of my departure, President Roh bestowed on me the highest Diplomatic Order for the contribution I have made to the promotion of Singapore and Korean relations.

My impression of South Korea is that it is a very Confucius-oriented society. This can be seen in weddings, funerals and the behaviours of the older generations. But the never ending student demonstrations all over the country have created a different impression. Confucius never encourage students to defy the authorities and to stage violent demonstrations. In my chapter no 'Confucius dreamland', I tried to explain the reasons behind the demonstration and the traditional anti-government mentality of young people in Korea.

Lately, the students have gone too far in showing their anger. They openly humilated the Prime Minister when he visited a university campus to give lectures. They threw rotten eggs on him and beat him up. The television carried the scene and since then, their popularity declined and support waned. I believe it is a matter of time before the students would be able to distinguish between a good government and a bad government and it would be better for them and their country to restrain their action.

Singapore was the last country in Asean to set up an Embassy and we now have an Ambassador. I have recommended setting up an Embassy ever since I set foot on Seoul for I saw the potentials of the hard-working Koreans and their fast expanding economy. It took Singapore a long time to decide on sending an Ambassador for it was not easy to find a suitable candidate.

With my departure from Japan and Korea, I have served the country in eight countries lasting eleven years between 1968 and 1974 and from 1984 to 1988. It was a rich and interesting experience. I have served in a country which was the centre of the Arab world — Egypt ruled by once a military strong man Nasser; then to a country ruled by Islam — Pakistan; a feudal African state dominated by the greatest of all Kings Haile Selasie; a psydo-Communists country run by leader of the non-aligned world Tito, a charismatic leader who brought six countries together as one nation and who dared defy Stalin and a country which was once heaven turned hell - Lebanon. In all these five countries, I have served from Cairo with only three home-based staff. Then I spent four-and-a-half years in Indonesia, our closest and greatest neighbour, patching up hurt relations and making it possible for Lee Kuan Yew to be officially invited to Indonesia. Except for President Suharto, the other Presidents and Emperors have passed away.

After ten years of continued political career, I called it a day and resumed my diplomatic career again in Japan and Korea for more than four years.

It was a satisfying experience. It gave me an opportunity to perceive the world at close quarters, understand the lifestyles of various peoples as well as their cultures, traditions and thinkings. The assignments enriched my life and my mental scope. I never regretted having accepted the first assignment in the first instance. These assignments also gave my daughters an experience with life outside of Singapore.

Looking back, it gave me a sense of satisfaction. I was never trained as a diplomat, but I acted as one and gained experience by practical day to day dealings. Wherever I went, I would study the language of the host country, research on their cultures and traditions, mixing with peoples from all walks of life and understanding their feelings. I never spent my time travelling from office to residence, but went out of the way to cultivate friendship. I have come to the conclusion that the best diplomat would be one who would try to understand the characteristic of the people, their culture and tradition and would analyse their behaviour motives, incentives and reasons for doing the things they did and do. Without this proper attitude, it would be difficult for an Ambassador to perform his task adequately. Life would be boring if an Ambassador does not take an interest in the language and culture of the people and try to understand their thinking. I have seen many of my diplomatic colleagues travelling from office to homes and attending cocktails and who always complained of the handicaps they experienced and the ideosyncracies of the local population. In Japan I met the Dean of the Diplomatic Corp who complained to me that he could not understand the Japanese. Being the Dean he had served in Japan for nearly 20 years. I asked him a simple question: 'Do you speak Japanese?' His answer was 'No'. After 20 years and he did not speak a single word of Japanese. How could one really understand the Japanese when one does not even bother to learn simple Japanese? I thought.

In the winter of my life, it is better for me to jot down my diplomatic experiences which might be of some use to the younger generations. If I should procrastinate, these experiences could easily be buried in the ashes of fading memories and the swifting sand of history.

1

'Excellency' in Cairo

'What about becoming an ambassador to Cairo?' Mr S Rajaratnam, Singapore's former Foreign Minister asked me. It was just after the 1968 elections when the People's Action Party had won all the seats in Parliament and everyone was anxiously waiting for the Cabinet to be announced. The question caught me by surprise. For having laid the foundation for the Arts Council and having been interested in culture, I thought they would put me in Culture. My immediate reaction was no. My reason was that I had from my first deceased wife two sons who were between the ages of fourteen and sixteen and who were in the middle school. It was a critical time they had to face and I had to leave them behind. My youngest daughter was only six months old. Rajaratnam explained to me the reasons for wanting to send me to Cairo. We had begun to train our army and when we had enough soldiers to occupy the Farrer Park camps, the Malaysian soldiers who were stationed there refused to leave. We were also looking for military advisers and instructors from various countries including the United Kingdom, America, India, Egypt and other friendly countries. But no friendly country would come forward to train our army. It was quite difficult for them because they were afraid to antagonize the Malaysians. Then came the Israelis who offered to train our troops and we got Israeli military instructors and advisers.

This, explained Rajaratnam, had antagonized many Arab countries, who were fighting the Israelis. But Egypt had remained friendly, though displeased. It was a matter of time

Bird's eye view of Cairo

before we had to recognise Israel and my mission was to find out which was the most appropriate time to do so and how to ease the situation with Egypt and other friendly Arab countries, when the time came.

I gave Rajaratnam the reasons I had to turn down his request. Next morning, the Prime Minister, Mr Lee Kuan Yew, called me up to the Istana. We had a long discussion on why I should go to Cairo. In those days, personal problems did not come to the minds of our leaders. It was a challenge and I accepted it the next day. I did not know what it was like to be an ambassador. Nobody could tell me what diplomacy was; for we had just achieved independence. Apart from Kenny Byrne, the former Minister for Labour, who was sent to New Zealand as High Commissioner, I was the first Member of Parliament who was sent out as ambassador.

I took my three daughters along, leaving behind the two sons. My little six-month-old daughter I left in a carry-cot in front of my seat in the plane. When we approached Cairo, I saw from the air nothing but desert. I remembered Cairo in 1949, when I was on my way to London for studies. I was then quarantined at the airport, because there was something wrong with my health documents. I was put up in a little dingy room without ventilation like the black hole of Calcutta. Little did I realise that 21 years later I would be back in that country as ambassador.

My immediate problem was housing. When we arrived, the protocol officers and our staff took us to see the quarters occupied by our former colleague, Ahmad Ibrahim. It was too small for my family and my liking. I decided to stay in Hotel Nile Hilton for the time being. I chose the West Wing because it was facing the Nile which was always peaceful and calm. It was real summer and the hottest temperature was 120° F. The radio had warned us not to go out of doors because we could get sunstroke. The sun shone on the glass window of our rooms and the heat made the airconditioner ineffective. During the day the rooms were like ovens and the children screamed. The smell of ghee pervaded the air for the Arabs use much ghee. For two weeks we had no appetite and we had to get our cook to our counsellor's house to cook and had the food brought to the hotel.

We finally found a lovely house in Maadi, a suburb about fifteen minutes drive from town. It was quiet and cosy with a beautiful garden. Then the problem of mosquitoes. There were mosquitoes everywhere and big ones too. They found their way into airconditioned rooms. Every night, my little daughter had her whole face bitten till it was red and swollen. I went round Cairo looking for mosquito nets and mosquito coils. The shopkeepers had never heard of such things. I had to write back for a mosquito net and it took something like a month before it arrived. In the meantime, nothing could be done but just let the mosquitoes bite. We went to the doctor and got some ointment. It was interesting fighting the mosquitoes at night. They were all over the room, so we got wet towels and we threw them against the mosquitoes when they landed on the ceiling. The mosquito war went on until we got the repellants from Singapore. Our room boy Abu slept open-air in the garage. He seemed to be immune to mosquitoes.

Then the food problem. There was no 'tau yu' or 'cheow cheng' — a sort of sauce made from beans — in Cairo. So for a whole month we had to use salt as a substitute. A month later, when the 'tau yu' arrived from Singapore, we really treasured it.

Does a Muslim country sell pork? My friends from Singapore felt sorry for me for not being able to eat pork for two years. I went to the market with my wife one day and discovered that there was plenty of pork and at cheaper prices too. There was a whole row of shop houses selling pork. The sellers were all Christians. They got them from a pig farm run by Christians. We asked for pork bones and this took them by surprise. One seller said, 'Oh, pork bones, there are plenty of them there', pointing with his finger at a corner near by. He said, 'We give them to the dogs. Why? You eat them? You can have them for free.' We looked embarrassed. We went to have a look at the bones, but they were dirty.

There were about more than a million Christians in Egypt. The Christian community was quite united. Just like minorities everywhere, they complained of discrimination by the regime. One of them said, 'Look we have only one minister who is a Christian. Most of the top people are Muslims.'

In the Mumbuna market, most of the hawkers wore Galibaya — the type of loose gown worn by Egyptians. There were blind people who would carry your basket for you for a *bakhshish*. There were a few people selling little sparrows strung in a bunch. Arab markets are the noisiest. The Arabs shout at the top of their voices, quarrelling over half a piastre. Beggars like mosquitoes pestered you while you moved around the stalls looking for what to buy. They were persistent and would not go until you parted with one or two piastres.

It took some time for us to settle down. There was the problem of language, food and friends. Cairo was a big city of 5 million population and the centre of the Arab world. There were 96 foreign embassies and it was customary for a new ambassador to call on every one of them. There were so many national days and social functions of the diplomatic corps that one could hardly find time for anything else.

Except for a few ambassadors who became close to us, the rest were just addressed as 'Your excellency'. The first time when someone addressed me as 'Excellency', I felt rather strange. Then I got used to it and started to address ambassadors as 'Excellency'.

There were three words which one soon picked up and they were very useful. The first word was *malesh* — meaning 'never mind'.

The Cairenes are a remarkably cheerful lot, raucous-voiced and fiery tempered but also humorous, easy going and democratic. It was only 17 years since the revolution led by Gamal Nasser and the Egyptians still had the peculiar, half-tamed energies and impulses of a recently liberated people to whom rulers used to mean robbers or tyrants coming to tax, compel or conscribe. They took things easy and would say *malesh* even if they knocked and damaged your car. Every morning when I travelled from Maadi to my Chancery in Doqqi about twenty minutes away, I used to see passengers clinging to buses or their rooftops. Buses were so crowded that passengers had to cling outside or sit on rooftops. Some fell and died. There was no fuss at all about the whole matter. They just covered the face with some dirty paper and said *malesh*.

Getting on and off a bus is an art, sport and proof of one's spirit in Cairo. Boarding is to take a running leap and clutch at whatever you can, window or door openings, bumpers or fellow passengers who often extend helping hands. Getting off is the real challenge requiring what one connoisseur called 'the flying dismount', which was to leap from the moving bus and run furiously to compensate for the loss of forward momentum, spinning, dodging and darting around oncoming traffic and would-be passengers swarming to get on the bus. There were many deaths from travelling on buses.

The other word is *bakhshish* meaning tips. My first encounter with *bakhshish* was during my stay at Nile Hilton. I did not know that one had to give *bakhshish* every day. I thought I would give the maids a lump sum at the end of my stay. On the third day of my stay, I discovered that they did not make my bed. I thought it was an oversight. The next day, not only did they not make the bed, the pillows were taken away. I lost my temper which I should not as a diplomat. I called up the manager and told him what had happened. He summoned the maids and gave them a good scolding. Then things looked better. Then came the time for us to leave. Hotel maids, waitresses, sweepers and the rest of the gang queued up from my room to the stairs waiting for *bakhshish*.

On the day when I presented my credentials to President Nasser, my car came out of the Chancery and there were a few people outside clapping hands. I was happy for I thought that they were clapping for the good occasion of the Singapore Ambassador going to present credentials to their President. When everything was over and we were celebrating with champagne with some friends, a few strangers turned up and asked my third secretary for *bakhshish*. What for? They said they had earlier clapped hands.

There were so many occasions when we had to give *bakhshish* to people. The doorman at the hotel opens your car door and you give *bakhshish*. When you leave the airport, the policeman would give you a good salute, and he expected a good *bakhshish*. It was *bakhshish* everywhere, but it was not acceptable to our Treasury.

Then the word *bogkrah* meaning tomorrow. When your air-conditioner is out of order or when you have no lights and you ask somebody to repair them, they will say 'okay *bogkrah*'. You wait for *bogkrah* and he never turns up. There is another *bogkrah* and yet another *bogkrah* until maybe a month later and then he suddenly turns up.

The Egyptians generally had no sense of time and urgency. I found when speaking to Egyptian leaders and people generally, they had a different concept of time. Perhaps it is because Egypt has 7,000 years of history that the people take time lightly. What is time after all when so much has happened. When you invite someone for a dinner party, he turns up one or two hours late and never bothers to apologise. He may even forget and never turn up.

Not contented with only three words, I started to study Arabic. I had a Chinese teacher who came from China. A staunch Muslim, he migrated from China after the Communists took over. A lot of Muslims migrated from Sinkiang to Saudi Arabia and other Arab countries. This man was Abu Bakar, his Chinese name Fu Ern Chuen (胡恩均). He was fat and short, middle-aged and rather lethargic. Sometimes during the teaching he would fall asleep and I had to wake him up. He explained to me that he had this disease of not wanting to do anything. I learnt a lot about Islam from Abu Bakar.

According to Abu Bakar, Egyptians are real fatalists. They have developed this fatalistic attitude towards life and have no ambitions. When you succeed in life it is 'Al hamdudilah', meaning with God's blessing or thanks to God, and nobody brags about it. You do not say 'I have succeeded. I willed it. I am happy I made it with my own effort.' If you do that then you would be criticised as irreligious because it is God's will that made you succeed. If you fail, nobody blames you that you have not made the effort and that you have failed. They just say, it is God's will that you have failed. And there is nothing to be ashamed of. The important word to remember is 'Insha'Allah' which means by the will of Allah. Even when you ask someone 'Shall I meet you tomorrow?' he would reply, 'Yes, I shall come, Insha'Allah'. And when he does not turn up, it is God's will and not his.

It is a common sight to see along the streets and pavement, people praying at one o'clock. They bow to Mecca to pray. The streets are crowded and you can hardly walk.

Jaywalking is the rule; pavements are primarily used for outdoor cafes, peddlars, cigarette and newspaper stands, barbers, shoeshine boys, car repair shops and garbage dumps. In

Cairo's 8,000 cafes, the Cairenes, most of them illiterate peasantry imbued with the fatalistic acceptance of medieval Islam, sip tea and smoke water pipes, listening to the echoes of the muezzin's call. They joke, gossip and listen to President Nasser's speeches and complain.

For Egyptians have much to complain about. There is no public housing. Egypt simply has no land to spare. It has only 2.3 million cultivated hectares along the 1200 km of the Nile and 5060 hectares a year are already lost to urbanisation. So shanty towns go up on the rooftops, where as many as half the Cairenes may now live. Another one million people are squatting in the tomb-houses of the City of the Dead, a vast cemetery once inhabited only by corpses and ghosts. This reminds me of Manila's Chinese estate for the Dead where rich people build huge houses to accommodate their beloved dead. The living go to play mahjong at weekends. The Cairo City of the Dead comprises various sizes of tombs built for the dead, but are inhabited by the living souls, without water supply and electricity. How a million living souls could cram into the tombs meant for dead souls and take shelter is something most difficult to imagine. There are more souls above than below. Those who went down below would not rest in peace with the noise above. At night, if a moonless night, the whole city would turn into a fairyland of candles.

Despite the crammed situation, the Egyptians generally are happy-go-lucky. Nobody goes hungry for one thing. Prices of basic commodities and food were pretty low during those days when I was there. You could have a nourishing and filling meal for 10 cents. It included *ful* or cooked broadbeans, *tacamia* or baked balls of breadcrumbs, a salad and two slabs of Arab bread — a rounded piece of white brownish bread somewhat like the Singapore chapati. Egyptians are great eaters. I once saw a fat Egyptian eating one chicken by himself at a restaurant. After the chicken, he asked for a steak and then ice-cream and chocolate. When the coffee came, he had fallen asleep in the chair. Whenever I invited Egyptians to dinner, I would prepare enough for twenty even if only ten were coming. And after dinner there would be plenty of chocolates. Egyptians are very generous with their guests. They would put a lot of food on your plate and expect you to finish it. If you do not finish it, they will feel offended.

In Cairo, they take a kind of thick coffee which is Turkish. The cup is small but the coffee is very thick. The Egyptians tell fortune from coffee cups. Once a friend of mine took me to see a coffee cup fortune-teller. She was about 45 years old, not a professional fortune-teller but was famous for telling fortune to close friends. Out of curiosity I wanted to know how she read fortune by coffee cup. We went to her house somewhere in the outskirts of Cairo. She asked me to drink a cup of coffee which was very thick. After I had drunk it, she turned the cup upside down and let the sediments dry. There were contours when the sediments dried up and she read from the contours. She said, 'You have just arrived, and will stay here for two years. In between you will visit a few other countries.' At that time, I did not know that I would be accredited also to Pakistan, Ethiopia, Lebanon and Yugoslavia. Strange as it may seem, it turned out to be correct.

Although it is an Islamic country, the Egyptians are a superstitious people. Beneath the facade of Islam, there are many superstitious beliefs and customs which are un-Islamic. When people get sick, they would see a medium who would go into a trance. The man or woman who does the trance would run round the sick person many times until he or she faints. He would mumble some words which would be the prescription.

In Cairo, whenever a person dies, the whole family goes around crying in the street. In ancient days, Egyptians would put mud all over their faces and run around the streets crying with their hair uncombed. Today, the Egyptians just go around crying with their hair uncombed but without putting on mud. The places that are dressed up for a funeral often use red and bright colours, quite contrary to the Chinese Taoist and Buddhist who use black as the mourning colour. I once nearly mistook a funeral parlour for a wedding ceremony.

Speaking of weddings, I noticed that upper middle class Egyptians were still very class conscious despite seventeen years of Arab socialism. My Egyptian friend told me that one of the sons of a very important person had asked for the hand of his daughter. He was high up in the political ladder, but my friend's answer was no because the other man's ancestors were from the lower class. They would go into family history to find out everything about the prospective partner before a match is concluded.

My eighteen-year-old butler Abu who stayed in the garage was ill one day. I called up my family doctor who came immediately and asked who was sick. I told him it was the Egyptian butler and this took him by surprise. He went to the garage and soon came back. I asked him for the prescription but he refused. I was rather annoyed with him that he refused to give the prescription. On the other hand, he was annoyed with me for having called him to cure an Egyptian. He said the boy was suffering from typhoid and advised me to move him to the hospital. I got him admitted and he died the next day. Abu's mother and a few other Egyptians came afterwards and demanded money for compensation. They asked me who had treated him and a number of other questions. I gave them some money and they left without creating a scene. When the doctor came again, he explained to me that if Abu had died in the garage and if the parents knew that it was he who gave medicine, then both of us would have been in great trouble.

Class distinction is glaring in Cairo. Whilst millions suffer, a few rich enjoy. They are referred to by the newspapers as 'Fat Cats'. Egyptian politicians claimed that the nation now had more than a hundred times the number of millionaires it had under King Farouk and demanded a government explanation of how a 'fat cat' class could develop in a socialist country. One politician charged in Parliament that Egypt had 500 millionaires compared with four before the 1952 revolution in which Gamal Abdul Nasser ousted Farouk. Critics of the regime charged that a vulgar display of wealth by Cairo's 'new class' could only increase social pressure in a country where per capita income was US$250 a year. A columnist in the daily newspaper *Al Akhbar* said that 'the cats could not grow fat unless they enjoyed the support of senior officials from the public sector.'

The Egyptians, rich or poor, love music. They were intoxicated by the songs sung by Omm Kolthourm an elderly lady singer who had a golden voice and was raved over by the whole of the Middle East. When she sang, the whole of the Arab world was at a standstill. Everyone would be holding on to their pocket radios to listen to her.

One evening I was invited to a concert given by Omm Kolthourm at a downtown theatre. I went with my wife to see this marvellous singer. The Hall was packed like a sardine can and the crowd outside the theatre was thick trying to purchase tickets. They had all been sold out.

When the show began, loud applause greeted this little lady of well over seventy who looked forty on stage. As she sang, she waved her handkerchief from right to left and they cheered. Her voice was a lingering one, loud, sharp but brilliant. She was accompanied by my friend the *kanon* player, Mohammad Abdul Saleh (deceased), the most famous in Egypt. Abdul Saleh was superb on his *kanon* (Egyptian harp) whilst Omm Kolthourm sang repeatedly and waving her handkerchief.

I did not understand a word of what she sang, but I appreciated the music and the voice. The crowd who sat there shouted aloud and clapped their hands when she sang. It reminded me of the Beijing Opera where the crowd would shout back at the stage and make noises during the performance. The crowd also brought food to their seats and ate during the show.

The Egyptians were most unpunctual. The ticket mentioned 8 pm as the cut off time for the show. But the show did not start until 9.30 pm. The audience included well-dressed ladies with their finery and ornament and the poor in slippers; the very old and little kids. There were also a few blind men.

This was the first time Omm Kolthourm appeared on stage after the June defeat of 1967. She had been responding to the Government's war on shows to mourn the defeat in the war against Israel. This mourning period was over, and she appeared to raise money for the National Defence Fund.

Omm Kolthourm's success was not sudden. She grew up in poor surroundings accompanying her father to sing from house to house in the streets of Cairo. Her talent was discovered by a musician who trained her up from small. With her beauty and charm, she soon became famous. The aristocrats patronised her and even King Farouk fell in love with her voice. He honoured her with awards. Soon the whole Arab world came to know her and the Arab kings invited her to sing at their palaces.

Omm Kolthourm became a millionaire. When she was well over forty, she married a doctor and settled down. She then sang only for fund-raising. She used to sing Egyptian classical songs but later sang Arab classical tunes. The lyrics of the song she sang that night were composed by a Lebanese poet George Gordani and the music was by Mohammad Abdul Wahhab. It was called 'My Night'.

Omm Kolthourm's records were bestsellers in the Middle East. In Cairo, there was a two-storey coffee house which played only Omm Kolthourm's songs day and night. It has been packed for the last forty years, since it opened.

At the back stage, I met my host the Maestro Abdul Halim Muera, the brother-in-law of the late President Sadat. His wife, who was the younger sister of Sadat and a prominent journalist, was also present when he introduced me to this remarkable lady Omm Kolthourm. We had lunch together at my home a few days after the concert. As she spoke only Arabic, conversation was rather difficult. Omm Kolthourm died sometime in 1977 and the Arab world lost a great singer.

2

Recognition of Israel

The time had come for me to present credentials to President Nasser. I waited for three weeks. Others, I was told, had to wait for two to three months. I brought along with me my credentials signed by the late President Yusof. First, I met the Protocol Officer who arranged for me to see the former Foreign Minister, Mahmud Riad, to whom I presented a copy of my credentials.

There were five outriders. When we reached the Palace, a uniformed guard blew the bugle. It was a simple ceremony with no Guard of Honour. The chamberlain came to receive me and asked me to wait in a room. Five minutes later, he brought me into the inner chamber and there I met President Nasser who was accompanied by his Foreign Minister, Mahmud Riad. It was the second time that I saw Nasser. The first time was at Bandung, when we attended the Afro-Asian Conference in April 1955. He was then in military uniform and was young and handsome. His speech at Bandung was not at all impressive. He was reading a speech with eyes fixed on a written text, never lifting his head at any time. This time he looked much older and haggard. He was about to leave for Georgia for a ten-day treatment.

I read out my speech which briefly said that we were moving away from the year of political ideals and working class solidarity to one where it was increasingly the young who saw in independence the freedom to translate their own political ideals into practical terms. I emphasised that 'In them the opportunity to obtain for themselves and future generations the fruits of modernisation and freedom from want, which has plagued previous generations, seems more meaningful than slogans of the past.'

After the speech, we shook hands and then sat down to talk. He told me that he had just quit smoking and was feeling a little nervous because of it. He asked me about Lee Kuan Yew and his relationship with Tengku Abdul Rahman. He said when he met Lee Kuan Yew last, he was told that relationship with Malaysia was not so good. I told him that all was well and that after three years of separation, we were on our own feet. The rest of the conversation was casual. I was warned beforehand not to talk too long. I took leave of the President and went back to the Chancery to celebrate the occasion.

Having presented credentials, I had become a full-fledged ambassador and it was time to call on the diplomatic corps. Meanwhile, the one thing which was uppermost in my mind was to find out how to cushion off the impact when we in Singapore had to recognise Israel. What would be the reaction of the Egyptian officials? What would they do to us? I had kept my mission secret and did not divulge it to any of my staff.

I started to gather information on the subject discreetly. I got to know Sir Harold Beeley, the British Ambassador who was an expert in Arabic and the Arabian affairs. He was a tall gentleman, bespectacled, with thick eyebrows and big eyes. He had a habit of twitching his face and stammered a little. When we talked in his quiet room, I was always distracted by the grandfather clock which ticked away the seconds with hypnotic power. I tried to sound him out on the question of recognising Israel. According to Sir Harold, most of the French-speaking African countries and also most of the English-speaking African countries had recognised Israel. Some had already established diplomatic relations. The U.A.R. Government, he said, did not take much offence in the case of those countries which had recognised Israel previously, particularly before the June war. But he warned that they would be very annoyed and agitated about new recognitions because this meant moral support to encourage Israel to continue its aggression and to continue to defy the United Nations resolutions. He told me that when Ethiopia had diplomatic relations with Israel, the Ethiopian

Ambassador, Mallas Mikael Andom, who was the Doyen of the Diplomatic Corps, had a tough time. The Ethiopian Embassy was surrounded by police ostensibly to protect the Embassy from attack by angry students.

The Morrocan Ambassador, Mr Mahdi Mrani Zentar, who was an outspoken and frank person, disclosed to me that during his conversation with UAR leaders, he gained the impression that they had reconciled to the fact that Israel was there to stay. In his mind, the UAR stand was that they were prepared to recognise the existence of Israel and even have a proper boundary drawn if the Israelis would withdraw from Egyptian soil. He said Morrocco had the same stand. He said all Arab countries would not tolerate the Israelis' inhuman act of destroying Palestinian homes and their attitude towards the refugees. But it would be unrealistic not to recognise the fact that Israel was there to stay. From the conversation with the Morrocan Ambassador, I got some insight into the views of the Arab leaders. I knew that the Egyptian leaders and for that matter most moderate Arabs realised that Israel was there to stay and that they could not do anything about it. I also realised that Egyptian leaders were prepared to recognise the existence of Israel.

The new Director of Asian Desk, Ezz El-Din Ramzy, was a cordial, understanding and outspoken man who gave me a great deal of insight into the thinking of the Egyptians. We became friends very quickly and were in a position to talk frankly. He had just returned from Burma as Egypt's Ambassador and was very fond of golf and perhaps the only Egyptian golfer in the Ministry of Foreign Affairs. Speaking to him, I got the impression that the Egyptians did not mind at all if we recognised Israel but we had to make our stand towards the Arabs clear. In other words, we would not condone Israeli occupation of Arab territories and that we still supported the United Nations' resolution No 22.

I reported the reactions back to Rajaratnam. Then on 22 February 1969, I received a cable from Singapore which said that Singapore would be establishing diplomatic relations with Israel, possibly in early March, and that the Prime Minister had written to Nasser indicating Singapore's intentions to do so. The cable assured that our stand in the United Nations and other international bodies regarding the middle east issue would continue to be in accordance with what Singapore considered to be just. The cable advised me to make the announcement in a very casual way and in low key.

Subsequently, Rajaratnam wrote to me on two occasions. The first was on 31st March 1969 telling me that he had informed the Israel trade representative in Singapore that we would raise the level of their representation to that of an Embassy by May 15 and a suitable announcement would be made. He had sought the cooperation of the Israeli Government not to overplay this development and if possible to keep the announcement in low key 'so as not to generate undue hostility among our Arab friends'. To this the Israelis had agreed and assured us that a short announcement would be made on that date.

In the second letter dated 21 April 1969, Rajaratnam said he would be releasing the news of our establishment of diplomatic relations with Israel on the evening of 10 May embargoed for the press on 11 May. I had made arrangements to go to Yugoslavia to present credentials to President Tito on 6th May. The letter reminded me that it was necessary for me to be present in Cairo during the announcement 'for otherwise it might be construed that you are purposely keeping out of Cairo during this important announcement.'

Rajaratnam had chosen 10 May because on the same day, news of our establishment of diplomatic relations with Israel would be overtaken by the general euphoria following the announcement of the Malaysian election results. The press would probably have little space for the news. Rajaratnam in this letter assured me that he would 'take care of the point you have stressed' and arrange for a copy of his statement to be relayed to me well in advance so that I could show it to the UAR officials if they chose to raise it with me on the day the announcement was made.

I had earlier stressed home the point that when we establish diplomatic relations with Israel, we should make it clear to the minds of the Arabs that we still supported the Arab cause in wanting the Israelis to withdraw from occupied territories.

On 2 May I received the letters which the Prime Minister had written to President Nasser and the letters Rajaratnam had written to his counterpart, Mahmud Riad and I was asked to deliver them immediately. I rang up the first Chamberlain of the President for an appointment with the President and was told that he had gone to spend the Bairam (Hari Raya Haji) with the military officers on the frontline. He told me to hand the letter to President Nasser's personal adviser for Foreign Affairs, Dr Mahmud Fawzy. He was one of the brains behind the 1952 revolutions although he did not take part in the military operations. He was once Foreign Minister and also Egyptian Ambassador to the United Nations. He had served as Ambassador to Japan for six years. Easily the brainiest of all the leaders, he is well read and respected in intellectual circles.

On Saturday noon, I went to Dr Fawzy's private residence. It was a humble house in the countryside along a canal not far away from the Pyramids of Giza. Surrounded by fruit trees, the simple house made of planks gave away the honesty and frugality of the owner. When I first called on Dr Fawzy at his office, he was rather stern-looking and he had a secretary taking down notes. I expected the same treatment, but he was an entirely different person. He was alone and was very casual. We had a cup of coffee and chatted about the advantages of living in a quiet countryside before we came to the main topic. When I handed over the letter to him, he put it aside and never read the contents. I think he knew the contents for we had informed the Egyptian consul-general in Singapore, Dr Makluf, on 30 April about our intention to recognise Israel. Dr Makluf must have cabled back to Cairo to inform his government.

Dr Fawzy put aside the letter and never read it. I was anxious to know his reaction. So I told him the content and explained to him frankly the difficult circumstances that we were faced with when we were evicted from Malaysia as well as the new situation brought about by the unexpected early pull-out of the British troops from Singapore by 1971.

I expected him to ask questions but after listening to me he said calmly in a philosophical mood: 'We understand your difficult position.' He then volunteered to tell me a secret. He said during Malaysia's confrontation with Indonesia, President Sukarno was angry with Egypt for not siding him. Sukarno had asked Nasser one day: 'Are you not our blood brothers? Why are you not with us?' Nasser told Sukarno that 'we wanted our blood brothers to cooperate and befriend your neighbours, not to treat them as enemies.'

Dr Fawzy said Singapore's geographical position made her useful in providing the necessary services to South-East Asian neighbours. These countries had the natural resources and 'you have the facilities and knowhow.'

He added: 'We realise your difficult position of cooperating with neighbours which have a large hungry population.'

Hinting at Sukarno, he said: 'It is a pity that political leaders made hasty decisions when they were tired and such decisions affected the lives of many people.'

The topic then drifted to world affairs generally. He told me he was leaving for Paris on Monday to see President De Gaulle. I asked him what he thought of the prospect of peace in the Middle East and he replied: 'I am afraid we are heading for hard times. The situation is very critical.' He was optimistic about the future for the Afro-Asian people. He said: 'Afro-Asia have great potentialites. We have vast natural resources and the manpower. What we lack is the capital and know-how to exploit such resources. This takes time. We may be a little too impatient. After all, Afro-Asian countries have gained independence only very lately. A time will come when the surplus manpower in Afro-Asia will become an asset to the development of our wealth and prosperity.'

We then talked about the problems of youth and how to spend our leisure hours. He told me that his present hobby was farming. He also likes painting but has been putting off learning how to paint day after day. He particularly likes Chinese and Japanese painting and has collected quite a few on his decorative wall. He also possesses a certificate for flower arrangement and art which he learnt when he was six years in Japan as Ambassador.

The conversation ended on a promising note for future closer personal contact through our common interest. I promised to teach him my method of Chinese painting — a method without tears and sweat.

Everything went off very well, I thought. If Dr Fawzy's personal reaction to the recognition of Israel could be the yardstick, then I had nothing to worry about.

The Prime Minister's letter to President Nasser mentioned our intention to recognise Israel, but that our stand in the United Nations and other international bodies regarding the Middle East issues would be in accordance with what we considered to be just.

The Prime Minister said that justice must be done to the people and countries of the Middle East, and the Palestinian refugees, whilst in the meantime we accept the existence of the State of Israel as a fact and her frontier was safeguarded.

On 6 May, I left for Yugoslavia to present credentials to President Tito. I returned to Cairo on the 11th, a day after the announcement was made because of plane delay. I heard from my first secretary that no one in the Foreign Ministry had asked to see me to explain our announcement on establishment of diplomatic relations with Israel. So far, only the *Egyptian Gazette* and the *Al Ahram*, the most influential newspaper in Egypt, had published our statement. The *Egyptian Gazette* published the full text of our statement in one column heading. The heading was 'Singapore Embassy for Israel.' There was no editorial comment. The *Al Ahram* published only two sentences and a precis of our statement in a small column heading 'Singapore raises diplomatic relations with Israel to Ambassadorial level.'

From the way things went, I had a feeling that the Egyptian leaders were not too angry with us because we had explained in the statement that 'Singapore remains committed to the belief that no country however big or small should be denied the right to exist, the fruits of conquest should not forcibly be converted into spoils of war.' In other words, Singapore does not condone Israeli occupation of Arab territories.

Soon after my return from Belgrade, I received an invitation from the Director of Asian Desk, Ambassador Ramzy to a dinner at his residence. This was an indication that the Egyptians had taken the matter philosophically. During the dinner, no mention was ever made about the recognition of Israel. All was well for the Singapore Embassy. Three months later, when the Rumanians recognised Israel, the Egyptian Government withdrew her Ambassador from Rumania, and Iraq, Syria and Sudan broke off diplomatic relations with Rumania. On the day when the Rumanian action was published, the Egyptian Director of East Europe Department Saad Afra summoned the

Rumanian Ambassador Titua Sinus to his office and demanded an explanation for his country's decision. A statement was issued on the same day by the Director accusing Rumania of her unfriendly act. When the Rumanian Ambassador tried to defend his country's policy after having received instructions from Bucharest, the Egyptian Government announced the withdrawal of her Ambassador from Bucharest.

All ambassadors of Arab countries boycotted the Rumanian National Day celebrated on 21 August 1969.

Rumania has in fact been giving aid to Egypt on several projects, two of which were the exploration of oil and of phosphate financed entirely by Rumania. But economic assistance meant nothing to the Egyptians when their anger was aroused. Many foreign diplomats were surprised that Rumania got such a heavy blow whereas Singapore got away so lightly for having done the same thing. In fact many congratulated us for our good fortune. When I met the Malaysian Ambassador, Hamid Jumat (deceased) at a party, he said: 'You are lucky. How was it that Singapore got off so lightly? After all, you did the same thing.' I merely said that it was a matter of approach. Come to think of it, we did the right thing in having made our stand clear vis-a-vis Israeli occupation of Arab territories. The statement issued by us had helped to soften the blow a great deal.

One serious mistake made by Rumania was to accredit her Ambassador to Jerusalem instead of Tel Aviv. The Egyptian Government and other Arab states considered the appointment of an ambassador at Jerusalem as a hostile act because it meant recognition and condoning Israel's occupation of Arab land as the question of Jerusalem was still a matter to be settled by the United Nations. Rumania did not take the necessary precautions before the announcement. She did make a statement later on to clarify her stand after it was demanded by the Egyptian authorities, but it came in too late.

In the game of diplomacy, it is necessary to be conscious of the feelings of the host country. We would have suffered the same fate as the Rumanians if we had not taken into consideration the feelings of the Arabs vis-a-vis the Israeli-occupied territories. We made our stand clear in this respect and escaped the wrath of the Egyptians when we recognised Israel.

I had fulfilled my mission.

3

Cairo's Diplomatic Circles

A Congolese tourist booked in at Cairo's Nile Hilton. He fell 'in love' with an Egyptian lift girl and got permission from the parents to marry her. They had a 'honeymoon' in a suite at the hotel. A week later, the Congolese man disappeared and his room was locked from inside. Soon the management discovered that something was wrong with the room and got the master key to open it. They found with horror that the girl was naked and the best parts of the bride had been eaten up.

Nobody knew who the Congolese was or his whereabouts. He gave his profession as a 'diplomat'. There was an item in the newspapers that the police was looking for a Congolese who ate up an Egyptian girl. He must have left the country.

This happened just after we had left the Nile Hotel for Maadi where we found our home. The news of the cannibalism of a Congolese diplomat spread like wild fire amongst the diplomatic corps and this affected cocktail parties given by African diplomats for no Asian ladies would attend them.

Cairo then had 96 foreign embassies, easily the busiest diplomatic centre of the world. There was an average of two national days in a week and several other social functions. Not skilled in balancing a teacup or hoisting a cocktail glass, I still had to attend the national days of my diplomatic colleagues and the various functions when we were invited. There were normally at least two parties a night and we had to hop from one to the other. One needs a strong physique, plenty of energy, and a good stomach and, most important, a sense of humour. For sometime we talked about the Congolese 'diplomat' who ate up the girl, and the Congolese Ambassador was most embarrassed.

As an Ambassador, I had to call on every Ambassador who was more senior to me starting from the doyen of the diplomatic corps. They in turn gave me a return call. Our embassy is a bungalow situated in Babel Street, Doqqi, a quiet residential area where there is little traffic. I had a cosy room adjacent to my office where I met all my guests. It was from the conversations with the guests and from cocktail-party gossips that we gathered information which may or may not be useful to us.

Among the African Ambassadors, the doyen of the diplomatic corps, Mallas Mikael Andom of Ethiopia was quite friendly to me. He was in fact brought up in Cairo and spoke fluent Arabic. He liked Cairo and got permission to stay on because the temperature and altitude of Addis Ababa was not good for his heart. He was a tall man with thick glasses and spoke quite loudly like most Arabs. When I had to present credentials to Haile Selassie, I saw quite a lot of him. When Haile Selassie was overthrown, he stayed on in Cairo.

In Cairo, I met many African Ambassadors, who were mainly divided into English-speaking and French-speaking. I was closer to the English-speaking ones. The Ghana Ambassador Haji Abu Wemah explained to me how his former President Nkrumah had nearly ruined his country and her relations with neighbours. President Nkrumah was deposed during his trip to China. His Egyptian wife stayed in Cairo.

Ambassador Haji Abu said that during Nkrumah's regime, many of Ghana's youth were sent to Cuba for training and they came back to infiltrate into other African countries trying to overthrow their governments. This had caused a great deal of unhappiness and suspicion among neighbouring countries towards Ghana and relations were strained. The Haji said Nkrumah was merely interested in personal glory and personal gain. After he was ousted, Ghana's relations with her neighbours improved.

The Zambian Ambassador Chief Mapanza Morris Katowa was an energetic young man who had been a school teacher.

He explained to me his country's plan to build a cross-country railway linking Zambia and Tanzania which would bypass Rhodesia. They had approached many countries for help without success. China came along and sent 200 Chinese technicians to Zambia for the construction of the railway which was vital to the economic stability of the country. He however explained that Zambia encountered some minor problem with the Chinese technicians who brought along the Red Book of Mao Tze Tung's thoughts and badges. They were trying to distribute them to shops and the Zambian authorities had to put a stop. This led to some misunderstanding.

The Tanzanian Ambassador could not distinguish one Asian face from another. He mistook me for the Mongolian Ambassador. This took place when I attended his National Day celebration and he started to talk of things which sounded rather strange to me. When I realised that he had mistaken me for someone else, I politely reminded him that I was from Singapore. He apologised profusely. One has to be patient, forgiving and polite. He had just called on me the previous day and we had about an hour's talk. Strange that Africans could not identify one Asian from another just as it is difficult for us to differentiate one African from another. African diplomats generally do not have a good name in Cairo. The Chief of Protocol told me that they bought cheap things from the tax-free shop and sold them in the black market.

When I was in Cairo, the Chinese Ambassador was Huang Hua, who became the Foreign Minister of China. Since my arrival, my personal assistant had been trying many times to contact the Chinese Embassy to fix an appointment for me to call on the Chinese Ambassador. I made courtesy calls on all ambassadors irrespective of whether we had diplomatic relations. It was the custom in Cairo's diplomatic circles. But the reply was 'No' or that the Ambassador was too busy. I met Huang Hua on several occasions at cocktail parties. We shook hands, but he appeared to be trying to avoid a conversation. I too refrained from intruding into his conversation, normally with Communist delegates and African delegates who had close ties with China. On one occasion, we had the opportunity of meeting face to face at the North Korean National Day celebration. I asked Huang Hua in Mandarin: 'When can I pay you a courtesy call?' He replied: 'We will make separate arrangements.' Seeing that he was not eager to continue with the conversation, I took leave of him. He left Cairo before me and we never had an opportunity to talk.

During the Chinese cultural revolution, I heard that his wife Wang Ju-mei had gone back to join the revolution leaving him behind in Cairo. The Chinese Embassy maintained a sizeable number of home-based staff who were non-diplomats purporting to be drivers, cooks, butlers and office boys. I was told that these were in fact Red Guards. I once saw them in the Embassy compound wearing singlets. The Embassy compound was saturated with wall-posters glorifying Mao Tze Tung. The Red Guards saw to it that such things were done. There was a strict ruling that no staff, whether diplomats or home-based, could leave the Embassy singly. This meant that they had to watch each other's actions. However, they seldom left the self-imposed bamboo curtain.

The only time the Red Guards with arm-bands moved out collectively was sometime in March 1968 when they surrounded Nile Hilton to demand the handing over of a Chinese official, Kuan Yu Sam, who had escaped from China. The Cairo police had to disperse them. According to Mr Ramzy, the Asian Desk Chief, Kuan Yu Sam was a political officer attached to the Afro-Asian Writers' Union. He spoke good English and Japanese. He was doing good work for the Union, receiving guests from abroad. When the cultural revolution came, he was severely criticised by all his colleagues and in fact was isolated. His main guilt was that one of his ancestors happened to belong to a rich family. He tried to explain to the authorities and in fact made several statements proclaiming his loyalty to Mao and Mao's thoughts, but he was not trusted because he was a descendant of the bourgeois class. When the conference of Afro-Asian writers took place early in 1968 in Peking, he was assigned to escort a Japanese writer. He made use of the Japanese writer's passport, borrowed Japanese clothing, booked a ticket under the writer's name and escaped to Cairo. He asked for political asylum and expressed his desire to go to Moscow.

Ramzy disclosed to me that three governments were interested in Kuan Yu Sam. The Chinese Embassy had been pressing hard for the return of this 'turncoat' who had escaped from

China; the Japanese because he took away the passport belonging to a Japanese; and the Russians because Kuan's desire was to settle down in Russia. Kuan Yu Sam was put into a Cairo prison where he stayed for a year and a half before being let out. The last definite news of him was that he had left Cairo on an SAS plane for Brussels.

This had caused Huang Hua a lot of headache and he failed to get Kuan back to China. That may be one of the reasons why Huang Hua was left at his post during the cultural revolution — the only Chinese Ambassador abroad at that time. The reason for Huang Hua's avoiding me was perhaps due to the cultural revolution. He did not want to be seen with a representative of a government which the leaders of the cultural revolution thought was 'reactionary'.

I do not blame Huang Hua for having avoided me for it was during the height of the cultural revolution and all the Chinese Ambassadors throughout the world had been called back to China except for Huang Hua who apparently had not completed his task of bringing back Kuan Yu Sam.

The Chinese Ambassadors who returned home to Beijing were persecuted by the Red Guards. They were accused of being too friendly to foreign countries, and leading bourgeois lives abroad. They were interrogated by the Red Guards. Some were punished and disgraced by being made to walk through the streets with banners around their necks. Others had to attend re-orientation classes. Chou En-lai had to put a stop to this practice of disgracing their own Ambassadors.

Huang Hua recently stepped down as Foreign Minister when he was still in Moscow attending the funeral of Brezhnev. He was replaced by Wu Hsieh Chien.

The Swiss Ambassador Andre Paradi who attended the Chinese National Day celebration told me there was a conspicuous absence of Egyptian Ministers and Government officials. The people who attended the celebrations were Palestinians and just ordinary men in the street who brought even their wives and children. There were wall papers surrounding the whole compound telling stories of the Chinese cultural revolution. There was a big portrait of Mao and whenever an Ambassador came near to it, photographs were taken. Badges of Mao and leaflets were made available to the guests who wanted them.

Judging from the attendance, the Chinese were adopting the policy of making direct contact with the masses who mattered more to them in the long run. Some of those who attended the functions were Palestinian commandos who were real fighters for the liberation of Palestine and who could be the nucleus of a future Arab cultural revolution.

When I was in Cairo, Communist China had lost out completely to the Russians politically and diplomatically. The Chinese were trying to get a tangible foothold in the Middle East by supporting the Palestinian commandos. For many years Chinese influence in the Middle East has been cold-shouldered by the Arab countries because of lack of diplomacy. The strained relation between China and the UAR has never recovered since Khalid Bagdesh, the leader of the Communist Party of Egypt, was allowed to criticise the UAR in Beijing at the Chinese National Day celebration in 1959.

Realising the possibility of being sold out by their own Arab brothers who seem so keen to look for a political settlement, the Palestinian commandos now rely on China for arms supply and support because China, during my stay in Egypt, appeared to be the only country which could help them and which was keen to fish in troubled waters.

The UAR government's attitude towards China was clearly reflected in the coverage given to the Chinese National Day in the official organ *Egyptian Gazette*. The Egyptian concern for the National Day was represented by only one paragraph, lost in a jumble of advertisement-like news items under the 'Official and Personal' column, with the remarks 'President Gamal Abdul Nasser yesterday sent a cable of congratulations to Chinese Premier Chou En-lai on the occasion of the Chinese National Day.'

In the same paper, the same day, prominence was given to the celebrations marking the centenary of the birth of Mahatma Gandhi. There was not only Gandhi's photograph but a long article on the legacy of Gandhi — an appreciation of the man as well as a separate news item under the heading 'UAR to observe Centenary', quoting Dr Okasha, Minister of Culture, and announcing that a main street or square in Cairo would be named after Gandhi, and that 'a commemorative stamp would be issued by the Postal Authorities to commemorate the great man.'

When I paid my courtesy call on the Thai Ambassador, Mr Somchai Anuman Rajadhon, a man nearly 60, he asked me to read the writings on the wall of the Chinese Embassy which was in front of his residence. There it was written in bold red 'Our great Mao Tze Tung, Long Live Mao Tze Tung; Down with the US Imperialist including its stooges in front' (meaning the Thai Embassy). The Thai Ambassador was rather annoyed and said 'These people have no manners.' The Chinese Embassy is surrounded by high brick walls and one could see the portrait of Mao Tze Tung from outside.

It is ironical that China today considers Thailand a close ally in the fight against Vietnamese domination of Cambodia. I am sure the writings on the wall of the Chinese Embassy in Cairo including the portrait of Mao must have been removed.

Speaking of Cambodia, her Ambassador in Cairo was a short and stout gentleman by the name of Sarin Chlak, who became quite close to me. He had short hair, small eyes and a big nose. We used to talk about the future of Cambodia, of Vietnam and China. At that time, the American troops were still occupying Vietnam. His view was that once America withdrew from Vietnam, the whole of Asia would come under China's direct influence. He said: 'China is too powerful. Historically and geographically, China has been in control of Indo-China for 150 years before the arrival of the Occidental. China is too near. In Cambodia alone there are 400,000 Chinese half of whom are still Chinese citizens loyal to Beijing although they appear to be quiet. There are hundreds of thousands of Chinese, in other states of South-East Asia. So, how can the Russians compete with China?'

The Ambassador said Cambodia did not believe that China had any territorial ambition. What she wanted was to make South-East Asia a buffer zone, a protective defence line against possible aggression from China just as Vietnam has been serving its purpose as a protective zone. He said in this respect, China would support its neighbouring Asian countries in case of outside intervention.

Sarin Chlak told me that the North Vietnamese were not happy with Beijing because the latter tried to break up the Geneva peace talks. He said China wanted the war to drag on to drain off US finances and manpower at the expense of Vietnamese lives; at the same time China did not want the war to escalate, leading to US bombing of Chinese territories. The Russians and the North Vietnamese, however, would like to see an early settlement. As far as Cambodia was concerned, the Ambassador hinted to me that she was not eager to see a settlement. He said: 'You are far away but we are near. Apparently Cambodia is scared of North Vietnamese expansion, and a peace settlement would mean that the Ho Chi Minh regime would swallow the whole of Vietnam and probably exert its influence on neighbouring countries including Cambodia and Laos.'

My impression from the talk with Sarin Chlak was that Cambodia feared China and had accepted the inevitability of China's supremacy in Asia in the years ahead.

Later on when Lon Nol took over from Sihanouk, I met Sarin Chlak at the non-aligned conference in Dar-es-Salam representing the Sihanouk regime. And when I left Cairo for home I met with Panouk (former chief minister of Prince Sihanouk) in a plane on the way to Beijing. Sarin Chlak later became Cambodian Foreign Minister in exile in Beijing. When the Khmer Rouge swept into Cambodia, he must have accompanied Sihanouk back to Phnom Phen and we never heard of him since.

The North Vietnamese Ambassador Nguyen Xuan was a short and thin man who spoke broken English. When I met him at the extraordinary conference organised by the Afro-Asian People's Solidarity Organisation in support of solidarity with the Vietnamese people in their struggle against US imperialist aggression in Cairo, he was surprised that the Chinese delegates did not turn up. He looked a little worried and said: 'China was invited but she did not attend.' China had boycotted the conference because of the Russian intervention in Czechoslovakia for the conference was manipulated by the Russians. Singapore was then represented by L P Rodrigo and Prime Minister Lee Kuan Yew sent a message which was read out amidst applause. The Vietnamese Ambassador was very pleased with the message.

Referring to the Chinese aid to Vietnam, Nguyen Xuan said: 'The Vietnam war is quite different from the Korean war. In the Korean war there were large numbers of Chinese volunteers and the American weapons were not so powerful

Author chatting with the former Permanent Secretary of the Ministry of Foreign Affairs

The Thai Ambassador Somchai with author

Author disclosing a secret to the Japanese Ambassador at a cocktail party

Cairo's diplomatic corps — Author with Ambassadors in Cairo

The Asean Ambassadors in Cairo

Author playing the Chinese harp for an Arab audience at home

Apa Pant the Indian Ambassador to Egypt having a chat with the author

The Author and his wife (second from right) with the former Cambodian Ambassador Sarin Chlak who was at one time exiled Foreign Minister for Prince Sihanouk

The Vietnamese Ambassador Nguyen Xuan and his wife with the author

Diplomatic gathering in Cairo. (From left) – The British ambassador Sir Harold Baley, the Lebanon ambassador Dr Halim Abu-Izzeddin, the Jordanian ambassador El – Sayed Mohamed Adid El – Amery and the author

then. In the Vietnam war, there is not a single Chinese volunteer and the United States used modern destructive weapons. All the soldiers are Vietnamese.'

He then emphasised more than once that Vietnam wanted only aid and not interference from outside countries.

The Russian Ambassador Vinogradov can be described as the then 'overlord' of Egypt. As Egypt was completely dependent on the Soviet Union, her Ambassador became the most important person. The Russian Ambassador behaved like one. When the Russian Embassy celebrated its National Day, nearly the whole cabinet turned up. The road leading to the Embassy was choked with cars and the people queued up to shake hands with the Ambassador. The Ambassador was a 61-year-old seasoned diplomat. He was instrumental in extending Soviet Union's influence in the UAR. He had been a diplomat since 1931. He was a short and stout man with a serious-looking square face. He had altogether 52 diplomats and a large number of other non-diplomatic staff.

I called on him and he was one of the earliest to return compliments. I asked the Soviet Ambassador what would Soviet Union do if the Israelis refused to withdraw and the Jarring Mission failed. He paused a little and said smilingly: 'You have put a delicate question to me.' He then continued: 'We will make the Egyptians stronger and that is the only way to ensure peace. We want a peaceful solution.' I told him that I could not find any sign of militancy since I arrived here among the Egyptians. He replied: 'The Egyptians have not been fighting a war for the last 1,000 years. They are by tradition peace-loving people, but the Army and the Air Force are well-disciplined and strong enough to defend their country. They are not ready for offensive. This will take time.'

The Russian Ambassador seemed more interested in Singapore Chinese since I told him that 75 percent of the population there were Chinese. He wanted to know the attitude of the Chinese towards Mao Tze Tung.

The Russian Ambassador was easily the most powerful man in Egypt as there were 5,000 Russian military instructors and advisors in the Egyptian Army. With so many instructors in the Army the Soviet Union would demand a say in the planning of Egyptian strategy and diplomacy. Incidentally, I was told that the Russian instructors were not too popular among the Egyptian rank and file for they were too stern and demanding in their training. To the man in the street, the Russians did not pay *bakhshish* and therefore were not too popular either.

There was no US Embassy for Nasser had severed relations with the United States.

The Indian Ambassador Apa Pant was from a royal family and was a yogi. He was slim and tall, always wearing a collarless Indian coat. Every Wednesday morning, we would go to his residence for yoga lessons which he described as Surianamaskar, and then adjourn to an Indian breakfast. The exercises involved fast breathing which necessitated contracting the stomach and a lot of bending of the knees. He wrote a book on Surianamaskar translated into Arabic. Several Ambassadors from the European countries including the Dutch and Canadian Ambassadors attended the functions. The breakfast consisted of little Indian tit-bits and 'Puttumayam' which I enjoyed very much.

The Indian Ambassador was a knowledgeable person close to President Nasser, and a very useful source of information. He had once worked with Jomo Kenyatta of Kenya who was then the head of the Mau Mau, and he used to tell us some of the interesting stories of Mau Mau operations. Apa Pant has now retired in Pune, India.

The Indonesian Ambassador Lt.-Gen. Ahmad Junus Mokoginta was a jovial and popular person in Cairo. He was a Dutch-trained military personality having joined the military officer cadet training at the age of 18. He was 48 and had received his training almost at the same time as President Suharto. He fought the Japanese during the second world war and became a prisoner of war. After the Japanese surrender he also fought the Dutch during the independence struggle. During the September 30 1965 coup, he was with Subandrio and 20 other Cabinet Ministers and he was instructed by Suharto to have them kept under house arrest. I got very close to Mokoginta and we became good friends. Whenever I felt like having some satay I would visit his residence which was really grand. It had a large garden and a beautiful dining room and the lounge was spacious.

Then one day he rang me up frantically and said he wanted to see me. He had asked me to convey to Singapore his government's plea not to hang the two Indonesian marines who were sentenced to death. They had thrown bombs into Macdonald House and had caused the death of three persons. They appealed to the Privy Council but had failed. As I was the Minister of State for the Prime Minister, he thought I could do something to stop the hanging. I promised to cable home the message. But nothing could be done. The two Indonesians were hanged. On 18 October 1968, the Indonesian Embassy issued a press release which was published by *Al Ahram, Al Goumhuriah* and *Al Akhbar*, stating that General Suharto, President of Indonesia, had called for revenge against Singapore for execution of the two Indonesian marines, and that thousands of Indonesians staged a noisy demonstration during which they forced their way into a number of buildings searching for the Singapore Ambassador P. S. Raman.

On the next occasion when I met the Indonesian Ambassador, he refused to speak to me. This went on for several months until tempers had cooled down and he spoke to me again. We became friends again and he introduced many important personalities who became useful to me when I was transferred to Indonesia.

In diplomacy, one may be in the best of terms one day but the next day when the tables are turned, one could be regarded as an enemy for reasons of state. This is what I would call 'the national feeling'. When two nations were on good terms, their Ambassadors behaved cordially, but once the nations quarrelled, the Ambassadors found it difficult to maintain the personal friendship.

I have yet to see the North Koreans and the South Koreans speaking to one another publicly. On one occasion when we were celebrating our National Day near a swimming pool (I had left Cairo by then) the North Koreans and the South Koreans fought one another and one of them was pushed into the swimming pool.

The Japanese Ambassador Yoshimitsu Ando, nearing 60, was an old-time career diplomat. He was an attache in Beijing during the Lu Kou Chiau battle (the outbreak of Sino-Japanese war on 7 July 1937) and told me how he escaped and found his way to Japan. During the war, he was Head of the Asian Desk and after the war became Ambassador to the United States and was responsible for the signing of the San Francisco Treaty. His last appointment was as Ambassador to Iran before coming to Cairo. He was thin, tall and weak. Despite his weak health, he still played 18 holes of golf and I saw him once panting profusely after the game.

The Japanese Ambassador, being a seasoned diplomat, talked very little. He felt that UAR was too dependent on the Soviet Union. He said it was not likely that the UAR would swing over to Beijing for support in case they want a hot war with Israel, the reason being that China was not in a position to supply sophisticated weapons and it would antagonise the Soviet Union who might even withdraw all her aid including the construction of the Aswan Dam.

Among the Arab Ambassadors, those close to me were the Kuwait, the Jordanian, the Lebanese, the Algerian and the Moroccan. The Kuwait Ambassador, Hamad Issa El-Rujuaib, was a top official from the Ministry of Social Affairs. He spoke little English and had a lady interpreter. We became friends because he was a good *kanon* player and I was beginning to learn how to play the *kanon*. He once invited me to his house to have dinner and to listen to him playing the *kanon*. The *kanon* is an Arabic instrument similar to the Chinese Ching or harp. In the case of *kanon*, one has to use two fingers whereas the Chinese harp would require three.

My wife and I arrived at his residence one evening and we were entertained to a really sumptuous dinner. There was a roasted sheep and we had to eat with our hands. At the beginning of the dinner, my host put his fingers and dug out the sheep's eyes and put them on my plate. This was supposed to be a delicacy for the Arabs and it was considered an honour. The sheep's eyes kept looking at me and I had to pick up courage and swallow them one by one, followed by the yellow sticky rice and some water. I said 'Oh, it's fine'. In fact, it was horrible and it was lucky that I did not vomit the eyes out.

When the dinner was over, we adjourned to a separate room and listened to him playing the *kanon*. It was beautifully played and I enjoyed the evening except for the sheep's eyes.

Kuwait is the richest country in the whole Middle East. Since the June defeat, Kuwait had been supporting the UAR with £3,250,000 a month to help rehabilitate Egypt. Referring to this financial aid, the Ambassador said: 'When we help the UAR and other countries we are in fact helping ourselves.'

The Jordanian Ambassador El-Sayed Mohamed Adid El-Amery was in fact a Palestinian who had just relinquished his post as Foreign Minister of Jordan. He was bald-headed, bespectacled and very friendly and frank. He suggested that I should visit the refugee camps and the front-line bordering Israel and also pay a courtesy call on King Hussein. This suggestion came after we had a frank discussion on the Palestinian problems and the Middle East crisis generally. He was one of those who would have liked to see a peaceful settlement and realised that existence of Israel is inevitable. He told me that many leading government officials in the Arab states were Palestinians.

I wrote back to Singapore asking for permission to visit Jordan but there was no reply.

The Lebanese Ambassador Dr Halim Abu-Izzeddin was a lawyer by profession and had studied law in Beirut and later in Paris. He was Governor of one of the northern provinces and had written a book about Lebanon and the five provinces. He is young and energetic and friendly. He had visited Singapore twice — first in 1954 while he attended the Afro-Asian conference in Bandung, and the second occasion in 1961. Although I was at the Bandung conference, we never met.

I told him that I was about to be accredited to Lebanon and he was happy. He said Lebanon was a free country and was the 'window' of the Middle East where one could have a 'peep' at world events.

He added: 'It is a wise move on your part to have a diplomatic foothold in Lebanon where there is a freer atmosphere and you will hear all shades of opinion. There is parliamentary democracy in Lebanon because we have had such a tradition for a long time. You can't blame the other Arab countries for not practising parliamentary democracy which you will agree needs time to develop.'

But what has happened to parliamentary democracy in Lebanon now? It is nothing but chaos and disaster.

The Algerian Ambassador Lakhdar Brahimi was an old friend of Singapore having come to make arrangements for the visit of Algeria's first provisional President Dr Ferhad Abbas. There was a big rally at the City Hall steps to welcome Dr Ferhad Abbas organised by us. When I first met him, he said: 'Oh, it is you. We have met in Singapore.' I was Parliamentary Secretary to the Minister of Culture when he came. He was the Head of the Provisional Government office in Jakarta during the revolution and knew many personalities in Singapore.

He asked about Lim Chin Siong, Said Zahari and Samad Ismail. I told him about Lim Chin Siong's attempted suicide and Zahari's involvement with the Brunei revolt and Samad Ismail was then working for an English newspaper. He seemed surprised. He said he would never forget the support which Singapore had given to Algeria during its struggle for independence, particularly Prime Minister Lee Kuan Yew.

Speaking of Arab disunity, he attributed three factors which had caused the disunity:

(i) Ideological differences: Some countries want the socialist system and its promise of better distribution of wealth, while the others were still feudalistic.
(ii) Economic vested interest: Big powers had economic vested interest in each Arab country and they wanted to preserve such interest by dividing them.
(iii) Personal power: There was always the question of wanting to maintain personal prestige and power in one's own country. Once you have one Arab world, the leaders of smaller countries will have less power and less prestige.

He liked the way of my description: 'It is better to be a big fish in a small pond than to be a small fish in a big pond.'

As ambassadors we met one another very often at national day parties, cocktail parties or at social functions. We also met one another at the airport to either receive important guests or send them off. These were usually at well past midnight for planes arrived at Cairo at odd hours of the morning. It was all right for those whose residences were at Heliopolis which was near the airport. But for those who stayed in town, it was quite a distance. When you have to get up at 1 a.m. and travel to the airport for the 2 a.m. arrival, and then shake the hands of the VVIPs and dash back to bed, you knew life is miserable. In Cairo, the ambassadors had to do this quite often. They only had the obligation to receive and send off the VVIPs visiting Egypt but not the privilege of meeting them at cocktails or dinner.

The ambassadors and diplomats go to various clubs. There was the Gezirah Club, which was once the haunt of British rulers. It had all the facilities for games and sports and other social activities. It was situated right in the middle of the city with an 18 hole golf course. Being in the desert, one should not expect a green. There was the shooting club where one could shoot clay pigeon; a riding club where one could go for riding. In Maadi where I stayed, there was the Maadi Club which was smaller in size, but had a good swimming pool, games and a weekly open air cinema show.

There were plenty of nightclubs in town where business went on till the early hours of the morning. Off the Pyramid track across the desert was the Sahara City where one could see belly dancing. The desert is hot in the day time but cool and refreshing at night.

There was also the Kanhalili traditional shopping centre where one could bump into one or two ambassadors or diplomats doing their shopping for pouffes and other Egyptian traditional handicrafts.

There were only two Chinese restaurants, one called the Peking restaurant and the other the Fu Shing. The best Chinese food they could provide was springrolls. I once gave a party at the Peking to ambassadors and they seemed to like the food there. There were many fat ducks which resembled Peking ducks swimming in the lake in Cairo where one could row boats, but none of the cooks in the two restaurants knew how to roast a Peking duck.

And of course, there was the famous Cairo zoo, the paradise for children.

There were many occasions when ambassadors gathered to listen to President Nasser at the National Assembly premises. President Nasser became bolder and bolder. Sometime in November 1969, he described the efforts of the United Nations and its envoy Dr Gunnar Jarring and the Four-Power talks 'as a waste of time' and spoke of the inevitable battle in which the Arabs would have 'to march in a sea of blood and under a sky of flames.' After the speech, he went to Moscow to meet the Russian bears.

Then on the morning of 28th January 1970, while I was chatting with a visitor in my Maadi residence, a series of bombs exploded around the corner and shook the whole building. The Israeli planes which let off the bombs flew very low and loud. We did not hear any siren. Soon after the planes left, a large number of villagers in galabia clothes passed my house and rushed towards the direction of the bomb site. They had heard rumours that an Israeli plane was shot down and they were curious to see it. The explosions were so loud that my nervous cook put up both of his hands and ran from outside into the house and hid himself under a kitchen table. The wife of the First Secretary of the Malaysian Embassy, who also lived in Maadi, was hysterical and cried over the telephone telling her husband what had happened. Many school children including my daughter in the American School of Maadi saw the fire that had gutted the military camp opposite and started to scream.

It was the biggest air raid carried out by the Israelis since the defeat of the Rabat Summit. We discovered later that the military recruitment centre and military installations around Maadi were bombed resulting in three deaths and 22 injured. At the same time, another Israeli plane bombed Dahshur near the Pyramids. Only two days back Israeli planes bombed Helwan military installations. This pattern of Israeli raids had become almost a weekly if not a daily affair.

Some ambassadors and their families evacuated. I cabled home to find out whether we should also evacuate in case the bombing became heavier. The answer was to stay put until most of the ambassadors had evacuated. We were told that we could evacuate to Greece when it was necessary.

When the Israeli bombs dropped, it reminded me of the Japanese bombs in Penang in December 1941 when I had to hide under a bridge. I said to myself: 'Do I have to suffer once more the agony of evacuation?' This is one of the risks which an ambassador has to take. When relationship between nations becomes bad, an embassy is likely to be bombed or burnt down or the ambassador taken as hostage or even assassinated. It was fortunate that the bomb did not fall on my residence because it was quite near the recruitment camp. Every morning, we used to hear shouts from the new recruits doing their daily exercise. That morning, there were no shouts but instead the bombs.

We stayed on in Cairo, and the air raids diminished as the days went by. Life returned to normal after sometime.

4

Nasser—Who Dreamt Too Long

'The Lion is dead', 'The Lion is dead', cried the people of Egypt who had heard from the radio announcement from the Vice-President, Anwar Sadat, of the death of Abdul Gamal Nasser, Egypt's President. The 'Lion is dead' echoed throughout the Nile where the Egyptians flock to, in time of grief and emotion. The people came out to the street, at first a group, then hundreds, then thousands and tens of thousands and very soon the streets were choked. They all shouted 'The Lion is dead'. Cairo streets were crammed with millions of people who came from the countryside and from abroad. The trains were stopped but people still came by donkeys and on foot.

The whole of Cairo was at a standstill for grief. Five divisions of troops moved in to control the mourners but the mourners were so enormous that the troops were swept away. The people tried to grab Nasser's coffin and managed to tear three flags away and at the Railway Square the President's body had to be taken from the gun carriage which was in danger of being wrecked and put on an armoured car. Eventually, the coffin reached the mosque after a tumultuous seven-mile procession. This mosque was close to the apartment where he lived at the time of his coup, and a little further away was the Army Headquarters which the Free Officers took over from King Farouk on 23 July 1952.

President Nasser was buried beneath a marble tomb inscribed with words from the Koran which were broadcast by Anwar Sadat when he announced his death.

What sort of a leader was Nasser? Why was he so loved by his people? What were his achievements and what were his drawbacks?

When Nasser wrote his 'Egypt's Liberation — the philosophy of the Revolution', he set his target very high. He pointed out that 'half the proved reserves of oil in the world lie beneath Arab soil, the remainder being divided among the United States, Russia and the Caribbean area and other sections of the globe.' He spoke of the Arab circle, and then of the continent of Africa which could not remain aloof from the terrible and sanguinary conflict going on there today between five million whites and 200 million Africans.

'The people of Africa will continue to look to us who guard their northern gate, and who constitute their link with the outside world.' He said, 'We will never in any circumstances be able to relinquish our responsibility to support with all our might the spread of enlightenment and civilization to the remotest depths of the jungle.'

He added, 'I will continue to dream of the day when I will find in Cairo a great African institute dedicated to unveiling to our view of the dark reaches of the continent, to creating in our minds an enlightened African consciousness and to sharing with others from all over the world the work of advancing the welfare of the peoples of this continent.'

Then he talked of the third circle and said: '. . . . my belief in the possibility of extending the effectiveness of the Pilgrimage, building upon the strength of the Islamic tie that binds all Muslims, grew very strong.' He said Islam should not be regarded as only a ticket of admission into Paradise after a long life, but should become an institution of great political power and significance.

And he ended with these words: 'And now I go back to that wandering mission in search of a hero to play it. Here is the role. Here are the lines and here is the stage. We alone, by virtue of our place, can perform the role.'

Obviously, Nasser had taken upon himself to perform the role. His horizon was not confined to the Arab world, but to the African continent and the Islamic world. He wanted to be the 'hero' or leader of these three worlds.

I first met Nasser at the Bandung Afro-Asian Conference in 1955. He was in military uniform, tall, slim but smart. He walked over to the rostrum with the written speech in his hand. He spoke with a monotonous voice and never raised his head, straining his eyes on the paper, and read out the speech till the end. As a speaker, he was not at all impressive. He was not a rabble-rouser, but said his words slowly and solemnly. He introduced the Palestine issue and made reference to the continuance of colonialism in North Africa and racial discrimination in South Africa, with Israel — the aggressor.

When I saw him on the stage, I least expected that I would be presenting credentials to him 13 years later as Singapore's Ambassador to Egypt.

In 1955, Nasser had already designated Egypt as 'Arab', for on 23 July 1954, the second anniversary of the revolution, he had announced: 'Compatriots, Egypt has started a new era of relations with the Arabs — an era based on true and frank fraternity, facing up and thinking out problems and endeavouring to solve them. The aim of the Revolutionary Government is for the Arabs to become one nation with all its sons collaborating for the common welfare.'

It was at Bandung that Nasser got to know Chou En-lai who introduced him to the Russians from whom he got the arms. The Americans had refused to give arms to Egypt because Nasser refused to join the Baghdad Pact. Nasser had returned home as a 'hero of Bandung and champion of peace and liberty.' His role at Bandung was acclaimed by the Egyptian press as marking the 'emergence of Egyptian diplomacy from its old shell into the wide world.'

Anwar Sadat, then a journalist writing for the Cairo daily *Al Goumhuriah*, had said: 'Nasser's voice will echo everywhere in Asia and Africa as a new symbol of hope; the people of Egypt, Palestine, Tunisia, Morocco as well as those oppressed in the jungles of Kenya will forever be proud of him.'

Nasser himself told an Indian journalist on his way home from Bandung that he appraised the Bandung Conference 'as one of the two most important events of modern history' — the other being the discovery of atomic energy.

There can be little doubt that the Bandung Conference marked one of the crucial turning points in Nasser's political thinking, and indeed of Egypt's foreign policy. Bandung appeared to have affected Nasser most strongly of all the participants. His contact with Nehru, U Nu, Sukarno and to a certain extent Chou En-lai opened up new vistas in international relations and brought him fairly and squarely into the camp of the militantly non-aligned. It was Nasser's full conversion, far more than Nehru's, which was to transform the policy of non-alignment into the dominant trend in Asia and Africa. In the years following Bandung, it was he who set the pace of militancy and who gave birth to the new concept of positive neutralism.

Sometime in July 1968, I met Nasser again, this time in Cairo at his Palace. I went there to present my credentials. I could see that the effect of the defeat in the seven-day war with Israel in 1967 was still troubling the tranquillity of his mind. The conversation lasted only about ten minutes and I bade goodbye to Nasser. I returned to the Singapore Embassy and had a cocktail party among the staff and friends of Singapore.

Nasser then went off to Georgia for medical treatment.

Nasser had mentioned the difficulties of merger for he had the experience in January 1958 in Egypt's merger with Syria. He had decided to call Egypt the United Arab Republic because of the merger. The union lasted until the autumn of 1961 when Syria left the union and was on her own. But the name 'United Arab Republic' continued to be used by Nasser.

The Moroccan Ambassador in Cairo, Mahdi Mrani Zentar, a young and handsome man, was right when he described UAR as a 'misnomer.' The Ambassador said that retaining the name of UAR indicated that President Nasser in fact 'had not given up the hope of trying to drag nation after nation into the orbit of his control.' This reflected the feelings of an Arab Ambassador towards Nasser and his ambition at the time before his death.

Mr Zentar added: 'Although we were Arabs, a large proportion of our population were Berbers.' He envisaged that a day would come when there would be a federation of the states in North Africa — Algeria, Morocco and Tunisia, the countries formerly ruled by the French, and Libya.

The Ambassador said: 'It is too much for President Nasser to expect to become an Arab as well as an African. They should confine themselves to the fertile crescent, meaning Egypt, Iraq, Lebanon, Saudi Arabia, Kuwait and Syria and leave North Africa alone.'

Even among Egyptians, there was a campaign by intellectuals to make people remember the glory of being an Egyptian instead of an Arab. Around August 1969, a long series of articles glorifying ancient Egyptian civilization appeared in the *Al Ahram*, Egypt's leading Arabic national newspaper. The introductory article referred to Cairo as a city of 5,000 years instead of 1,000 years of history. The article indirectly hinted that as an Arab, Cairo has only 1,000 years of history behind it, but as an Egyptian it has 5,000 years of civilization. I met Professor Abu Bakar, a leading Egyptian archaeologist at a dinner party given by an artist friend of mine Prof N Kamil, who is also lecturing at the Cairo University. Prof Abu Bakar expressed his views very frankly and told me that he was the editor of the articles written by a number of Egyptian experts. He said the purpose of the whole exercise was to:

(i) remind our people that we should be proud of our Egyptian heritage instead of wanting all the time to be only an Arab, and
(ii) make the people forget the term 'UAR' which is after all a misnomer in the present context.

Prof Abu Bakar speaking to me privately had said: 'Why should we get ourselves involved in other people's affairs? If we had properly utilised the resources spent in minding other people's business in Yemen, Syria and other Arab neighbours, we as Egyptians would be very much better off. It is time that we reminded our people that we are Egyptians in the first instance.'

After the dinner, Prof Kamil took me to see his oil paintings in his underground studio. We came across a painting of Nasser which was sandwiched between rolls of canvas. He said casually, 'Do you recognise this portrait? This will fetch a better price when the person is gone.' I kept quiet but silently noted the feeling of yet another intellectual.

But Nasser never gave up his idea of a United Arab Republic. Since December 1969, the success of the Sudanese and Libyan revolutions had eked out the balance of power within the inter-Arab power struggle in favour of Nasser. There was talk of the three 'progressive' states of Arab Western Front which geographically and economically speaking belong to one unit, forming a federation. The 27-year-old Libyan revolutionary leader Gaddafi was in fact arrested in 1961 while he was still a student for involvement in the 5th October demonstration in protest against the separation of Egypt and Syria. He said in an interview with the Press recently, 'We believe in the unity of Arab Revolution. The Arab revolutionary movement should be one in purpose and we are against multi-revolutionary theories.' But after much talk no federation was formed.

By the time of his death, Nasser only had a weak Egypt under the name of United Arab Republic. His dream of an extended hand in the African continent was buried with him. And his third circle, the Islamic world, was wrecked by the Muslim Brotherhood within his own country which made an attempt on his life. He detained most of the Muslim Brotherhood leaders.

One afternoon, during the end of January 1969, I suddenly received a call from Chia Chiong Fook, First Secretary of our London High Commission, indicating that our Prime Minister would like to visit the Abu Simbul during his visit to Cairo. I was rather worried because Nasser would not allow his visitors to fly by plane within Egypt because it was too dangerous. I told Chia that I could not promise but I would try.

It happened that the night before Chia's call, I had invited the chamberlain in charge of the Presidential Palace, Fuad Taymour, for dinner. For some reason, he did not turn up and never even phoned. The host and guests waited until almost 10.30 p.m. and there was no sign of Fuad. We went ahead with our dinner without him.

The next morning, he frantically rang me and apologised for not attending the dinner for he had forgotten about it. He apologised over and over again. I thought it was an opportunity for me to ask him for a favour at a time when he was apologetic. I said I had some important matter to discuss with him and requested an interview. He immediately gave me an appointment. At the interview, I told him my urgent request and hoped that he could be some help. He looked at me open-eyed and said: 'Normally, we do not allow our guest to fly by plane within Egypt at this hour because it could be dangerous. However, I will do something about it.'

He immediately called up his assistants and told them to make the arrangements. After about half an hour, he said to me: 'It's all done, the Abu Simbul visit is on.'

It was a stroke of luck that Fuad forgot to turn up for dinner and he was doing everything possible to redeem his guilt.

The Prime Minister and Mrs Lee arrived in Cairo on the 21st of January 1969 and left on the 24th. At the airport they were received and sent off by Anwar Sadat, who was then Speaker of the Parliament and a leading member of the Higher Executive Committee of the Arab Socialist Union. Sadat was third in hierarchy, although he was actually the second because Hussein Shafei, who was supposed to be second was more of a religious figure. The Minister of Justice, Mohamed Abu Nusseir, was the Head of the Mission of Honour who accompanied Prime Minister Lee Kuan Yew's party throughout their visit.

Prime Minister Lee had a frank talk with Dr Fawzy on international affairs generally with particular emphasis on the Middle East crisis. Dr Fawzy was the former Foreign Minister and later became the Adviser to Nasser on foreign matters. Later he had one and a half hours discussion with Egypt's Foreign Minister Riad. Riad told our Prime Minister of the strained relations between the UAR and Beijing. He spoke of Beijing's instigation that the Arabs should fight without giving regard to the actual situation and of the Arab capabilities. He also mentioned the Chinese Ambassador's constant demand for the return of an 'insignificant' Chinese Kuan Yu Sam who escaped from Beijing to Cairo. Riad said it was the policy of the UAR to provide political asylum to those who arrived at Cairo. This included the recent political refugee from Greece.

The Prime Minister also had a private discussion with President Nasser. It was at Nasser's dinner for our Prime Minister at his Presidential Palace that I met him for the third time. The President's dinner was attended by Anwar Sadat, Dr Fawzy, Riad, the Minister of Justice Mohamed Abu Nusseir and the newly elected Speaker of the National Assembly, Dr Mohamed Labib Shukeir and Abdel Mohsen Abdu Nur, formerly Minister of Local Administration, and their wives.

The dinner was an informal one. Nasser was in lounge suit. As usual, he was tense and seemed to have lost the art of relaxation. He had recovered a great deal after the Georgia treatment. He chatted with the Prime Minister like old friends and they seemed to get along well. Nasser's wife was a simple woman who dressed simply and behaved very humbly. She did not put on any jewellery. Nasser was very friendly and hospitable to his guests. He was natural but there was something in him that was difficult to fathom. Something was unsettled within him and he seemed to be bothered with it.

The reception was warm despite the fact that we had recognised Israel. During the visit, none of the UAR leaders or officials had queried us about our stand vis-a-vis the Arab cause, nor had they asked any embarrassing questions.

The day after the Prime Minister's departure, the *Egyptian Mail* carried a front-page three-column article entitled 'Lee agrees on Need for just Mid-East Solution.' The paper quoted a spokesman of the Prime Minister as having said that 'President Nasser explained to the Singapore Premier the true dimensions of the Middle East problem. The President and the Premier agreed on the necessity of solving the Middle East issue on the basis of justice.'

The Prime Minister's party visited the Abu Simbul, by taking a special plane. The visit was so hurriedly arranged that the host forgot about our lunch and it was not until nearly 4 pm that we had some soft drinks and sandwiches. The Abu Simbul which sank into the sea was entirely lifted to the ground through the help of UNESCO. It was a most impressive historic monument with giant figures of Egyptian pharoahs. The Egyptians were right in wanting to preserve it.

I had many subsequent occasions to see Nasser. I saw him attending the Arab Socialist Union meetings when guards would line up the streets along the routes leading from the Palace to the ASU Congress building. The streets would be clean and there would be people welcoming him. I saw him opening some factories and again the streets leading to the factories would be lined up with security guards — one at every ten feet. I saw him speak at the Parliament and his speeches were fiery and lengthy. He had learnt the art of speaking and was much more impressive than the time I last saw him at Bandung. But I had a feeling that Nasser did not know what was really going on in his country.

One of the paradoxes of Nasser's life was that while he was a rebel, he was also a dreamer. He was taught to believe that Hell was horrible and that children could go to heaven. At the age of seven, he and another boy decided to commit suicide. They went to the Post Office where his father worked as a clerk and stole some wax which his father had always warned was poisonous. They ate it and lay down to die. But instead of going to heaven, he got stomachache and was beaten up by his father.

That naivete stayed on with him all his life. He was never interested in women or money or food. After he came into power, the cynical old politicians tried to corrupt him but they all failed miserably.

In 1953, one year after he took office, the Americans tried to bribe him with $3 million. It was a bribe offered through the mistake of the US Ambassador Caffery. The American government had intended to aid Egypt with $43 million, $40 million of conventional financial assistance in accordance with their laws, and $3 million of unvouchered funds directly from the President's budget. When Ambassador Caffery received word of the $43 million or rather the $40 million plus $3 million he thought of the idea of a 'personal gift' to Nasser. The next day, he visited Dr Fawzy, the then Foreign Minister, to inform him of the $40 million in aid, but said not a word about the $3 million. The US Embassy staff consulted Hassan, the head of Nasser's bodyguard unit what they should do with the $3 million. Hassan in turn consulted Nasser who saw no reason not to accept the money. When the money had arrived from Beirut, they took the money in two suitcases in hard cash and took them to Hassan's house in Maadi. Nasser's reaction to the 'attempted bribe' was a mixture of annoyance and amusement. His first inclination was to send it back, possibly announcing to the world that a bribe was offered to him. But this was not Nasser's style. Instead, he ordered that the money should be spent on constructing something ugly to remind the Americans of their foolishness. The result was the ugly looking Cairo Tower which graces the landscape of Gezira island, across the Nile and taller than the Pyramids.

There was no doubt as to the integrity and honesty of Nasser. His family life was impeccable. He always tried to lunch with

President Nasser talking to author after the presentation of credentials

Abu Simbul — Egypt's most impressive historic monument, lifted from the sea

Premier Lee and Mrs Lee visiting the Abu Simbul in 1969

his wife and three sons and two daughters. His only hobby was to watch films and sometimes listen to his wife playing the piano.

The Americans had misjudged Nasser. They thought that he could be bribed into supporting their Baghdad Pact which comprised Iraq, Turkey and Pakistan to stop the expansion of Communism from the Soviet Union. Immediately after Nasser came into power, he had cut the army's budget and had used the £70 million he had confiscated from King Farouk to build hospitals, schools and roads. He had asked the United States during the early days of his regime for $40 million. Then after negotiations, the figure went down to $20 million and finally 'just two or three million dollars worth of parade items' — helmets, pistol holsters, and various kinds of shiny equipment which would look good when the army was parading through the streets of Cairo and give officers and soldiers a feeling of pride.

Until recently, Nasser had been ruling the country with his comrades in arms of the Free Officers Committee who had helped him into power. The inner circle of the Free Officers Committee became the inner circle of the Revolutionary Command Council and later the ruling clique of the Cabinet. Of the five top men in his inner circle, General Ameer, his righthand man, was politically ambitious and was capable of succeeding him. The other was Zakaria Mohieddin, formerly Deputy Prime Minister, who was a pro-West rightwinger in favour of closer relations with the West and of taking more stringent measures to improve the economy.

The third was Aly Sabry who was a pro-Moscow leftwinger and who was Deputy Prime Minister and Minister for Local Administration. When I was in Cairo, Moscow was anxious to see Aly Sabry elected as Secretary-General of the Arab Socialist Union. The other two who were less ambitious were Hussein E Shafei, more of a religious figure, and Mohamed Adeky Soliman who was Minister of Electric Power and High Dam. These were Free Officers who had fought with Nasser during the 1952 Coup.

The change of the power structure in the Nasser Cabinet came about immediately after the June defeat in 1967. Soon after the disastrous defeat, Nasser told Ameer privately that since both of them were responsible for the defeat, they should both resign. At the same time, it was suggested by certain quarters that Nasser should step down to enable pro-West Zakaria Mohieddin to save the situation. Nasser accepted the idea perhaps to test the ambition of Zakaria Mohieddin who had privately agreed to shoulder the burden. Then on 9th June 1967, when Nasser announced his decision to resign over the television, he mentioned that 'In appreciation of Article II of the Provisional Constitution issued in March 1954, I have entrusted my companion, my friend, my brother Zakaria Mohieddin with the position of President of the Republic and to work in accordance with the constitutional article decreed. After this decision, I have placed everything I have at his disposal and in the service of the dangerous and serious circumstances through which our peoples are passing.'

As he made the historic announcement, he got his supporters to engineer a countrywide mass demonstration to demand for 'No other leader except Nasser' to rule the country. Meanwhile, Ameer had already tendered his resignation and it was subsequently accepted by Nasser when he became President again.

Soon after Nasser got back into his saddle, he found Ameer a good scapegoat for the June defeat and events ultimately led to Ameer's suicide. Can Ameer be blamed when Nasser in his television broadcast had admitted that it was the American President and the Soviet Ambassador who had asked 'me' not to fire the first shot? On the day when he made the broadcast announcing the resignation he took all the blame and made no mention of Ameer. One year later, after the defeat and long after Ameer's suicide, he said in a speech to the ASU National Congress that 'our officers and men were ready to die for the country, but no orders came.' He did not explain who did not give the order, leaving people to guess that it was Ameer.

Who did not give the order? As Commander-in-Chief of the Army and the Air Force, Nasser was kept informed to the last minute before the outbreak of the June war. He had disclosed in his resignation speech about contacts with President Johnson and the Soviet Ambassador who appealed to him not to fire the first shot. Who else could be blamed for not giving the order?

I said earlier that Nasser had announced the appointment of Zakaria Mohieddin as President to replace him when he resigned. Zakaria who privately accepted knew that he fell into the trap when mass demonstrations were held demanding Nasser to stay on. He immediately made a statement declining the offer and pledged his support that Nasser should be the only leader for the country. Although he was appointed as one of the four Deputy Prime Ministers on 20 June 1967 after Nasser was returned as President, he was destined not to remain long in the Nasser Cabinet. When the second reshuffle took place, in March 1968, he was dropped from the Cabinet and it was rumoured that he was kept under house arrest. With his exit, Aly Sabry was also dropped in order to keep the balance between the left and right factions in the inner circle.

With the new Cabinet reshuffle, 18 Army officers who can be considered as 'old guards' of the 1952 revolution lost their positions in the Cabinet. They were replaced by civilians comprising trusted permanent secretaries, academicians or university professors and lecturers who were popular among the university students and the intelligentsia. None of the 19 new Cabinet Ministers took part in the 1952 revolution. They were technocrats. Some were appointed because of their special knowledge and experience. The appointment of some of the professors was to pacify the university students who began to show discontent towards the top heavy military complex of the previous Cabinet set-up.

The Cabinet I found in Cairo when I arrived was a balance of power between trustworthy 'old guards' and technocrats who had not participated in the 1952 revolution. The Cabinet members were appointed after each of them was interviewed separately by President Nasser just as civil servants going through the Public Service Commission interview for promotion.

With this new Cabinet reshuffle, Nasser's position seemed more secure than ever before. That explained why he could afford to take three weeks' leave in Georgia.

Nasser brought about his secured position by instituting the ARAB SOCIALIST UNION. After 16 years of revolution, the Army was still the only cohesive force in the country. There was no written constitution. Political parties were non-existent and the people, 80 percent of them illiterate, were disorganised. Nasser had formed the Arab Socialist Union to bring about some form of 'guided democracy'.

He had announced the March 30 Programme, after the riots in Helwan and Cairo University. There was discontent, particularly among the intellectuals, with the way things were run despite the lesson of the June defeat. An opportunity to demonstrate their frustration and discontent came when the military tribunal passed too light a sentence on those military officers who were alleged to have been responsible for the June defeat. The students protested against the light sentences, and riots occurred but were later suppressed by the authorities. To overcome the difficulties, Nasser immediately reshuffled the Cabinet and brought to the ministerial posts technocrats and academicians described by him as the cream of the nation's youths to satisfy the intellectuals. On March 30th, he announced his plan to reconstruct the Arab Socialist Union. The announcement, later known as the 'March 30 Programme', was accepted by the people in the general referendum held on May 2 the same year.

For the first time in 16 years, there was some form of election in Egypt. Six million members of the ASU in July 1968 cast their votes for 180,229 candidates for executive posts in the Basic Units in the villages. The 71,000 successful candidates became elected members of the Basic Units who would choose delegates to the districts, the factories and the governorates up to the National Congress consisting of 1,700 members. The 1,700 members elected the Central Committee of 150 members who would then elect the Supreme Central Committee. The whole structure was like a pyramid.

The National Congress elected Nasser as President of the ASU, the highest authority in the country. The Congress would supervise the work of the Government and would also have a say in all legislations before they were presented to the National Assembly which was a separate body. The Congress would help the Government to formulate policies.

The National Congress had also been entrusted with the task of drawing up a permanent constitution for the UAR. This draft constitution when approved by the Congress would be put to a national popular referendum.

This in brief was the set-up of the Arab Socialist Union and Nasser was putting his heart and soul into it, because it was believed when the constitution was accepted by the people, he would be democratically elected by the people as UAR's President.

But as things were, it seemed to me that the efforts made so far were merely trappings and formalities. Nasser still derived his strength from the Army. On the mobilisation of the masses through the ASU, I was doubtful of the results. The ASU as it were would not accomplish the task. There was no proper training of cadres, and no definite ideological concept except vague slogans of Arab Socialism and the enemy Israel. Most of the time spent on the Congress meetings were statements of self-glorification of the Government's achievements in economic expansion and the Armed Forces. There was no sign of any mass movement to bring literacy to the 80 percent, nor to make the people more militant.

One would have thought that the first thing the Government or the ASU should do was to extend the working hours instead of continuing with the system of having a long siesta after 2 pm every day and having 18 official holidays a year. One would have expected the radio and TV which was Government owned to instil some sense of urgency and militancy in the people by patriotic songs and other more serious programmes. Instead, the radio and TV were still saturated daily with soft and sleepy music and romantic items of entertainment. I was told that they tried once with patriotic songs but had to give them up after two months' experiment. The people were just disinterested.

A typical example of the lack of discipline could be found in the behaviour of the policemen in Cairo. It was not an unusual sight to see a policeman shabbily dressed, smoking a cigarette while on duty, or listening to a pocket radio, not for news but for soft music.

The only time policemen appeared smart and alert was when they lined up, every five yards, along the road for Nasser to pass by when he was on his way to meetings or functions. The streets were usually dirty except when the President was scheduled to pass by.

My chauffeur told me that his son who had had seven years of education did not know how to write his name in Arabic. The teacher who was underpaid was more interested in asking the children to get money from their parents — not legal school fees but money for their own pockets, otherwise no lessons.

Was the President aware of such things and what was the ASU going to do about them?

My impression of the ASU was that it was a political party with its trappings but had yet to develop into a movement to change the leisurely ways of the people, bring about efficiency to the Government service and to rid corruption which was rampant in Egypt.

Since the June defeat, the UAR had to depend more and more on Russia. The Soviet Union had replaced all the planes destroyed or captured by the Israelis and had supplied more arms. In Nasser's own words, 'We owe the Soviet Union so much and yet they never asked anything back from us.' He was naive. Nasser had admitted in his speech at the ASU National Congress that there were 5,000 Russian instructors and military officers training the Egyptian army. So long as the Soviet military officers remain in the Egyptian Armed Forces, there is no question of any coup or success of any coup attempt by local officers. This would mean, however, that Nasser's own security would depend more on the generosity of the Soviet Army officers. The moment he tried to switch line or was out of step, who would guarantee that a new military junta more acceptable to the Russians would not stage a coup with Russian blessing?

It seemed difficult for him to get out of the Soviet grip without endangering his own safety and security as the Soviet military instructors got an upper hand in the Egyptian Armed Forces.

Then came the Russian invasion of Czechoslovakia. President Nasser was convalescing in Alexandria. According to *Al Ahram*, on 22 August 1968, the President received an urgent message from the Soviet leader at 4 pm (Cairo time 21 August), informing him of the Warsaw Pact countries' decision to send forces into Czechoslovakia. The Soviet leaders were keen that Nasser should hear their views on the situation before the forces entered Czechoslovakia.

Nasser was caught in a dilemma. What should he do or say? The world was waiting for the campaign of non-aligned countries to say something. But Nasser had not said a word about the event.

I tried to contact Czechoslovakia's Ambassador Otto Klicka whom I met a day before the invasion. What Otto Klicka could do was to send to all ambassadors in Cairo the text of the Note of Protest from his Government to the invaders. The only newspaper that commented on the Russian invasion was the UAR official organ, the *Egyptian Gazette* published in English. The editorial entitled 'Contract' did not mention a word of protest against Soviet invaders, but instead compared the invasion to what happened 14 months ago when Israelis invaded Egypt.

I was told that all newspapers were warned to lay off the issue until Nasser had made up his mind. How long would Nasser remain silent? The fact that he was hesitant to judge the Soviet move confirms my belief that he was under the grip of Moscow. His silence was an indication of Russia's success in neutralising him.

The Russian invasion had generated anti-Russian feeling in Cairo. I have met editors of Arabic and English newspapers, foreign correspondents, shopkeepers and those whom I knew and for the first time they had become vociferous in their anti-Russian attitude. Even my own chauffeur, an Egyptian, a quiet person not keen on politics said: 'These Russians cannot be trusted. If they do this to us, we will kill them.'

Meanwhile, no Arabic newspapers published in the UAR so far have criticised the Russians. Instead, cartoons appeared to ridicule the Americans for trying to exploit the Czechoslovakian situation. The Egyptian newspapers instead diverted public attention by playing up the UAR Revolutionary Court's verdict on two former Ministers and the former Director of Intelligence for plotting to overthrow the Nasser regime in August 1967. The Revolutionary Court announced its verdict in three major cases involved with the plot to topple the regime by force. The former War Minister Shams Badran, the former Minister for the Interior Abbas Radwan, the former Director of Intelligence Salah Nasr and the former Commander of Shock Troops Galal Haradi were sentenced to hard labour for life plus repayment to the State Treasury of a large amount of money. The total number of the accused was 63. These former Ministers conspired with the late Marshal Ameer (alleged to have committed suicide) in an attempt to overthrow the regime on 27 August

1967 after the June defeat. They plotted to overthrow the Government when Ameer was relieved of his duty as Deputy Commander of the Armed Forces.

But the prominent political commentator and editor-in-chief of *Al Ahram*, Mohamed Massanien Heikal, whose articles were known to reflect President Nasser's thinking, had come out with a long analysis explaining why Arab countries particularly the UAR had been quiet about the Russian aggression. Heikal put his comment in such a way as to indicate that there was vested interest in the Arab countries vis-a-vis the Russian move in Czechoslovakia. According to Heikal, certain influential leaders in the Czechoslovakian Government including the Deputy Prime Minister Ota Sik were pressuring for the resumption of diplomatic relations with Israel. Heikal said that those leaders had alleged that the Soviet Union had coerced Czechoslovakia into breaking her relations with Israel after the Middle East war. Heikal's articles went on to relate the influence of the Jews and Zionists in the Czechoslovakian Government. The article said that one of the agreements of the Bratislava talks was that Czechoslovakia must not resume diplomatic relations with Israel. Had it not been for the Russian intervention, Czechoslovakia might have resumed diplomatic relations with Israel which would be detrimental to the Arab interests.

Heikal's view on the Russian aggression can be summed up in the following sentences: 'I would not support the military intervention of the Warsaw Pact countries in Czechoslovakia, but I would not condemn it. I would not support it in principle and would not condemn it on the basis of circumstances.' This reflected the views of Nasser.

The editorial of the *Daily Star* of Beirut aptly described the feelings of most Arab leaders: 'They too must have been alarmed at the Russian moves against the legal government of Prague, yet, while the world joined in condemning this invasion, these 'friends' of Moscow — many of whom are here in the Arab world — have kept silent. They dare not, it must be admitted, condemn the Soviet Union; they stand to lose much if they do, nor can they welcome the Soviet action, for only 14 months ago, some of these countries were themselves victims of aggression.'

'One must sympathise with these leaders: their dilemma is even more acute than that of the Czechs — the latter at least know where they stand.'

When Nasser met Tito again after the Czechoslovakian invasion at Aswan, Tito had questioned him for remaining silent. Tito had said, according to Heikal in his book entitled *Nasser — the Cairo document*, 'We are non-aligned, we must state our position on these matters.'

Nasser replied: 'You must see the realities of my situation. Part of my country is occupied. I cannot be completely non-aligned. No nation which is partly occupied can be completely independent.'

He asked Tito: 'What if my relations worsened with the Soviet Union? What would happen if I attacked them over Czechoslovakia? It would mean that my position in the Middle East would be lost completely because the Soviet Union is my only hope of getting the arms I need to regain the lost territory.'

In November 1968, three months after the Czechoslovakian incident, students at the universities of Mansoura, Alexandria and Cairo staged demonstrations and rioted. The authorities had to suspend the universities. The student incident was the worst in Mansoura about 200 kilometres from Cairo resulting in the death of three students and an old parent of a student, injuries to five students and casualties to nine police officers and 36 policemen. This happened after 5,000 students tried to seize the police headquarters. They beat up policemen with iron bars. When the police force of 63 were forced to retreat the students tried to capture the police headquarters and the police had to fire to kill.

Outside the Cairo University, students clashed with the riot squad when they stoned the police and tried to stop buses. Ostensibly, the students demonstrated in protest against the new rulings announced by the Minister of Education. Briefly, the rulings demanded the final-year students of secondary schools to leave school after they had failed twice in their final examinations, and all the university level students who failed in two subjects would have to take a re-examination before they were promoted. The students wanted the education authorities to withdraw such ruling, for in the past they were allowed to continue for as long as they liked.

Nasser had promised every secondary student a place in the University, and they stayed on as long as they liked. The enrolment of university undergrads of each university was astronomical in figures and the country could ill afford this free for all policy.

Instead of tackling the problems from the root source, Nasser put the blame for the student riots on the Secret Agents of the Israelis. This time, Nasser did not blame the Muslim Brotherhood, nor any foreign embassy. He claimed that the Egyptian authorities had successfully tracked down and approached members of four spy rings working on behalf of Israel. Investigations had revealed sensational secrets in connection with Israelis' nefarious practices of recruiting agents with the lure of money, sex and promises. These cases involved a press photographer, editor of an American News Agency, a reserve officer, a Spanish captain and a former official of the Ministry of Foreign Affairs.

The problem remained unsolved and after the lifting of the rulings the students went back to their classes.

Then about the same time, Egyptian authorities re-introduced religion into all schools. Religion has now been made a compulsory subject. This was the first time Egypt had done so since the 1952 revolution. Apparently, Nasser and his colleagues were beginning to discover that neither nationalism nor socialism was able to arouse the sentiment of the people in their preparations for war with the Israelis. After 16 years of preparation and of talking, the people were still apathetic. In fact, even religion was gradually losing its grip on the people. Almost on every street in Cairo you find cabarets and nightclubs functioning up to the early hours of the morning and sometimes until 6 a.m. The radio and TV programme consisted of nothing but comic sketches, western pop songs and exotic dancing. I have yet to see any programme to make the people realise that the country was preparing for war.The leaders also realised that Communism was equally unacceptable to the Muslim population who in fact was concerned that the Russian influence in Egypt was growing. They had therefore fallen back on religion as a weapon to arouse the feelings of the people to participate in this 'holy war'. They had exploited the fourth Muslim Ulemas Conference which was held in Cairo in September 1968 into a political forum to whip up the feelings of Muslims throughout the world to support this 'Holy War'. The conference declared on 6th October that 'sacrifice of blood and money in the 'Jihad' has become the duty of all Muslims all over the world.'

All these statements of religious fanaticism and the call for a 'holy war' appeared only in the Arabic newspapers. Not a single line appeared either in the *Egyptian Gazette* or the Cairo press review. Apparently, the Egyptian leaders were speaking on two wavelengths — one directed towards the Muslim world appealing for support of the 'holy war', and the other a mild statement directed towards the non-Muslim world.

To understand Arab politics, one must know whether an Arab leader was saying what he means or whether it was meant for home or external consumption or for both. This was indeed a very difficult job, but it was the basic principle in understanding Arab politics.

As Nasser boasted of building a one million strong army to liberate Arab land from the Israelis in early January 1969, the Israelis launched a series of dramatic air raids right into the heart of Egypt to call Nasser's bluff. Since the failure of Rabat Summit, it seemed clear that Israel had launched this major psychological offensive to discredit Nasser, to mar his image in the eyes of the world. Foreign diplomats in Cairo were exchanging notes about the unbelievable success of the Israeli raids, particularly the carrying away of the brand new Russian built 7-ton radar station from the Egyptian shores of the Gulf of Suez near Ras Gharb on December 26. Some diplomats described the successful pinching of the Egyptian radar station in an Israeli helicopter as something similar to the fables of the *Arabian Nights*. Rumours also circulated that when the radar dismantling took place the Egyptian soldiers fled and rang up their superior officer who was reported to have retorted, 'Don't talk nonsense. You are always drunk.'

The bomb struck Maadi, the place where I stayed. They hit the trainee camp which was opposite the American school where my daughter was studying. It shook the whole building of my residence.

Nasser's prestige and image was much affected by Israeli bombs.

The time had come for me to pay my farewell call on President Nasser after two years of assignment. I was told that Nasser normally did not receive any departing ambassador unless he had respect for the ambassador. For instance, the Burmese Ambassador who had stayed on in Cairo for six years had failed to obtain an audience with Nasser before he left the country. In fact the Malaysian Ambassador, Hamid Jumat, threw a challenge at me that Nasser would not receive me because of our relations with Israel.

I arrived at Manseit El Bakri, the Palace where the President gave a dinner to Prime Minister Lee Kuan Yew. While I was waiting in the guest room, I had a glance at the photographs of world leaders displayed around the room. I noticed that he had on his table photographs of dead friends like Nehru, or deposed leaders such as Sukarno and Ayub Khan or even leaders whose countries sometimes became not too friendly such as Chou En-lai. This to me seemed to reflect Nasser's sentimentality towards friends.

The President normally appeared stern and serious in public functions. I remember when I first presented credentials to him he was quiet and stern and had nothing much to talk. This time as he walked into the room, he immediately showed a sense of intimacy in a relaxed, cheerful and friendly mood. We talked about many things — his health, family, Egypt's future, the 1967 war, the Super Powers, about Arab unity and about South-East Asia.

We started off by talking about health. Nasser appeared to be fit and healthy. He said he played tennis twice a week and with only his instructor because the balls would have to be manipulated to his arm's reach without his having to run for them. The other days, he would spend his time walking four miles in his own garden. He said he put on four kilos after the ten-day holiday in Aswan because the scenery there was beautiful and he ate too much. Now he found it difficult to reduce the four kilos.

As we discussed family matters, he told me that his wife played the piano well, and that he had a son who was now receiving naval training and that his two daughters were already married — one to an Army officer and the other to a civilian and she was now working in the Publication Section of the *Al Ahram*. She got £25 a month and with her husband's earnings they could survive. He said: 'She has to earn her own living, you know.'

Speaking of the Egyptians, he said: 'The Egyptians are patient and enduring people. They like to joke and live but when there is a crisis they will pull themselves together and overcome their difficulties.'

'In our long history we have been invaded by many people — the Romans, Napoleon, the British and the others but the Egyptians have always driven them out.'

'The Israelis are now invaders trying to colonize and build a new Empire in the Arab land. If they think they can succeed by force, they are mistaken. No amount of bombing will make the Egyptians surrender. There will be no direct talks until and unless the Israelis withdraw completely from Arab occupied territories. We cannot have direct talks when they are still occupying our land.'

The President was apparently well-informed about the activities of all ambassadors. When he spoke about the recent Israeli bombings, he said: 'Oh you live in Maadi. How was it during the bombing recently?' I told him about my daughter's experience when she was still in the American School and how the children cried and ran under the tables when the bomb dropped only a few kilometres away from the school.

Speaking of how they lost the June 1967 war, Nasser said: 'We lost because the US gave electronic warfare equipment to the Israelis. They had special electronic equipment which could automatically detect our radar stations. Then they had other types of electronic equipment to jam our radar stations. As a result of this equipment we were helpless and our anti-aircraft were rendered motionless during the 1967 war.'

I chipped in, 'Why don't the Russians give you more aid?'

He replied: 'They are giving and will continue to do so but we are handicapped by the shortage of pilots. We lost 45 pilots during the 1967 war and it takes time to replace them. It takes about three years to train one pilot.'

Nasser seemed to be losing hope of the Americans steering an unbiased policy in the Middle East. He seemed to think that the US was now backing Israel 100 percent because of its vested interest in the Middle East oil. He said: 'Israel had no Phantoms or Skyhawks during the 1967 war. They only had Mirage. After the war, the Americans gave them 50 Phantoms and 100 Skyhawks. They not only gave them the planes but the pilots who were American Jews having dual nationality. Some of them had fought in the Vietnam war. This is the advantage of the Israelis. The Americans think that they can make us give in by force but they will be proved wrong.'

The President said the UAR's demand was simple. The Egyptians wanted the Israelis to withdraw and the refugees adequately compensated. He said: 'We want peace and justice.'

I interrupted by saying that the problem today had become more complicated because it was no more a problem of compensation of refugees but the Palestinians wanted a state of their own and that they would not be satisfied with mere compensation. He answered: 'You are quite right. If the Jews can return after 2,000 years to form a state, why can't the Palestinians who had been driven out of their homes by force only 10 years ago not have the right to form their own state — a multiracial state?'

I told the President quite frankly that the trouble with the Arab world was disunity among the Arab states. He answered: 'It is true. There are certain basic contradictions among the Arab states. For instance, King Feisal is afraid that if things were settled he would be the next target. King Hussein accepted the UN Resolutions just because we have accepted them. But Egypt alone shall be strong enough in time to come to face the Israeli challenge.'

We reached the end of our conversation, when he asked about my next appointment. When I mentioned Indonesia, he said: 'Oh yes, I was there during the Bandung Conference.' And I said I saw him too speaking at the Conference when I was a journalist. Then he asked whether I knew what was happening to Sukarno. He supplied the answer. 'Is he under house arrest in Bogor?' He said Sukarno was a jovial chap who liked to travel and have fun. However, he had done his part for his country. When I told him that Suharto had appointed Dr Hatta to be adviser to an anti-corruption committee, he said: 'I met Dr Hatta when I was in Bandung. He is a clever man.'

Talking of China, he seemed to think that if Chou En-lai was in full control, China would sober up and be more stable.

Before I left, the President thanked me for the two marble lions which I had brought from Singapore and presented to him.

When I left his residence my driver told me that the guards outside were feeling rather uneasy because I stayed a little too long.

Two months later, President Nasser died.

Soon after Nasser's death, an Egyptian delegation led by Dr Labib Shoukair, who was chairman of Parliament, went to Beijing and met Chou En-lai who immediately asked about Nasser's death. Why had Nasser died so young? He was only 52 years old. The delegation was puzzled by Chou's question and said it might be God's will. Then Chou said: 'Let's not blame God for what has happened, there must be a reason. Gamal Abdul Nasser was young, fifty-two years is young. I am seventy-two and I am still working and as you can see, I am in good health.'

Chou said: 'It is the fault of the Soviet Union. They deceived him. They pushed him into a situation and then they left him. They allowed his heart to be broken.' Ironically, it was Chou who had introduced Nasser to the Russians for the supply of arms.

Nasser was a man of integrity and honesty. He meant well for his country and his people. But he dreamt of establishing one Arab world and of extending his influence to the African continent, and of uniting the Muslim world. He was naive and too ambitious. He dreamt too long.

Anwar Sadat coming to pay last respects to Nasser

Nasser's Funeral Procession

Nasser's Funeral in Cairo

5

Sadat and the Muslim Brethren

It was the Vice-President, Anwar Sadat, who announced to the world the news of Nasser's death. Sadat was apparently closest to Nasser. He was one of the few revolutionaries left from the 1952 revolution who stuck to Nasser till the time of his death. When Nasser was alive, Sadat was always in his shadow, never aroused his suspicions and always behaved properly. Nasser trusted Sadat because he was the least ambitious.

I met Sadat several times when I was Ambassador in Cairo. I had the occasion to get closer to him when our Prime Minister, Lee Kuan Yew, visited Cairo in January 1969. He was at the airport to receive Lee Kuan Yew, and while waiting for the plane, we had a chat. It was about the Middle East situation and he stuck to Nasser's line of approach. He never revealed his inner feelings. I had occasion to meet him again at the Arab Socialist Union premises during the ASU meetings. His distinguished moustache, the slightly bald forehead, the high majestic nose and his smokeless pipe he held in his hands left a deep impression on my mind. Behind the dreamy eyes and thick eyebrows was a sense of unusual calm and tranquillity. Although he spoke loudly like any Arab, he appeared to be frank, outspoken and friendly. His handshake was tight and warm. He was talkative, but his words had substance. He gave one the impression that he was at ease with himself and there was no inner conflict.

I met Sadat again in September 1975, when Prime Minister Lee Kuan Yew visited Egypt on his way to Iran and Yugoslavia. That was soon after he had a showdown with the Muslim Brotherhood. It was the first time Lee Kuan Yew had met him after he became the President.

The two leaders discussed bilateral relations between Singapore and Egypt. Lee Kuan Yew invited President Sadat to send Egyptian technical officers to Singapore to learn the basic principles of our system in free trade zone, customs and inland revenue so that they could modify them to suit Egyptian conditions. Lee said once the system had begun operating in Egypt, Singapore could then send its experts to see how it worked.

Sadat looked strong and fit, welcoming us in his Palace with a pipe in his right hand and always smiling.

It was the first time I revisited Egypt after my two years assignment in 1968–70. Things had deteriorated in the overcrowded city which was crammed with eight million people. Prices of foodstuff and commodities had more than doubled and rental of houses was two-and-a-half times that of 1970. Frequent blackouts and water rationing were annoying the poor and middle income groups. Such hardship had made the people welcome the disengagement in Sinai, and Sadat's surprise victory in 1973 over Israel. They expected the Government to spend more money on the welfare of the people than on war.

When Nasser passed away, he was the first political leader to be informed. He went to Manshiat Al-Bahri Palace where Nasser was lying. He was immediately brought into Nasser's bedroom. Nasser was in bed surrounded by doctors. They told him that he had died an hour before. He lifted the veil to see Nasser's face. He put his cheek against his and did not feel the chill of death. He turned to the doctors and said: 'It is not true, what you're saying is wrong . . . It can't be right.' He could not believe that Nasser was dead. He burst into tears and asked the doctors to try to revive Nasser. But the doctors said they had tried very hard for two hours, but the will of God could not be reversed.

In his autobiography *In Search of Identity*, Sadat said that when Nasser died, he was reluctant to be elected President. In his speech to the nation, Sadat said that Nasser had declared that presidential elections would be held only after the 'consequences of the Israeli aggression had been removed'. So, he would carry on as Vice-President until he had removed the consequences of aggression and then allow elections to be held.

But circumstances had compelled him to change his mind. At the top, domestic intrigues had started. Certain strong men, alternatively referred to as the 'central power bloc' who relied on Soviet Union for support, wanted to exploit the situation. The Soviet agents were organising effectively. These men were aspiring to take over power on the pretext that they were the legitimate heirs of Nasser and were therefore responsible for maintaining his political line.

Sadat summoned his top officials and told them that he had changed his mind and then got the Supreme Executive Committee of the Arab Socialist Union to endorse his decision to stand for the Presidency.

The central power bloc had a showdown with him. On the first day when he became President, Sami Sharaf, who was Nasser's confidant and Minister for Presidential Affairs, called on him with a heap of papers. They were tapped telephone conversations between certain people being watched. Sadat lost his temper and told Sami that he did not intend to follow Nasser's footsteps. He said: 'I couldn't possibly do things the way Nasser did, simply because we were different men. True, we never differed in general principles but we did differ completely on the means of reaching our goals.'

In his autobiography, Sadat said he wanted to put right many of the conditions which he was convinced had for so long been wrong. He said: 'I knew that human values had been violated, if not shattered altogether but I also knew that I could redress the situation by instituting and vindicating my own ideals and principles and not by oppression.'

Sadat said he had the opportunity to observe that the gravest injustice done to the Egyptian people was the 'cultivation of fear'; rather than trying to build up the inner man, they did all they could to destroy the soul of an individual — and the soul of a people.

He said: 'People were thus turned into dummies. They became puppets in the hands of rulers, who did what they liked with them. Travel abroad was forbidden. No one could say anything that appeared to contradict the official line of thinking (the penalty being arrest and loss of livelihood). People's passivity increased daily until one day no man felt he could be secure unless he had completely kept to himself, cut himself off entirely, both from public events and from the very stream of life around him, as though he wanted to see nothing, hear nothing, and say nothing.

'It is this that makes me say that just as the July 23 Revolution was colossal in its achievements, so it was equally colossal in its mistakes . . . '

'By nature,' said Sadat in his book, 'Nasser tended to suspect others. He was too preoccupied with his own 'security' either to have a clear vision of the future or to pay due attention to the advancement of his people as human beings — to that humanity which is the most precious asset of a given community. Worse still, as a result of his preoccupation with 'security' and of the doubts that preyed on his mind, the Egyptian people's horizons dimmed and their opportunities for self-fulfilment increasingly narrowed down. Regrettably, grave mistakes were committed in Egypt against man's humanity, the very asset we should have guarded most zealously.'

Sadat came from a poor family and lived in a poor village. He had experienced poverty but did not admire the rich. When he finished secondary school, he joined the Military Academy. He had great admiration for the Turkish hero Kemal Ataturk, and wanted very much to be a revolutionary to drive off the British colonisers. His opportunity came when he was with the Free Officers Organisation where he started to conspire with his colleagues. He was imprisoned several times for his involvement with the revolution. After the revolution, he became a Member of the Revolutionary Command Council, then Secretary-General of the Islamic Congress and also Editor-in-Chief of *Al Goumhuriah* and then Speaker of the National Assembly. His last post was as Vice-President.

When Sadat was Vice-President, he was hiding his feelings all along when he was working for the Nasser regime. All these feelings exploded when he took over as the President.

No one had expected that Sadat would turn the tables, denounce the Soviet Union and become friends of the United States. No one had expected that Sadat who was close to Nasser would change the country back to Egypt instead of the

United Arab Republic, and go to Israel to have direct talks with the Israeli leaders. And most important of all was the fact that Sadat swung the same crowd that had packed the Cairo streets mourning Nasser over to his more liberal method of running the country and of releasing Egypt from the grip of Moscow.

The first thing Sadat did when he became President was to release from the Cairo prisons several thousands of members of the Muslim Brotherhood — an ultra religious and conservative movement which was easily the most powerful in the Arab world. The leaders and the supporters of the Muslim Brotherhood were responsible for the assassination attempt on Nasser on 26 October 1954. The Nasser regime had tried the Muslim Brethren and hanged a large number and more than 300 were given long terms of hard labour and another 11,000 landed with sentences of various lengths.

Sadat issued a Presidential decree to pardon even those leaders who had fled to Saudi Arabia in 1954 rather than face sentences of hard labour. These figures included Sheikh Mustafa Alam, who had returned to Cairo, Sheik Ashnawi Suleiman, who paid a visit to Egypt and was even interviewed on television and Said Ramadan, who had also returned to Cairo. All the three had been sentenced to life imprisonment for trying to kill President Nasser in 1954 at the trials which heralded the repression of Muslim Brotherhood then so powerful that the Government could not dissolve it like any other political party.

When I was in Cairo, Nasser revealed at the Arab Socialist Union National Assembly sometime in September 1968 that the Muslim Brotherhood was trying to form an underground army and that was why 800 of the 6,000 connected with the Muslim Brotherhood were still under detention. Nasser said these 800 members had been trained in the use of weapons and represented the clandestine organ of the Muslim Brotherhood. He said their action was based on armed operation, assassinations and sabotage.

Nasser added that in fact one feared that if they were released, everyone of them would form an armed cell and start arming themselves once again for destruction. There were certain people who were now abroad in West Germany and Switzerland who had offices there and were financed by the American intelligence.

Sadat had released the Muslim Brethren to prove that he was different from Nasser. By declaring that 'Nasser died for good with the defeat in the six day war on 5 June 1967' he finally cleared up a longstanding misunderstanding with the Muslim Brotherhood.

The main practical steps he took to differentiate Sadat's Egypt from Nasser's Egypt was to release those who had been imprisoned for their political beliefs and to re-establish the authority and independence of the law courts. He declared that no one was to be gaoled on the basis of his opinions. He went further to dismantle Nasser's political organisation — the Arab Socialist Union — and replaced it with a multi-party parliamentary democracy. He chose the tactic of tolerating and even encouraging Muslim activities as a counterweight to his Marxist and Nasserite critics. While the Muslim Brotherhood was never legalised, it was not suppressed and its newspaper *Al Dawa* was generally left untouched.

Sadat, whilst following a relaxed policy at home with his Muslim Brethren, was taking a tough stand vis-a-vis the reoccupation of Sinai, the territories lost to Israel. He took steps to strengthen his army and air force. He visited the battlefield very often and gave the soldiers courage and encouragement.

Then on a Saturday afternoon, on 6 October 1973, came the zero hour for the air force to cross the Canal. A total of 22 supersonic jets took part in the first wave and accomplished their mission in twenty minutes. The air strike was according to plan and scored a stunning blow to Israel. It achieved 90 percent of its targets. It had hit the command posts of the Israeli headquarters. It destroyed all aerial combat headquarters, air defence and jamming centres (the electronic warfare equipment), all Liaison points, missile batteries and gun emplacements in Sinai. It took the world, both East and West, by surprise.

Sadat became a hero to the Egyptian people. He congratulated the air force commander, General Husni Mubarak who had planned and executed the air strike. With the admirable air strike, the Egyptian air force recovered all it had lost in the 1956 war and the 1967 defeat and had restored confidence in the Egyptian armed forces. It also restored the world's confidence in Egypt and exploded the myth of an invincible Israel.

Sadat later asked General Mubarak to abandon his military uniform, put on civilian clothes and assist him as Vice-President.

Meanwhile, the Muslim Brotherhood, with the release of their members, managed to recoup and reorganise themselves. They were still aiming at establishing an Islamic State of Egypt.

In May 1975, Egyptian security forces smashed a plot believed to be associated with the Muslim Brotherhood to overthrow the Sadat Government. The plotters arrested were charged with attempts to overthrow the Sadat regime, change the country's constitution by force, illegal acquisition of arms and immoral behaviour.

The ringleader was alleged to be a twenty-eight year old university student, Shukri Ahmed Mostapha.

News of the arrests came just three days before sentence was due to be passed on 92 Muslim fanatics accused of taking part in the murderous attack on Egypt's Technical Military Academy in April 1974. Eleven people including five soldiers were killed and 27 injured in the raid, which was designed to seize weapons with which to overthrow President Sadat. The three principal defendants among the 92 were found guilty on May 10 and faced the likelihood of execution.

According to *Al Akhbar*, the subversive group arrested had lived in mountain caves near Minia, in Upper Egypt, where they were trained in the use of arms. The group who believed that women should not work and should be veiled, persuaded many girl students to abandon their studies and marry them without parental consent.

Then in early September 1981, President Sadat suddenly made a swoop on the Muslim Brotherhood, dissolved the organisation and arrested 1,500 people. In a decree announced in Parliament on 5 September, he also toppled the patriarch of the 23 million strong Coptic Christian Church. He shut down seven religious and opposition journals and carried out a purge of journalists, broadcasters and university professors. Among those arrested were Abdul Hamid Jazzar, the Islamic student coordinator, the famous blind preacher Abdul Hamid Kishk, the veteran Muslim Brother Omar Alemasani, secular politicians of all colours and generations such as Fuad Serageddin, Fathi Radwan and Hilmi Radwan, journalists such as Mohamed

Heikal, the famous journalist who was Nasser's confidant, and the Marxist Lufti el-Knoly as well as the Coptic Pope Shenouda III.

According to *Al Ahram*, the government newspaper, most of those arrested belonged to the Muslim Brotherhood, which had been calling for a government run according to Islamic religious law and denounced Western materialism. Flushed by the success of the ayatollahs in Iran, the group had denounced the peace treaty which Sadat had signed with Israel.

Sadat had repented his lenient measures against the Muslim Brethren. He became even tougher than Nasser in persecuting his political opponents. The Egyptian Government took over 40,000 privately owned mosques and tightened its supervision of Muslim preachers. The Ministry of Wakfs (religious endowments) took control of 65 mosques that were formerly run by Islamic fundamentalist societies. Sadat 'nationalised' the country's 40,000 private mosques revealing his grave weakness. He instructed that Friday sermons should be cleared of political content. Even Nasser at the height of his power could not control the independent mosques. Sadat had outdone Nasser in this respect.

In his speech, Sadat severely attacked the Muslim Brotherhood and the shadow Islamic fundamentalist societies for their 'sectarian sedition'. He produced a huge pile of documents in Parliament to prove their illegitimacy. Sadat said: 'I wish to say that the Muslim Brotherhood as a society does not exist officially — it is illegitimate.'

Waving a copy of the movement's publication, *Al Dawa*, Sadat said he had been maligned in it and his policies distorted. He said he had 'tolerated the presence of the Muslim Brotherhood and other fundamentalist groups and both the Christians and the Muslims thought we were weak.'

'The Muslim fundamentalists tried to call for a jihad or Holy War. This is absolute impudence. They have to pay the price. I was wrong in being lenient with them.'

Soon after this purge of the Muslim Brotherhood, Sadat ordered more than 1,500 Soviet officials and advisers out of Egypt, claiming Moscow had incited the recent Muslim-Christian strife in Cairo. The Cabinet gave Soviet Ambassador Vladmir Poylakow and six members of his staff 48 hours to leave the country. It also ordered a Hungarian diplomat expelled on grounds that he too was 'involved' in the conflict between Muslims and the Christian minority.

The Cabinet also terminated the contracts of about 1,500 Soviet technical advisers, expelled two Soviet journalists, including the Cairo correspondent of the Soviet news agency Tass, and closed the Soviet military liaison in Cairo and its Egyptian counterpart in Moscow. An Egyptian Cabinet statement accused the Soviets of 'exploiting religious strife and escalating the sectarian conflict, in which about 70 people had died in the year.'

Then on 6th October 1981, Sadat, dressed in black military uniform with the Star of Sinai medal round his neck and spurs on his black boots, took the salute at the annual October 6 military parade to celebrate the 'glorious Arab victory in October 1973 against Israel.' The parade was to celebrate his greatest military triumph. That day, eight years ago, Egyptian troops had successfully launched a surprise attack across the Suez Canal into the Israeli-occupied Sinai Peninsula.

While he was receiving the salute from the military parade, two young bareheaded men in Egyptian army uniforms on the back of a moving jeep suddenly fired at the reviewing stand. They leaped from the moving vehicle and charged at President Sadat. They shouted 'Glory to Egypt. Attack. You are agents, you are intruders.' Five bullets hit Sadat and he fell. Sadat went into coma immediately. Clergymen, diplomats and military men were also hit by bullets. The crowd of military men and government officials stampeded, screamed and fell over each other. Ambulances with sirens wailing pushed through the crowds to get the wounded. Sadat had been assassinated.

Sadat was brought to the Maadi Hospital. Doctors found two openings on the left of Sadat's chest, a bullet in the neck and another near the collar bone. The fifth bullet had entered his left knee and passed through his left thigh. They tried their best to save him, but it was hopeless. Sadat never recovered from the coma. He died in the hospital.

A strange, almost eerie calm atmosphere prevailed in Cairo after Sadat's assassination. Some people stayed up all night, talking quietly in groups around street vendors selling roast lamb. Downtown, the only outward sign of the year-long state of emergency decreed after Sadat's death was the heavy concentration of troops around the national television studio and other crucial buildings.

It was a tremendous contrast to the scenes of hysteria after the death of Sadat's predecessor Gamal Abdul Nasser in 1970, when millions packed the streets, sobbing and screaming. Ordinary people expressed sadness but little surprise, perhaps reflecting a general acceptance that Sadat's assassination had become just a matter of time.

Sadat was laid to rest under the Unknown Soldier Monument, which was built in 1975 to honour all Egyptian soldiers killed in the four wars against Israel. The Monument which was ordered built by Sadat rises 20m high on the opposite side of Military Parade Avenue where he was assassinated. It was built in three months at a cost of 750,000 Egyptian pounds. The architect, Sami Rafeh, once said the inspiration behind his creation was the ancient Egyptian belief of immortality.

It was a quiet and heavily guarded funeral attended by the world's dignitaries. Within a few days of Sadat's death, Egyptian security forces had overpowered about 100 armed Muslim fundamentalists in the southern town of Asyut on the banks of the Nile River. The Egyptian troops fought with the Muslim fundamentalists and regained control of Asyut, about 400 km south of Cairo. The Muslim fundamentalists attacked the central police headquarters in Asyut with sub-machine guns. Witnesses said the trouble started when police tried to prevent Muslim worshippers from praying in public in defiance of a year-long ban on street demonstrations imposed after Sadat's assassination.

Asyut was a stronghold of Muslim fundamentalists and the scene of past battles between Muslims and the town's Christian Coptic minority. Military authorities said that the leader of the assailants who killed Sadat was a Muslim fundamentalist officer and that weapons used in the attack were brought in from southern Egypt. The fundamentalists who took their cue from the Iranian religious leader Ayatollah Khomeiny wanted to turn Egypt into a theocratic dictatorship.

When Sadat passed away, Mubarak took over as President. Two weeks after he took office, he clamped down on Muslim fundamentalists. In late October 1981, Egyptian security forces fought gunbattles in Cairo for a few days with Muslim fundamentalists plotting to overthrow the government. The police raided a hideout in the garden suburb of Maadi (where I stayed before), exchanged fire with two gunmen, killing one of them. The police arrested 397 members of the fundamentalist groups which were responsible for the murder of Sadat. They found in the densely populated Gamaliya area a hideout where weapons such as sub-machine guns, automatic rifles, pistols, grenades, dynamite and hundreds of molotov cocktails were discovered. They also found US$20,000 and thousands of Egyptian pounds in the possession of members of the organisation. Those arrested made detailed confessions of their plans to stage a 'Khomeiny type' revolution in Egypt. They had planned to kill officials and sabotage vital installations.

When Sadat was still alive, Vice-President Mubarak visited Singapore in 1977 on his way to Australia. I met him when our former Foreign Minister Rajaratnam was giving him and his party a dinner. Mubarak was tall and handsome. He looked more a military type than a civilian. Always smart and alert, Mubarak spoke fluent English. He was a good conversationalist and was frank and outspoken. No stranger can escape the impact of his dynamic personality and self-confidence. When we were chatting at the Mandarin Belvedere, we least expected that he would be the No 1 man in Egypt.

It was Sadat who picked Mubarak as Vice-President when the latter successfully planned the October 1973 surprise attack on Israel that shook the world. Now that Sadat has died, will Mubarak follow Sadat's policy of compromise with the Israelis? From the measures he has taken, it would seem that Mubarak has his own policies since his personality might not be the same as that of Sadat. After Egypt had taken over Sinai from Israel, Mubarak gradually soft-peddled Sadat's legacy of animosity and differences with the Arab world, and tried to reach a compromise with the Arab countries.

In December 1982, the half-brother of the late President Sadat, Esmat Sadat, was charged in court for corruption, fraud and peddling of influence. Esmat, 58, a bus driver, and his 15 sons had misused their influence and their relationship to the late President and traded on the black market. The charges listed 29 cases of seizing real estate illegally, extorting money, importing foodstuffs not conforming to government specifications and sale of construction materials on the black market. Sadat who began life as a bus driver for a monthly salary of less than US$100 was said to have become a multi-millionaire owning seven import and export and maritime companies, a fleet of trailing trucks, houses and villas in Cairo and Alexandria and several pieces of land.

In February 1983, he and his three sons were gaoled for a year each after being convicted of corruption and fraud.

Mubarak would not tolerate corruption even if the persons involved were the relatives of the late President Sadat. But he warned the press not to overplay corruption in the country for it might drive away foreign investors. Commenting on the Sadat case, Mubarak said: 'To me the case proves only one thing, that no one is above the law.'

According to Mohamed Heikal who was once detained by Sadat and who was close to Nasser, Sadat became more concerned with being a superstar than a real leader of Egypt. Heikal, who was formerly editor of the Cairo Daily *Al Ahram* and one of the most influential journalists in the Arab world, wrote a new book entitled *Autumn of Fury* which strongly criticised Sadat.

In the book, Heikal alleged that Sadat spent his last days drinking vodka and building new presidential residences and watching uncensored foreign movies as well as videotapes of himself in his heyday. He retreated into an isolated world of his own after the failure of his peace talks with Israel and his historic visit to Jerusalem in 1973.

Heikal criticised Sadat for spending millions of dollars in restoring his residences at a time when most historic monuments in the land were crumbling because of lack of funds to maintain them.

Heikal alleged that Sadat loved commandeering national treasures and gave them away to his friends such as the Israeli Defence Minister Ezer Weizman and the Shah of Iran. And he was fond of saying 'my friend Giscard', 'my friend Schmidt', 'my friends Nixon, Ford and Carter' and 'my friend Onassis', plus a string of Hollywood stars including Frank Sinatra and Elizabeth Taylor.

In May 1983, Egypt, Saudi Arabia and other Arab countries banned Heikal's book and said it was malicious.

In April 1983, Mubarak also made efforts to clear the way for the normalisation of the strained Egyptian-Soviet relations. He told the weekly newspaper *Mayo*, organ of his ruling National Democratic Party, 4 April 1983, that once Cairo and Moscow exchanged ambassadors again, relations would be 'ordinary as with any other country.'

Mubarak said no problems stood in the way of normal relations between Egypt and the Soviet Union. He said 'The time will come when we resume normal relations. The Soviet Union is a superpower which we cannot ignore.'

Egyptian-Soviet relations were crisis-ridden during Sadat's regime, which expelled 17,000 Soviet military personnel following its ban on Muslim mosques.

This is the irony of history. Sadat was a good follower of Nasser. But when he took over power from Nasser, he turned the tables and changed all his policies. Mubarak was a follower of Sadat, but after Sadat's death, he cracked down on corruption and brought Sadat's brother to trial to prove that there was corruption during Sadat's regime. He also tried to reconcile with the Arab countries and the Soviet Union which Sadat was hostile to.

This is what I would say about the influence of personality on politics. Whichever leader comes into power has his own way of ruling the country and often he would try to impose his personality and try to outshine his predecessor.

6

The Pyramids

As a kid in school, I learnt about the pyramids. In Chinese, they were called stupa of the letter Gold. (金字塔) I do not understand why the Chinese called the pyramid by such a name. Perhaps it was because it resembled the top portion of the character Gold. But the text in Chinese books merely stated that it was one of the wonders of the world. When I arrived in Cairo for my assignment, the first thing I did was to put down my luggage at Nile Hilton, and proceed immediately with my family to the western desert to see the pyramids of Giza.

As our car approached the desert we saw the Giza group looming up in the heat haze, dominated by the greatest pyramid of all — the Cheops, the most powerful monarch of the Old Kingdom. As we drew nearer, the immense bulk of Cheops' monument overshadowed and awed us. Its gleaming limestone sides, more than 450 feet high, flung back the glare of the sun. There was a group of western tourists descending from their buses. We saw the Arabs in their white flowing galibaya approach them with their camels. But my eyes were fixed on the pyramids. For the Giza pyramids were beyond doubt the supreme expression of Pharaonic majesty and power.

It was noon time in summer, and the huge limestone sides leaning against the blazing August sky resembled a flight of heavenly stairs. Framed as they were against the western desert, it was not the size that impressed one who first saw them but their colour, a warm shining gold stippled with black shadows

The Sphinx and the Pyramids

thrown by the rectangular blocks of which the pyramids were built. Each of these blocks weighing two and a half tons rose stepwise from the base to a peak of 136 metres high. And 2,300,000 of these blocks made up the Great Pyramid of the Giza built by King Cheops in about 2720 BC. It was no doubt the most fabulous and mightiest of all human achievements. *No traveller, emperor, businessman, warrior, poet or artist can tread on these sands and not gasp in awe. King Cheops, Pharaoh of the fourth dynasty, had built the highest monument known to mankind in those days.* The area the pyramid covers is vast enough to hold St Peter's Cathedral in Rome, the cathedrals of Florence and Milan, Westminster Abbey and St Paul's all put together.

Considered from the tip downwards, the pyramid is like the sun's ray, bursting through a gap in the clouds. The pyramid is a perfect combination of simplicity and magnitude. The interplay of its angles makes the best harmony of shape and volume. It was architecture's purest achievement for it relied on straight lines alone. Never had straight lines been drawn with so much mastery, skill and strength.

In the western desert, there were other less magnificent pyramids like the pyramids of Khephren, built on a slightly smaller scale and the pyramid of Mykerinos, smaller but no doubt impressive. And there were hundreds of other smaller pyramids.

Since my first visit to the pyramids, I was so attracted to them that whenever I had an opportunity I would never fail to make my way there. I would sometimes go to the Sahara Desert and have a glimpse of the pyramids from the top. Early in the morning, I could get a glimpse of the morning sun shining on the golden tip from right across the valley. Or one could go there at dusk when the climate was cool and one could perceive the silhouettes of the pyramids' straight lines against the multi-coloured sky until darkness gradually swallowed up the entire complex. Or during winter, one could sit comfortably in the open-air to see and listen to the spectacular Son Et Lumiere (Sound and Light) produced regularly for tourists. When I had more time, I would sit and paint the pyramids with my Chinese brush. I found the straight lines most difficult to handle.

As I was painting the pyramids I sometimes paused to wonder how it was possible for the ancient Egyptians to build this magnificent structure without modern tools. The blocks of stones had to be dragged down to the Nile from quarries in the Arabian range of hills. Stone by stone it had to be built from earth to heaven. Each stone averaged two and a half tons in weight and 2.3 million of them were hoisted up and laid one upon the other. The finest ones of pure granite were dug up in the quarries of Aswan whence they came by boat, carried by the flooding of the Nile. In front of such superhuman effort can one believe in the legend of the whip? A hundred thousand men laboured constantly for twenty years to complete the superstructure. One of the earliest European visitors — Herodotus, the Greek historian — who came to Egypt in about 450 BC got the information from the priests who told him that the pyramid was built in steps. After laying the stones for the base, they raised the remaining stones to their place by means of machines formed of short wooden planks. The upper portion of the pyramid was finished first, then the middle and then the part which was lowest and nearest the ground. There was an inscription in Egyptian hieroglyphs on the pyramid which recorded the quantity of radish, onion and garlic consumed by the labourers who constructed it. According to Herodotus, when the pyramid was completed it was covered from top to bottom with a smooth polished casing of fine limestone and capped by an apex gilded to catch the first rays of the sun. On the Great Pyramid nothing remains today of the limestone casing. It had been completely stripped off so that instead of a smooth gleaming surface we see a series of steps. We do not see the pyramid as its builders or even Herodotus saw it.

How did they lift the stones? There was no crane as we know it today. There was no evidence in the tomb paintings to suggest that the Egyptians possessed any machinery more elaborate than the lever, the roller and the inclined plane. Even the largest blocks in the Great Pyramid, the 56 roofing beams in the King's Chamber, could have been raised by leverage, though each weighed 54 tons.

Herodotus described Cheops as a sacrilegious tyrant who exhausted the manpower of the kingdom in building his colossal monument. But other experts pointed out that during the year, there were three months of inundation when the men were unable to work in the fields and would therefore have idled away their time. It was during these three months that King Cheops ordered them to float the quarried stone across the Nile. Manoeuvring the heavily laden barges across the fast flowing river must have required considerable skill. Then the blocks had to be hauled on sledges up the causeway to the pyramid plateau.

One wonders what they were like, these unknown thousands who laboured for 20 years to raise the greatest stone monument in the world? Did they feel themselves to be slaves of a megalomaniac tyrant? Or did they perhaps identify themselves with the power and aim of the King as subjects of modern dictatorships conditioned to worship the state? As I looked around Cairo, it was hard to believe that the men in the street were descendants of those who built the pyramids.

Why did the Old Kingdom Pharaohs choose the pyramidal shape for their tombs? The Pyramid Texts, the earliest religious documents known in Egypt say: 'A stair-case to heaven is laid for him so that he may climb to heaven hereby.' The true pyramid was nothing more than a large-scale reproduction of the sacred symbol of the sun-god. The angle of the pyramid resembled the rays of the sun shining down through a gap in the clouds. When standing on the road to Sakkara and gazing westward, it was possible to see the sun's rays striking downwards at about the same angle as the slope of the Great Pyramid. The purpose of the pyramid was to be a material representation of the sun's rays.

Why were the pyramids built? The answer is simple. They were the tombs of kings. All of them, from the largest to the smallest, contain sarcophagi and most bear the names of the kings who were buried there. Thus the Pyramid of the Cheops once contained the sarcophagus of King Cheops; and that of Khephren of Khephren. All the pyramids were in fact tombs of greater and smaller kings, queens and princes. The whole Western desert is a cemetery for the burial of the royal families.

The ancient Egyptians believed that the dead body of a person should remain intact after his death. That was why they mummified the body so that after death his *bai* or spirit could come back. The *bai* seems to have been the spiritual element in man which was separated from the body when he was dead but was still dependent on the presence of the body.

There was also another spirit entity called the *ka* which was the reality of the soul of the person. These spiritual entities could survive after death only if the physical body was preserved and supplied with the means of life.

The Egyptians considered death an interruption, not the end of life; a change in a man's personality, not its annihilation. Their belief in the continued existence of the dead was shown in a striking manner by the fact that in certain emergencies they addressed letters to dead relatives. In their tombs the bodies, carefully prepared and dressed, were buried with their personal belongings and ornaments, including toilet requirements. The offerings at the tomb were specially made to a man's *ka*, to his vital force. A person who died was said 'to go to his *ka*', for while it was clear that this vitality had left his body, he needed to sustain the vitality or *ka* by the offerings.

The ancient Egyptians communicated regularly with their dead and concretely shared their company. They visited the tombs not only to make offerings to the *ka* but they gathered there on feast days to have a meal at which the dead were supposed to be present. This custom has, in fact, survived in Egypt to this day.

But how could the relatives of the dead be sure that his spirit would receive the food they brought for it? The Egyptians overcame this difficulty in their usual practical way. Inside the pyramids they built a chamber to contain the life-sized statue of the deceased, fashioned to represent him exactly as he appeared in life. This beautiful statue was never intended to be seen by the living. Each was walled up in its dark chamber known to Arabs as the *serdab* (cellar), only a narrow slit at the eye-level of the statue enabling it to 'see' into the offering chamber beyond. Thus, the spirit of the dead man, recognising his likeness in the statue, could inhabit it and so partake of the offerings. Most of the masterpieces of the Old Kingdom sculpture which now adorn the museums of the world came from these tombs. They may look magnificent as pieces of works of art, but they were in fact designed for a practical purpose. Fearing that the later generations might neglect them, some ancient Egyptians even carved offerings at their tombs. To the Egyptian mind, the carved representation of the offerings were good enough to ensure that the *ka* would never perish through neglect.

Since the slope of the pyramid was built according to the sun's rays, it was meant for those who were buried in the pyramids to go to heaven faster. In the case of Cheops' Pyramid, King Cheops' body was buried in the centre of the pyramid and when I was there the Egyptian authorities were building the sun-god's boat beside the pyramid to enable King Cheops to travel his nightly journey through the Underworld.

Once I made an attempt to climb into the Cheops' Pyramid to see what was inside. I was led by an Egyptian official. We came to the Ma'mum's hole, climbed a number of blocks and came to a gate. The passage was only four feet high and three feet six wide. It could only allow one person to go through. When two men were abreast of each other they could not move. There was very dim light inside the cave. We had to bend our backs and move upwards. The steps were uneven and the air was stuffy. My torch gave but a faint light. I could however clearly distinguish the principal objects. When we reached the top of the ladder, I saw a sarcophagus and had expected to see the mummy of King Cheops. The sarcophagus contained nothing but rubbish. I was greatly disappointed and we immediately returned to the exit by lowering our backs. When we reached the gates the Egyptian officials explained to us that the mummy and treasures of King Cheops were stolen by some tomb robbers 2,000 years ago. It was during the troubled times of the Seventh to the Tenth dynasty when tomb robbers were rampant. Eight centuries later, an Arab Khalif Ma'mum thought that the pyramid contained treasure and hacked out of the west face a tunnel which is still called the Ma'mum's hole. Ma'mum's men attacked the wrong spot at the beginning but later came across the granite plug block which sealed the entrance to the Ascending Passage. It was a dramatic moment when the men heard the great stone fall in the depths of the pyramid. Guided by the sound they started tunnelling west and finally broke through into the original entrance passage. Earlier they stormed up the great gallery and into the King's Chamber in the heart of the pyramid but found that they were thirty centuries too late. There was only an empty sarcophagus.

Outside the pyramid tricks were performed in the past. There was once a young man who could run barefoot up the pyramid to the top and down again within five minutes. Tourists often gathered to see him perform, and they would tip him. But the Egyptian authorities put a stop to it because it was found to be dangerous. If he were to slip there would be an ugly incident and the publicity would not be too good for Egypt.

Just a stone's throw from the Cheops' Pyramid was the Great Sphinx, a huge figure with a man's face and the body of a lion. His nose was broken by the Muslim Arabs who first conquered Cairo 1,000 years ago. He was a handsome figure when he was originally built. The Arabs came and disfigured his nose because they did not want people to pray to idols. The Sphinx was there to look after the Cheops' Pyramid. In other words, he was the pyramid's bodyguard. I sometimes looked into the melancholic eyes of the Sphinx and thought of many things. For five thousand years, whenever the sun rose each morning, its first rays touched his face. He has seen the history of Egypt in its first glow. He has been the Pharaoh's companion since his death. He watched over the plateau of Giza, over all its monuments, over all the tombs of the Kings. He bore witness to the will of Cheops and saw Anthony and Cleopatra pass by. Alexander the Great, Caesar and Napoleon paused at his feet. He saw the ambitious dreams of conquerors whirling like dead leaves. He saw conquerors reflect before him and bow their heads. He saw Alexander the Great, handsome as a barbarian, thoughtful as a prophet. He saw Caesar one evening staring at him and Egypt's last queen bearing him a son. He saw Napoleon and his burning eyes. Then he became despondent when an irascible emir of the Middle Ages, who disliked his smile, thought he was pagan and disfigured his nose.

He looked ugly and no longer did anyone come to pray at his feet. Then for sometime the Sphinx was nearly buried in sand.

The Sphinx was once used by Turkish riflemen for target practice. He was originally a knoll of rock shaped by the royal artisans into a recumbent lion with a human head. He was probably coated with plaster and painted with gay colours like most Egyptian statues. The Greek word 'Sphinx' by the way may be derived from the Egyptian word meaning 'living image' and between the paws of the fabulous beast was a slab of red granite put there over a thousand years ago by Tuthmosis IV. It bears an inscription stating how Tuthmosis, while still a prince, was hunting in the neighbourhood and decided to rest in the shadow of the monument. Falling asleep, he dreamt that the Sphinx, who was regarded as the embodiment of the sun-god Harmachins, spoke to him, promising that if Tuthmosis would clear away the sand which encumbered the statue he would inherit the Double Crown of Egypt. The prince agreed to do so, and presumably on his accession, set up the inscription in gratitude to the Sphinx.

In 1817, when the Sphinx was rediscovered in a sand excavation, it was perceived that all the internally joining surfaces of the blocks were full of figures of animal-headed gods of the most profane Egypt.

The Sphinx was supposed to look after the Cheops Pyramid and the other pyramids of the Western Desert but what happened was that at the beginning of the Eighteenth Dynasty, about 1,600 BC, there was hardly a king's tomb in the whole of Egypt that had not been rifled. All the mummies of the kings and queens and the gorgeous luxury, gold and treasures that were buried with them were ransacked by tomb robbers. By the Twenty-first dynasty, all attempts at guarding the tombs, including the tombs at the Valley of the Kings in Luxor, seemed to have been abandoned and the royal mummies were moved about from place to place in a desperate effort to preserve them. No fewer than thirteen of the royal mummies were moved at one time or another to the tomb of Amenhetep II and here they were allowed to remain. Mummies of other kings were eventually collected from their various hiding places and placed in a well-hidden tomb cut in the Deir el-Bahari cliff. This was the final move, for by accident the exact locality of the tomb was lost, and the mummies remained in peace for nearly three thousand years.

The word mummy is derived from Arabic which means a body preserved by wax or bitumen. According to Herodotus, when someone died, his family members besmeared their heads and faces with mud and then leaving the body in the house, wandered about the city and beat themselves. This custom of the bereaved family running about crying aloud is still the custom in Egypt. When they have done that they brought out the body to be embalmed. There were persons who were appointed to do that job. The people who practised the art of embalming belonged to a class of men in whose families this profession was hereditary. The embalmers were held in high honour and were treated with much consideration because they were friends of the priest and were allowed to enter the sanctuary as if they were ceremonially pure.

There were many ways to embalm depending on the price. The most expensive manner was to draw out part of the brains through the nostrils with an iron hook and then the rest by infusion of drugs. With a sharp Ethiopian stone they made an incision in the side of the stomach and took out all the bowels and having cleansed the abdomen and rinsed it with palm wine they sprinkled it with pounded perfumes. They then filled the belly with pure myrrh pounded and cassis and other perfumes, and frankincense and sewed it up again. They finally steeped it in natron leaving it there for 70 days after which they washed the corpse and wrapped the whole body in bandages of flaxen cloth and smeared it with gum.

The bodies of the poor were preserved by two cheap methods, one consisting of soaking in salt and hot bitumen and the other in salt only.

When the first great find of royal mummies was made at Deir el-Bahari in 1881, a considerable number of the coffins bore inscriptions written in ink, recording the restoration of each respective mummy, or the steps taken to preserve it from destruction by removing it to another tomb. The robbers in their search for treasure had taken away the bandages, and damaged the bodies, and the pious restorers had to set about rebandaging these battered remains.

When I was in Cairo, I went to the National Museum and saw the mummies of the various Egyptian kings. They looked awfully dried up and pitiful. It was never the intention of the kings to be seen in such a fashion by later generations of people. The Museum has now prohibited tourists from entering this chamber. What they needed was quiet and solitude. That was why the Kings of the Old Kingdom had taken all the trouble to build pyramids to hide their corpses. That did not prevent the tomb robbers from breaking into them for the pyramids were too conspicuous. The Egyptian kings who came later went into Upper Egypt and hid their corpses in an unknown valley which later came to be known as the Valley of the Kings. But the tomb robbers again went for the treasures the Kings had brought with them into their graves. What was left of an ancient

Egyptian civilization were the tombs of these kings in the form of pyramids and the Valley of the Kings where they buried themselves in great splendour.

The mummies became much sought after in the Middle Ages when physicians believed that when crushed to powder they were valuable as medicine. It was believed that when the mummy was ground to powder and then mixed with vegetable oil till it had attained the consistency of an unguent or salve, it could be taken and proved efficacious in treating sprains, inflammation, pleurisy and pneumonia. European merchants travelled all the way to Egypt to buy the new cure. In the 16th century, the trade was in full swing. Farmers spent their time digging for mummies during inundation. For centuries, the chief supply of mummies was from Sakkara near Cairo.

This is cannibalism after death. What was the point in preserving one's body to be robbed and eaten by people of later generations?

7

The Valley of the Kings

Six hundred miles up the Nile River is a small town called Luxor, for many years the paradise for archaeologists. Here stood the Imperial city of Thebes which ruled over the Egyptian empire for more than 1,000 years. It was here that some of the most romantic and spectacular discoveries were made. The archaeologists found the 36 royal mummies at Deir-el-Bahari in 1881, and the opening of the kings' tombs in the Valley of the Kings, culminating in the discovery of the world's famous sepulchre of Tutankhamen. How can one leave Egypt without seeing these historical relics? There is a saying that those who have not been to Luxor have not seen the real Egypt.

Thus one early morning, in the winter of 1969, the UAR plane took my family to Luxor. I have never seen the sun so huge and so red rising from the East from the plane. The Nile River resembled a green meandering snake and on both sides of it were large stretches of desert sand. Within 45 minutes we reached Luxor. We had brought our overcoats along, but found them redundant. An old bone-shaker car took us to the Winter Palace, an old-fashioned hotel full of Egyptian antiques.

Luxor was once an important market. It controlled the routes to the gold mines in the Nubian mountains and collected the produce of the Sudan such as gums, ostrich feathers, gold dust and slaves. In the Eighteenth dynasty when the warrior kings ruled this city, rich tributes flowed in, enabling the monarch to build gigantic temples and monuments such as the Karnak.

Looking westward across the river from the hotel in the evening we saw the purple-coloured cliffs of the Theban hills, the burial ground of the Pharaohs at the height of Egypt's imperial power. The large, red sun was setting and the whole Theban hills turned purplish red and they looked beautiful against the palm trees that line the Nile River. Luxor is situated on the east bank of the River where the easy-going people lived with the splendour of its temples — the Amun Re, the royal palaces and the haunting sadness and mystery of that vast city of the dead hewn out of the Western hills across the river.

The next morning we took a boat across to the Theban hills. The turbaned boatmen waited at the landing stages to take us across the Nile just as their predecessors did their passengers in the Pharaonic times. There were some Americans with their sun-hats, cameras and a gaggle of long-legged, chattering daughters. A group of French-speaking tourists chatted loudly when the boat was about to leave.

When we landed on the shore of the West bank, a jeep took us through a mile of broad plain until we reached a range of limestone cliffs which were cracked into gullies by the sun and wind. They were not very high, between 800 to 1,000 feet, but to us the Theban hills have been something which were unparalleled anywhere in the world. For 2,000 years, they have become the resting places for embalmed kings, and nobles of seventy generations.

Until the Eighteenth Dynasty (1555 BC), the Theban kings seemed to have been buried on the eastern side of the mountain. They still adhered to the pyramidal form of their tombs which were robbed by pyramid robbers. This had led later Pharaohs to seek to conceal their sepulchres. The Pharaoh who broke with tradition and thought of going underground instead of upwards was Tuthmosis I, the third king of the Eighteenth Dynasty. He went to the Thebes and found an amphitheatre in the hills, a very remote and unearthly sterile place to bury his body. This was the beginning of the Valley of the Kings. From Tuthmosis I onwards throughout the Eighteenth, Nineteenth and Twentieth Dynasties, king after king had his tomb hollowed out of cliffs of the valley and buried their sepulchres.

The earlier kings and queens had their tombs sited in remote and mysterious places and their entrances were inconspicuous. But later even such precautions did not prevent secrecy from leaking out and their tombs were also robbed. They finally gave up trying to hide their secrecy and began to open their tombs boldly and tunnelled out long broad galleries which descended for hundreds of feet into the heart of the mountain. They began to protect their bodies with concealed burial chambers and massive granite sarcophagi. From the twelfth century onwards (1200–1090 BC) no more kings were buried in the Royal Valley. Under the weak government of the Ramesside kings, tomb robbery became more rampant and we learn from the papyri the trials of some of the daring robber gangs. Eventually the Valley of the Kings had most of its tombs stripped and empty, and the valley was abandoned. The Pharaohs' might, respect for the dead or even the fear of god had all proved less powerful than the lust for gold.

When Christianity came to Egypt, the copts built their cemetery nearby and some of the hermits lived in the tombs of these Egyptian kings. When the Arabs came they searched for buried treasures. Only the descendants of the ancient Egyptians now poor and conquered lived in the ruins of their ancestors' monuments and sometimes within their tombs. The Egyptian authorities have now taken over these tombs and made them into a tourist sight.

We visited the tomb of Sethi I, son of Rameses I, who was the third king of the Nineteenth Dynasty (1350–1200 BC). He came to the throne when the Bedouin took advantage of the long peace and was causing trouble in South West Asia. The energetic king wiped out the Bedouins and went further to attack the Libyans, Egypt's Western enemies, and reopened the routes to gold mines in the South East. He reigned Egypt for twenty years and his workmen hollowed out great tombs which descended into the mountain through a series of galleries and extensive halls for no less than 450 feet below. From the entrance of his tomb were a broad flight of stairs leading downwards. As we entered we found a long corridor which sloped downwards covered with religious symbols. Above our heads were rows of painted vultures stretching their wings and on each side were the symbols of Amun Re — the God of the Sun, the King of gods and the patron of the Thebes. He has the head of a ram and a human body. And there was also Mut, the Queen of the gods with eagle head and human body and their son Khonsu with the head of an owl. The Egyptian gods

Underground path leading to King Tutankhamer's cave

were like human beings and many produced children. As we saw more animal headed gods in the galleries we knew we were entering the Underworld.

The rock-hewn passages and chambers represented stages in the journey in the Underworld. The deceased sailed through them at night in the boat of the ram-headed Sun God surrounded by his retinue. As they passed from one leg of the journey to another they had to go through massive gates each guarded by huge serpents.

As we descended a steep flight of stairs we came to the second corridor which had thirty-seven forms of the Sun God depicted on the upper part of the recesses on both sides. As we descended to the third corridor, we saw Maat, goddess of truth, with her outstretched wings above the doorway, and then Isis, the sister of Osiris who was the King of the Underworld. On the walls of the third corridor we witnessed the Book of Dead. Osiris, the creator of law and agriculture, had once ruled on earth. He had been a just and much-loved ruler who was slain by his jealous brother Set. Set, as the myth went, conspired against Osiris and at a banquet persuaded him to enter a chest which was then sealed and thrown into the Nile. It was carried down to the sea. The broken-hearted Isis wandered far and wide in tortured misery seeking the body of her loved one. Isis eventually found the body entangled in a tamarisk bush in the marshes of the delta. She hid the body but Set who went out boar-hunting found it again and cut it into fourteen pieces, and scattered them in all directions. Isis continued her mission, collected the pieces and sought the help of the jackal-god Anubis who became god of embalmment to prepare it for the netherworld. Isis, the myth continued, raised her son Horus in the marshes until he was strong enough to avenge his father's death by slaying Set. He then set out to seek his father and raised him from the dead. This risen Osiris, however, could no longer reign in the kingdom on earth and now became king of the underworld.

On the walls of the tomb chamber were dramatic representations of the whole story.

Towards the middle of the left-hand wall, the sun boat was driven through the netherworld by seven gods and seven goddesses and in front of it marched four gods and the goddess Isis. On the right-hand wall, the Sun God and his retinue were drawn through a land inhabited by demons and monsters and we saw a serpent with three heads, wings and human legs.

From the third corridor onwards, the quality of the colour on the reliefs was superb. It was hard to believe that after nearly three thousand years, the reliefs on the wall could be preserved so well as if they were done only recently. The reliefs were the work of unknown ancient Egyptian artists who were ordered by the Pharaohs to carve them. These artists who always remained anonymous had exact precision and beauty of the lines.

After the third corridor we entered a square chamber with four pillars. On the pillars themselves the Pharaoh was shown before the various deities: Isis and Nephthys, Hath, or the goddess of joy and love to whom the cow was sacred, Selket the goddess to whom the scorpion was sacred and Horus the son of Osiris. In a superb mural, the four races of men known at the time — the Egyptians, Asians with beards and coloured aprons, Negroes and Libyans with feathers on their heads and tattooed bodies — stood before God Horus. On another wall, we found murals showing the journey to the underworld; the sacred cow, ram, bird and human head guarding the procession against the fiery serpents. We saw the enemies of the Sun God being burned under the supervision of the hawk-headed Horus in strange furnaces while fire-breathing goddesses stood watch with swords.

We descended further down. The tomb had an ante-chamber that contained the alabaster sarcophagus of the Pharaoh. Adjoining the tomb chamber were four side-rooms. The first one had the text of a myth that concerned the rebellion of mankind against the Sun God, their punishment and final rescue. On the rear wall was a magnificent relief of the heavenly cow. In another room was more dramatic representations of the Pharaoh's journey to various provinces, safeguarded by the spells of Isis, the sacred Ibis and the ostrich feather — the symbol of justice and truth. Spirits and demons greeted the procession. The foes of Osiris were beheaded by a lion-headed god, the dead were restored to life, and serpents with heads of genii upon their backs, or with swords in their hands, rising in unison to annihilate the foes of the Sun God at the end of the Journey.

With the help of the Sun God, the Pharaoh would overcome all obstacles and would be able to eat and drink again imbued with life so as to reign again. This was his ultimate hope and all the murals depicted his journey to the Underworld and how he overcame difficulties.

Finally he would have to appear in the Judgement Hall of Osiris where his heart would be weighed in the balance against a feather.

Thoth the ibis-headed god of the truth would record the result. If the heart is heavier than the feather, then he would go to hell. If the feather and the heart are of the same weight, then the owner goes to heaven. Before he reached the Judgement Hall, he had to pass through many gods who would ask awkward questions, and faced many demons. But, by the time of the New Empire the priesthood had produced many elaborate and lengthy books of magical spells, and 'manuals of infernal geography' by the aid of which the soul might make the journey through those perilous regions unscathed. From such books the dead man or woman would find all the questions they would be asked and the correct answers to give. These scrolls including the inevitable verdict of acquittal were sold by priestly scribes to anyone who could afford to buy them. These products of the priestly imagination had side-tracked the development of Egyptian religion into dubious subways. The purchasers of these magical spells hope to put the gods into their pockets.

We also visited the tomb of Tutankhamen. This was the only tomb that had escaped the tomb robbers and had hit the world's headlines in 1922 when an American Egyptologist, Thomas Carter, discovered the tomb. The tomb was built on much less elaborate lines than those built in the Theban manner. Instead of an elaborate series of corridors, sunken staircases, protective wall and further descending passages, antechamber and a series of storerooms, his tomb had only a sunken entrance staircase, a descending passage and antechamber with an annexe, a burial chamber and one storeroom. All these rooms were small and of the simplest kind. The burial chamber was rectangular. Depicted on the east wall was a scene of the funeral procession: the deceased Tutankhamen was being drawn by courtiers to the tomb. The mummy was shown supported upon a lion-shaped bier, within a shrine, on a boat which rested upon the sledge. Over the dead king were festoons of garlands; on the boat in front of the shrine was a sphinx rampant. Nephthys and Isis were mourning.

The mummy of Tutankhamen was fashioned to symbolise Osiris. The beaten gold mask, a beautiful and unique specimen of ancient portraiture, bore a sad but calm expression suggestive of youth overtaken prematurely by death. Upon its forehead, wrought in massive gold were the royal insignia — the Nekhebet Vulture and Buto Serpent, emblems of the two Kingdoms over which he had reigned. The chin had conventional Osiride beard, wrought in gold-coloured glass. Around the throat was a triple necklace of yellow and red gold and blue faience disk-shaped beads, pendant from the neck by flexible gild inlaid straps was a large black resin scarab that rested between the hands.

The actual contents found inside the Tutankhamen tombs surpassed the wildest dreams. When we gaze at the contents which now lie in the Cairo Museum, we can imagine the exhilaration, suspense and amazement of those who first saw these fabulous treasures inside the tomb. According to Carter who spent ten years cataloguing the contents, there were 171 objects in the first room alone. When he had made a small opening in the door of the tomb chamber, he had been faced with what appeared to be a wall of solid gold. Inside there were a stone sarcophagus and three mummy coffins. The one holding the pharaoh's remains was in solid gold and alone weighed 2,488.8 lbs.

The mummy was found to be resplendent in gold, with a solid gold mask on the head. There were bracelets, chains, collars, gold beads and necklets of precious and semi-precious stones, engraved scarabs and garlands of flowers. Only the inner mummy case which contained the Pharaoh's mummy had been left on the site. The rest were in the Cairo Museum.

The paintings on the walls were in almost perfect condition. They were representations from the Book of the Dead.

There were signs of disorder in the tomb. The disorder was indicative of a hurry, as was the lack of decoration on the tomb walls. It was clear that the young king met a sudden death and was buried in haste. Was it suicide or murder? The results of anthropolitical and skeleton examination of the Pharaoh's mummy, carried out by the Departments of Anatomy of Cairo and Liverpool Universities, were now at hand and it appeared that death could have been caused by a blow on the head. If the young Pharaoh proved to have been murdered after all, who was the murderer? Was it his tutor who coveted his young wife and probably married her after Tutankhamen's death? Or was it General Harmbab who had designs on the throne and actually succeeded in seizing it from the blue-bloods at the beginning of the Nineteenth Dynasty?

The tomb paintings in the Royal Valley were more than 3,000 years old, but they opened up a window of the way Egyptians had lived, their hopes and aspirations, their customs and traditions and their religion. In the tombs of the Lords and other high officials who were not Pharaohs, the walls were full of paintings of fishing, hunting and feasting. They hoped to enjoy in the next world the happiness they had experienced in this.

When I went down the tombs, I had the feeling similar to that of going down the London tubes except it was not by escalator. Imagine that you were beneath the deepest depth of the London station and around you were the fresh mural paintings of the Egyptian mythology, the many animal-headed gods; and the pharaoh's journey to the Underworld and then the sarcophagus. I have seen China's Ming tombs and that of Empress Dowager, and they were nothing compared to the Valley of the Kings.

One cannot leave Luxor without seeing the temple of Amun at Karnak, the blueprint of the power and glory of a golden era, a temple of splendour and unimaginable proportions dedicated to the King of Gods Amun Re. We took the little donkey-drawn *arabiyas* (a kind of cart) and clopped our way towards Karnak. As we got off the *arabiyas*, we were suddenly struck by a double row of ram-headed sphinxes. These have sun discs on their heads and a statue of the Pharaoh between the forepaws showing the Sun God as strong as a lion, as docile as a ram. They were there to protect Pharaoh Rameses II who placed them there. Before us rose the massive first pylon which dated from the Nubian Dynasty and which was never completed. It was 113 metres wide, 43 metres high and 5 metres thick. On the doorway leading to the Great Court was an inscription recording the latitude and longitude of the chief temples of the

Karnak Temples, Luxor

Massive gold mask of Tutankhamen

Statue of Rameses II — Luxor

The Great Hypostyle Hall — Karnak Temples, Luxor

Pharaohs as calculated by the group of scholars accompanying the army of Napoleon to Egypt.

The Great Court which was built during the 22nd Dynasty covered a massive area of 8,919 square metres. Then, there was the Temple of Rameses III and the Triumphal Monument of Sheshonk I and then we came to the Great Hypostyle Hall, the fruit of Egypt's power and wealth and one of the most massive of human creations covering an area of 4,983 square metres. There were 134 columns arranged in 16 rows. The whole of the cathedral of Notre Dame in Paris could be comfortably accommodated within its walls. Each of the columns was 69 feet high and nearly 12 feet thick. It was easily the largest single chamber of any temple in the world. As I stood in the middle of the columns and looked up, I sensed that only people who were a hundred feet tall could have conceived of this idea. You were lost in the jungle of giant columns and you felt really minute. It has terrifying strength, massiveness and power. One felt crushed by the weight of masonry, columns carved out of a single block of granite and weighing 140 tons. One was overpowered by their titanic size and weight.

Karnak is not beautiful but it is powerful and massive. The importance of Karnak as the home of the King of Gods explained why generations of Pharaohs lavished the wealth of an empire on the building and enlargement of its temples. These temples belong to that rare species of architectural marvels that will continue to awe many people.

Each pylon told a story of the Pharaoh. On the seventh pylon was a gigantic carving of Tuthmosis III, his left hand grasping a group of bounded captives, and his right hand brandishing a mace with which he was about to dash out their brains as a sacrifice to Amun. Nearby was the daring description:

'From the mysterious lands as far as the boundaries of Asia . . . His Majesty brings back prisoners to make a great massacre of them . . .' These were all written in hieroglyphs.

Pharaoh after Pharaoh added halls and pylons and obelisks to commemorate their victories and as thanks offering to their God, until the Great Hypostyle Hall reached its present magnificence.

The letters written on the stones and walls of these columns and those in the caves of the Valley of the Kings were all in hieroglyphic. It was a sign language like Chinese which followed the shape of things. How could modern people understand the hieroglyphics or the Egyptian language of five thousand years ago? It happened at the time of Napoleon's short-lived conquest of Egypt in 1799. He brought with him a number of distinguished French savants who made a survey of the country. In August the same year, a detachment of French soldiers was working on the fortifications at Rossetta in the Nile Delta and they found an irregular-shaped stone of ancient origin built into the wall of an Arab fort. The stone was inscribed in what appeared to be Greek and in hieroglyphic. The stone was despatched to the Institute National in Cairo for examination. Napoleon himself was personally interested in it and ordered ink copies to be made and distributed to the scholars of Europe. In 1801, under the treaty of Capitulation important Egyptian antiquities had to be handed over to the British as spoils of war and among these was the Rossetta stone. The Rossetta stone finally landed in the British Museum. An Englishman Dr Robert Young and a Frenchman J. F. Champollon succeeded in deciphering the inscriptions on the stone. It was found that there were alphabetic hieroglyphs and from then onwards the secret of ancient Egypt came to life. The hieroglyphs which had baffled generations of students at last gave up their secret and the road was open by which men could travel back 5,000 years to rediscover the world of ancient Egypt.

The Egyptians, like the Chinese, used hieroglyphs in ancient times as a sign language to communicate. The Egyptian language was buried with their pyramids, and the walls of the Valley of the Kings not to be rediscovered until the early nineteenth century. It was nearly lost to mankind, whereas the Chinese had succeeded in transforming their hieroglyphs into a modern language. And the language is still being further simplified.

The Egyptians had a religion which was preoccupied with death and their Pharaohs spent all the national resources of the country in preparation for the next world. The Chinese were more practical, had no religion but down-to-earth philosophies like Taoism and Confucianism which dealt with how to make life and society more contented and happier on earth. The former perished and the latter survived.

8

Pakistan in Turmoil

Four months after I arrived at Cairo, I received a cable from Singapore Foreign Ministry accrediting me to Pakistan. On 10 November 1968, I took a KLM plane destined for Karachi. In the early hours of the next morning, I was awakened by the sudden flash of light inside the plane, followed by an announcement that the plane could not land in Karachi because of a heavy fog. The plane took us instead to Bombay in India, a country which was still hostile to Pakistan.

What can one do in Bombay Airport in the early hours of the morning? The long benches meant for transit passengers were all occupied by sleeping tourists, some with shoes on. I went to the bookshop to pass away my time. I bought a walking stick and a book entitled *Kundalini*, a book which one could obtain only in India.

A few hours later, I took a BOAC plane and flew to Karachi. When we were about to land at the Karachi Airport, a thick layer of white cloud covered the whole city and visibility below was nil. From the plane, the white cloud resembled a huge white bear trying to swallow the whole city. The plane flew around Karachi for nearly half an hour and just when the announcement came that we had to fly off to New Delhi a streak of sunlight pierced through the fog and Karachi emerged from below. Everyone in the plane was tongue-tied when finally the plane touched down at Karachi. There was a sigh of relief from all the passengers.

I took the Pakistani Airlines and flew to Rawalpindi, the capital of Pakistan which was having a curfew because of the riots which took place the night before. In fact, the heavy fog which prevented us from landing turned out to be a bad omen, for on that very day an assassination attempt was made on President Ayub Khan's life. We read from the newspapers in front page headlines that someone had attempted to shoot Ayub Khan. Ayub was speaking to a 20,000 crowd when suddenly a young man shot at him but missed him. The assassin holding a pistol in his right hand was dumbfounded and was taken away by a police inspector, before the furious crowd pounced on him.

On the same page of the newspaper was the news of the assassination attempt on the American President Nixon by four Yemenis who were also arrested.

I stayed at Hotel Intercontinental, the place where Ali Bhutto had aroused anti-government sentiments leading to a riot. The police clashed with students who supported Ali Bhutto, and killed two students and another man. I saw cars overturned, buses burnt and shops looted. A curfew was imposed and Ali Bhutto detained.

It was nearing election time and opposition parties were whipping up their campaign against Ayub Khan. Ali Bhutto who was the most prominent opponent of Ayub Khan seemed determined to get himself arrested. He openly supported the violent demonstration of University students who were dissatisfied with the authorities over certain education policies. They had demanded that:

1) The third grade students from secondary schools should be admitted to the university;
2) The students should have representatives in the University Council;
3) The University Ordinance should be abolished (the Ordinance provides wide powers to the authorities, one of which is the power to deprive a graduate of his degree).

The day before my arrival at Rawalpindi, the students gathered outside the Intercontinental Hotel to receive Bhutto. They shouted slogans to cheer Bhutto but the demonstration was peaceful. It was the tactless mishandling on the part of the police that brought about the clash when the police fired at the crowd and killed two students. When that occurred, the students ran amok and started burning buses and destroyed every traffic light in town.

On 12th November, the Chief Protocol Officer Mr Anwar Khan, accompanied by an assistant, came with a state car to Intercontinental Hotel to take me to the President's residence. I have never seen a more nervous person than the Chief Protocol Officer. Inside the car, he closed his eyes and mumbled something to himself. Apparently, he was praying aloud in front of a stranger, perhaps to give him strength because he had to meet the President. I took the book written by the President entitled *Friends not Masters* with me, hoping to get the autograph of the President. When I raised this matter with the Chief Protocol Officer, he said: 'Oh, no, please don't do that. Don't talk about politics to my President.'

I was received by the President's military Secretary Major-General Mohamed Rafi Khan, who took me to the waiting room where I sat for five minutes, and then I was escorted to see the President next door. Ayub who was in plain clothes got up from his seat and walked towards us. We shook hands and I presented my credentials. He then returned to his seat facing the three of us, with the Chief Protocol Officer on my left and the Military Secretary on my right. The ceremony was simple and short. No speech was necessary and no other formalities.

The President started the conversation by asking me how Prime Minister Lee Kuan Yew was. I told him that the Prime Minister was having a holiday in Canada and doing some research. On hearing this, he said: 'He is a lucky man. Few Prime Ministers can afford this relaxation. I remember I played golf with him and Tengku Abdul Rahman when they were in London for the Commonwealth Prime Ministers' Conference.' Ayub was inquisitive about conditions in South-East Asia — our relations with Malaysia and Indonesia. He seemed well-informed including the recent incident with Indonesia. He spoke about the raid at our embassy in Jakarta and that our Ambassador had to go into hiding when we hanged the two Indonesian marines. I explained the latest situation and emphasised to him the necessity to abide by the rule of law.

The President appeared to be least ruffled by the assassination attempt on his life. He looked calm and collected and never showed any sign of nervousness. I was tempted to raise the matter but since the Chief Protocol Officer had warned me earlier not to talk about politics, I made an indirect approach by talking about the student riot in Singapore. On hearing this, Ayub said: 'Oh yes, we too have student troubles. The opposition tried to exploit them. Invariably, opposition parties do not have concrete proposals but only slogans and invariably opposition parties are normally leftist inclined.' He did not mention the assassination attempt and I left it at that.

He then turned the topic to the Middle East. He expressed delight that President Nasser had made a good gesture by sending a congratulatory message to the US President-elect Nixon for his victory. He then added: 'We must realise that small nations will not change the policy of big nations. It was a mistake to break relations with the United States.' The conversation between us took about twenty minutes and we did discuss politics.

Before I left for Rawalpindi, I had written to Singapore to ask for permission to bring my personal assistant along to help me arrange for appointments. The answer was 'No. This is not the usual practice.' So, after presenting credentials I was on my own. I hired a rental car, put on the national flag myself and drove off to my appointments. As Ambassador I had to call on the doyen, then Ministers and then my colleagues. Without a personal assistant, how do I call on another Ambassador? I cannot pick up the phone and call on another Ambassador and say to him: 'I am Ambassador so and so, can I see you.' This is not the way diplomacy is conducted. There are certain rules of decorum and etiquette to be observed. I made use of the telephone operator in the hotel as my temporary secretary by paying her a handsome tip. She acted as my secretary and rang up the doyen and Ambassadors and made the necessary appointments. But after the experience I wrote back to Singapore and said that I would not like to be accredited to another country again without a personal assistant. And they gave me one when I went on other assignments.

I called on the Foreign Minister, who was then Arshad Hussein. He was an old-time diplomat, having been posted to the Soviet Union and later to India. The Foreign Minister was glad that at last Singapore had established diplomatic relations at ambassadorial level with Pakistan. He hoped however that we would set up an office in Rawalpindi.

Arshad Hussein explained to me why Pakistan had to take a 'tight-rope' foreign policy of balancing between her relations with the East and the West. He said Pakistan was convinced of India's aggressive motive and that India had not reconciled to a co-existence with Pakistan. Under the pretext of arming herself against a possible attack from China, India was in fact trying to prepare herself for aggression against Pakistan. He added that by increasing her military capacity India tried to coerce Pakistan into giving up her claim over Kashmir. Up till now, India still refused to abide by the Security Council resolution that the Kashmir issue should be settled by a referendum by the people, 80 percent of whom were Muslims.

Touching on the Kashmir issue, the Foreign Minister politely expressed his dissatisfaction over Singapore's stand in the matter. He drew my attention to the joint communique issued by our then Foreign Minister Mr S. Rajaratnam and the former Minister of External Affairs of India Shri Mohamedali Currim Chagla, when the latter visited Singapore from May 8 to 10, 1967. He referred to the second sentence of paragraph 7 (which was underlined) as follows:

'The Foreign Minister of Singapore noted these efforts and expressed the hope that the two countries could find a basis for resolving their differences by direct discussions without any outside interference, as peace between the two countries would contribute to the prosperity and happiness of the peoples of India and Pakistan.'

The Foreign Minister pointed out that by using the word 'differences' instead of 'dispute' and by the clause 'direct discussions without outside interference', Singapore was in fact siding India.

The Kashmir issue, he emphasised, was still a dispute and not a difference. By saying that there should be direct discussions without outside interference India tried to ignore the Security Council resolution by which both parties had agreed to hold a referendum by the people. There can be no repudiation of an international agreement of this nature. Under the Tashkent Declaration, India was honour-bound to negotiate on Kashmir. He hoped that Singapore would be fair and would abide by the Security Council resolution on the Kashmir issue. He disclosed to me that Pakistan would soon be reviving the matter in the Security Council and hoped that Singapore would this time support Pakistan in the name of justice and fair play.

He added: 'So long as the Kashmir dispute is not settled, there will be no peace between India and Pakistan.'

Rawalpindi was a small town with a few main streets of tarred roads. There were a number of four-storey high buildings scattered here and there along the main road. The rest were dilapidated houses made of plank sprawled out along narrow muddy untarred roads. When a horse cart passed by the dust burst into one's face. To the veiled Muslim women who covered their faces and resembled moving black mosquito nets, the dust was no bother at all. I took a ride on one of those horse-drawn carts which were meant for giants with long legs and went round the town sightseeing. My legs could not touch the bottom when I leaned back. There was really nothing much to see in Rawalpindi.

About seven miles from Rawalpindi was the new capital Islamabad where the foreign embassies and the ambassadors' residences were situated. Islamabad was under the lee of the Margalia Hills. Spread over 350 square miles of the Potwar Plateau, the site was a panoramic expanse of natural terraces and meadows rising from 1,700 to 2,000 feet above sea level with a backdrop of mountain ranges. Ayub Khan had chosen this site for the capital because Pakistan had two provinces — East and West Pakistan — separated by long distances. It would be better to choose a neutral place and a common platform. The place had a rich history. It was claimed that it was one of Man's earliest homes, dating back four hundred thousand years, as shown by the Stone Age relics of the Sohan Culture found in the Potwar Plateau by Sir Mortimer Wheeler. Later, inhabitants of this part of the world built a centre of their power at Taxila, on the other side of Margalia Range. Taxila was a notable seat of civilization and learning long before the dawn of the Christian era. It was the cradle of Gandhara art.

Islamabad might be beautiful in scenery, but to a diplomat who was accustomed to the life of Ginza in Tokyo it was hell. The Malaysian High Commissioner Tengku Indra Putra who

A goat market in Pakistan

was Ambassador to Japan had just been transferred to Islamabad with a Japanese wife. As soon as he arrived, he looked around and got into a panic. He went to the house of the Japanese Ambassador and said: 'What do I do in this desert place for two years?' This story was told to me by the Japanese Ambassador Mr Tanaka when I called on him. He advised the Malaysian High Commissioner to be patient. I met Tanaka again when he was transferred to Indonesia. Around 1974 he was sent back to Japan because of illness and died soon after that. To the doyen of the diplomatic corps, the Iraqi Ambassador who was an Imam, Islamabad was paradise. He stayed there for 16 years and refused to return to his own country. Whenever his term ended, the Muslims in Islamabad would send a petition to Iraq pleading to the Iraq Government to allow him to stay on. He had already become their Imam and they respected him.

Tengku Indra Putra invited me to dinner one evening with his Japanese wife at his home. I had a wonderful curry meal and we talked about the loneliness of the place.

Karachi is a much larger city, the only port for West Pakistan. It was once the capital of Pakistan. It is situated on international air routes and even before independence was a centre for foreign commercial firms. After independence a large number of Muslim men of money and business acumen migrated from Bombay, Kathiawar, and other places in India to Karachi, and the town soon developed into the principal commercial and industrial complex of the country. With the influx of refugees and industrialization under Ayub Khan's administration, its population began to grow rapidly and civic facilities began to deteriorate. A city of some 250,000 in 1941, it had grown by 1968 to a population of about three million.

The first time I went to Karachi was in 1949 when I was on my way to London for further studies. The second time was when I accompanied Tengku Abdul Rahman's merdeka mission to London; the ship 'Asia' brought us to the last stop at Karachi before we boarded a plane for our destination. This was my third trip. During the second trip, Karachi was full of refugees. About nine million refugees had poured into Pakistan. The continuing animosity of Hindus and Sikhs, and the economic and social boycott brought about one of history's most tragic migrations. Before Ayub, the political regimes were interested in keeping this problem alive and refugees became a pawn in the game of party politics. Karachi became a centre of agitational politics.

Politicians found that they could collect mobs with the help of industrialists and businessmen and brought all kinds of pressures to bear on the government. A time came when one large public meeting attended by a riotous mob could determine the fate of the government. Moreover, the Central Government Ministers got embroiled with the affairs of Karachi's local administration. That was why Ayub moved the capital to Islamabad.

When I met Ayub Khan, he was nearing the tail end of his political career. Opposition to his leadership had mounted following the arrest of Ali Bhutto, his former Foreign Minister. Ali Bhutto resigned from Ayub's cabinet because of disagreement with the President over the Kashmir issue. He also had a personal grudge against Ayub. He was only 32 when he was made a Minister. He was first appointed as Minister of Commerce in the Revolutionary Government formed in 1958. From 1960 to 1963, he was Minister for National Reconstruction and Information. During most of that period, he also held charge of the Ministry of Fuel, Power and Natural Resources and the Ministry of Kashmir Affairs. He was later appointed Foreign Minister in January 1963. He later published a book called *Political Situation in Pakistan* which was highly critical of the Ayub regime and called for the overthrow of the Government. The book was later banned. Ali Bhutto's main platform was to bring back democracy to the people of Pakistan. When I was there, the country was run on the system of 'Basic democracy' which Ayub imposed upon the nation on 27 October 1959.

Under this system, the country was initially divided into 80,000 constituencies which were equally shared by the two provinces of Pakistan — East and West. Each constituency with an average population of 1,000 to 1,500 elected on the basis of universal suffrage a representative who was called a Basic Democrat. About ten such Democrats formed a primary body called a union council which was referred to as committee in towns and cities. Each primary body would have Government-nominated members who were to exercise control over the council committee. These primary bodies were entrusted with the development programme in their respective areas. Under the constitution of 1962, the 80,000 Basic Democrats of the country were to elect the President, the National Assembly and the provincial legislators. All would serve a term of five years.

The main characteristics of the authoritarian system were that it suppressed the politics of opposition, restricted universal franchise and brought East Pakistan firmly under the West Pakistan-dominated national fold. Naturally the most implacable opponents of the system were the Bengali elites of East Pakistan who wanted to achieve the liberation of their province from its economic, linguistic and political bondage to West Pakistan.

Ayub had genuinely believed that the constitution would work for Pakistan. In his book *Friends not Masters*, Ayub had explained that his people were mostly uneducated and their politicians most unscrupulous.

'Unfettered democracy can therefore prove dangerous, especially when Communism from within and without is so quick to make use of its weakness. We therefore have to have a controlled form of democracy with checks and counter-checks,' he said.

'We must not forget that democracy is a means to an end and not an end by itself and that there is no set pattern of democracy that can be applied to every country without modifications. It would be advisable therefore to enable people to elect a college of people in each sub-unit, who in turn elect members for the provincial and central legislatures. Such an election system would be more easily manageable and would make for a good deal of responsibility.'

But, Ali Bhutto wanted to do away with the system of Basic Democrats, and return universal suffrage to every eligible voter. Students in Rawalpindi and other parts of Pakistan were demonstrating to demand for the release of their 'hero' Bhutto whom they described as the 'pride of Asia' and 'great leader'. The students in their clash with the police chanted a 'death to Ayub' slogan. Rawalpindi was deserted as most shop-owners responded to the appeals by student leaders for a city-wide strike. Virtually no public transport was available. Elsewhere lawyers kept up their protests against the Government, with processions in at least six cities, including Karachi, Lahore and Dacca to demand for the release of political detainees and asked for political reforms.

In his bid to topple the government, Ali Bhutto had unscrupulously supported Mujibur Rahman's demand for East Pakistan's regional autonomy. So far he had been always opposed to Bengali separatism. It was more a tactical move than an overall strategy.

Bengali political elites were the most frustrated under Ayub's regime. The Basic Democracy had cheated them of what they considered their legitimate right in the selection of their own leaders. They became even more disgusted when the Indo-Pakistan War of 1965 came along when they had to fend for themselves to defend the 55,126 square miles of territories and 75 million people with barely 10,000 soldiers.

Mujibur Rahman in 1966 put forward his six-point plan which demanded full regional autonomy (financial, military and political) confining federal responsibility to only matters of defence and foreign affairs, and direct election to legislatures on the basis of adult franchise. Ayub had Mujibur arrested.

By the time I went to Islamabad, the whole country was almost paralysed by the general strikes called by opposition parties. Administration had virtually collapsed in East Pakistan, where mobs of people roamed the streets, burning houses, looting and killing prominent personalities who supported Ayub. By 10th March 1969, Ayub made his last attempt to save the country by calling up opposition parties and conceded their demands for a federal parliamentary system of government with regional autonomy and the election of legislatures by direct adult franchise. But, Ayub would not concede to Mujibur Rahman's demands for separate autonomy for East Pakistan. On 25 March 1969 Ayub stepped down from the Presidency, handing over power to army's Commander-in-Chief, General Yahya Khan, who forthwith abrogated the 1962 constitution, declared martial law and appointed himself as the chief martial law administrator. Not long after that, Ayub died.

Yahya decided to play the role of an arbitrator among the conflicting and perhaps irreconcilable political groups. He announced in November 1969, that elections would be held in 1970 on the basis of universal franchise. On 7 December 1970, Pakistan went to the polls for the first time since its independence.

Mujibur Rahman's Awami League won the election, capturing 160 (over 53 percent) of the seats. Ali Bhutto's People's

Progressive Party came second, capturing 81 (27 percent) of the National Assembly's seats.

The Bengalis had voted en bloc for Mujibur Rahman's party. In fact, two nations had voted separately for their respective national parties. Mujibur Rahman claimed the headship of the Government and threatened to opt for an independent Bangladesh if not granted. Yahya faced the most difficult task by trying to negotiate with Mujibur Rahman and Ali Bhutto. But the negotiations reached a deadlock. Then Mujibur started his Civil Disobedience movement and delivered an ultimatum asking for autonomy for East Pakistan within 48 hours. Yahya had Mujibur arrested and the Awami League was banned and press censorship imposed. A large number of Bengali civilians were killed during clashes with the police. The following day, the Awami League launched its resistance to the Pakistan army and declared the independence of Bangladesh. The new nation Bangladesh was pronounced on 16 December 1971 when Pakistani army unconditionally surrendered to the Indian forces at Dacca. Indian intervention became imminent when India faced the problem of supporting about ten million East Pakistani refugees. India declared war on Pakistan when Yahya Khan himself ordered the bombardment of a few Indian airports in the Punjab-UP region.

With the defeat and disintegration of Pakistan's army the second authoritarian phase in the country's history came to an end. On 20 December 1971, Yahya Khan handed over power to Bhutto.

The first problem of Bhutto was to settle the demand by the National Awami Party in the provincial legislatures of Baluchistan and North West Frontier Province for regional autonomy. Its leader Wali Khan demanded an independent Pakhtunistan state comprising the North West Frontier Province and perhaps the Pushtu-speaking areas in Baluchistan. Faced with such opposition from the very beginning, Bhutto abandoned whatever idea he might have had about reviving democracy. In February 1975, he banned the National Awami Party on the grounds that it had been attempting to establish an independent state of Pakhtunistan through large-scale insurgency, terrorism and sabotage.

In the 1977 elections, nine rightwing opposition parties united and formed the Pakistan National Alliance to contest the election. But, Bhutto won the election, acquiring 155 of the 200 seats in the National Assembly. The opposition launched a nation-wide civil disobedience movement against the Bhutto Government. In April 1977, martial law was imposed on three of Pakistan's main cities and from then onwards, Bhutto began relying on the army for the restoration of law and order. On 5 July 1977, General Muhammad Zia-al-Huq, the Pakistani Army Chief-of-Staff, overthrew Bhutto's Government, suspended the constitution, dissolved the National Assembly and provincial legislatures and began his martial law regime. Zia projected the image of an unambitious soldier of Islam. The very day he took over the government he said his martial law regime intended to restore elections within three months. He released Bhutto to enable him to campaign for elections.

Bhutto could draw large crowds, for he was still a political force. On 3 September 1977 Bhutto was arrested in connection with a political murder which had taken place in 1974. On 19 March 1978, the Punjab High Court found Bhutto guilty and sentenced him to death. In the early morning of 4 April 1979, despite appeals by various governments and protest from within, Bhutto was hanged.

In less than ten days after Bhutto's hanging, Zia's faith in Western-style democracy and his determination to hold elections suddenly changed. On 16 October 1979, Zia cancelled the general elections, banned all political parties, imposed strict censorship on the press and imprisoned a few hundred politicians including Nusrat and Benazir Bhutto, the wife and daughter respectively of Bhutto. A few days later on 21 October, Zia declared that he would create an Islamic state which would have no room for the secular democratic system of the West and the Western-type elections based on universal franchise. In Zia's Islamic state only practising Muslims were to be nominated as election candidates and not every one was to have the right to vote, certainly not the majority of the Pakistani women. This might at least succeed in destroying the prospect of a woman like Nusrat or Benazir Bhutto from standing for election and becoming the President of Pakistan.

Pakistan was formed on 14 August 1947 for Muslims millions of whom streamed into the country. It was a dream for Muslims and people thought that religion could bring the nation together and work for common good. The Pakistanis crossed a river of blood on independence. People were uprooted and driven like millions of dry leaves by a turbulent gust of fanaticism and blind passion. They were trampled and crushed under the feet of communal fury. Hundreds of thousands of men, women and children were butchered and the sub-continent was engulfed in a bloody civil war.

Then, it was free-for-all in Pakistan where there was no constitution. This resulted in the Rawalpindi conspiracy and then the assassination of Prime Minister Liaquat Ali Khan. Between the period of Liaquat Ali Khan's death till 1958, there was chaos and disorder. The central government was at loggerheads with the provinces and a great deal of intrigues and dog-fighting was going on within the central government itself. There was the leading personality of Khan Abdul Quyyun Khan who was going round the country spitting fire and preaching civil war. Khan Abdul Quyyun Khan built up the Muslim League National Guards of about 60,000 strong. They paraded in the streets wearing uniforms and steel helmets and carrying rifles. Prime Minister Malik Firoz Khan Noon announced that there would be little chance of free and fair elections if every political party had a private army of its own. What was more dangerous was that some of the politicians like Quyyun Khan had started making contacts with certain members of the armed forces. Then on 4th October 1958, Martial Law was proclaimed throughout Pakistan and Ayub Khan took over.

Ayub Khan introduced his Basic Democracy until March 1969 when he stepped down in favour of parliamentary democracy. Ali Bhutto took over and now Zia has once again swung the country back to Martial law.

Ayub Khan had done a great deal in building up the country and the army. What went wrong with him? It was his son Gohar Ayub Khan and his family who spoilt his image when he abused his power by monopolising business opportunities in Karachi. By December 1968, he was made to sever his ties with Gandhara Industries. His ties with the firm had been a source of opposition charges that members of the President's family were "enriching themselves through favoured treatment in private business."

What had gone wrong with Pakistan? The Pakistanis had come out of India because of religion. But religion alone could not unite the people. From one country, it split into two — Pakistan and Bangladesh, and nearly into three — Pakhtunistan. There is a lot of truth in what Ayub Khan had said in his book *Friends not Masters*, that 'We Pakistanis are a great mixture of races and of types. Individualistic in our outlook in civil life, we do not easily make a team and yet when disciplined, we make first class soldiers. This offers every budding leader an opportunity to make a team of his own. We are apt to be emotional and do not always take a realistic view of things. No demagogue can resist the temptation of working on our emotions and misleading us. We criticise everybody except ourselves and as there is a dearth of people with knowledge and experience there is a scramble for office. All this accounts for the distressing and dismal conditions in which the country found itself after the first few years of independence.'

The major conflict in Pakistan today is between the ulemas and the educated classes. All that was material, temporal and secular was identified with the educated and all that was religious and spiritual became the monopoly of the ulemas.

Whoever rules Pakistan must contend with the ulemas, who in some cases were well versed in Arabic and had made a special study of religious matters, and were regarded as the custodians of Islam. Among them were many, who did not hesitate to exert their influence in politics and had gradually built up for themselves a strong political force, opposed to that of the western educated groups in society. The conflict between these two classes has a long history. The educated regarded the ulemas as relics of the past and the ulemas treated the educated as heretics and unworthy. The ulemas would always demand that the government should agree to adopt an Islamic Constitution, leaving it to the ulemas to decide whether any law or measure was Islamic or not. It was a well-known fact that a number of Muslim ulemas openly opposed the concept of Pakistan. Some felt that Pakistan was essentially a territorial concept and thus alien to the philosophy of Islamic brotherhood which was universal in character.

The conflict between the educated Muslims and the ulemas was started in the early years of British rule and reached its culmination during the struggle for Pakistan. For decades after the British had consolidated their position in India, the ulemas kept the Muslims away from all sources of western knowledge. Not until the middle of the nineteenth century was this barrier of prejudice broken down. After Pakistan was formed, the ulemas reorganised themselves and began to exert pressure on the Government and to spread their influence on the population. They insisted that a constitution could be regarded as Islamic only if it were drafted by the ulemas and conceded them the authority to judge and govern the people.

It seems that Western Parliamentary democracy has again failed in the soil of Pakistan.

Author presenting credentials to President Ayub Khan

9

Haile Selassie—the Conquering Lion that lost his teeth

I met Emperor Haile Selassie, the 'Conquering Lion of Judah', 'King of Kings' and 'Elect of God', at Singapore's Sri Temasek, the Government rest house, when he visited Singapore in 1968. We were giving him a dinner in his honour. Haile Selassie was a minute figure, slim and short, bearded, and with a pair of big piercing eyes. He always had a supercilious look and it was most difficult to strike up a conversation with him. We sat next to one another and he just remained quiet with his eyes looking straight ahead. He was so stern and serious that one was easily influenced by his solitude.

He was always with his pet chihuahua, Lulu, the size of a doll who toddled around the dining room from underneath the tables. Off and on, the Emperor would call out his name, and he would come running and jump up to his lap. He would stroke the fur on the upper neck down to the spine and Lulu would feel comfortable and relaxed.

Least did I expect that months later, I would be presenting credentials to this Emperor at his Palace. I was in Cairo in early February 1969 when I received a cable notifying me that Singapore would like to establish diplomatic relations with the Kingdom of Ethiopia. I passed on the information to the Ethiopian Ambassador in Cairo, Mr Ato Mallas Mikael Andom who was the Dean of the Diplomatic Corps. He told me that the ceremony for the presentation of credentials in Addis Ababa would be very formal. I needed a tail coat and a special top-hat and white gloves and these were very expensive. I had them specially made, for the shops for hire had none to suit me.

I left for Addis Ababa on 29th March with my personal assistant the late Saim Noordin. We arrived at a time when both the Emperor and the Foreign Minister were busy with the State visit of the British Prime Minister Sir Harold Wilson. We therefore had to wait until April 4 when I presented a copy of my credentials to the Foreign Minister Ato Ketema Yifru.

On 5th April at 10.00 a.m. the Emperor's Deputy Chief Aide-de-Camp, Brig-General Tafesse Limma (he led the Ethiopian troops that participated in the 1950 Korean war and was A.D.C. to the Emperor during the latter's visit to Singapore) arrived with a Royal State car to receive me with five outriders. A short briefing on the procedure of presentation took place at the Guest Room of the Neon Imperial Hotel where I stayed.

At 10.00 a.m. we proceeded to the Jubilee Palace in the Royal State car with our Singapore flag fluttering in front of the car. At 10.15 a.m. we arrived at the Palace and I got down to inspect the Guard of Honour. I took the top-hat in my right hand, and with tail coat, I inspected the Guard of Honour which comprised one platoon of Imperial ceremonial guards. As I stood at attention to the playing of our national anthem by a special Imperial Guard band in front of the Palace, I noticed some lions roaming the garden unchained. After the Guard of Honour, I was escorted by the Brig-General to the entrance where I was met by the Foreign Minister. As I entered the Palace, I saw an unchained lion on my right lazing along the corridor and on my left was a leopard strolling up and down the corridor. Both of them stared at me as I entered. They were apparently tame. But it did give the new visitor a psychological jerk. It was the usual style of the Emperor to put his opponents at a disadvantage.

We were escorted to a guest room, but before we could sit down, news came that the Emperor was ready to receive us. I left my top-hat and white gloves on a table outside and proceeded to the entrance of the colourful and majestic Imperial Court room which was brightly lit. I stood in front of a red carpet which led to the other end of the room where the diminutive figure of his Imperial Majesty, Haile Selassie I, was standing in front of a magnificent throne. He was as usual in military uniform with full military decorations on the right side of his chest. The usher announced my name and designation and I made my first bow followed by my personal assistant Saim Noordin and the Brig-General. We proceeded to the centre of the court room and made our second bow, then walked towards the Emperor and halted five steps in front of him. He looked as usual stern and supercilious, casting his eyes on me from the top platform. I made my third bow and walked towards him and presented the credentials.

After that we shook hands. I stood aside and introduced my personal assistant to him. After shaking hands with the Emperor, Noordin retreated to the corner with the ADC. It was the normal practice in Ethiopia that the Ambassador, after presenting his credentials, introduced his staff members to the Emperor. I was then introduced by the Foreign Minister to Prime Minister Tsehafe Taezaz Aklilu Habte Wold who stood to the right of the Emperor and then the Minister of Commerce and Industry and Tourism on the left hand of the Emperor and we chatted for about five minutes.

The Emperor said he was grateful for the warm welcome he had received during his tour of the Republic of Singapore. With my appointment as Ambassador to Ethiopia, he said, he was confident that the friendly relations between the two countries would be further strengthened. I conveyed to the Emperor the best regards from our President and our Prime Minister. I told him that we in Singapore had heard much about what he had done for his country. Before presenting credentials I found out that the Emperor who was 77 years old liked to talk of the past especially his historical speech which he made at the League of Nations in 1936 against Mussolini. I did some homework and read up the speech. When I met the Emperor, I told him that I had read his speech 33 years ago at the League of Nations. He smiled and appeared to be pleased with the remark. I also expressed the hope that he would visit Singapore again. He replied that he would do so when he could find the time.

The Emperor was not in the mood to talk for an earthquake had occurred in Ethiopia resulting in tremendous damages including deaths and there were student riots and the Parliament had just passed Emergency Regulations initiated by him authorising the Government to detain anyone for three months without trial.

During our conversation, Lulu, the little pet of the Emperor came and urinated on my shoes. The Emperor pretended that nothing had happened. Then when the time came for me to say goodbye, I shook the hands of the Emperor and had to retreat by walking backwards. I made the first bow, then retreated to the centre of the room, bowed the second time, turned around and walked towards the entrance, turned around again and made the third bow. Just as I was walking towards the entrance, Lulu came running and barking at me and then as I bowed the third time, ran back to the Emperor.

Lulu did this stunt from time to time. Once Lulu urinated on an Indian Ambassador's leg when he presented credentials to the Emperor. He was a Brahmin and got rather angry. But what could he do in such circumstances?

On another occasion, I was told that an Ambassador presented credentials to Haile Selassie. The personal assistant made a mistake and took a wrong envelope which contained the certificate of a pedigree and presented it to the Foreign Minister. When receiving the credentials of the Ambassador, the Emperor said: "This is the first time in my life that I have received credentials from a dog." The Ambassador was embarrassed but laughed it off as the Emperor's great sense of humour.

All ambassadors including those from the Super Powers had to make the three bows going to and returning from the Emperor. To all the six bows, I noticed, the Emperor reciprocated.

The Emperor was so fond of Lulu that he brought him along wherever he went. Once he brought him to Canada on an official visit. When the plane arrived the ground officer refused to allow Lulu into the airport because they were very strict with animals. The Emperor just kept quiet and refused to land when the first 21 gun salute was fired. Lulu instead ran down the red carpet till the bottom of the steps, urinated and ran back to his master. That was meant to be a sign of protest. The Emperor refused to budge and finally the authorities had to allow Lulu to accompany his master.

When Lulu died after a long and comfortable life on the royal lap, the Emperor built him a marble mausoleum and buried him in the Palace ground. The fine headstone inscription reads:

'To Lulu — Our Beloved Dog. He has been with us in Europe, Latin America and Asia.'

The Emperor also liked animals. He had at least a dozen lions and leopards in the Palace ground and employed many trainers to train them. Every day at least one bull was slaughtered to feed them.

After signing the Register at the Imperial Palace, the Brig-General escorted me back to the hotel. I immediately took off my clumsy tail coat and put on an ordinary suit and went to the Crown Prince's Palace to sign the register and then proceeded to the patriarch's (head of the Coptic Church) house to give a card as required by protocol.

During my stay in Ethiopia, I paid courtesy calls on a dozen ambassadors — the Liberian (the Doyen of the Diplomatic Corps), Canadian, Nigerian, Indian, British, Japanese, American, Soviet, Indonesian and Thai. The Malaysian Charge d'affairs, Ajit Singh, who had a Chinese wife, was particularly friendly and helpful. Ajit told me that the Malaysian Government had nominated Hamid Jumat (deceased) as the Ambassador to Ethiopia. After three months of waiting, the Emperor turned down Hamid Jumat's appointment. Diplomatic circles in Ethiopia also knew about the unpleasant incident when the South Vietnamese Ambassador-designate stayed three months in Addis Ababa waiting to present his credentials and finally had to return home without presenting them because the Emperor had refused to accept his appointment. The South Vietnamese were utterly embarrassed particularly as publicity had already been given about his arrival to present credentials. Considering these facts, diplomatic circles were particularly surprised that I could present credentials within a week, for even the British Ambassador had to wait for ten days. All these could be a clear indication of the friendship and regard the Emperor had towards the Republic of Singapore.

I arrived at Addis Ababa at a time when the Ethiopian Emperor was beset with disturbing internal and external problems. Student demonstrations against Selassie's 'fascist' rule, competed with the mounting countrywide demonstrations staged by Ethiopian citizens against Syria's interference in Ethiopia's internal affairs — inciting the Eritreans to secede from Ethiopia. The day I arrived, an Ethiopian airline Boeing 707 jetliner was bombed at Frankfurt Airport by a Syrian-based fanatic group.

For nearly 40 years, except for a short period of Italian occupation, the 77-year-old Emperor had this rich empire of poor people under his grip. The 'King of Kings' was the only monarch in the world who actually reigned and survived several attempted coups including the one in 1960 when his own son, the Crown Prince, was involved and which nearly succeeded.

Not since the Middle Ages has one ruler so stamped his personality for so long on a nation. The great-grandson of King Sahle Selassie and son of Ras Makonnen-Menelik's cousin and one of his ablest generals and governors — the young Tafari was a provincial governor by the age of sixteen. In October 1928, he assumed the title of 'King', stepped up his reform programme, and provoked the northern Rases into open rebellion in 1930. He defeated them in battle at Debre Tabor, but the event precipitated the death of Empress Zauditu, and on 2 November 1930, Tafari Makonnen was crowned Emperor, taking the name of Haile Selassie, which meant 'Might of the Princes.' He wanted to modernise the country, and sent many young men abroad to gain the educated skill to help him achieve his aim.

After his coronation, he developed a kind of schizophrenia. His centralising administration was aimed less at greater efficiency than at giving him tighter control of his fragmented empire and limiting the opportunities for provincial rulers to rise against him. He established a Parliament but only allowed it to function according to his wishes. Throughout the 40s and 50s he presented Ethiopia as an example of a progressive, stable and prosperous African nation — a rarity in the emerging continent. Few visitors could see beyond the charisma of this diminutive monarch to the realities of the country where the gap between the rich and the poor was unbelievable and there was blatant corruption.

The Emperor trusted no one and no one trusted him. Several attempts were made to overthrow his kingdom, the most notable one being in 1960 when he was visiting Brazil. Within a few hours the rebels had control of Addis Ababa, and had arrested several leading members of his regime. They also detained the Crown Prince, Asfa Wossen, and persuaded him to broadcast anti-establishment statements and to declare that he would become a salaried monarch. The 'Red' Ras Imru, a well-known socialist, was pressed into allowing himself to be declared Prime Minister. Within two days however, a successful counter-coup had been organised and the Emperor returned to find the country back in loyal hands.

The 1960 coup had little to do with the population. It was a struggle between rival factions in the establishment and the military aimed at ousting Haile Selassie than ending the feudal regime.

Several factors conspired to make the Emperor ever so powerful: the myth which has been written in the constitution that by virtue of his Imperial blood (descendant of King Solomon and Queen Sheba), the Emperor was 'sacred', his dignity inviolable and his power 'indisputable', the immense power of his Coptic Church (the population being 90 percent Coptic) which could make or break a leader or could even play king-maker; and the illiteracy of the people — 97 percent of whom still could not read or write even the Amharic, the only written language in Africa.

However, I wrote on 15th April 1969 that the myth would not last long unless and until some urgent measures were taken to narrow the gap between the rich and the poor. Whilst beggars and young uneducated idlers roamed the streets of Addis Ababa, thousands and thousands of acres of rich volcanic virgin land awaited cultivation and rich minerals remained unexplored. We did not know how sincere the Emperor was in his land reform, but the royal families, the nobles and the corrupt political leaders owned four-fifths of the land. The other one-fifth belonged to the Church. So far there was still no registration of land title, and as a result whenever a piece of land was allocated, litigation followed in the courts.

In the streets of Addis Ababa were innumerable beggars lying in the gutter or ditch at the side of roads. Occasionally, a few para-military police would come along, jump out and kick a bundle of filthy smelly beggars and round them up. The street urchins and their cargo of human flotsam would be taken to special compounds well out of sight of the casual traveller where they were kept for perhaps several days. This routine would be performed prior to any visit to Addis Ababa by important visitors. After all, such blatant poverty could not be allowed to tarnish the good image of Haile Selassie.

When visitors arrived at the International Airport, they passed the south-eastern outskirts of Addis Ababa along wide, tree-lined dual carriageways towards the city centre where there were luxurious and often impressively designed modern homes of ambassadors, and where the Ethiopian aristocracy and senior military and government servants lived. But behind the main streets were floorless, mud and dung, tin or turf-roofed huts, the homes of the average Ethiopian citizens.

Along the streets, one was invariably confronted with the street boys and the hawkers who crowded around trying to sell brass crosses, monkey skins in white and black (which is illegal), nylons, cassette tapes and chewing gum. Men relieved themselves openly wherever the need arose, for there were no public toilets. The women squatted in the ditches, their modesty protected more by accident than design by their long, full skirts.

There were many modern shops and departmental stores for the rich Ethiopians. The majority did their shopping in the Mercato — an enormous bazaar which was reputedly the biggest market place in Africa.

The jobs the ordinary people could get consisted of service in the homes of diplomatic staff, foreign businessmen and other expatriate residents as maids, cooks, gardeners and 'sebanyas' — the guards that were needed day and night at every Western-style home because of the prevalence of theft. It was a country where 97 percent of the people were illiterate, where 70 percent had no recognizable form of employment; where most people lived in the most primitive conditions, scraping their existence from soil that was tired and eroded, and their drinking water was contaminated with every intestinal parasite known to medical science. The first thing when I arrived was a warning from Ajit Singh that we should never drink the water without boiling. He brought a bottle of boiled water to me every day. And when you purchase the fruits, you should soak them in prepared chemical solutions for otherwise you might contact hepatitis. In Addis Ababa, hepatitis, typhoid, smallpox and tuberculosis were endemic and frequently epidemic.

At night, there were red light districts everywhere. The number of people who suffered from venereal diseases was the highest in Africa. There were 350,000 prostitutes operating in 10,000 brothels. Lepers loitered in the streets in thousands.

Despite appalling poverty, the Ethiopians remained a proud people and considered themselves superior to the blacks from further South. I was told by the Canadian Ambassador that the former Zambian Ambassador's wife often went home crying because when she went to the grocery shop she was made to wait as her skin was darker. Ethiopians never liked to be referred to as black. They regarded themselves as the whites in black Africa.

By nature, the Ethiopians were courteous (they kowtow like the Japanese), proud and arrogant. In most feudalistic countries, the people learn to bow. The Ethiopians have reason to be arrogant and proud for the Amharas, the minority ruling class, has a written language, apparently the only written language in the whole of Africa. The Amharic language has become the official language apart from English, although it was the language of the minority tribe. No census has yet been taken in Ethiopia, but it was estimated that there were 4 million Amharas, 6 million Tigrenyas and 12 million Galas. The Amharas were in all key government and military positions.

There was a particular tribe of people who called themselves the *Rayas and Azebo* who had a weird custom of taking pride in emasculating visiting male humans. It was reported that as a trophy for the hand of the daughter of any family of the Rayas and Azebo, the suitor must, as testimony of his prowess and daring exploits, have in his possession at least one pair of human male testicles cut out from another male human. These human testicles must be preserved and exhibited as trophies around the neck. The satisfaction of the family, and the daughter's social prestige were increased in proportion to the number of such trophies the sweetheart was presented. One would hang around one's neck the gallants of human scrota as ceremoniously and as proudly as one would hang the Grand Cordon of the Order of Solomon.

I met the author of a book called *The Musical Bride,* Dave Talbot, a West Indian, one-time editor of the *Ethiopian Herald* and press consultant to the Imperial Ministry of Information. The book described the custom of this tribe of people and the adventure which he had experienced with them. According to Dave years ago, during the tribal wars, the enemies of the Rayas and Azebo tribes took away their girls, married some of them and enslaved the others. The Azebos were very jealous of their women. As part of their punishment for their enemies, every prisoner that was caught alive would be emasculated and transformed into eunuchs for their service. This act became a mark of prowess, for each warrior's gallantry and daring was measured in terms of how many such trophies he had gathered on the field of battle.

The Rayas and Azebo did not pillage the land of their enemies nor steal their livestock, but they devised this method of tribal protection. Their enemies abducted their women in order to subdue them; they in turn met that assault by castrating them and killing their soldiers in battle.

After the wars with their enemies in those far off days, their heroes were in great demand. They were sought after and admired by women. By some corruption, it became the vogue that any Rayas and Azebo man to be worthy of the hand of a deserving virgin must be a hero who could gather enough testicles. The custom still persists, and could not easily be wiped out. It has become a social ritual. In the month of Tirr (January to February), the beginning of the season of engagements, the young men of this area go out to collect such trophies.

One victim of such a custom was the famous painter who did the glass murals on the wall of the Organisation of African Unity hall. The painter was in fact a eunuch because one day as he was travelling along Kobo, someone came from behind with a knife, pushed him down and cut off his testicles. He was alive but had lost his manhood.

I happened to pass through Kobo, the village where such incidents took place. Knowing the story I was secretly afraid that someone might pop up from behind the bush and do the same thing to me.

Haile Selassie had decreed that it would be a crime to do that miserable act, but the ancient custom still persisted.

At the hotel dining room, a musical orchestra was playing Ethiopian music when I dined there one night. The music sounded oriental, somewhat Japanese and somewhat Korean. I asked the hotel manager, who was an Ethiopian, why they were playing Japanese songs in this far-off place. He replied, 'They are playing Ethiopian songs.' Strange, how could it be? It seems that during the Korean war, Ethiopian soldiers were sent to Korea to fight. They picked up some Korean songs and brought them to Addis Ababa. They became popular. Since then, Ethiopian composers have composed songs with a Korean flavour.

In Ethiopia, there is a special instrument which is played with one string. It looks like an ancient guitar.

Addis Ababa is eight thousand feet above sea level and the oxygen content of the air is very thin. One got tired easily. Climbing the steep steps up to the hotel would make one pant. Diplomats who were not used to such heights had to go to Sodore which was 150 kilometres south of Addis Ababa for a short spell of oxygen. Once the Thai Ambassador returned from Bangkok to Addis Ababa, and at the airport he collapsed and died of heart failure.

Sodore is a paradise for the rich and wealthy. I hired a car and went to Sodore for a short visit. To reach Sodore we had to pass a number of small villages. One of the villages we had to pass was Debre Zait, which was previously called Shiofu. Debre Zait was a Jewish name. It housed many Jewish Air Force instructors and there was a military air base. To name a village after the Jewish showed the closeness of relationship between Ethiopia and Israel.

On the way, we found at frequent stops a number of children, women and old folks holding chicken and little lambs in their hands trying to sell to passersby. At one stop I found someone selling an owl. I was told that Ethiopians ate owls.

In another village called Gala, the people wore Mexican hats and dressed like Mexicans. They held a stick in their hands and put on a white towel over their necks. Some were cycling and others rode on donkeys. The women walked with a water jar over their back. These people were so much like Mexicans. In Addis Ababa there is a Mexican Square where everything appeared as in Mexico.

Sodore's famous spot is the hot spring. There is a hot spring complex where there is a pool of hot spring about 50 yards long and 20 yards wide. There is also a small pool for children. Beside the pools are shady trees. The entrance fee is one Ethiopian dollar.

I saw many whites and blacks. Some whites brought black ladies along and the blacks were in the company of white ladies. The only yellow skins were the Japanese. I saw no sign of racial discrimination. They were all either swimming or resting under the shade of the trees, drinking Ethiopian beer and having fun. I took a dip into the hot spring. It was my third experience in a hot pool. The first time was in New Zealand in 1961, and the second in Japan in 1968. It was very refreshing after a hot spring bath.

Sodore is a small town with only a few streets. I drove back to Addis Ababa the same evening.

When I arrived at Addis Ababa, students of Haile Selassie University had been on strike for nearly a month. Being idealistic and impatient with the country's slow progress, they wanted a quick change. The students realised that although Ethiopia claimed to have 3,000 years of history unhampered by foreign domination, except for the short period of Italian invasion, economically the country was the most backward in the whole of Africa. The Canadian Ambassador seemed to think that it was precisely because Ethiopia had not been colonised by a European power that it was still backward.

Hitherto, the students had confined their demands to academic matters such as freedom of forming a students' union, academic freedom or reducing examination fees. This time, the students had gone further. They had put forward fifteen demands, the major ones of which included the dismissal of the Minister of Education (who happened to be the Prime Minister's brother) for changing the education system, the end of the 'fascist police methods' and the closing down of a number of Ethiopian embassies abroad because they were a waste of public funds. The Emperor gave way to demands of an academic nature but would not tolerate students meddling in political matters. He granted audience to the students described by the *Ethiopian Herald* as 'students begging the Emperor for forgiveness.' The students begged the Emperor to release the seven students detained and were about to be tried. But this request was rejected.

Then the day after I presented credentials, the students staged another demonstration and clashed with the police. At least 1,200 students were arrested though most of them were released. One student died. Some said he fell down from the lorry whilst others said he was shot by the police.

Till the time I left Addis Ababa, the students were still on strike.

Two weeks before my arrival at Addis Ababa, the Imperial Government deported six diplomats — three from the Russian Embassy and three from the Czechoslovakian Embassy. Of the three Russians, one was the Tass correspondent. They were deported because of their alleged involvement in the student trouble. The United States Ambassador Mr William O Hall told me that the Russians and Czechoslovakians were caught red-handed transporting, in their vans, students who were on strike. The Russian Ambassador Mr Alexei Shiborim, who presented his credentials after the trouble, denied that his Embassy staff were involved in the student trouble. He told me that the Ethiopian Government needed a scapegoat for the students' frustration at the slow pace of economic progress in the country. The deportation, he said, was a big embarrassment to his country for it was publicised.

I learnt from the Canadian Ambassador that the Communist embassies led by the Soviet Union had recently boycotted several official functions as a mark of protest at the 'unjustifiable deportation' of Communist diplomats.

Addis Ababa was a city of rumours. This time the rumour went to say that the Crown Prince who was away since the previous month was conspiring with certain military officers and one section of the Imperial Guards to overthrow the Emperor. This rumour, it seemed, was spread by Eastern European Embassies. In order to kill the rumour, the Emperor summoned back the Crown Prince who returned to Addis Ababa sometime in August 1968. The rumour then subsided.

At the time when I arrived at Addis Ababa, the *Ethiopian Herald* almost daily carried headline stories of demonstrations in Addis Ababa, Condar, Makale, Harrar, Arba Milnch and Dre Kawa and other towns throughout the Empire against Syria's 'interference' in Ethiopian internal affairs. The Imperial Government openly accused Syria of inciting the people of Eritrea to secede from Ethiopia.

Half of Eritrea's population were Muslims and they spoke Tigrenya which was written in Arabic script. Eritrea, which had their own self-governing Parliament before, was brought into the rule of the Emperor almost by force. Those who were dissatisfied with the feudalistic rule had joined the Eritrea Liberation Front which also had an army. It was believed that some of the student leaders who instigated the strikes were from Eritrea. Although Eritrea was not viable as a state economically, it controlled the sea route of the Ethiopian Empire.

The Emperor was trying to maintain a non-aligned policy in foreign relations and in fact aspired to be one of the leaders of the non-aligned movement. In order to remain neutral, he allowed both the Hsin Hua News Agency of Beijing and the Central News Agency of Taipeh to open branches in Addis. However, events proved that the so-called correspondent of Hsin Hua Agency, Li Yi Chen, was indulging in activities other than journalism. Li was in fact behaving like an Ambassador arranging trips to Beijing for Ministers and students. His wife Chen Chong Yin became a close confidante and interpreter for Chou En-lai when the latter visited Addis. Li's visa was finally 'not extended' when he applied to return to Addis from Beijing.

The Emperor tried to remain neutral in the Arab-Israeli conflict and appeared to be friendly with Nasser. But there was no doubt in anybody's mind that Ethiopia was pro-Israel. Apart from the blood ties with the Jews and the historically bitter struggle Ethiopians had with the invading Muslims, the Emperor feared that one of these days the Arabs in Yemen and Syria might conspire with the Russians and the Eritrean rebels to deprive his empire of any port in the Red Sea. The Israelis who were training the Ethiopian intelligence officers as well as the airforce could have poisoned the minds of the Ethiopians against the Arabs.

On 15 April 1969, I wrote back to Singapore to say that "There is always the possibility of the emergence of a 'Nasser' in the armed forces leading the young 'free officers' to stage a revolution backed by the students, in which case it will be a clash between the younger generation which want a republic and the older generation."

On September 12, 1974, a Major in the army by the name of Mengistu, a tough little soldier, half-caste Gala of negroid appearance, led other majors in the armed forces backed by the students to overthrow Emperor Haile Selassie, and ended his 50 years of iron rule. The Emperor was at prayer when the army moved on his capital of Addis Ababa. The troops surrounded the airport, the telecommunications centre, and the Commercial Bank. Soon they were patrolling the streets in jeeps and swaggering down the tree-lined avenues in battle dress. Overhead US-supplied F.5s of the Ethiopian Imperial Air Force roared menacingly, and an occasional burst of small arms fire was heard coming from the blue hills that ring the city. It was a stunning turn of events. The 81-year-old Emperor, the Conquering Lion of Judah, the King of Kings and the Elect of God was no longer in control. The Ethiopian Army had taken over.

For years, the Haile Selassie regime had become ineffectual and corrupt. The Government's ineptitude was demonstrated by their failure to deal with the drought that swept across the country in 1973. Millions of cattle died, crops were decimated, and perhaps 100,000 people starved to death before Haile Selassie's cabinet moved to meet the crisis. As a result of the drought, food prices rose abruptly. Then because of Arab oil politics, the cost of gasoline skyrocketed. In early March 1974, the high cost of living touched off riots in Addis Ababa — the outbreak ending only after the Government clamped on a semblance of martial law.

Then on 7th March 1974, the spirit of discontent spread to the armed forces. Noncommissioned officers and their men, who claimed they could not make both ends meet on their meagre salaries, seized control of Asmara, the capital of Eritrea province. Next, units of the Ethiopian Navy, garrisoned at the sultry Red Sea port of Mesewa, joined the mutiny and so did the air force units at Debre Zait.

At first, Selassie tried to brazen it out. He argued that the Government could not afford to pay increases for the military and ordered the mutineers to obey his commands. 'Our enemies will rejoice at our disunity,' he told the troops — an apparent reference to the Muslim separatists in the province of Eritrea and to the government of neighbouring Somalia, which had had designs on Ethiopian territory for some time. When the rebels remained adamant, Selassie agreed to pay the hike, but it soon became clear that the mutineers wanted more than money. They proclaimed their loyalty to the Emperor but they insisted that he dismiss his 19-man cabinet. Next day the rebels seized three of the four senior generals whom Haile Selassie had sent to Asmara to negotiate a compromise and threatened to keep them hostage until the Government agreed to all their demands. Meanwhile, the mutiny spread until it included nearly all of the country's 47,000 soldiers, sailors and airmen.

Panicked by the revolt, Aklilu Hapte Wold, who had been Prime Minister since 1951, quit as did his entire Cabinet. When the Emperor did not immediately accept Aklilu's resignation, dissident soldiers in full battle gear moved into the capital's streets. In a show of strength, they took control of Addis Ababa's banks, its airport and key buildings. At that point, Selassie capitulated. Appearing once more on radio and TV, Selassie granted the armed forces virtually the entire pay raise they demanded, pledged no reprisals and designated the popular career diplomat Endalkachew Makonnen, 46, the new Prime Minister. Perhaps more important, he elevated one popular general to army commander and named another to the key post of Interior Minister.

Venerated by his people and respected by other African leaders, Haile Selassie was still head of state and a symbol of authority. But, for the moment, at least, power in Ethiopia rested with the military. After Endalkachew took office, some army officers called for trials of many of the ousted Cabinet Ministers on the ground that they had enriched themselves at the people's expense, maintained fat foreign bank accounts and taken land illegally from the peasants. Thousands of students paraded noisily proclaiming support for the army and demanding freedom of the press and formation of political parties. As for the Prime Minister, he promised thorough economic and social changes — an indication that he intended to heed the army's yearning for Ethiopia to progress faster.

But Endalkachew's government did not last long. Later on General Aman Andom emerged as the new Head of State. In August 1974, the weekly magazine *Ethiopia* carried the public attack straight to the Emperor — accusing him of 'Squandering the nation's money on lavish journeys abroad'. An Orthodox priest publicly questioned the Emperor's claim to descent from Solomon and Sheba, while other articles and letters accused him of being 'an expensive and unnecessary luxury.' Then on August 25 came the dramatic announcement that the Emperor's personal residence, the Jubilee Palace (where I had presented credentials), had been nationalised.

Haile Selassie was now utterly powerless, but he continued to function in the only way he knew, officiating on August 27, at the swearing-in of the new members of Michel Imru's reshuffled cabinet. He was still allowed to travel between his Palace and to a nearby church, but that was all.

On 28th August, the military regime announced the nationalisation of the country's biggest bus company — Anbassa — the Addis-based firm in which the Emperor and his family were the biggest shareholders. People who a few months ago were prostrating themselves in the mud every time the Emperor's car passed by, were now calmly accepting his public denigration. Students marched through Addis demonstrating against the Emperor. Radio Ethiopia in Amharic had quoted the slogans of the students who chanted 'Kill the Emperor', 'Hang the Emperor' and 'Down with the Emperor'. The TV began to show victims of the Wollo drought and alongside pictures of the Emperor in his fine clothes, feeding large chunks of meat to his beloved Lulu. One of the features of the campaign showed Lulu's marble mausoleum with the inscription on it.

Then came 12 September 1974, when a small group of military officers went to the National Palace just after 6 a.m., summoned the Emperor, Haile Selassie, frail, but retaining his dignity, to their presence and read out to him the proclamation that he had been deposed. He stood proud and erect despite his eighty-two years and allowed the officers to read the proclamation. He was accused of corruption and neglect and told that he had abused his powers for gain and profit to his family. His eyes glistened as it was said that he was too weak, mentally and physically, to shoulder the responsibility of office any longer. The Emperor broke the awkward silence and said: 'We have served our people in war and peace. If we have to step down for the good of our people, we will not oppose this.'

With obvious embarrassment, one of the young officers, addressing Haile Selassie as 'Your Majesty', asked the Emperor to come with them.

'Where?' he asked sharply.

'To a place of safety, you'll see,' was the reply.

The Emperor was brought into a small Volkswagen. There was no ceremonial of outriders, only a jeep in front and behind.

They were brought to a humble three-roomed mud hut in an army barracks.

Then followed a campaign of public denigration of the Emperor. They accused the Emperor of hoarding fortunes in Swiss banks and other more serious crimes.

World opinion had been almost entirely concerned with the fate of the deposed Emperor, and offers of asylum had come from Cameroon, Gabon and unofficially from friends in Britain.

General Aman, hero of Korea and the Somali front — where he earned the affectionate nickname 'The Desert Lion' — was in control at the earlier stage. He began to see himself playing the role of the first President of the Republic of Ethiopia. The General, being an Eritrean, genuinely wanted a peaceful solution and was prepared to negotiate with the Eritreans. He was a more tolerant man who wished to work things out more systematically and constitutionally. Meanwhile, there was another group who called themselves the 'Dergue', the nearest translation was simply a committee of equals. The Dergue consisted of 120 men none above the rank of major and led by Major Mengistu.

This group on 17 November 1974 presented General Aman with two demands. One was for authorisation to send additional troops to Eritrea for a major offensive against the Eritrean Liberation Front. The other was for his signature to a list of detainees to be executed by the firing squad. The list consisted of ministers, generals and officials of the old regime. General Aman refused on both counts, and threatened to resign. Then on Saturday, 23 November, Radio Ethiopia announced that sixty persons had been executed 'for crimes against the Ethiopian people'. The execution had taken place in the courtyard of the main civil prison, Akaki Jail. Among the list of dead were two former Premiers, Aklilu Habte Wold and Endalkachew Makonnen, Haile Selassie's grandson, Rear Admiral Eskinder Desta, two of the country's top noblemen, a number of former ministers and General Aman. It was three days before Dergue admitted that General Aman had died in a gun battle and had not been executed along with the others. This day was now known as the 'Bloody Saturday'.

The Ethiopian revolution had touched barely a fraction of the population. The active ones were the traditional dissenters —

the students, intellectuals, teachers, the tiny labour movement — and in no way to be called a 'revolution of the people.'

When the hard-liners under Mengistu took control of the movement, killed Aman, massacred the ministers and tried to drag their country into some instant socialist Utopia, they had replaced Haile Selassie's despotic feudalism with an equally rigid doctrinaire militarist tyranny.

Today, the Ethiopian press regularly refers to Mengistu Haile Mariam as chairman of the Provisional Military Government of Socialist Ethiopia (PMGSE) and the Ministers call each other 'comrades'. At the entrance of Addis Ababa Bole International Airport huge signs bear the legend 'Proletarians of the World, Unite.' and 'The Victory of Socialism is Inevitable'. Large canvases showing determined soldiers, workers and peasants spell out similar messages at every square and intersection in the sprawling capital. Giant portraits of Marx, Engels and Lenin dominate the Revolution Square and in many public buildings hang the stylized profile device featuring these three Communist saints. The halls of ministries are festooned with posters in Amharic, and occasionally English, proclaiming revolutionary slogans. Soviet flags flutter beside the red-yellow-green national banner in the city and in the countryside. From all this, a visitor arriving in Ethiopia for the first time is likely to conclude that this country has been rapidly and willingly transformed into a bastion of Communism.

Col. Mengistu has emerged as the most dynamic member of the Dergue and is increasingly visible as head of state and government. He rules as Haile Selassie did, from the Grand Palace built by Emperor Menelik II shortly after the founding of Addis Ababa in 1886. He has adopted many features of the old, highly personalised imperial style, travelling periodically to outlying regions, visiting developing projects and factories, and receiving delegations of local citizens. When Mengistu is not travelling, newspapers almost daily carry photographs of him — as they once did of Haile Selassie. Ethiopians expect their leader to be diligent and energetically engaged in the daily tasks of governing, meeting with ministers, approving plans and budgets, and personally managing the governmental machinery.

Has Ethiopia become part of the Soviet Empire? It is too early to say this is so. There is outward evidence of loyalty to communism in Ethiopia, but Mengistu's Government is still very much an improvised system which has been slow to evolve into permanent new forms. It is still very much dependent on Western educated civil servants who as young men had moved into higher positions in the 1960s and early 1970s. These people have assured continuity of government throughout the revolutionary period, providing basic services, maintaining highways and communications and skilfully managing the country's finances. The Dergue which seized control of revolution in the latter part of 1974 had no alternative but to depend on them.

Another obstacle to Communism is religion. Since the Middle Ages, Ethiopian nationalism had been closely linked to Christianity. Ethiopians saw their country as a Christian island in a sea of Muslims. In 1974, the military revolutionaries reduced Christianity to a less privileged status and made a number of conciliatory gestures to Ethiopia's Muslims who constitute 30 percent of the population. The churches are filled to bursting on Sunday mornings with believers of all ages including young men in business suits and young women in the embroidered white national costumes. The Revolutionary regime recognised from the very beginning the strength of religious feeling in the country and the manner in which religious tradition formed part of the very fabric of Ethiopian life.

Deposed Emperor Haile Selassie who died during the night at the age of 83, was the last representative of the world's oldest surviving monarchy. During his rule no one was allowed to approach the monarch without bowing three times. People in the countryside used to prostrate themselves at the sight of the 'Conquering Lion of Judah, King of Kings and Elect of God.' Had he stepped down earlier before his dethronement, the bearded autocrat would no doubt have gone down in history as one of Africa's great statesmen.

True enough, he was God to a group of people in the West Indies, particularly Jamaica. They were the adherents of a sect known as the Ras Tafarians (so called after Haile Selassie's pre-coronation name Ras Tafari) who were the descendants of Ethiopian slaves. They believed that Haile Selassie was a god and had built up a religious cult around him. Ironically in the land of their god there had never been more than 40 Ras Tafarians, and by 1974, their numbers had dwindled to about

25 adults, with some children, living an uneasy and harsh life in the south-west of the country. They had made a pilgrimage from Jamaica in 1969 expecting to be allowed to live and worship at the feet — or at least not far from the Palace — of their god. Instead, extremely embarrassed, Haile Selassie had grudgingly given them some unfarmable land near Shashamane some 250 miles south of Addis and left them to their fate.

Now their god had been deposed. But they still clung to their faith. The spirit of their god still lived and would live eternally no matter what was done to the people of the Emperor.

When I was in Jamaica in 1979, I saw many Ras Tafarians in town and the countryside. They left their long and curly hair uncombed (for it was against the cult to comb the hair) and all had a long beard. They dressed shabbily and roamed about the streets smoking ganja for it was part of the cult to smoke ganja. The shaggy head common to all Ras Tafarians symbolises the lion's mane. Though social noncomformists, the Ras Tafarians are industrious, artistic and friendly. They live in the countryside in communes and they abhor dishonesty, adultery, liquor and voting. They regard themselves not as Jamaican citizens but hope to be repatriated somehow and at some future time to their 'African homeland' — Ethiopia.

When Haile Selassie visited Jamaica in 1966 these Ras Tafarians came to the airport and bowed to the Emperor and kissed his feet. It was quite an embarrassment to their God.

Why did so many Ras Tafarians worship Haile Selassie? What has Ethiopia got to do with these Ras Tafarians? Long before Ethiopianism came to America, the term had been adopted in Jamaica by George Liele, the American Baptist slave preacher who founded the first Baptist Church in the island in 1784 — which he named the Ethiopian Baptist Church. This church grafted itself onto the African religion of Jamaican slaves and developed outside the Christian missions, exhibiting a pure native flavour. But, the movement that was to embody the Ethiopian ideology was the Back-to-Africa movement of Marcus Garvey, who was the prophet of African redemption. Through Garvey's writings and speeches, the glory of Ethiopia-Africa became the glory of things to come. Marcus Garvey returned to the theme of the superiority of the ancient Black race time and again.

The movement which Garvey organised was known as the Universal Negro Improvement Association. In a speech delivered at Madison Square Garden in New York on 16 March 1924, he described the movement in these words:

'The Universal Negro Improvement Association represents the hopes and aspirations of the awakened Negro. Our desire is for a place in the world, not to disturb the tranquillity of other men, but to lay down our burden and rest our weary backs and feet by the banks of the Niger and sing our songs and chant our hymns to the God of Ethiopia.'

In Marcus Garvey, Ethiopianism reached its highest development. From ideology, it became a movement. The god worshipped was the God of Ethiopia and all structures and orientation were aimed towards African redemption.

When Marcus Garvey left Jamaica for the United States in 1916, followers in Jamaica fell into disarray. Although the movement continued to exist with local leadership, no one could fill the void. This situation existed until 1930 when Ras Tafari, great-grandson of King Saheka Selassie of Shoa, was crowned Negus of Ethiopia. He took the name Haile Selassie (Might of the Trinity) to which was added 'King of Kings', and the 'Lion of the Tribe of Judah', placing himself in the legendary line of King Solomon. His coronation in St George's Cathedral, Addis Ababa, in November of that year brought representatives of all the great powers as well as journalists and correspondents from every part of the world. The crowning of a young Ethiopian king, with this Biblical title, together with the pomp and grandeur of the fabled empire, was more than a secular occasion. For the people of Marcus Garvey's leaning, this came as a revelation from God. In Jamaica, an almost forgotten statement of Garvey who, on the eve of his departure to the United States was supposed to have said: 'Look to Africa for the crowning of a Black King, he shall be the Redeemer,' came echoing like the voice of God. Possessed by the spirit of this new development, many Jamaicans now saw the coronation as a fulfilment of Biblical prophecy and Haile Selassie as the Messiah of African redemption.

Among those who took this crowning seriously were Leonard Howell, Joseph Hibbert, Archibal Dunkley and Robert Hinds. All four may have been original Garveyites.

Leonard Howell later became the leading figure in the movement. It was in Kingston that the movement had its period of incubation and from this point of inception, the movement gradually spread throughout the island.

No one knows how the name 'Ras Tafari' was adopted over the title 'Haile Selassie'. The name 'Ras' in Amharic is the title given to Ethiopian royalty, comparable to the English title 'Duke'. 'Tafari' is the family name of the King. Whatever the reason, this name has become not only a holy appellation and a ritual invocation, but also the name of the movement itself. The 'Rastafarians' is a Jamaican rendering of 'Ras Tafari' and is the name given to the members of the movement.

It is necessary to understand that movements of this type are not interested in empirical truths, but rather in the certitude of the doctrine. That is, if it fulfills an emotional need, it is enough. In this case, the inception of Rastafarians came in 1930 when Jamaica was at low tide economically and socially. Socially, people experienced the brunt of the depression as well as a disaster due to a devastating hurricane. Politically, Jamaica was gripped by colonialism and the future of the masses looked hopeless. Any doctrine that promised a better hope and a better day was ripe for hearing. Armed with this situation and possessed by a new messianic message, Leonard Howell and his men set out to make the crooked path straight and the rough places plain. Haile Selassie was now given divine status. The God of Ethiopia, of whom Marcus Garvey spoke, had appeared in the flesh, and all who needed redemption could now receive it from the most powerful ruler on earth before whom all kings had bowed. Black people throughout the world needed only to call on his name and the Lion of Judah would break all chains. Armed with this unique power, early Rastafarian leaders set out to preach the glad tidings.

The incubation period of the movement occurred in the slums of Kingston between 1930 and 1933. Satisfied with the success of the new movement and having set up a nucleus in the capital, Howell decided to evangelize its members throughout the island. To finance his project, he was reported to have made photographs of the newly crowned King Haile Selassie, and sold them at a shilling each as passports to Ethiopia.

Then in December 1933, Howell held an open-air meeting in the village of Trinityville, St Thomas and advocated six principles:-

1 hatred for the White race,
2 the complete superiority of the Black race,
3 revenge on Whites for their wickedness,
4 the negation, persecution and humiliation of the government and legal bodies of Jamaica,
5 preparation to go back to Africa, and
6 acknowledging Emperor Haile Selassie as the Supreme Being and only ruler of Black people.

Howell was arrested for sedition and was sentenced to two years' imprisonment. Following his release from prison, he organised the Ethiopian Salvation Society and recruited a large following and was the leader of a cult commune deep in the hills of St Catherine overlooking the city of Kingston. To avoid harrassment by the police, Howell headed for the privacy of the hills.

He purchased a piece of land in the hill country near Sligovikle (about twenty miles from Kingston) and named it Pinnacle. Howell served as the Chief and was reported to have taken thirteen wives for himself. For a living, they planted native cash crops, among them the famous ganja (marijuana) herb that has remained in the centre of the movement's ritual practice. Police raided the place and arrested twenty-eight Rastas and sent them to prison. Howell evaded the police but was finally apprehended and sent to prison for another two-year term.

By 1953, the male members of the Pinnacle began to grow their hair in locks — a custom that distinguishes the Rastaman to the present. They were called 'lockmen' now known as 'dreadlocks' or 'nattydread' but in their early period they were known as Ethiopian warriors. Ferocious dogs were used for security. To enter the commune one made one's presence known by sounding a gong at the gate. Early 1954, the police again raided the place and 163 members were arrested. Howell and his men were tried but this time the government had become tired of sending them to prison. The judge acquitted them as nuisances.

The great impetus came in 1955 when a leading official of the Ethiopian World Federation Inc visited Jamaica with an important message which was to energize the flagging Rastafarian movement. The message said that 'The Emperor Haile Selassie is now engaged in building up a Merchant Navy and the time was not far when ships from Addis Ababa would sail to American ports. There was the possibility too that ships would one day call at Jamaica.'

The Ethiopian World Federation of New York had informed the various branches in Jamaica that the Emperor had granted 500 acres of land to the black people of the West who through the EWF aided Ethiopia in its time of distress. The rich and fertile land was the personal property of the Emperor and was being given on a trial basis. If used successfully, additional grants would follow. The letter stipulated the types of people who would best profit from the land grant were farmers, carpenters, plumbers, masons, electricians and other skilled persons including nurses and doctors.

The vision of ships and new land in Ethiopia created what might literally be called a religious revival among the Rastafarians. 'Repatriation now' was the cry of the cultists. The news of return to Africa came at a time when thousands of Jamaicans were leaving to seek a living in Great Britain, a land which for them was strange, cold and unknown.

In 1958, the Rastafarians held a 'universal convention' in Kingston and 300 bearded men of the Rastafarian cult along with their women and children 'captured' the city. The police arrested many of them for possession of drugs. Then in 1959, a Rastafarian by the name of Claudius Henry who gave himself the title of 'The Repairer of the Breach' distributed thousands of cards bearing the certificate for shipment back to Africa. They were sold at a shilling each and many thousands of these cards were sold. On 5th October 1959, people from all over Jamaica flocked to Rosalie Avenue ready to depart to Africa. But there was no ship to take them away. The excitement created by this Henry fiasco was given little attention by the government for many days. Several days after the aborted repatriation scheme, Henry was finally arrested but the court freed him and ordered him to keep the peace for one year with a fine of $100.

Henry possibly misjudged the government's leniency towards him and became radically revolutionary and militant. News began to leak to the police that Henry was planning a military take-over of the island. A raid was made at his African Reform Church in Rosalie Avenue and they found arms and ammunition and he was sentenced to six years' imprisonment.

Soon after the Henry incident, his son Ronald Henry was reported to be in the Red Hills overlooking Kingston training a guerrilla band of Rastafarians with high-powered rifles reported brought secretly into the island from New York. The Royal Hampshire Regiment raided the hills and Ronald Henry was arrested after a gun battle. He was tried and sentenced to death.

The news of these tragic happenings related to the Rastafarian cult aroused Jamaican society from its slumber. At the request of the leading Rasta brethren, the head of the University of the West Indies authorised three scholars to study the doctrines and special conditions of the Rastafarians and to make recommendations to the Premier of Jamaica. The Manley Government accepted the recommendations. One of the recommendations was that the government of Jamaica should send a mission to African countries to arrange for immigration of Jamaicans. Though no large-scale immigration to Africa by Jamaicans was achieved, the sending of some Rastafarian leaders to Africa resulted in the movement's enhanced knowledge of African realities and probably diffused the movement's enthusiasm for immediate repatriation. Almost all of the recommendations have been carried out to some extent over the years, the last being the establishment of a branch of the Ethiopian Orthodox Church on the island. The present freedom of the Rastafarian movement on the island may to some extent be attributed to the far-reaching insight of these recommendations.

There are at least 50,000 Rastafarians in Jamaica including the world-famed reggae superstar Bob Marley.

Bob was the single most important figure in the dissemination of Rastafarian concepts. Some likened his role in the movement to that of John the Baptist. The Rastafarians familiarised themselves with new sets of beliefs, transformed self-conceptions with fresh, exhilarating ambitions. During the 1970s, thousands upon thousands of young blacks broke with their parents and surrendered themselves to the Rastafarian group. They believed in a new reality, a reality replete with an explanation of why they had struggled in ignorance for years, why blacks had been downtrodden for centuries and why their parents were still labouring. And indeed, why they had reason to be optimistic about their future. They believed that Haile Selassie was God but white slavemasters and missionaries concealed this from the black man by force-feeding him mistranslated versions of the Bible. Only Rasta had broken from this and were now re-educating themselves.

By early 1970s the Rastafarian movement had spread to Birmingham and later to Manchester because in England the West Indian community was pretty large. When confronted with the news that Haile Selassie had died, the Rastafarians dismissed it as 'Imperial propaganda' or 'The lies of Babylon.'

To the Rastafarians, Haile Selassie is still alive. All over the world, people are looking for their roots. The Rastafarians, I think, are some of those who are trying to trace their roots to derive inspiration from them.

Before the inspection of the Guard of Honour outside Haile Selassie's Jubilee Palace, the author was receiving a salute from the Chief of Palace Guard

Inspection of Guard of Honour before presentation of credentials to Emperor Haile Selassie

Author shaking hands with the former Foreign Minister inside the Jubilee Palace

Author with Emperor Haile Selassie after presenting credentials

10

Tito's Yugoslavia

When I heard that I would be accredited to Yugoslavia, I was a little excited, for it would be my first experience in a communist country. What would a communist country look like? How would it be to live in a communist country? These were some of the questions that crossed my mind when I heard the news.

I arrived at Belgrade with my personal assistant K. K. Menon on 6 May 1969, and was received at the airport by Dr Staniza Cvetkonio, Assistant Chief of Protocol, who took us to Hotel Slavia. The next morning, arrangements were made for me to see the Chief of Protocol, Lazar Lilic, who took me to see the Foreign Secretary (Foreign Minister) Mirko Tepavac and later the Assistant Secretary, Foreign Affairs, Dr Radivaj Unalio and then the Head of Asian Desk and Head of Political Department, Edward Klyun. The same evening I met Shestane, the Chief of Protocol of President Tito, and was briefed on the procedure of presentation of credentials and was told that I would be flown in a special plane to Brioni Island, the summer resort of President Tito, the next day.

The Foreign Secretary Tepavac had become Minister only six days earlier when I presented a copy of my credentials to him. He spoke through an interpreter, Dr Zvonimir Patnicki, who interpreted for our Prime Minister during his last visit to Belgrade. Tepavac was formerly President of the League of Communists of one of the member states of the Republic. He had yet to be sworn in. He was to take his oath together with

President Tito offering a cigar to author after he has presented credentials in Brioni Island

the other 15 Cabinet Ministers on the 16th of May. He was one of the six members of the inner Cabinet. He was 46 years old, quiet by nature and was a man of substance. I was told that his wife was a wellknown film star who was still busy with her theatrical career.

I met Tepavac at the Ministry of Foreign Affairs which was situated in a busy street in the heart of Belgrade. I was the first Ambassador he had met since he became Foreign Secretary. He was new to his job. We discussed generally the similarities between Singapore and Yugoslavia such as multi-racialism and multi-nationalism, and religious tolerance. He was keen to know whether we had succeeded in separating religion from politics. I told him that we had succeeded to a certain extent and explained to him the multi-lingual set-up of our society. He admitted to me frankly that Yugoslavia still found some difficulties in separating religion from politics. He said he had difficulty particularly with the Muslims, who wanted to be considered not only as a separate religion, but as a separate nationality. There were Turkish Muslims as well as Yugoslav Muslims and they demanded to be recognised as distinct ethnic groups.

We also discussed at length the arrangements for the non-aligned conference which was to be held in Tanzania. At that time Singapore was still not a member of the non-aligned conference and Tepavac asked whether Singapore was interested to participate at the Consultative level and subsequently at the Summit level. I told him that we would consider attending when invited. He said that Singapore would definitely be invited at the Consultative level because this was proposed by India and accepted by other Asian countries which participated in the Cairo Conference.

At 6 a.m. on 9th May, the Secretary in the Secretariat of State for Foreign Affairs Mr Stjepan Rakoci picked me up from the hotel for the airport. At 6.45 a.m. we took off in Tito's special plane for Brioni Island which is about 600 kilometres away on the west coast of the Republic. The Foreign Secretary Tepavac and the Japanese Ambassador Mr Akira Sono and his wife were on the same plane. The Japanese Ambassador who had served in Yugoslavia for three years was going to bid farewell to President Tito and to receive from him his Medal of Honour.

After about two hours' flight we arrived at Pula, an industrial port on the west coast. We travelled a short distance by car and then crossed the sea by ferry and arrived at Brioni Island at 9.30 a.m. After a short rest, the Chief Protocol Officer took me and my personal assistant in a State car and proceeded to Tito's White House. Before that he gave me a copy of the President's reply to my speech. It was now the practice not to waste time reading out the speeches at a presentation of credentials ceremony.

We arrived at the White House at 10 a.m. sharp. I inspected the Guard of Honour which was lined up from the place where we alighted to the entrance of the White House. I saw President Tito in ordinary suit standing at the centre of the hall waiting to greet me with a smile. After my name was announced by his Secretary I walked towards him, shook hands and presented my credentials. I then introduced my personal assistant to him.

The President was most informal and unpretentious. He tapped my shoulder and invited me to a cup of coffee. I conveyed to him the greetings from our President and our Prime Minister. The 77-year-old President appeared to be physically fit, although it appeared to me that age was fast catching up and the power of concentration waning. During our conversation the Foreign Secretary Tepavac was present. When the President learnt that I was stationed in Cairo, he asked about the Middle East situation. I told him that it was explosive and that there seemed to be no way out, and the President replied: 'I agree with you that there is no peaceful solution. The Palestinian resistance movement is getting stronger and stronger.'

He never mentioned a word about President Nasser. I was told by the British and the Japanese Ambassador before I met Tito that the old man was quite unhappy with Nasser that the latter had kept quiet after the Russian invasion of Czechoslovakia and that there was an exchange of long letters followed by a visit of Nasser's right-hand man Sadat to Belgrade to explain the reason for having kept quiet. It seemed that President Tito was quite disillusioned and worried that in case Yugoslavia suffered the same fate as Czechoslovakia, there might be similar silence from the non-aligned leaders such as Nasser and others. Nasser's silence over the Czechoslovakia

Author inspecting the Guard of Honour outside Tito's Presidential residence in Brioni Island

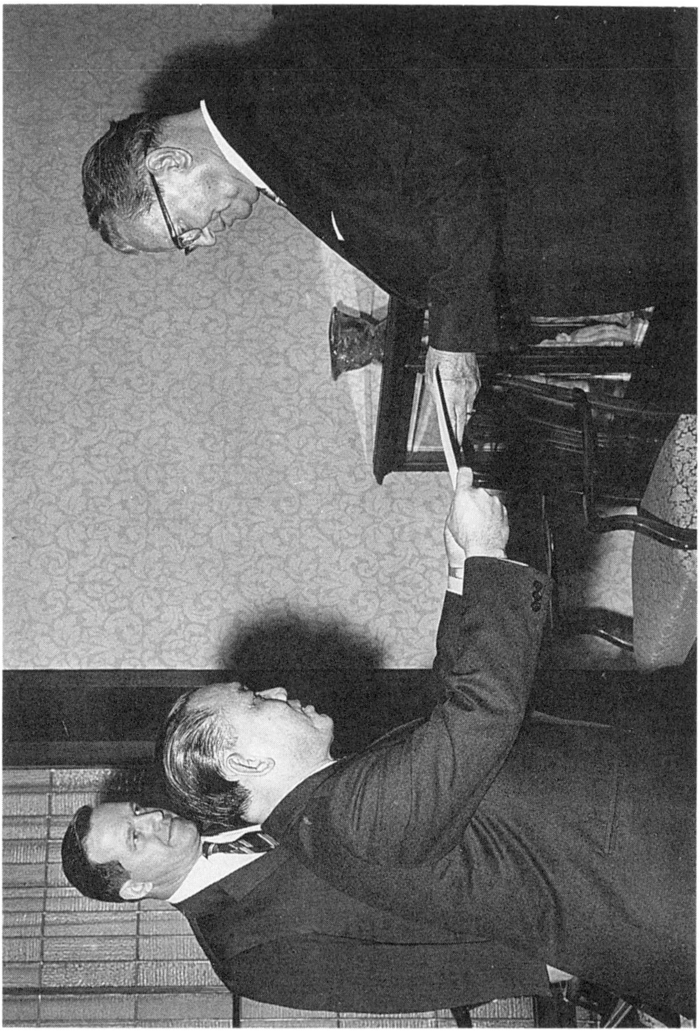

Author presenting credentials to President Tito in Brioni Island

incident had created a certain amount of misunderstanding between the two leaders.

The topic then turned to the Big Powers. He stressed the importance of convening the non-aligned conference and that non-aligned countries should not allow the Big Powers to infringe on their national integrity. He said that once the Big Powers got involved in any issue, it became difficult to settle. I thought he meant also the Middle East crisis.

He said there were today five Big Powers — the United States, Russia, France, Britain and China. He doubted whether Britain could be considered a Big Power today because her strength seemed to be diminishing.

Tito showed particular interest in getting Japan into the Non-aligned Conference. He told me that during his visit to Japan, he had a long discussion with Sato on the question of Japan participating in the Non-aligned Conference. He said Sato told him that although Japan sympathised with the non-aligned idea, she was still not in a position to participate at this juncture because of her arrangements with the US. Tito said there was a strong Japanese public opinion in favour of Japan taking a non-aligned policy. He said the Japanese Socialist Party might participate in the coming Non-aligned Conference as an Observer.

Tito seemed to think that Japanese participation would mean a great deal in strengthening the influence in the world of non-aligned policy.

Tito was keen to know what the power struggle would be like after the British withdrawal from South-East Asia. I told him that it would probably be a three-corner fight among the three countries — the United States, Soviet Union and China. I also told him that the United States might be interested to see Japan playing a more important role in South-East Asia not only politically and economically but also militarily.

'But Japan has no strong army,' said President Tito. I told him that in my opinion Japan might develop into a nuclear power after they regain Okinawa.

President Tito was anxious to see Singapore participating in the Consultative level of the Non-aligned Conference. When we were discussing this topic, he turned to his Foreign Secretary and asked whether he had consulted me on Singapore's participation. I again explained to the President that we would consider attending the Conference if invited. I also mentioned that I read his speech made on April 30th, in which he proposed that the Consultative Committee level of the Non-aligned Conference should be extended to countries which did not attend the Cairo Conference of 1964.

Referring to the possible site of the Main Summit Conference, President Tito said it would probably be held in India, since the first Summit Conference was held in Belgrade, a European country, the second in Cairo which was Africa, the third should be held in India which was Asia. He said Emperor Selassie was not interested in the Non-aligned Conference at Consultative level but he would like the Summit Conference to be held in Addis Ababa. The problem however was that if the Summit were held in Addis Ababa, the Arab countries would not participate. Therefore, India would be the ideal place.

After the 25-minute conversation, he gestured that I should take leave because he had another appointment with the Japanese Ambassador. When I rose to wish him farewell, he asked me to convey his greetings to our President and our Prime Minister.

After another inspection of the Guard of Honour, we were driven back to the rest house. We waited for the Japanese Ambassador to return and then joined by the Foreign Secretary we toured the island on horse cart. I was on the horse cart with the Foreign Secretary and the Japanese Ambassador was with the wife of the Assistant Secretary of State. It was a bright sunny day and the weather was cool. Brioni Island was so quiet and calm that we could only hear the sound of the gallops and their echoes bouncing back from the woods. We clip-clopped along the quiet garden planted with shady trees. We saw antelopes, deer, peacock, pheasants, rabbits and buffaloes roaming the island, grazing the green pastures.

We visited Tito's private zoo which has a collection of elephants, giraffes, zebras, camels, lions, tigers and wild goats. All these animals were presented by foreign dignitaries. The giraffe and the camel had just delivered their babies and were happily licking them.

Brioni Island was a holiday resort in the past for Roman and Byzantine emperors. A few monuments still remained.

Later on, a rich Yugoslav millionaire bought over the island as a private resort. His son, a great gambler, gambled away the island and committed suicide. At the end of the revolution Tito took it over and turned it into a semi-retirement summer residence. It retained the stamp of its original owner, in the days of the Austro-Hungarian Empire. Tito put in a zoo, for he liked to have game bred for him and liked hunting. A hotel for high government and party officials was built with everything of the finest quality. Tito's villa had a reception hall which could accommodate five hundred people. The construction of the island was largely done by prisoners.

After a sumptuous lunch given by the Foreign Secretary in our honour, we left for Belgrade in the same plane. I was told that it was a rare occasion for President Tito to receive credentials in Brioni. So far only 3 percent of the Ambassadors had the privilege of presenting credentials in Brioni. The President did this for only countries which he regarded as friendly and intimate. I met Tito thrice, the second occasion was when Mr Rajaratnam, then Minister for Foreign Affairs, visited Yugoslavia in 1969, and the third when our Prime Minister went in 1975.

It has been said that Yugoslavia is a mosaic of different nationalities. Indeed it is a mosaic in every respect one can possibly think of, from climate to architecture. Belgrade was devastated by war several times in history. Each time, however, Belgrade leapt to its feet again like some impetuous Phoenix, eager to restore what had been lost. Not all, of course could be restored, and little now remained of its past. The Kalemegdan Fortress, a single mosque to witness to the five centuries of Ottoman presence, the Laudanov Sanac, an entrenchment from which the Marshal of His imperial Apostolic Majesty defended the city against renewed Turkish invasion — these monuments apart, Belgrade is almost a city without a history. In its zeal to wash out the bloody stains of the past, each new epoch destroyed the relics of its predecessor. Belgrade's town planners did not have to worry very much about preserving the city's cultural monuments. The only one of any importance was the fortress built upon the bank that overlooks the confluence of the Danube and the Sava. On the other side of these two rivers, the Sirmian plain stretches into the distance. Just fifty years ago, this was all Austrian territory, and Belgrade stopped abruptly at the right bank of each of the two rivers. Now, it has begun to take possession of both banks. A whole new town, New Belgrade, is taking shape on the far side of the Sava, a city of skyscraper apartment blocks, a city of broad avenues and parks.

To a foreigner on a first visit to a communist country, Yugoslavia looked more like any non-communist state. Along the traffic-jammed streets of Belgrade, long-haired hippies rubbed shoulders with religious priests, some of them wearing Muslim songkoks. Yugoslav socialist commercialism had not yet caught up with the capitalist commercialism of Italy or America, but the difference was only quantitative. Life-size photographs of handsome men and women on the walls of tobacco kiosks bore advertisements with the words 'Be sure to smoke if you want to be handsome and happy like us.' Feature films in cinemas were preceded by slides which captivated audiences by praising the chocolate which was claimed to be 'superior to all other chocolates', the restaurant 'superior to all other restaurants.' I also found elaborate vulgarity in shop windows. At news stands, I found domestic film magazines in the same order as film magazines everywhere, cheap thrillers mostly translated from Western writers, inane comic strips imported from the United States. The newspapers carried human interest stories just like the western countries.

Jukeboxes had made their appearance. Besides the western pop tunes, rock and roll and twist blared from those corpulent boxes. There were antique stores where sofas and rugs were selling for more than what a man would make in a year. In the departmental stores, refrigerators, tape recorders and TV sets, some imported, were sold at high prices.

Along the main streets were high class hotels and ordinary restaurants, with ordinary food and service, and very fancy restaurants, bars and nightclubs. I noticed many imported automobiles, particularly Mercedes Benz sedans — often driven by chauffeurs, and large luxurious apartments. In the grand hotels, I saw a group dressed in tuxedoes and elegant evening dresses and fur coats. I also found President Tito's picture in every store, every office and every public room, absolutely without exception. Milovan Djilas seemed to be right when he wrote that a new class had formed itself to rule and enjoy the fruits of the new 'socialist state'.

I found in some of the old streets of Belgrade, many privately owned craftsmen's shops, bakers, tailors, mechanics that it was sometimes difficult to believe that I was in a socialist country.

The smells of roasting peppers and coffee beans were common in city streets, mingled with the smoke from chevapichichi stands, where little sausages were cooked over an open charcoal fire. In certain parts of Belgrade, one could see dress ranging from the latest western fashions to the long full skirts and many-coloured aprons of peasant girls. In restaurants, it was common to see a peasant in embroidered jacket mingling with a group of businessmen in gray-flannel suits. In shopping districts, one could find counters selling everything from lace to refrigerators. There were tiny shops of myriad artisans — tailors, bookbinders, quiltmakers, coppersmiths, tinsmiths, cabinetmakers, cosmetic makers, pastry cooks, bakers, watchmakers, repairers of fountain pens, shoemakers, brushmakers, skirtmakers, brassiere makers, rugmakers, sausage makers, glovemakers and men who repair nylon stockings.

The kafana is one of the great institutions of Yugoslav life, and it perpetuates the openness and outwardness of the Yugoslavian way of life. One can order one coffee and sit undisturbed from opening time to closing time, no matter how crowded the tables become or how many people were turned away. The kafanas perform the functions of a bar, restaurant, the gas station and the drugstore. They were never empty, even in midmorning. Yugoslavs who have travelled abroad often marvel that in other countries the coffee houses and bars are empty.

In Yugoslavia, people go out to the kafanas in the evening to drink and pass away the time with their friends and relatives. The most common drinks were beer, plum brandy and wine. The most common fare is chevapichichi. They were sold in orders of five or ten and eaten with mounds of chopped raw garlic or onion. This was the cheapest dish on the evening menu and even families with small income could afford it. Towards the end of the evening, people began to sing and drank noisy toasts to each other, throwing the empty glasses on the floor in good Slavic style.

Occasionally tempers flared and fights erupted in the midst of all this exuberant goodwill. By one o'clock everything was closed except for a few of the more expensive cafes which kept their gypsy orchestras and folk-singers until nearly dawn. In some of these kafanas, a stage was provided with a piano and anyone could go forward to play and sing. In some kafanas, there would be a group of singers with their violinists who would roam from table to table playing into the ears of the customers.

There were a few beggars who loitered around the cafes in the centre of the town, but they were well fed and wore very good shoes beneath their tatters. Begging was simply a profession, illegal but lucrative.

People appeared quite free to speak their minds, not just in private homes but in cafes and offices on the streets. The Government was not telling them where to go and what to do. They lived where they pleased and worked where there were jobs. My Yugoslav friends showed no sign of fear that their association with me would make them suspect. There was no climate of fear or looking over their shoulders when they met someone strange. The people showed every sign of liveliness, energy and gaiety.

I was staying at Hotel Metropole, easily the largest hotel in Belgrade. One night as I was feeling lonely, I went to the basement nightclub for dinner. To my great surprise, in the middle of the dinner there was a striptease show. And when she stripped, she really stripped until there was completely no cover.

When I had dinner with the Director of Asian Desk, Klyun, I asked him why was it that Yugoslavia allowed such striptease shows and did it not contravene Socialist principles? He answered: 'We are a free country culturally. The striptease shows have nothing to do with socialism.' He then went on to explain that in Yugoslavia citizens were allowed to own private property. One was allowed to own a flat and a holiday bungalow. If you had a family of five then you were entitled to have five bungalows and five flats and each of them was allowed to own a car. All these apart from the benefit of national security insurance and old age pension.

I had visited Dubrovnik three times, once on my own when I went there with my family, once with Mr Rajaratnam when he visited Yugoslavia and the third time when our Prime Minister visited the country. The Slavs in these parts of Yugoslavia accepted the cultural influence of their Italian adversaries, though never ceasing to resist them when occasion demanded. The superb results of this cultural grafting may still be seen in Dubrovnik. The island on the southern Adriatic coast is the best preserved Renaissance city in Yugoslavia. The old walled town dating from the time of Dubrovnik Republic is uniquely well preserved. Dubrovnik began to be built in the 7th century, on the site of an antique settlement. In the Middle Ages, it had the status of a city republic, and grew rich because of its merchant fleet. Napoleon's invasion put an end to the republic. During its centuries of independence, trade, crafts and the arts flourished. Many well-known writers and scholars lived and worked there. Today it is the most popular tourist city on the Yugoslav Adriatic coast.

In the centre of the city is a square where no cars are allowed. One could stroll leisurely without fear of the traffic, do shopping along the many shops lining up the square and feed pigeons which crowd around you in the middle of the square. I saw an old chap who played the drum and violin single-handed on the sidewalk, expecting listeners to throw a penny or two.

On my trip with the Prime Minister in 1975, we had an opportunity to pass through Sarajevo, a meeting place of East and West. The feel of the Ottoman Empire was still there; it was not only the minarets rising above the apricot trees in the gardens and courtyards of the Muslim quarter, which produced this impression. It was also the manner of dress and way of life of the people of Sarajevo. Not even the Austro-Hungarian Empire was able to expunge all the trades of their predecessors in the four decades of their dominion over Bosnia. The oriental exoticism of Sarajevo, the remnant of a past, was rapidly giving way before the pressure of modern life.

We were brought to a kafana for dinner. It was open-air and the waitresses in oriental costumes were busy serving a huge crowd who sat at rectangular tables along the pavement. A violinist was playing an oriental song sung by an old lady who could still sing at a very high pitch. They went from table to table and collected a handsome sum as tips.

Our trip to Sarajevo was short and memorable.

Unlike Singapore which is a nation of different races, languages and religions and cultures, Yugoslavia is not a nation in

A bird's eye view of Dubrovnik, Yugoslavia

that sense but a Federation of five nations comprising 7,806,000 Serbians (at 1969), 4,294,000 Croatians, 1,589,000 Slovenes, 1,046,000 Macedonians and 514,000 Montenegrins. There were also minorities of Shiptars, 915,000 Hungarians, 50,400 Turks, 181,000 Slovaks, 86,000 Bulgarians, 67,000 Rumanians, 61,000 Ruthnians, 81,000 Gypsies, 32,000 Czechs, 36,000 Italians. Yugoslavia is literally a multi-national country because we seldom find a Yugoslavian referring to himself as a Yugoslavian but takes pride in describing himself as a Serbian, Montenegrin or a Slovene. Klyun was proud to be a Slovene and he did not hide the fact that the Slovenes were superior to the Serbians, whom he described as 'lazy' and explained that perhaps it was due to Turkish influence. At one dinner, he complained that Slovenia has been subsidising too much to the other backward republics such as Macedonia and Montenegro. He said Slovenia will soon demand that they should have a larger percentage of representation in the Foreign Ministry.

Tito was a Croatian, the new Prime Minister was a Slovene and the Foreign Secretary a Serbian and the Director of the Singapore and Malaysian section a Montenegrin.

Of the six republics which make up what is now Yugoslavia, three were under the Turks for over four centuries: Serbia, Macedonia and Bosnia-Hercegovina. After several rebellions, Serbia gained full independence in the nineteenth century. Macedonia was freed only sixty years ago by the Balkan wars. Bosnia-Hercegovina was released by the Turks in the 1870s only to become part of the Austro-Hungarian Empire. Two of the other republics — Croatia and Slovenia — belonged for centuries to the Austrian Empire, and part of Slovenia was later taken over by Italy and held until World War II. The Adriatic coast was at various times under the Venetians, the Austrians and the Italians. Only the high barren mountains of the tiny republic of Montenegro remained independent. Mutual hatred divided Serbs from Croats, Macedonians from Serbs, Croats from Slovenes, and all of them from the large minority groups of Hungarians, Rumanians and Albanians. The cultural differences covered the whole range from West to East — from the Germanized Slovenes to the Muslim Macedonians.

In 1941, Tito and the Yugoslav Communist Party called for general armed rebellion and the call found response in varying degrees over the whole country. The heroic example of the Communist Party coupled with the incredible organisation of the Party made a disciplined army out of the spontaneous uprisings and popular bitterness of the people against the occupiers. This force, known as the Yugoslav Partisans, fought both occupiers and collaborators. After 1943, the Partisans had the material support of the Allies and later they received fighting assistance from the Russians on the Eastern Front near Belgrade. They liberated the country and became a socialist country under the revolutionary dictatorship of the Communist Party. In that struggle Yugoslavia lost about 1.5 million people, ten percent of their population.

In 1948, the Yugoslavs broke with the Russians to make a nation in their own independent way and build socialism according to their own way. The successful resistance by the postwar government to the pressures of Russia and the Cominform countries was due to the strong will of the Croatian leader Josip Broz, one of whose conspiratorial names was Tito. When 1948 came, the choice was between a Russian-dominated Yugoslavia or an independent Yugoslavia. Tito chose independence. The decision made in those years of crisis during and immediately after the war laid the foundations for present-day Yugoslavia.

Although Yugoslavia is a socialist country, President Tito and his other leaders were pragmatic and realistic enough to realise that strict adherence to the principle of socialism in this multi-national plural society might ruin the nation. Therefore, instead of following strictly the principle of free competition for the best brains in all political and other appointments irrespective of nationalities, the country was adopting a practical system of representation of nationalities in the Cabinet, the Party as well as the Parliament. For instance, Yugoslavia's cabinet was formed out of three top leaders from each of the six republics. The Prime Minister reserves the right to reject any of the nominations from the republics; but the republics also reserve the right to nominate new candidates in place of those rejected by the Prime Minister for the Cabinet posts. It was normal practice that when the President of a republic was a Serbian, the Prime Minister of the republic must be either a Slovene or a Croatian. This system of equal representation of nationalities was strictly observed in the formation of the governmental departments. There was no attempt to envisage the day when Yugoslavians will regard themselves as Yugoslavians and would hold positions according to their abilities, irrespective of nationalities.

When the revolution led by Tito succeeded nearly 34 years ago, virtually all the leaders who were entrusted with the power to run the country were young military officers who participated in the revolution. Many of them were promoted as Brigadiers and Generals when they were less than 25 or 30 years of age. They held high positions such as Cabinet Ministers or central Executive Committee members for a long time. Experience has shown that persons holding the same post for a long time went into a rut and there were signs that bribery, corruption and nepotism were creeping in. At the same time, the new crop of young leaders, the fruits of the revolutionary efforts, who had not experienced war, began to feel frustrated because they saw no immediate chances of sharing power. The younger generation demanded a say in shaping the destiny of their country.

In view of all these, Tito introduced a rotation system for the Cabinet, the Party as well as the Parliament. According to the amended constitution, Cabinet members cannot remain in office for more than two terms (each term of four years). When a Cabinet Minister has completed his two terms, as Cabinet Minister, he could serve in a different capacity either as Member of the Executive Committee of the League of Communists, or as Editor of the Party organ or in some other capacity. This system was to encourage a flow of new ideas and to enable a wider scope of leaders to have experience of running the country. Similarly a Member of Parliament could not sit in the Parliament for more than two terms. As a result of this rotation system, nearly 70 percent were new blood in the republics as well as in the Federal Parliaments. According to the Constitution even the President must resign after four years with the exception of President Tito who was given life term because of his great contribution to the country.

Both the Yugoslavian officials and the diplomats that I have met agreed that the Communist League of Yugoslavia was playing a lesser role in public affairs. I understood from Klyun, who was also a Communist party member, the organisation of the League of Communists of Yugoslavia was not so tightly knit as in the other Eastern European Communist countries or in Russia. For instance, there was no indoctrination of Marxism-Leninism or any form of ideology on members nor was there special training classes for cadres. Any citizen could become a member of the Communist Party if he was recommended by other members and there was no swearing-in ceremony or oath-taking of allegiance to anyone. He merely had to agree that he would not misbehave himself such as getting drunk or gambling. There were at present 1,100,000 members in the Communist Party (by 1969). The League of Communists did not impose its view by means of authority but through persuasion in the Socialist Alliance and various other organisations of self-government and representative bodies.

The Socialist Alliance of the working people of Yugoslavia was a broad-based political organisation. In other words, it was an open front organisation not entirely controlled by the League of Communists. This Socialist Alliance which was open to all citizens had 8,126,000 members. It had the right to nominate candidates for election in the republics and Federal Parliaments.

The British Ambassador Mr Garvey, who was an expert on Yugoslavian affairs and who was able to read and write the Serbo-Croatian language and had been consul-general in Yugoslavia for a long period, expressed the fear that too speedy a liberalisation and democratisation might be detrimental to the country. He said that just before World War II, there was anarchy in the country because of an open scramble for power by all nationalities. He said Tito was aware of this danger and had taken measures to tighten it a little.

The country's main internal problem was how to tackle the student unrest. There was a strike and demonstration in June 1969 by university students. They demanded:

(a) a say in running the University
(b) a change in the educational system and curriculum
(c) more scholarships
(d) a solution to the unemployment problem.

The University students were divided into three groups — pro-Russian, pro-West and pro-Albanian (meaning the Peking line in those days). All these groups were anti-government. The Japanese Ambassador, who had just received the highest honour from President Tito, was however quite critical in his political analysis of the country when he had a long private chat with me. He said that Suharto had to postpone his trip to Belgrade at the request of the Yugoslavian government because it feared that there might be student demonstrations in June to mark the anniversary of the student demonstration last year. The student paper recently said that only 'one drop in the ocean' of their demands were met. The student population constituted a major threat to the stability of the regime because of the conflicting views they held and because of their frustration over the mounting unemployment in the country. There were about half a million people unemployed whilst there was a big brain drain of well-trained university graduates such as doctors, engineers, and technicians because of better pay abroad. There was no restriction of this brain drain as the authorities were incapable of absorbing them.

Yugoslavia was still groping its way in the bold experiment of the self-management system in factories, hotels, restaurants and other enterprises. This self-management system, the first of its kind implemented in Socialist countries of the world, provides workers not only the right to decide how the factories should be run or what it should produce and at what prices but also the distribution of profits after taxes and running costs were deducted. The Yugoslavian ideologists claim that only the Yugoslavian socialists' self-management system abides by the spirit of Marx because this system will eventually lead to the withering away of the state as envisaged by Marx. Under the system, the role of the state was gradually decreasing. The state now no longer possesses direct control through its bureaucratic machine and the state has in fact returned 70 percent of all state-owned land and enterprises to the farmers and workers to be run on the self-management basis.

In Yugoslavia, every enterprise that employed more than five workers was run by self-management. In other words, every worker becomes a shareholder and has the right to vote. The workers have the right to choose their managers. In a hotel for instance, the waiter, the cook, the cashier and the manager were all shareholders. They all have a say in running the hotel and how to distribute the profits. The profits were distributed according to one's rank.

The system was having its teething troubles. The Japanese Ambassador pointed out the danger that the workers might tend to kill the golden goose when deciding on the distribution of profits. Human nature being such, they might want to enjoy the fruits of their labour instead of accumulating the profits into capital for further expansion. This was one of the reasons why there were more new cars in the cities and Yugoslavian products were becoming less competitive in overseas markets because of the high cost of production.

The Cuban Ambassador, who was the Dean of the Diplomatic Corps, was highly critical of Tito's liberal socialism and of the self-management system. He pointed out that the strike which took place in the motor industry in Kakanica was due to the dissatisfaction by one section of the workers against the payment of a better percentage of personal income to the technical section as a result of better results. According to the system, the payment of personal income was based on 'to each according to his ability.' He said the self-management system in factories was the cause of the sharp rise in the cost of living of the country. He was also critical of the liberal cultural approach in allowing youngsters to put on long hair and to do what they liked. He said that the self-management system was a 'bluff' because the State owned banks and exercised control over all enterprises.

The system of self-management was the product of anti-Stalin struggle. If after the 1948 confrontation with the Soviet Union, Yugoslavia had continued as an administrative system based on the Soviet economic model, Yugoslavia would have fallen into chaos, which might have undermined Tito's power. That would have given rise to the possibility of foreign intervention — primarily Soviet military intervention — which would inhibit national development for decades. In order to function effectively, economic enterprises and management were given autonomy, but only insofar as it did not infringe on Party authority. The same was true of culture, so long as it did not deal with subjects that were taboo, meaning the Party and the revolution. The concept of self-management was born from the struggle against Stalin's tyranny and from visions of a true democratic socialism. Self-management legalised criticism of the bureaucracy. It solidified gains towards a free-market economy and yet it did not substantially influence the character of power. Self-management was undoubtedly an achievement in the area of the rights of producers and a free-market economy, but it has no influence on power and the political system.

The Japanese Ambassador was right when he said that Tito actually implemented the system out of necessity and then went on to find an ideological explanation to justify it.

What makes Yugoslavia unique and contradictory is the fact that the Communist Party which was built up during the Stalin era has begun to organise society on the basis of ideas which is a mingling of western democracy and socialist theory. Power is being constantly transferred from the centre outwards. The commune, the business enterprise and the individual citizen and worker are daily finding more possibilities open for their initiative. The people on the whole enjoy democratic freedom and have a say in the means of production and yet the country is controlled by the Communist Party.

But what will happen after Tito? This was the question we were asking ourselves when we were last there in September 1975 during Prime Minister Lee Kuan Yew's visit. My impression was that the Yugoslavs were obsessed with persistent Russian overt and covert subversion to undermine the Yugoslav brand of communism and to pressurise them into following the Soviet hard-line policy. Tito's idea of forming the non-aligned group was to use it as a global voice and international protection against possible Russian intrusion against Yugoslav integrity and sovereignty. When I was there, the Yugoslav Charge d'Affaires to Singapore, Milutin Filipovic, told me that a few months back, 50 exiled pro-Russian Yugoslav Communist Party members returned to the outskirts of Belgrade and held meetings condemning the Tito Government of deviating from the principles of Marxism-Leninism. They were arrested and imprisoned after a trial for treason. The Soviet Union denied implications but the Yugoslav authorities had documental proof that these men were sent back by the Russians for subversion.

The adviser to the President of the Federal Executive Council for Foreign Matters, Mr Nikola Cicanovic, also told me that two months back when the Soviet Union celebrated their anti-Fascist anniversary, they distributed pamphlets which claimed that it was the Russians who liberated Yugoslavia. This had angered Yugoslavia. Tito made public speeches protesting against the misrepresentation of facts. Diplomatic protests were also made. The Russians explained that the documents were drafted by junior officials and that it was an oversight.

The danger facing Yugoslavia is that of whether the country will produce a leader who has Tito's guts, one who challenged Stalin who tried to control Yugoslavia. Tito had warned the Russian Ambassador in Belgrade after the Czechoslovakian incident that the Soviet Union should keep its hands off Yugoslavia. He was reported to have said: 'We did not sacrifice 1,700,000 lives for nothing. (Yugoslavia lost that number of people during their fight against Hitler.) We are prepared to sacrifice another 3,000,000 to uphold our national integrity. You can tell that to your leaders.' Will any other Yugoslav leader say the same thing when he becomes the President?

When I was last in Belgrade in 1975, Tito was only a symbol and a figurehead spending more of his time in his favourite island of Brioni, with casual visits to the republics, meeting foreign dignitaries and touring foreign countries when he found enough energy. The day-to-day administration of the country was in the hands of a 15-man Presidium and the Cabinet.

The Japanese Ambassador Mr Akira Sono had this to say about Tito in 1968: 'In my opinion, the Emperor of Japan knows more about what is happening in Japan than Tito knows of Yugoslavia. And Tito in fact lives more luxuriously than the Japanese Emperor.' I think the Japanese Ambassador was right.

Then on Sunday, 4 May 1980, after four months of illness, President Tito died in Ljubljana, capital of the Socialist Republic of Slovenia. The following morning, the coffin with the President's remains was carried by the Blue Train from Ljubljana to Belgrade, accompanied by the highest Yugoslav State and Party leaders.

On its journey to Belgrade, the train stopped in Zagreb, capital of the Socialist Republic of Croatia, where it was met by hundreds of thousands of people. On the same day, the train reached Belgrade where again hundreds of thousands of people were waiting. The coffin was then carried through columns of citizens to the building of the Yugoslav Assembly. The citizens of Belgrade and people from all parts of the country filed continuously past the coffin day and night. By the funeral on May 8, half a million Yugoslavs had paid their respects to their late President.

The funeral cortege then set out for Dedinje, the suburb of Belgrade where Tito was to be buried. The procession was headed by standard-bearers with the flags of Yugoslavia, each of its republics, the League of Communists, and 365 Partisan units in the National Liberation War. The march to President Tito's last resting place, the House of Flowers in the garden of his Belgrade residence, No. 15 Uzicka Street, where he was buried at his own request, took two hours. The coffin was then lowered into the grave close to the house where Tito had lived for much of the past 35 years. A simple white marble slab bears the inscription in gold letters: JOSIP BROZ TITO 1892–1980.

The President's funeral was attended by 209 delegations from 128 countries, 122 state delegations, 68 party delegations, four delegations from liberation movements and nine delegations of international organisations. The members of these delegations included 31 Presidents of republics, four kings, eight vice-presidents, six princes, 22 prime ministers, 11 presidents of national parliaments, 12 vice-premiers and 47 foreign ministers.

Tito will certainly be remembered by military historians as a great military leader, perhaps the greatest leader of irregular forces that history has ever known. When the history of the period comes to be written, he will be remembered for the stand he made against Stalin in 1948. The fact that at that time he was able to assert Yugoslavia's national independence and survive was of enormous importance not only in the history of world communism, but in the history of our era. I think we are still feeling the consequences of that today. If things had gone differently, if Tito had not survived, history would have been very different. He will be remembered for the self-management system which he had introduced into Yugoslav socialism, the new brand of socialism which represented the first break in the Communist system.

The First Guard of Honour by the bier of President Tito in the Yugoslav assembly

11

Lebanon—Heaven Turned Hell

Sometime in early September 1968, I suggested to the former Minister for Foreign Affairs Mr S. Rajaratnam that I be accredited to Lebanon because Cairo was a dead city so far as news gathering was concerned. There was strict press censorship in Cairo and we had to order newspapers from Beirut. This was a handicap. Articles that were critical or unfavourable to the Egyptian Government appearing in the *Times*, *Time Magazine* or *Newsweek* or other publications were normally torn off when put on sale in bookstalls. The only source of information in Cairo was the *Egyptian Gazette* and the *Egyptian Mail* which gave only the official version of events and views. Without diplomatic contacts one would be like a 'frog in the well' so far as the knowledge of the outside world was concerned.

My information was that Beirut was the only 'window' of the Middle East where one could have a peep at international events and obtain different shades of opinion. Almost every Arab country was subsidising or financing one Arab newspaper to expound their views in Beirut. There were for instance several pro-UAR, Pro-Syria, Pro-Jordan and Pro-Saudi Arab newspapers. Atmosphere in Beirut was the most free for diplomats. There was at least some form of parliamentary democracy in Lebanon and the press was quite free to criticise. In fact, Beirut was the asylum for political refugees from all over the Middle East.

On 9th November 1968, I received the formal note addressed to the Ministry of Foreign Affairs, Republic of Lebanon, proposing to appoint me as Ambassador to Lebanon. I immediately forwarded the note to the Lebanese Ambassador to Cairo, Dr Halim Abu-Izzeddin, who informed me that the Ambassador would need a formal morning coat which would cost about $500 Singapore currency. Dr Halim passed on the message to his government.

It was not until September 1969 that I was to present credentials to the Lebanese President. The reason was that Lebanon was in a crisis and there was no government for some months. The Lebanese politicians were bickering for power and position and quarrelling like cats and dogs. Premier-designate Rashid Karamy who announced his 14-man Cabinet had faced another Cabinet crisis following the resignation of two Ministers, Mr Pierre Gemayel, leader of the Phalangist Party and Mr Raymond Edde, leader of the National Bloc Party. They had insisted that the Cabinet included Camille Chamoun who was a member of the Chamoun tripartite. Apart from the differences in party politics, the Parliament was divided on the basic question of whether to take an all-out pro-Arab policy and to prepare the country for defence against Israel, or to invite UN Forces to the country's borders for protection. In Lebanon, the commando activities resulted in an open clash with the Lebanese army and police leading to the resignation of the three-month-old Karamy Government. Everything was topsy-turvy in Lebanon and my accreditation was postponed.

After nearly six months' delay, the Lebanese authorities despite the continuing political crisis, decided in May 1969 to establish diplomatic relations with Singapore. I sent the letter of our government's decision to accredit me to Lebanon with my biography to the Lebanese Government through Dr Halim who told me that the reply could be expected within two weeks. But the reply did not come until August 1969.

I made my first trip to Beirut and stayed at the Hotel Phoenecia, the largest and most modern hotel in Lebanon. In the morning of 8 September, the Deputy Chief Protocol Officer, Namiyo and the Director of International Affairs, Khalil Makkawi came in the President's Rolls Royce with seven outriders to the hotel. They briefed me on the procedure of the presentation. Escorted all the way by the seven outriders, I sat in the Rolls Royce and travelled 25 miles south of Beirut and arrived at the Baiteddin Palace.

As soon as I alighted from the car, I was greeted by the Commander of the Guard of Honour who carried a sword. We stood to attention near the military band and Majulah Singapura was played. After viewing the guard of honour, I alighted a flight of steps which led into a huge courtyard and then into the President's guest room. I was escorted by the President's Chamberlain, an oldish looking man, to another inner chamber where President Charles Helou (Sharl Hulu) and the Foreign Minister were waiting. I walked to a distance of about three metres away from the President and read out my speech. After that I handed the letter of credential to him and then retreated a few steps to listen to his reply in French off the cuff.

The President agreed with my speech that there were many similarities between Singapore and Lebanon and that with my accreditation he hoped that the friendly ties that existed between the two countries would become stronger socially, economically and politically. He also conveyed his greetings to our President. After this ceremony, we adjourned to a corner and had about ten minutes' chat over a glass of fresh orange juice.

The President seemed to have a vague idea of Singapore, admitting that he had read a few books about Singapore and its beauty and charms. I explained to him the multi-racial, multi-religious and multi-lingual aspect of our country and he seemed very interested. I expressed the hope that the President would visit Singapore one day and he replied that it was one of his ambitions to see the East, particularly Singapore which has so much in common with Lebanon. He added that he would do so either as President or as an ordinary citizen. The President will have to resign next year when his six-year term expires. Under the present Constitution, no President is allowed to stand for Presidency more than once unless the Constitution is amended by the Parliament.

After bidding farewell to the President, I was escorted back to the Guard of Honour where the Lebanese National Anthem was played. I got into the car and drove past the Guard of Honour and returned to the hotel.

Author inspecting the Guard of Honour outside the Lebanon Presidential Palace

Cheers to the health of President Charles Helou after the author has presented credentials to him

Fifteen minutes after we left the Palace, one of the motorcycle outriders skidded and fell from his motorbike. It was drizzling and the road was slippery. I suggested to Khalil that the car should slow down to find out the condition of the outrider, but he said it was a small matter and did not stop.

On the same night I had a dream. I dreamt that the outrider came to see me and told me that he was dead. I recognised his face because before we took off for the Palace, he came to ask for bakshish (tips) and I told my secretary K. K. Menon to give him one after the presentation of credentials. He was happy with the arrangement. In the same dream, I dreamt that I was collecting gold coins from the air. The coins just dropped from the sky and I started to collect them. I told my wife of the dream when I woke up. Fifteen minutes later, the telephone rang. A voice from the Foreign Ministry said: 'I regret to inform you that the outrider is dead.' What a coincidence. I had dreamt of his death before the telephone rang. And what about the gold coins? I told my wife that gold coins would be waiting for me at the Cairo airport when we returned to Cairo. When I arrived at the Cairo airport, the third secretary brought a parcel and presented it to me saying: 'Sir, here are your gold coins.' I had ordered the Singapore 150th anniversary gold coins previously and these had arrived. And the news came into my dream. This was a most unforgettable dream. How was it possible that a dream could tell you events before they actually happened?

I ordered my personal assistant to arrange for a wreath to be sent to the deceased and sent 100 Egyptian pounds for the funeral.

When I presented credentials to President Charles Helou, Lebanon had been without a government for more than four months. The crisis was worsened by another clash recently between Palestinian commandos and the security officers at Nahr Lbaree Refugee Camp near Tripoli. Despite political turmoil inside and outside the country and despite the fact that the country had been without a government for four months, life in Lebanon, and particularly in Beirut, went on as normal without any excitement. In fact the money-minded Lebanese seemed to think that Lebanon could get on without political parties and a government.

Hotel Phoenecia, the hotel where I stayed, was a super-class ultra modern hotel, crowded with Arab oil tycoons who lavished their money like sprinkling water. At the lobby which was gigantic and grand, one could see them in beautiful white galibaya with a ring on their heads chatting loudly in little groups. Beirut was the centre of relaxation and entertainment for most Arabs who had made money in the Arab hinterland. Arab royalty, oil tycoons, and whoever had the money to spend made their way to Beirut where there was a freer atmosphere and where one can do practically anything under the sun without having to look over one's shoulders. One can let the hair down for a change.

Beirut's western orientation and preponderant Christian element was closely attuned to the West in its sympathies than any of the Arab states. Its people boasted that nature had endowed it with a greater variety of attractions than any other area of equal size. Where else, they asked, could one swim in the sea and ski on the heights on the same day? Of the seven skiing centres, the one near the famous Cedars about 90 miles from Beirut has an altitude of 6,300 feet, where lovers of winter sports can take a chair-lift to the summit. That was 9900 feet above the sea with the Lebanese forest providing an impressive background. Most fashionable among the resorts were Ayn Sawfar (Safar), 15 miles from Beirut and 4265 feet high, near the mountain spine; Alayh (Aley) 9 miles from Beirut and 2,790 feet high; and Duhur al Shuwayr, 15 miles from Beirut and 4,085 feet above the sea.

In summer, Beirut's night clubs and entertainers migrate to some of these resorts, all of which were provided with fairly comfortable hotels and boarding houses. The caressing breezes of the mountain offer a welcome relief from the hot weather below. The sight of the rising sun crowning the hoary summits with its rays and of its golden disk sinking slowly in the distant horizon behind the blue Mediterranean was one of those not easy to forget.

There was colourful display of different shapes of stones in a cave in one of the show places in Lebanon.

Other attractions were archaeological such as the unsurpassed Roman ruins of Ba'labakk to remind the Lebanese of their origin. The Ba'labakk, colloquially known as the

Ruins of Ba'labakk – in the outskirt of Beirut

Ban'albak was originally a temple dedicated to the worship of that great Aramaean deity Hadad, god of lightning and thunder, who sent rain to fructify the earth and also sent floods to destroy crops and flocks. The ruins of the acropolis have throughout the centuries so excited the wonder of writers and visitors that they were included among the seven wonders of the world. None from Roman days were comparable to them, not even in the imperial capital itself. Within the area south of the Jupiter-Hadad temple lie the ruins of a smaller and better preserved temple of Atargatis, commonly attributed to Bacchus. Indeed, this is the best preserved and most richly ornamented ancient temple in the entire area. Its colossal sculptured doorway, 45 feet high and 25 feet wide was reckoned among the grandest products of Roman architecture. The shrine of Jupiter was surrounded by a peristyle of large columns of yellow stone with Corinthian capitals and a frieze above. Of these columns six hold themselves proudly erect to this day, facing Mount Lebanon in majestic grandeur. Aside from the colossal magnitude of the pillars and the huge size of the stone blocks, it was the wealth of detail in ornamentation and the figure work in friezes that constituted a feature of the surviving groups of buildings. The decorations comprise wheat and poppies (emblems of life and death), winged genii lifting a veil and cupids with bows and arrows or mounted on dragons and dolphins. Geometrical figures, interspersed with foliage, and busts of emperors and deities adorn the ceiling.

Then there was the famous Casino Leban, situated some distance away from Beirut. It was the paradise for the rich to squander away their wealth or try their luck for further riches. The casino had a stage show which was the grandest I have seen. It was easily the biggest stage in the world. I have seen stages in Paris, London, New York and Las Vegas, but they were nothing compared to that in Casino Leban. One could see the scene of a volcano, the roar of the bursting lava, with horses running about on the stage. Then at the end of the show, at the press of a button, the whole scene was turned into a sea, with ships sailing and one of these ships sailing right in front of the audience when the floor split wide open with water flowing from underneath one's feet. I visited the Casino and had dinner, with a floor show.

Lebanon was a paradise for the well-to-do. But its Arabic language and large Muslim population have made it gravitate into the Arab states' orbit. Threats loomed from without and within. The rulers of Syria dreamt of a greater Syria to include Lebanon. The Christians who comprised half of the population would prefer to remain neutral and independent. They did not wish to be absorbed into the Arab orbit. Lebanon presented a conspicuous exception. It remained Christian in faith and Syrian in speech for centuries after the Islamization and Arabicization of the entire area. Among the Christians in Lebanon, the most powerful were the Maronites who owe their name to the patron saint of their church, an ascetic monk who lived in the latter part of the fourth century and died about 410 in the wilderness between Antioch and Cyrrhus to the north. As the tidal wave of Arab conquest engulfed inner Syria and the maritime plain, resulting in the gradual supplanting of the religion of Christ by that of Mohamed, Lebanon emerged as a Christian islet in a sea of Islam. The Maronites moved downwards and colonised north Lebanon. The Maronites were an offshoot of the Syriac-speaking Church of which the two other offshoots were the East Syrian and West Syrian communions. Their church which may be considered the national church of Lebanon, has retained to the present day its Syriac liturgy, a derivative of that ascribed to St James and the non-celibate clergy.

Then there was the Druze (al-Duruz) who derived their name from a missionary (dai) of Turkish origin, Muhammad ibn-Ismail al Darazi (tailor) a confidant of the sixth Fatimid caliph in Cairo, al Hakim (996–1021). The Druzes' favourite name for themselves was al-Muwahhidun (unitarians), the believers in one and only one God. The basic doctrine of Druzism was a continuation of the Ismalite teaching, held by the followers of the Imam Ismail, seventh successor of Ali, hence their other name Seveners. From its cradle at the southern tip of Lebanon Druzism worked its way northward in the mountain, avoiding the maritime and inland plains. There were also the Shiites and the Sunnis among the Muslims, and Greek Catholics and Greek Orthodox among the Christians.

One persistent factor in Lebanon's turbulent political history has been the self-interested manipulation of the country's factional and sectarian rivalries by outside forces, from the

Middle Eastern region and the world at large. Since the Ottoman times, hardly any major conflict among the Lebanese has been free from external intervention. In nearly all cases, Lebanese discord has been used by external powers, in one way or another, to serve diverse aims which have little to do with the Lebanese themselves. Most important is the historical division of the Lebanese along religious and sectarian lines and consequently, the lack of solidarity among them as a people or a nation. This peculiarity of the Lebanese as a segmented society has made the country a fertile ground for internal discord and an attractive target for external political investment in local situations of discord. The failure of the Lebanese to overcome their sectarian conflicts, and their failure to build up a solidarity against outside intervention, have frequently transformed Lebanon into a battlefield where Lebanese factions, often unknowingly, have fought the undeclared wars of other nations by proxy.

The three civil wars which Lebanon has experienced during the last two centuries — in 1860, 1958 and the ongoing one since 1975 — seem to have two main features in common. First, all three wars have involved an awakening of dormant religious sectarian tensions, which grew on every occasion to overshadow other expressed or implied sources and causes of conflict. Second, all three wars have been either initiated by regional or foreign powers to serve their own interest. The massacres of 1860 between the Maronites and the Druzes resulted in about 18,000 deaths on both sides. The death toll shocked both the Druze and Maronite leaders and as a result they were ready to submit to the Turkish authority. Under Turkish auspices, they immediately signed a peace treaty in which they declared that their autonomy had engendered anarchy, and asked that Turkish authority be effectively and continually exercised in the affairs of Lebanon. But the European powers — Britain, France, Russia, Prussia and Austria-Hungary — would not respect this treaty. They all compelled Turkey to join them in an international commission to work out a system for the administrative reorganisation of Lebanon that would guarantee its continued autonomy. The representatives of the five powers finally signed a protocol on 9 June 1861 authorising the administrative reorganisation of Lebanon. As amended in September 1864, this protocol became the charter of an autonomous Lebanese province which enjoyed autonomy until the outbreak of World War I.

World War II brought Lebanon closer to independence. When Paris fell to German troops in the summer of 1940, nationalist leaders in both countries knew that France, too weak to defend itself, could not hope legally or morally to defend its continued presence in the Lebanon. The Maronite and Druze leaders found an understanding for the maintenance of an independent, sovereign and viable Lebanon. This Muslim-Christian understanding came to be called al-mithaq al-watani or the National Pact of 1943. With the consent of the Christian and Muslim leadership, the President and Prime Minister committed the two communities to the following principles:

First, the Christians gave up the idea of an isolated Lebanon and accepted an independent and sovereign Lebanon within the Arab world. The Muslims in return gave up the idea of giving back to Syria the territories which had been annexed to Lebanon; and also the aim of uniting Lebanon with the Arab world.

Secondly, the Christians gave up the idea of foreign protection, either by way of occupation, military outposts or the concluding of treaties with the Western Powers. In return, the Muslims agreed to stop working to make the Lebanon submit to Syrian or Arab influence.

Thirdly, the number of seats in Parliament was to be distributed in such a way as to ensure a majority to the Christians. Also the President of the Republic was always to be a Christian while the Premier in the Government was always to be a Muslim.

Since the Christians were a slight majority, they were given a slightly larger representation within the Chamber of Deputies, in accordance with a set ratio of six Christian to five Muslim deputies. Agreement on this ratio had been reached only after a crisis threatened to disrupt Muslim-Christian cooperation.

The balance of power thus established in the Chamber of Deputies was continued by virtue of the National Pact into the executive branch of the government. The Pact of course merely followed a trend that had been set during the mandate period: the presidency was reserved for the Maronites, the largest community, and the premiership for the Sunnis, the second largest community. Previously these two communities had stood at opposite poles with regard to the future of Lebanon; the Maronites generally favoured isolation from the Arab world, the Sunnis had pressed for integration within the Arab world.

To give the other major sects the same peace of mind, the Cabinet would include a Greek Orthodox, a Shii, a Greek Catholic, a Druze and a Maronite. In the spirit of conciliation of 1943, the Shiis were accorded the right to the presidency of the Chamber. Henceforth deputies would elect their own president from among their Shii colleagues.

This political arrangement between the Christians and the Muslims was generally referred to as 'confessional politics'.

A revolution broke out in 1958 because of the discontentment against President Chamoun's foreign policy. President Chamoun who had supported the Eisenhower Doctrine as a means of pressuring the nation into granting him a second term in office was strongly opposed by the Damascus-Cairo centre Muslims who felt that Lebanon was deviating from the Arab world and becoming hostile to Cairo. A compromise was reached when the nation chose as President General Chehab who was in command of the 6,000 strong army and who remained neutral during the civil war.

When General Chehab finished his term in 1964, Charles Helou to whom I presented credentials took over. Charles was known to be a public relations man and not a politician. He did not belong to any political party. He won the title of 'Fire extinguisher' long before he became President. He worked hard during the 1958 trouble between the Lebanese fighting factions and brought about an end to the civil strife. The fact that he was on talking terms with both sides of the fence won him the admiration of many Lebanese who saw no purpose or sense at all in the troubles. During the crisis, Charles always applied a sense of public relations for which he became famous. The entry of a large number of Palestinian refugees and the emergence of the Palestinian commando activities have however made the task of public relations extremely difficult for President Charles Helou. When I was there, press reports and diplomatic circles were talking about the year 1970 as to who would succeed Charles Helou. I was told that Charles wanted to retire to write books. He was once the editor of a French language newspaper *Lejour* and before that he was Lebanon's first Ambassador to Vatican. So far the people in Lebanon respected President Helou as a pious and devout Christian Maronite and an honest and straightforward man. In Lebanon politics, however, the main criticism against President Charles Helou was that he wanted to keep everyone satisfied at the same time. Rumour was circulating that the United States was trying to convince the present Commander-in-Chief of the Armed Forces to stand as a candidate for the next Presidency. It was felt that Lebanon needed a strong man at this stage and not a public relations man.

From conversations I had with diplomats and other people in Beirut, I gained the impression that Lebanon was controlled by big business monopolies. Their influence was felt in almost every government department and was in fact controlling the government through their purse. Even political parties were under their influence. Rumours which were against the Tripartite Alliance — the alliance of the National Bloc Party led by Raymond Edde, the National Liberal Party led by the former President Camille Chamoun, and the Phalangist Party led by Pierre Gemayel — were that they were all American stooges. These leaders represented a large proportion of the Christian population. Politics in Lebanon meant nothing to the man in the street except a means to get rich and was synonymous with corruption, bribery and power. The Tripartite Alliance wanted to retain Lebanon's sovereignty and independence without being absorbed by the Arab countries. This faction, comprising mostly Maronites, was against the stationing of Palestinian commandos in Lebanon as this would give the Israelis an excuse to attack Lebanon from time to time. On the other hand, the Parliamentary Democratic Front led by Prime Minister Karamy supported by Sunnis wanted the Government to support the Palestinian commandos and wanted Lebanon to identify itself more with Arab states. The Druze leader, Jumblat who led the Progressive Socialist Party, was backing Karamy in wanting the Government to support the commandos. President Charles Helou seemed to be the only man at that moment who could rally the country together because he was a non-party man.

The biggest problem facing Lebanon was the existence of Palestinian refugees and commandos. In 1948, about 140,000 Palestinian Arabs came to Lebanon and took up residence in various Lebanese cities and villages. Since 1950, the United Nations Relief and Works Agency of Palestinian refugees set up an Agency to look after them. By 1968 the number of refugees rose to 223,000 which was more than ten percent of the Lebanese population. Although the Lebanese authorities required refugees to obtain work permits, at least 100,000 Palestinians were working in Lebanon without permits. The authorities were closing one eye to this fact because Lebanon stood to benefit from the presence of Palestinians there. The UNRWA was said to spend an average of 30 million Lebanese pounds on the Palestinians in Lebanon every year. The total of UNRWA expenditure in Lebanon over the past 20 years was therefore estimated at 600 million. Furthermore, the Palestinian labour force was relatively less expensive and it played an important role in the implementation of various major projects in the country. The Indian Ambassador A. K. Dar said quite rightly: 'Without these Palestinian refugees, all the major projects here will be held up. The Lebanese are not hard workers. Therein lies the paradox.'

The Palestinian refugees also produced a large number of tourist souvenirs at very cheap prices which was also a contribution to the tourist industry. Being Palestinians, the refugees quite naturally supported the cause of the commandos.

A country which was working on a system of free enterprise required cheap labour but at the same time wanted to get rid of the cream of the cheap labour who participated in commando activities against the Israelis.

The British Ambassador Mr King who was an Arab expert explained to me the external problems which Lebanon had to face. Briefly, Lebanon had trouble with almost every Arab state. It had trouble with Syria — because traditionally and historically Lebanon had been trying to fight against merger with Syria.

Iraq — because of press comments against Iraqi's persecution of the Shiite community. When I was there, the Iraqi Government ordered all Iraqis to leave Lebanon. So far 7,000 had left. I heard from the Indonesian Councillor Mr Rashid stationed in Beirut the true reason behind the Lebanon–Iraq dispute; it was caused by the son of the Iraqi President General Bakr. According to the story which was being circulated, General Bakr's son was involved in a brawl in a Beirut night club and was taken in by the police. He protested strongly and tried to throw his weight around. It seemed that he shouted aloud that he was the son of the Iraqi President and that he should have immunity. The police carried out their duties. The son wrote to the father, who got angry and started to take all measures against Lebanon under other pretexts.

Saudi Arabia — because Lebanon had turned down its application to start the third oil refinery in Lebanon. Saudi Arabia threatened to boycott trade with Lebanon if she insisted on the refusal.

Egypt — because the Egyptians had sent their agents to Lebanon to incite trouble since 1958 during the Nasser regime. The bloody riots of 1958 between the Christians and the Muslims were partly due to instigation from pro-Nasserite elements within Lebanon. It was a well-known fact that President Charles Helou would not visit Cairo and that Nasser would not visit Beirut.

The problem facing the Palestinian commandos was that they tried to create a state within a state in Arab countries. Unlike Vietnam where the Vietcong had a legal territory to operate from, the Palestinian commandos were in fact political squatters on sovereign Arab states. Backed by Arab leaders the commandos believed that they had a right to operate in these countries according to their own plan and, more often than not, ignoring the orders of the State Governments and sometimes taking the law into their own hands.

The events which led to the sharp crisis in 1969 were caused by a bid by the commandos to move from the slopes of Mount Hermon in the Arkoub area down to the central southern area, near the old 1949 Armistice Line with Israel. They had apparently been driven off by the Lebanese Army resulting in the now commonly known Majdel Silm 'massacre' — a clash between the commandos and the Lebanese Army.

The Lebanese authorities were against allowing the Commandos to have bases in the central area near the Armistice Line for two reasons:

(i) The Lebanese Government officially announced in August 1969 when it complained against Israeli raids on some southern villages that the only arrangement that existed between Lebanon and Israel was the 1949 Armistice, because Lebanon was not a party to the 1967 ceasefire agreement which replaced the 1949 Armistice for Egypt, Jordan and Syria. Lebanon had emphasised that the 1949 arrangement did not exist any longer — which was interpreted as reflecting Israeli expansionist ambition against Lebanon.

(ii) A Lebanese statement had earlier explained with regard to the Majdel Silm incident that the Commandos had tried to move into the densely populated area which would endanger the livelihood and security of the Lebanese inhabitants there, which meant that the Commando presence there would invite Israeli attacks. Furthermore the central southern area was an important agricultural section, particularly due to the tobacco crop there on which a large section of the southern population depended for their livelihood.

The commandos had established a de facto presence in South Lebanon without the advance approval of the Lebanese Government. The problem facing Lebanon was to find a workable solution whereby Palestinian Commandos would be allowed to operate freely without endangering the security of the country and at the same time safe-guarding the sovereignty of Lebanon. When Nasser was still in power, he managed to bring about a temporary agreement between the Lebanese authorities and the Palestinian Liberation Organisation in Cairo.

The situation in Beirut was tense throughout the early 1970s when the US sixth fleet was standing by in the Mediterranean and the Soviet Union had warned the United States and other foreign countries against interference in Lebanese affairs. Meanwhile, the then Israeli deputy Premier Allon had warned that Israel would not stand 'idly by if the Beirut Government was overthrown by foreign forces.'

Then in 1975, something tragic happened. The Christians and the Muslims started their communal brutality that took the lives of some 40,000 people. The civil war destroyed Lebanon as the commercial crossroads of the Middle East and carried that small tortured country to the brink of annihilation. Lebanon was being smashed mainly because the Lebanese Christians, the country's dominant faction, had become a minority — their lower birth rate and higher emigration rate meant that they now accounted for about 40 percent of Lebanon's estimated 2.5 million people and deeply feared the consequent erosion of their power. In Lebanon, the Christian militants were supported by the majority of their own faith, who for years had lived peacefully alongside Muslim neighbours. The militant leaders feared that any change, however slight, to the constitutional arrangements that some 35 years ago gave the Christians a permanent administrative edge over their Muslim fellow countrymen would signal the start of a slide towards a Muslim state. In preference to this, the most militant would chop this small country into two even smaller parts. True, no single leader has yet said publicly that partition is his aim. On the contrary, they had all said that it was not. But the pattern of fighting was plainly directed at the consolidation and, within Beirut, the expansion of Christian-held territory. Those Maronite extremists whose target appeared to be partition must believe that a minuscule Christian state perched between Mount Lebanon and the Mediterranean could manage on its own. But would the foreign banks, companies and tourists that had provided Lebanon's gold share this optimism? Many of them had left for good. Those who might be enticed to stay or to return were even less likely to respond if they were invited to a Christian enclave surrounded by a growling Arab world.

On 10 November 1977, Syrian peace-keeping troops and tanks entered Beirut proper, marking an effective end to the unrestrained and suicidal violence of a civil war. The war in the south was punctuated by a major Israeli invasion in March 1978, but never stopped and sporadic but bloody fighting shattered the relative calm in Beirut.

The central issue of Lebanese politics was how to re-establish the authority of the Lebanese Government, challenged by Syria,

Israel and the more than 40 armed bands and sectarian-based private militias that wielded power in the country. Political dialogue was almost non-existent, and partition between Christian and Muslim enclaves had become a deepening reality. Beirut, once a great and vibrant city, suffered from increasing crime — robbery, extortion, smuggling, and narcotics-trafficking. Murder and kidnapping occurred on a daily basis; protection rackets flourished. A leading Lebanese commentator described the country as a republic of petty kingdoms. Lebanon, the paradise of Middle East, had turned hell. The confessional system of politics was at stake.

On the Christian side, the dominant factions were the Phalange and the National Liberal Party (NLP) who were joined in a Lebanese Front led by a former President Camille Chamoun. The Phalangists, the larger of the two parties, had become a state within a state, maintaining cooperatives, health clinics, a bus service, a radio station, and a party security police in addition to a militia of some 25,000 men including 10,000 'regulars' . The Phalange seemed determined to win control of the Christian heartland in the northern mountains. Its leader Pierre Gemayel argues that 'there are two peoples and two lands (in Lebanon) and anyone who tries to ignore this fact is deluding himself.' The NLP's Dory Chamoun, the former President's son, declares that 'ideally we want a state based on a Christian democracy though not based on religious patterns.' Allied to Chamoun was the Front for the Preservation of the South, which blamed southern conditions on Palestinians. Some Shii Muslim leaders had also moved towards cooperation with the Christian right.

The Lebanese Front was not politically unified and fewer than 10 percent of Lebanon's Maronite Christian community were said to be active Front supporters. Its coercive tactics had alienated many Catholic and orthodox sects. The Franjishs, a Pro-Syrian Maronite clan headed by former President Suleiman Franjieh, had accused the Phalange of attempting to eliminate all other Christian movements, of working towards partition, and of imposing its will through 'terror, money and imported ideas.' They rejected the Maronite alliance with Israel, referred to Phalangists and National Liberals as 'treacherous agents of Zionist enemy,' and favoured reconciliation with the Muslim community.

Meanwhile, the Lebanese army was weak and fragmented. The polarization of political forces had rendered the Lebanese army into a military arm of the Christian authorities. Historically Christians took important positions in the Lebanese army. It was utilised by Christian Presidents in previous confrontations with Palestinian guerrillas. In November 1975, rightist Christian pressure prevailed on moderate Muslim Premier Rashid Karamy to commit the army to quell the escalating conflict between the regulars and the Palestinian guerrillas. This time, sectarian loyalties proved overwhelming. When it was finally committed to the conflict in the winter of 1976 the Lebanese army disintegrated. Christians threw in their lot with Christian units and continued to call themselves the Lebanese army. The army command at Yarze near Beirut remained Christian. Muslims deserted en masse and some ultimately formed a new fedayeen-sponsored 'Lebanese Arab Army'. Many from both sides merely went home and tried to sit out the war.

The country was now being maintained by the Arab Deterrent Forces 9 (ADF) but they cannot be expected to remain forever. Nor could the ADF pacify the remaining area of violent conflict in the extreme south.

As for the Israelis, they would only recognise the Lebanese army which was being rebuilt. To the Muslims, Palestinians and Syrians, however, an exclusive Christian unit would not be acceptable. It would merely serve as an adjunct to the southern Christian militia.

Meanwhile, the United Nations took action in March 1978 when it created the United Nations Interim Force in Lebanon (UNIFIL) for the purpose of 'restoring international peace and security' and assisting in the returning of effective authority. But the UNIFIL was confined to patrols south of the Litani River, leaving the PLO and other related factions free to function at will. Down the south Lebanese villages across what was once the country's quietest border with Israel, Metualla was held by a Christian soldier Major Sa'ad Haddad, commander of the Christian forces, with the help of the Israelis. Major Haddad's ragtag Free Lebanese Force had its own clinics all along the barbed wire and sandbagged border, with Israeli doctors and Lebanese nurses working side by side tending the sick and wounded, brave enough to cross over.

It was this area that the UNIFIL found difficult to control and Major Haddad was accusing the United Nations forces of siding the Palestinians.

The increased tempo of fighting in the south and elsewhere had devastated the economy. Roads to farm and market were blocked by the militia. Ships avoided Beirut after the battles, and 95 percent of Beirut's industry was shut down because of the lack of security in the capital and the scarcity of materials. So far, only one half of the 700,000 emigrants who left during the war had returned. In early 1978 over one million Lebanese were reportedly in need of welfare, while more than 125,000 were homeless. Several hundred thousand Lebanese and Palestinians temporarily lost their homes during the Israeli invasion, creating a difficult situation in Beirut, where refugees broke into vacant apartments or huddled in makeshift shelters. By October 1978 virtually all primary and secondary schools in Lebanon had closed.

Israel, which views herself as the protector of Lebanon's Christian community, seemed to have two aims in Lebanon: to prevent Syrian control of the country and to thwart Palestinian domination of the south. Israel has been a major source of arms for the Christian militias and she has provided training for them. Estimates of Israeli advisers with the militias in east Beirut range from 100 to 1,500. In July Israeli officials warned the Syrians that Israel would not permit the annihilation of the Christians, underlying the warning by sending fighter planes over Beirut.

Syria wanted a strong centralised Government in Lebanon, but one that was amenable to considerable influence from Damascus. The Syrians undoubtedly feared the Christians' deepening ties with Israel, and they had urged the government to discourage dissident army officials who had openly cooperated with Israel in the south. The official Syrian daily *Tishrin* had accused the right of preparing to declare a Free Republic of Lebanon, whose existence would be guaranteed by a 20-year defence treaty with Israel. As a patron of PLO, Syria also wanted to preserve the Palestinian resistance in Lebanon, under strict Syrian control.

No lasting peace in Lebanon seems possible without an overall Arab–Israeli settlement, including a solution to the

Palestinian problem. The Lebanese Front demanded Palestinian withdrawal from the south before it would discuss a settlement with the Syrians and the other Lebanese factions. Camille Chamoun has stated that there could be 'no political solution before the evacuation of all armed forces without exception from Lebanon.'

Clearly the old warlords had learned little from the years of bloodshed and destruction. The left is too weak to effect a solution on its own, while the right, supported by Israel, was in no mood to compromise.

Many of Lebanon's problems would be simplified if its inhabitants could view themselves as citizens of a country rather than members of a clan or community. For obvious reasons, the Palestinians of Lebanon were unable to do so. Muslim Lebanese, while certainly regarding themselves as citizens of Lebanon, still have strong community ties but it was the Maronite Christians above all who, to most observers, seemed enmeshed in a mass of family, clan and religious loyalties that blinded them to state loyalty. Such a view, however, ignores the Maronite historical memory which recalled the massacre of Maronites in 1860 during which about 18,000 lives were lost. Maronites view the recent Syrian actions as a threat to their very survival. They regard themselves as rightful masters of a country they had dominated since independence from France in 1943. They see themselves as intellectually and culturally superior to their Muslim compatriots and above all, they fear to live under any Muslim-dominated Lebanese government which may emerge. 'What', the Maronites ask, 'would be our place in an Arab Lebanon with Islam as the state religion?'

The tragedy for Lebanon is that it is now probably too late for its people to rediscover the many bonds which could unite them. What compounds the tragedy is that Lebanon's future depends to a great extent on the operation of factors and factions outside its control. It is only strong international pressures exerted on all parties to the dispute which could now bring about any movement towards a negotiated compromise.

Lebanon, a country of heavenly pleasure, has turned into a miserable hell.

12

The Uphill Task at Jakarta

Singapore was without an Ambassador in Jakarta for nearly nine months after His Excellency, the late P. S. Raman, suffered a heart attack. Some months earlier the Singapore Embassy was raided by anti-Singapore elements following the hanging of two Indonesian marines in 1967. The two Indonesian marines were charged with murder for having thrown bombs into MacDonald House killing three persons and they received the death sentence. They appealed to the Privy Council but the appeal was rejected. Before the hanging, President Suharto appealed to Singapore not to hang the two marines but his appeal was unsuccessful. When the two were hanged, the Indonesians asked for their bodies to be returned. When the bodies were returned to Jakarta, the rioters raided the Singapore Embassy burning the Singapore flag. Our Ambassador later had a heart attack. He returned to Singapore and took a long rest.

When Adam Malik met S. Rajaratnam one day at the Cameron Highlands at an Asean meeting sometime in 1970, he asked when Singapore would send an Ambassador to Indonesia since there had been no Ambassador for so many months. Raja replied that he could not get a Malay to be the Ambassador thinking that it would not be proper to send a Chinese. Adam Malik replied: 'Why is it necessary to be a Malay? Send anyone even if he is a Chinese.' That remark sent Raja's mind racing. Who should he send? He finally thought of me. I was then in Cairo; having served for two years I had some experience in diplomacy.

So he wrote to me on 12 January 1970, and among other things, he mentioned that the Ambassadorship in Indonesia had been vacant for some months. This together with Kuala Lumpur, he said, was diplomatically one of our most important posts. It would require an Ambassador with considerable political skill, tact and perception and he had been cracking his brains for sometime over the matter. He added: 'I am not indulging in flattery when I say that you are the Ambassador whom I can really trust to handle this very delicate and important assignment. I had postponed making a final decision on this because I was reluctant to saddle you with another difficult assignment. I have since discussed the matter with the Cabinet and the agreement is that you are the man to be trusted with the post in Jakarta.'

This letter came as a big surprise to me, for I had just finished my assignment in Cairo and was about to return to Singapore. The Cairo assignment was by no means an easy one, and I was looking forward to meeting my constituents who had missed me for two years. Elections were around the corner and I had to be with them. I wrote to Raja turning down the offer and explained that as a politician, I could not afford to be away from the ground for too long. The reply was a coded cable which I received on 2 February 1970, stating that 'Cabinet decision about your reposting is firm. Have taken note of your observations in your letter and will explain later.'

A letter from Raja followed stating that my anxiety in regard to prospects in my constituency was unfounded. Raja said: 'I agree with you that personal contact with your voters is necessary but I think our voters are sufficiently sophisticated these days to know that you have been selected by the Government to perform duties in Indonesia which are vital to the welfare of Singapore. In any case, you will come back to your constituency well in advance of the time for the next elections. Anyway, we can discuss this fully when you return to Singapore prior to taking up your appointment in Jakarta.' My appointment was meant for one and a half years. It lasted four and a half years and it was only after I had asked to be sent home was I allowed to conclude my assignment.

My first reaction to my Jakarta assignment was that I would be going to a city where one had to chase away the flies in restaurants with both hands, and cockroaches could be found inside the bottle of tomato ketchup. I had the experience of staying in Hotel Nusantara, the then biggest hotel in Jakarta when I was there in 1960 arranging for the Prime Minister's first visit. My room leaked at midnight and the whole room was raining and I had to sleep outside on the verandah. When the Indonesian Information Officer in Singapore, one Mr Sujono, came to see me in the morning, he found me sleeping outside and was surprised. He asked: 'Why do you sleep outside, is it too hot inside?' My reply was: 'It is raining inside.' He laughed and said he would find out what had happened. Half an hour later, he came back and said: 'The pipe upstairs burst. This happens once in twenty years.' He moved me to another better room. This story and my general impression of Jakarta came back to me and, frankly speaking, I was not too keen to go. But interest of the nation came before self-interest. I accepted the offer.

Whilst in Cairo, I did my spade work. I contacted General Mokoginta, the then Indonesian Ambassador to Egypt, a friend of mine, and told him of my assignment to his country and he was delighted. He immediately wrote back to Jakarta and informed his colleagues, Ali Murtopo and Alamsjah and told them what sort of person I was and asked them to assist me. I had got my introduction made to two important persons in the Indonesian Cabinet before my arrival. Mokoginta was close to me in Cairo and knew very much that I had an Asean outlook and understood Indonesia. He recommended that I should read some books on Indonesia for I knew the country only through my contacts as a journalist when I attended the Bandung Conference, and when I went to pave the way for the Prime Minister's visit, as Parliamentary Secretary to the Ministry of Culture.

Sometime in June 1970, I arrived in Jakarta. It coincided with the death of Sukarno and the date of presentation was delayed for a week because the country was mourning. There had been great prominence in all newspapers and television given to Sukarno's death. It was interesting to note the editorial in the *Indonesia Raya* on 23 June 1970 entitled 'Lessons from Sukarno' written by Mochtar Lubis, which warned that Sukarno had failed because he did not care for the law and he considered himself as above the law. Mochtar Lubis also warned that Sukarno had allowed others to use his name in various kinds of dealings including business. The editorial hoped that President Suharto would take heed of this lesson and should not allow his private assistants to interfere with the affairs of the various departments and put an end to corruption.

Sukarno's death brought my mind back to 1960 when I met him at the Istana. I remember when I accompanied Prime Minister Lee Kuan Yew and his delegation to see Sukarno at Istana Negara, he made us wait for fifteen minutes. Then the young and handsome Sukarno, smartly dressed in bush jacket and a topi, holding some sort of walking stick in his right arm, came out from the room and greeted us flamboyantly. He was serious and brief when speaking to Lee Kuan Yew. They spoke in Bahasa for about twenty minutes, then he got up, shook our hands and walked back to the room without observing even the courtesy of sending us to the door.

My impression of Sukarno from this experience therefore was that he was arrogant, treating us as delegates from a small country paying him a tribute. The preparations for the visit, I must say, were well organised.

That was the only occasion that I met him face to face. And now he was gone, ending an 18-year era — an era of slogans and speeches.

Jakarta was a different city from the one I had known in the 1960s. The city now had skyscrapers, the roads were wide, and there were many posh hotels with air-conditioned facilities. There were grand Chinese restaurants with central air-conditioning and I need not chase away flies with my bare hands. I put up at 53 Imam Bondjol, a stone's throw from Hotel Indonesia — the grandest hotel then in Indonesia.

On 2 July at 8.45 a.m., the Acting Chief Protocol Officer accompanied by the ADC to the President came to my residence. We had a chat and when the time was ready, as confirmed through walkie-talkie, we proceeded to the Palace accompanied by five members of my staff with diplomatic status. When I arrived at the Palace, the Army Band played the Majulah Singapura while I inspected the guard of honour. I waited for less than a minute before I was called to the Presidential Hall. President Suharto, as usual, was with a smile. He stood in front of me, flanked by the Foreign Minister Adam Malik, his State

Secretary Alamsjah and top Ministry officials and ADC. The press and television men were around. After delivering the letter of credence, I stepped back and delivered my speech in Bahasa Indonesia. This took everyone by surprise. President Suharto listened attentively and watched me with his piercing eyes all the time, perhaps trying to fathom my soul. Whenever I lifted my eyes to look at him, his eyes were fixed on me.

After my speech, he delivered his speech in a dim and soft voice, which could hardly be heard ten yards away. He started his speech by saying that with my long years of experience as a journalist I would be able to understand the Indonesian people, their way of life, their aspirations and problems. He said it would be a great help in achieving my aim of promoting better understanding and cooperation between the two countries. He stressed the importance of cooperation among Asean countries in the field of economic and cultural exchange. He said that there were bound to be differences between Singapore and Indonesia in the field of economic development because of the leftovers from the days before Independence. He said it was quite natural for individual countries to adopt economic measures which were necessary and suitable to the national interests of the respective countries. Whatever measures that might have been taken by Indonesia would be taken purely with a view to promoting the national economic interests.

President Suharto then praised Singapore for its achievements in economic development. He said: 'You have succeeded in raising your status as the prominent country in this region in both industry and social services and in raising the standard of living of your people.' He stressed that Indonesia and Singapore should work together to promote bigger projects for mutual benefit.

After his speech, President Suharto introduced me to the Foreign Minister, his State Secretary Alamsjah and his Presidential staff, and I in turn introduced my staff to the President.

Suharto was in a happy and relaxed mood. We spoke in Bahasa. Adam Malik said to the President: 'We have been old friends for 20 years.' I replied: 'But you still look young.' Adam Malik replied: 'Yes, young only at heart.' And we had a good laugh. Suharto then mentioned the Pulau Batam project and he said he was glad that there would be cooperation between Singapore and Indonesia to make the project a success.

The author presenting credentials to President Suharto at the Istana Negara

President Suharto, Adam Malik, the former Foreign Minister and the author toasting at Istana Negara after the ceremony of the presentation of credentials

President Suharto talked about life in general in Indonesia. He said in many parts of Indonesia, people could live easily from the soil and river. He said some people just put their hooks into the river and got their fishes within minutes. Then he added, 'That is why they get lazy.'

He then tried to elaborate on his speech about the economic measures taken by Indonesia for national interests. He said for instance when Indonesia started the processing of rubber and other products, this should not be misunderstood. This was not meant to destroy the economic interests of other countries. He said that it was quite natural for an independent country to look after its own national economic interests and that it was quite natural for Indonesia to wish to have its own processing for its own products. Similarly, Singapore might take certain measures which would be in the interest of Singapore. But he emphasised that we should cooperate in projects which would be of mutual benefit to the two countries.

I took the opportunity to tell the President in front of Adam Malik of my Prime Minister's proposal to visit Indonesia and he seemed quite pleased. Although he mentioned that the Prime Minister could come any time, he said that he would be busy preparing for National Day and that he would be visiting Europe early September. The best time would be towards the end of the year. Since it was the first time I met the President, I thought it was not an appropriate time to discuss the matter further.

Before I bade farewell to the President, he asked me whether I played golf. I said I was just starting to learn. I also told him that I saw him about two days ago when he was about to start his golf at Rawamangun and he chipped in, 'Yes, I also saw you and I thought it must be the new Ambassador of Singapore.' Then he said, 'One of these days we must play together.'

I left the Palace after inspecting the guard of honour and after the Indonesian national anthem was played. We had a little celebration with champagne and cakes with the Indonesian officials and the embassy staff and some Singaporeans whom we knew.

I learnt after the ceremony from my First Secretary, Yap Eu Win, that the State Secretary to the President, Alamsjah, had told him, 'Your Ambassador has struck the right chord. It was good that he spoke in Bahasa.' Hugh Mabbet, correspondent of the Straits Times, also told me at the party in my residence that Hafas, Editor-in-Chief of *Nusantara*, the newspaper which had not been too friendly to Singapore, also said to him, 'Oh, we are friends of Singapore and we should cooperate.' The general response was good and all seemed to augur well for the future relationship between Singapore and Indonesia.

Incidentally, the day I presented credentials was Thursday, 2 July. Normally the President receives Ambassadors only on Saturdays. Several colleagues of mine including the Ambassador of the United States, Frank Galbraith, commented, when I told him that I would be presenting credentials on Thursday, that it was unusual for the President to receive credentials other than on Saturdays. Mr Galbraith said, 'It is a good omen.'

The first thing I did was to call on leading journalists in Indonesia. Having been a journalist myself, I realised that journalists were most in touch with society and they generally knew the people at the top as well as the bottom. Moreover, they were all my journalistic friends. I met Mochtar Lubis of *Indonesia Raya*, Dr Hafas of *Nusantara*, Rosihan Anwar of *Pedoman* and B. M. Diah of *Merdeka*. Apart from *Merdeka*, the other three newspapers were banned by Sukarno. They were revived only after 1966.

It was unusual for an Ambassador to call on journalists. But I did it in order to better understand Indonesian society and to seek their cooperation on future publicity matters.

I met Mochtar Lubis in Singapore after his release from prison when he went to see Othman Wok. Mochtar Lubis was the first person to tell me about the mystery of the Javanese mind. Mochtar said: 'As a Sumatran, I find it difficult to understand the Javanese mind. The Javanese generally believe that their ruler is sent from heaven to lead them and that they will never fail. God has given the leader the power. Sukarno had bluffed the people for 17 years and yet the Javanese still worship him after his death. When his power was taken away by force, the Javanese said that God had taken away his power.' Mochtar Lubis said Suharto still believed in mystic power.

Mochtar told me that Sudjono Humardhani had gone to Bali to look for Gadja Mada's mask and had placed it at the

Palace for one thousand days. He was smiling away in disbelief when he told me the strange stories. I made up my mind to study Javanese mysticism.

He said Suharto had to act quickly against corruption. According to Mochtar Lubis the students had given Suharto until 15 July 1970 to declare his stand on the recommendation of the Four-men Commission. The four-men commission was led by Dr Hatta to look into the problem of corruption in Indonesia. It was appointed by Suharto.

Dr Hafas, Editor-in-Chief, had been writing editorials of late advocating that the Government should do something to curtail the economic monopoly of non-Bumiputra (he did not want to be branded as anti-Chinese so he used the word non-Bumiputra, meaning those who are not of Indonesian origin). In an editorial he claimed that the non-Bumiputra was holding 70 percent of the money in circulation in Indonesia and that this grip on the Indonesian economy should be got rid off.

I met Dr Hafas in 1957 in Australia when we were members of the Asian Journalist Team touring Australia. He was then a very young editor, stout and handsome and I remember he punched Michael Goh, a Singapore reporter, in the bathroom because the latter was impolite to him. Dr Hafas who had grown much older seemed to have good relations with me and came to visit me at my office quite often.

Commenting on Indonesia's confrontation against Malaysia, Dr Hafas said: 'You know as well as I do that it was all Sukarno's bluff. Indonesia's gun boats had been rusty and idling. The aircraft were grounded. Indonesia was and is not in a position to confront anybody. The confrontation was merely a PKI excuse to get the communist youth, Permuda Rakyat, trained militarily so that they could use the arms smuggled from Peking to overthrow the Generals.'

Rosihan Anwar said Suharto had a 'minute mind' which looked into details. He could remember figures such as how much money should be spent in which province. He got the impression that Suharto had not forgotten the humiliation as a result of the hanging of the two marines by the Singapore Government.

Diah was formerly Ambassador to Czechoslovakia, Hungary and Thailand. His last appointment was Minister for Information until 1968. The Diah family had started a 1.5 billion Rupiah 250-room hotel in Jakarta called the Ambassador Hotel. Diah offered me the services of his paper to publicise Singapore and bring about better relations between Singapore and Indonesia.

When I called on the ministers and officials, they looked at me with curiosity and they were conscious that I was a Chinese. They did not seem very friendly.

General Alamsjah, the State Secretary to the President, was the first person who started arranging for Premier Lee's visit. When I met him in late July 1970, he told me that Adam Malik had asked him to approach the President about Lee Kuan Yew's visit to Indonesia. Alamsjah told me that he had heard from his Cairo Ambassador Mokoginta about me and that he should treat me as a Singaporean and not a Chinese. He said he was impressed with my speech in Bahasa and so too were the Ministers and the generals.

Alamsjah was short and stout with a rounded face. He was consciously aware of his power and influence. He was one of the organizers of the student demonstration against Sukarno which brought about the downfall of Sukarno. Being State Secretary to the President, he was close to the centre of power. He told me that although Suharto's schedule might be tight in August, he thought it could be arranged between 20 August and 25 August 1970. He would speak to the President and would let me know. He suggested that the Prime Minister stay two days in Jakarta and then move on to Lake Toba in Sumatra. The Prime Minister could then return to Singapore through Medan.

Alamsjah said he had often advised the President to forget the past and to cooperate with Singapore. Alamsjah was the first Indonesian official to touch on the hanging of the two marines, and he said he tried to persuade the President to let bygones be bygones. As he spoke to me quite frankly, I also explained to him quite bluntly that owing to Sukarno's expansionist policy such as sending the two marines to subvert Singapore, it was quite natural for Singaporeans to get the impression that Indonesia had ambitions on Singapore.

He replied, 'Why should Indonesia want to grab Singapore? We are too big and too rich. We need only

Singapore's services just as China needs Hongkong's services. Singapore has the facilities, we can make good use of these for mutual benefit.'

On 29th July, when I was called to Adam Malik's office I thought that I would be asked to discuss details of the Prime Minister's visit. Instead, he asked me whether I had received any definite news from Alamsjah whom I met last week. He told me that the President had agreed in principle on the Prime Minister's visit but had not given a definite date. He said Alamsjah had rung up his Acting Chief Protocol Officer asking him to prepare tentatively to receive the Prime Minister between the 20th and 25th August 1970.

One reason for the delay, according to Malik, was that President Suharto had just rejected Lon Nol's proposal to visit Indonesia and he felt rather awkward that having rejected Lon Nol, he would now welcome Lee Kuan Yew. Lon Nol wanted to come to Indonesia after visiting Bangkok, but Suharto had been advised not to allow Lon Nol's visit before the Lusaka Conference in order not to prejudice Indonesia's neutral stand. My First Secretary heard that Suharto had been invited to open a sugar factory sponsored by the Polish Government in Maluku between 20th and 25th August 1970.

Alamsjah paid a surprise visit to Singapore and met with his Ambassador General Sunarso to discuss the Prime Minister's visit. After his return from Singapore one would have expected something to move, but nothing happened. Something had gone wrong somewhere. With less than ten days to go before the proposed date for the Prime Minister's visit, I had yet to receive any definite official confirmation as to whether the trip was on or off. I did not hear from Alamsjah again. He was later transferred as Ambassador to the Netherlands. Alamsjah made a comeback to politics after his return from the Netherlands. In 1978, he was appointed Minister of Religion, and after the Presidential election in 1983, he was appointed Minister of State in charge of five ministries. In Indonesia, a Minister of State is higher in status than a Cabinet Minister. When I met Adam Malik at our National Day celebration, he told me that the visit might have to be postponed to next year. He said: 'You are right, there are obstacles in the way.' He hinted to me that the Aspri (personal assistants to the President) were against the visit.

On 19th August 1970, I met Adam Malik at a party and he told me that the President had the impression that the idea of the Prime Minister's visit was that of General Sunarso and that he had to speak to his military leaders. It was an open secret in military circles that Sunarso was not in the good books of Ali Murtopo, head of the OPSUS and Chief Personal Assistant on political matters attached to the President. OPSUS (Operasi Kursus) was an organisation similar to America's CIA, collecting information about people.

I understand that it was Ali Murtopo who was misled into believing that Singapore businessmen could pressurise the Singapore Cabinet to reprieve the two marines. I also understand that Ali Murtopo's men had spread the warning before the hanging that if the two marines were hanged, they would have no more business from Indonesia and it was to their good to pressurise Singapore into giving way. Somehow the OPSUS men were given the impression that Singapore would give way and so Ali Murtopo had advised Suharto to write the appeal. Ali Murtopo and Suharto therefore felt humiliated when the two marines were hanged in Changi Prison.

On 23rd March 1971 when I was playing golf with Brig. Sudjono Humardhani, Economic Adviser to the President, he told me that he would like to convey a personal message from the President to Prime Minister Lee Kuan Yew. He asked whether I could arrange for him to see Lee Kuan Yew. He did not tell me what the message was about. It could be just to size up Lee Kuan Yew to see what sort of a person he was. Javanese leaders like Humardhani believed that a leader like Lee Kuan Yew must possess certain powers to make Singapore so dynamic and progressive. Humardhani was then the lobby man for Japan and Suharto often sent him to contact Sato or Fukuda and others before Suharto actually saw them. He was leaving end of the month to see Prime Minister Sato on behalf of the President and would probably arrive at Singapore on 13th April 1971. Humardhani preferred to convey the message personally to the Prime Minister because he was not on good terms with Ambassador Sunarso.

I made arrangements for Humardhani to see the Prime Minister on 13th April 1971. Sotopo Yananto went ahead to Singapore to wait for his arrival. I got Prof Yeoh Ghim Seng

Author shaking hands with Brig. Sudjono Humardhani, Economic Adviser to the President Suharto

and Sim Kee Boon who knew the General well to play golf with him. Col Mallal went back to Singapore specially to finalise arrangements. He went to the hotel to pick up the General and sent him to City Hall where the Prime Minister was working.

When he went to the hotel, he found Humardhani meditating. He was not to be disturbed. When he entered the Prime Minister's office, Col Mallal saw him kissing the baton which he was holding. For a few minutes, he was dazed and was mumbling. Then he was himself again and they spoke for 45 minutes.

I was at the airport to receive Humardhani when he returned to Indonesia on 16th April. The first thing he said when he met me was: 'I met your Prime Minister for 45 minutes. We had a very frank and open discussion on matters of common interest and on world affairs generally.' He was very much impressed by the Prime Minister's frankness and hospitality. He said he was forewarned that our Prime Minister was tough, snobbish and arrogant. But instead, he found a soft-spoken, humble and frank Prime Minister. I heard that Humardhani being a chain smoker was a little nervous because he refrained from smoking for 45 minutes. The Prime Minister is allergic to smoke and prefers that his guests do not smoke in his presence.

Humardhani promised that he would do his utmost to bring 'the two leaders', meaning Lee Kuan Yew and Suharto, closer together. He said his purpose in seeing the Prime Minister was to convey Suharto's message to invite him to Indonesia after the opening of the Parliament.

I had crossed the second hurdle and the Aspri were now with me. I am sure Humardhani must have told Ali Murtopo, his close colleague, about his trip to Singapore.

Soon after the return of Humardhani from Singapore, I called on Ali Murtopo, Indonesia's strong man, the most feared of all generals, who was in the inner circle of Suharto's regime. He was the strongest Aspri in charge of political affairs and was a close colleague of Humardhani. I got to see him through Sutopo Yananto, for the Foreign Ministry did not think it was necessary for me to pay him a courtesy call because he was not a Minister. Although he was a most talked-about personality he seldom appeared in public except when President Suharto received Heads of State at the airport. On several occasions when he appeared in public, I found that most of the Ministers and other generals were rather reluctant to go near him. Because of his shrewdness and ruthlessness, the Chinese circles in Indonesia referred to him as 'Tsao Tsao' the shrewdest and most powerful personality in the three kingdoms in Chinese history. Unlike many other generals, he did not mix socially, did not drink and never attended nightclubs. He was one of those rare ones who was serious in his work.

My intention of seeing him was to try to size him up and I thought it would be useful to get to know people in the inner circle. I met him in the morning at his home during breakfast time. As he came out to see me in his military uniform, several Chinese Cukongs were waiting for him at the other corner of the sitting room. The house buzzed with activity.

When we started our conversation he whisked away Sutopo Yananto and asked Col Ramli, who was Ambassador Sunarso's deputy in Singapore, to join in the conversation. Col Ramli explained that he just happened to be there. Ali Murtopo said he knew about my assignment before my arrival from Sim Kee Boon and General Mokoginta, who was then Ambassador in Cairo. He told me that he wanted to be frank with me like a brother since I knew Indonesia well. He then went about trying to convince me that it was he who had been advocating an independent Singapore whereas most of the Asian leaders were against the idea. He claimed that in his discussions with Tengku Abdul Rahman, the former Foreign Ministers of Japan and the Philippines, Chiang Ching Kuo, son of Chiang Kai Shek of Taiwan and Chou En-lai of China, he found that they were all against the existence of an independent Singapore for different reasons. He said most of these people were still alive and the facts could be checked.

Ali Murtopo said that Sukarno was against Singapore's independence because of the Peking-Jakarta axis. He revealed to me that Sukarno had in fact set up a special task-force in readiness to invade Singapore. They had separate units for the Army, Navy, Air Force and even a missile section. When the debate was on whether or not to occupy Singapore, he claimed that he was against the idea. He said he told the group of generals that if they wanted to invade Singapore, he would guarantee it could be done in 24 hours. He said because he was against the strategy of occupying he had antagonised many people. Soon after President Suharto took over, he recommended that the special unit for capturing Singapore be disbanded. The generals in charge of the separate units were later posted to other assignments; one of them was then the commander-in-chief of Menado, another was posted as Ambassador. (I think he was referring to General Hartono, who died in Jakarta when recalled as Ambassador to North Korea. He was the one who openly advocated the invasion of Singapore when the two marines were hanged.)

Ali Murtopo took some pains in trying to explain his strategy of wanting Singapore to survive. He gave his reasons as follows: China is a major power comprising a population of 900 million and has an expansionist policy. She would always use overseas Chinese as agents of subversion. Taiwan is also a force to be reckoned with so long as she is still a member of the United Nations and one of the founders of the organisation. (At that time Taiwan was still representing China at the United Nations.) Peking and Taipeh were forever competing for the loyalty of the overseas Chinese. Without an independent Singapore, the overseas Chinese throughout the world, particularly those in South-East Asia, would forever be divided in their loyalty between pro-Peking and pro-Taipeh, which caused instability not only among the overseas Chinese themselves but in the country where they resided. The success of the Chinese in forming a nation outside China and Taiwan with the cooperation of other non-Chinese races was a useful experiment which would have great bearing on the psychology of overseas Chinese. If Singapore succeeded in turning a multiracial society which was 80 percent Chinese into a nation with its people loyal to Singapore, it would be an eye-opener to other overseas Chinese that there was an alternative to them apart from having to choose between loyalty to Peking and to Taipeh. This would encourage overseas Chinese in this region to be loyal to their country of domicile. All this would mean stability for the whole region.

That was why Ali Murtopo said it hurt him very much when Singapore hanged the two marines despite President Suharto's personal appeal. He said he had advised 'Pak Harto' to make the appeal because he was given to understand that the appeal would carry weight. (I looked at Col Ramli and he looked rather embarrassed.) Ali Murtopo said that he could show me a pile of signatures which he had received from Singaporeans comprising leaders of all walks of life supporting the reprieve of the two marines. Without these signatures, he said he would not have advised President Suharto to make the appeal. When the hanging took place, he felt very sad because he became a laughing stock to many of those who advocated invading Singapore. They had proved that his strategy for an independent Singapore was a mistake.

Ali Murtopo said Suharto had not forgotten the humiliation. It would take some time for the wound to heal. He claimed that he had been pacifying the President and advising him to let bygones be bygones for he still believed in the wisdom of his strategy. He emphasised that it would not be too difficult to occupy Singapore but that would be disastrous to Indonesia and to the region and the world as a whole in terms of stability. The overseas Chinese would have no alternative but to cling permanently to their traditional loyalty of pro-Peking or pro-Taipeh. He said that Suharto was now in a better mood in that there was better understanding. Soon after the general elections, arrangements would be made for Prime Minister Lee Kuan Yew to visit Indonesia and he hoped that all would augur for the good relationship. We were conversing in Bahasa all the while.

I explained to him the rising spirit of Singapore nationalism particularly among the younger generation and that they have been taught to be loyal to Singapore and not to China or Taiwan. The curriculum and textbooks of Chinese schools were changed long ago and that when the older generation passed away there would be less and less and in fact virtually very little connection between the Chinese in Singapore and those in China or Taiwan. I explained to him that it was also our deliberate policy to build a multi-racial nation and that we were aware of the role we had to play in the region as an independent nation practising a democratic system and not receiving orders from any foreign country. I assured him that the experiment of Singapore's nation-building would be a success.

Ali Murtopo in fact told me that if Singapore were occupied

at that time it was intended to make Tjokropranolo, who was then the Security Chief to the President, Governor of Singapore.

Before we parted, Ali Murtopo said: 'We are brothers and you can come and see me any time you like.'

After the 1983 general elections, Ali Murtopo, who was the Minister for Information, dropped out of the Cabinet.

At the beginning, it was only Adam Malik, Sultan Hamengku and then Alamsjah who were talking favourably about Singapore. Now, we had Humardhani and Ali Murtopo on our side as well.

My relationship with the Aspri became closer and closer. I could go to Humardhani's home almost in slippers and without warning.

But when the general elections were over in July 1971, nothing happened to the Prime Minister's visit. What could be the obstacle? My relations with Suharto's inner circle were good and I became rather popular among the Generals and Ministers. What could the snag be? I was asking myself the question over and over again. One day in 1972 when I returned to Singapore and met Dr Goh Keng Swee at his office for a chat, he told me frankly: 'KC, I think you have made your point. It is no use. They will not invite the Prime Minister to visit Indonesia. You better come back.' I said to him: 'No, I will not give up. I believe they will do something quite soon.'

Sometime in April 1971, I had a game of golf with General Sumitro, the Deputy Commander of KOPKAMTIB (the Internal Security Department) who was known to be the most powerful military leader in the Suharto regime. Although General Panggabean was the Commander of Kopkamtib, Sumitro was in fact the real power with direct access to Suharto in matters of national security as well as foreign policy. He had just completed an unofficial tour of Pacific countries including Singapore as personal envoy of President Suharto with a view to formulating a policy on Indonesia's strategy in the region. He was also responsible for the clamp-down on the movement of diplomats in Indonesia following the publicised, alleged Russian subversive activities in Central Java. Persons close to General Sumitro told me that although he had a ready smile he was known as the 'thunder'. When his temper flared, he would even throw paper weights at his opponent. He was also known as Bima, the Javanese hero who had a hot temper and would speak out his mind.

Sumitro was unhappy that he could not meet Prime Minister Lee Kuan Yew when he visited Singapore. He only spoke to Dr Goh Keng Swee and Wong Lin Ken, the then Minister for Home Affairs. During a golf game, he hinted to me that Lee Kuan Yew was quite 'unapproachable and sombong'. He said he tried to make an appointment during his trip to Singapore but failed. He knew that I had arranged for Humardhani to see the Prime Minister. It struck me that Sumitro could be the obstacle to the Prime Minister's visit. As Hankam's (Defence Ministry) representative he could have objected to the Prime Minister's visit. I immediately replied: 'Lee Kuan Yew is not sombong. Nobody on the Singapore side knew that you wanted to see him.' 'Is that true?' he asked. 'Could you arrange for me to see the Prime Minister, for I have something which President Suharto wants to clarify with him.' I told him that I could easily arrange for the meeting. I said: 'Just give me a date and I shall arrange for the meeting.' Then he gave a date in early April 1972, and told me not to inform Ambassador Sunarso.

'Keep it a secret and I will teach that person a lesson,' he added. I flew back to see the Prime Minister and got a date for Sumitro. And on that date, I flew back to Singapore to wait for his arrival. General Sumitro arrived with his assistant Sugent Djared, a leading member of the Bakin (Intelligence Department) who followed Sumitro as political adviser when he visited foreign countries and was his close confidant. I took them from the airport straight to the Istana, and was present when the Prime Minister met both of them.

After the introduction, Sumitro conveyed greetings from President Suharto and went straight to the point. He explained that he was sent by President Suharto to clear up from Prime Minister Lee Kuan Yew personally certain doubts about Singapore's stand on certain problems. He said the purpose was to bring about closer relations between Asean countries and that he would like to see the development of a personal friendship between Prime Minister Lee and President Suharto.

Sumitro explained that Suharto fought very hard against the late President Sukarno in order to establish relations with Malaysia including Singapore. As a soldier he said President

Suharto understood the plight of a soldier. He said Suharto could not understand why Singapore had rejected his appeal not to hang the two marines. He asked whether there were pressures from the British or from other sources that led to the tough decision taken by the Singapore Government. He said in Indonesia when rebellions were suppressed in Sumatra and North Sulawasi, the rebels were pardoned. The two marines were after all taking orders from the late Sukarno regime. Since Suharto had fought very hard to bring about diplomatic relations with Malaysia, he thought that the two marines could be pardoned, that was why he made the appeal. Sumitro thought it was unfortunate that when Prime Minister Lee met Suharto in Lusaka, there was no opportunity for an explanation on this matter.

Sumitro wanted to know our stand on the Straits of Malacca. He said both Indonesia and Malaysia would not consider the Straits as international waters and that they had the right to control traffic in the Straits in order to ensure safety and security. He spoke of the Soviet Union's strategy of encirclement of China and of the Russian threat to the security of countries in South-East Asia. He said the three countries, meaning Indonesia, Malaysia and Singapore, should work together to ensure the safety and security of the Straits of Malacca and to prevent subversion.

Sumitro also wanted to know why Singapore had engaged Israeli military advisers and instructors. He said he gathered information that Singapore's position was the same as that of Israel in the Middle East. He also expressed the concern that Singapore would develop into a country like Israel with similar policies in South-East Asia.

After allowing Sumitro to finish, the Prime Minister replied point by point. He explained to Sumitro the background of the psychological and political approach of the present leadership in Singapore, who had fought very hard for many years to bring about the merger with the then Malaya. He said the British had wanted to retain Singapore as a military base because of its strategic position from where they once ruled their colonial territories in South-East Asia. He said this had been the basic concept of the present political leaders to make Singapore, not only part of the then Malaya, but also to serve countries of South-East Asia. Unlike Israel, the population of

Singapore was not one of sudden transplantation from abroad such as the persecuted Jews that had gathered in Israel. Singapore's population was the result of natural growth, having social, economic and later political links with Malaya and now Malaysia. Singapore's independence was brought about by an expulsion from Malaysia.

The Prime Minister also explained that after separation, Singapore had not even one soldier and that Malaysian troops were stationed on Singapore's soil. He said he had written to the late President Nasser and the late Prime Minister Shastri for help to train Singapore's soldiers. The requests were turned down, perhaps because the Egyptian and Indian leaders did not want to antagonise their friends in Malaysia. Then Singapore explored the possibility of training its troops on the Finnish, Swiss or Israeli patterns. The Israeli method of military training was found to be the most suitable because of the similar size of population. Singapore could only afford the citizen army like that of Israel without having to tax the national resources required for economic expansion. It happened also that at the time of crisis after Singapore became independent, the Israelis were the first to recognise our independence and offered to train our soldiers.

The Prime Minister then went on to explain another important factor which was vital to the understanding of the psychological background of the present Singapore leadership. He mentioned that most of the present leadership including himself were trained in Britain and that they had been 'brainwashed', if one liked to use the term, into accepting the rule of law and respect for the constitution. He explained that Singapore was still practising the British system of separation between the executive and the judiciary and that the rule of law was sacred and it provided safety and guarantee for the people as well as foreign investors. He said no Minister in the Singapore Cabinet including himself as Prime Minister could pick up a phone and instruct judges of the courts what to do and what not to do and once court judgement was passed, the sentences would be executed. This sort of training had become institutionalised and as a result, it had created confidence, which in turn brought about stability and prosperity.

On the Straits of Malacca, the Prime Minister explained that the Straits had been international waters for centuries where all ships had passed. Being trained to think constitutionally and act constitutionally, Singapore leaders would prefer that matters relating to these territorial rights of free passage and of safety, pollution and security be referred to international bodies. Singapore would deal with Indonesia and Malaysia on measures recommended by international bodies for safety, anti-pollution and security. However, Singapore would not want to be involved in any action that would lead to cold war with Russians, the Japanese or any other people using the Straits. He warned that the Japanese now using the Straits for their oil tankers would in five or ten years' time be a formidable naval power in Asia and might challenge whatever measures that might be taken to restrict their oil tankers in the Straits. For the moment, he said, the Russians might start by sending an oil freighter to defy whatever obstacles that it might be confronted with in its passage through the Straits. However, nothing would prevent them from sending later, more modern naval vessels armed with nuclear weapons. By the time the Russians were prepared to ignore world opinion and marched their troops into Czechoslovakia, they had decided on a new brand of policy relating to international relations. Will it be wise to stop the Russian warships when they are in this mood? The Prime Minister again stressed that Singapore respected international law and would abide by the decision of international bodies regarding the usage of the Straits and would not like to get itself involved in any international incident.

Having explained the constitutional-mindedness of the present leadership, the Prime Minister then said that the hanging of the two marines was the logical consequence in a country where the rule of law is respected. He assured that it never occurred to him or to Singapore leaders that President Suharto would take the matter so personally. In fact, it was thought that the appeal was only a matter of formality. The Prime Minister mentioned that it was unfortunate that at that time there was no Indonesian Ambassador in Singapore and that the Charge-d'affaires as well as our Ambassador in Indonesia were unable to explain the significance of the psychological background and of the respect for the rule of law in Singapore which had not been taken into account when they made the appeal.

Sumitro then interrupted and agreed with the Prime Minister that the line of communication between the countries should be strengthened. He said that he established a channel of direct contact for Ambassador Lee to President Suharto so that at any time of emergency, they could meet and discuss. Similarly, he hoped that the same arrangement could be made for Ambassador Sunarso or whoever might become the next Ambassador to meet Prime Minister Lee from time to time when necessary.

Sumitro then explained that President Suharto was in the process of launching the 25-year plan for the economic development of Indonesia. The emphasis now was on economic development and not on political slogans. The Prime Minister chipped in and expressed the best of wishes for the success of Indonesia's economic development.

Touching again on the Straits, Sumitro hinted strongly that Indonesia would take measures to exert her rights of sovereignty over the Straits. He said if the Russians were trying to get tough, Indonesia would not hesitate to face the confrontation. He said in quite a serious tone that if the Russians liked, they could try to occupy Indonesia and see whether they could succeed.

Before he left, Sumitro thanked the Prime Minister for having given him an opportunity to have a frank talk and that he would convey the gist of the discussion to President Suharto on his return to Jakarta.

I met Sumitro after he had seen the Prime Minister. He said to me: 'I am really very happy. It is nonsense to say that your Prime Minister is arrogant. I appreciate that he has been very frank. I want to thank you very much for having arranged this meeting.' It had been his impression that Lee Kuan Yew was an arrogant man, difficult to talk to. He had asked President Suharto to forgive him if he had to walk out of the discussion if Lee Kuan Yew became too arrogant. It was therefore a pleasant surprise to Sumitro that Lee Kuan Yew was after all not arrogant and had in fact spent one and a half hours with him. The same night we went to Maxim's to celebrate the occasion whilst Sugent and Prof Pang Lye Kim prepared the report about Sumitro's talk with the Prime Minister. It was to be submitted to President Suharto.

As I crossed the third hurdle and all was set for the visit of the Prime Minister, I received a death threat. Two dark tall men came in a Volkswagon one afternoon sometime in early April to my house at 53 Imam Bondjol. I saw them from my sitting room window. I had just had my lunch and was taking a rest. I asked Din, my butler, to see what they wanted. They handed Din a letter and asked whether they could see me. I opened the letter and then asked Din to tell them to go off. The letter was written in English. It said:

"Safe greeting!
It has become a fact that the flow of Chinese capital to Indonesia via Singapore is aimed at dominating the Indonesian economy.

Singapore politics, which can be easily differentiated in every discussion when compared with other Southeast Asian countries, is proof that this country purposely works to break apart the harmony of Asian peoples.

By permitting smugglers to operate unchecked between Singapore and Sumatra, and their determination to wound the Indonesian nation by openly hanging two Indonesian nationals (KKO — Shore Navy Patrol) a while ago, clearly reflects the enemy-like character and malicious jealousy of Singapore toward Indonesia.

Therefore, we hope that the Ambassador will immediately urge the Singapore Government to alter such politics.

We are not responsible for the safety of the Ambassador and his Embassy staff in Djakarta if, during the month of April, the Ambassador does not make public alterations in the attitude of his Government.

Representative of the Association of Anti-Chinese Movements in Djakarta.
Sastro Damul."

I took it as a threat and intimidation to my safety and that of my staff. I made photocopies and handed one copy to Bakin, the security branch of Indonesia and another copy to the

Ministry of Foreign Affairs in Singapore. I flew back to Singapore asking for a security guard who could be disguised as my driver. My request was not acceded to because it never was the practice to provide the Ambassador a security guard. As I took the matter seriously, I went to Thomson Road Police Training School and practised shooting with my revolver. I spent a few days practising target shooting. I did not tell my wife about the death threat nor of the shooting training. I took my revolver along with me and when I returned to Indonesia, I told the Police Chief, General Widodo, that I would shoot anyone who tried to be funny with me. I took my pistol with me wherever I went. Even at cocktail parties, I took the revolver along.

I was staying alone at the residence. I put the revolver below my pillow every night when I went to sleep. A slight noise at night would wake me up and I was vigilant. This preparedness went on until well after April when I found nothing had happened to me. Meanwhile, the Bakin gave me a telephone number and asked me to contact Osman in case something really happened.

Apparently, the whole scheme was a test of nerves. As things were going well between Singapore and Indonesia, some anti-Singapore elements were trying to frighten me so that I would quit the job and when a new man took over, he would have to start all over again. I told my wife about the whole story only when I had said goodbye to Indonesia and when the plane landed in Singapore.

This was something which an Ambassador had to face. There have been many murders and kidnaps of Ambassadors in hostile countries and one was expected to have nerves of steel. When May and June passed without any incident, I began to forget about my revolver and went about without it.

Meanwhile, nothing transpired about the visit. I became a little worried. I asked myself what could be the snag?

I had crossed the third hurdle in the preparation for the Prime Minister's visit. Sumitro had given a good report to the President and it was now left to the President to decide the date for the Prime Minister's visit.

It now appeared to me that only one snag remained and that was face-saving. How could Suharto invite Lee Kuan Yew to

Indonesia when he was humiliated by our rejecting his appeal for pardon for the two marines? A face-saving device must be found. I met Sumitro on the golf course and he came out with a good idea. He suggested that Dr Goh Keng Swee should first visit Indonesia, bringing along a letter from Lee Kuan Yew inviting President Suharto to visit Singapore. Suharto would then reply to say he was busy and instead Lee Kuan Yew should visit Indonesia first. I wrote back to Singapore and persuaded Dr Goh Keng Swee to visit Indonesia with the letter.

When Dr Goh went to Indonesia on 23 October 1972, the military leaders gave him red carpet treatment. They went out of their way to be hospitable, friendly and helpful. On arrival at the Kemayoran Airport he was received by high-ranking generals from the Hankam (Defence Ministry) headed by vice-admiral Subono, Head of the General Affairs of Hankam. When we arrived at the Hankam Headquarters, Dr Goh was received by General Panggabean, Minister of State for Defence and Security and concurrently Deputy Commander of the Armed Forces. Dr Goh paid a courtesy call on General Panggabean, before they proceeded together to the Presidential Palace to see President Suharto.

President Suharto was in a good mood and did the talking most of the time. He touched on Indonesia's foreign and defence policy and gave his views on the critical situation in South-East Asia. He stressed the importance of closer cooperation between leaders of South-East Asian countries.

It was at this juncture that Dr Goh handed the Prime Minister's letter to President Suharto inviting him to visit Singapore. He appeared quite pleased with the gesture and remarked that it was only a matter of time before arrangements could be made for Lee Kuan Yew to visit Indonesia. After the courtesy call on Suharto, Dr Goh's party returned to the Hankam Conference Hall where one of Panggabean's intelligence experts General Hassan Habib, gave an hour's briefing on Indonesia's policy and strategy.

The host provided a Jet Star plane to take Dr Goh's party to Bandung on the second day to visit the Seskoad (the Army's Staff and Command college, the highest training centre for military personnel) and the Pindat, Indonesia's army industry centre. On the third day, a specially arranged Hercules plane took Dr Goh's party to Medan. Gen. Panggabean accompanied Dr Goh all the way from Medan to Lake Toba and back to Medan before the party left for Singapore. When Dr Goh arrived at Siantar, half-way between Medan and Perapat (a village on Lake Toba) in a convoy of air-conditioned cars all the chieftains of the eleven Batak tribes gathered in front of the rest house to greet the party in typical Batak fashion. There were Batak music and dances all the way with a sprinkling of rice and repeated chanting of 'horas' meaning 'welcome' in Batak. At the evening reception in Perapat Dr Goh was given the highest honour by the Batak community by being crowned with a Batak headgear and the sarong. It is equivalent to the conferring of chieftainship, rarely accorded distinguished visitors. The same honour was given to Mrs Goh. It was done ceremoniously at the reception given at the Conference Hall attended by the Batak community.

Dr Goh's visit to Indonesia with the Prime Minister's letter was a breakthrough in the relations between Singapore and Indonesia. Comments on the visit in all the major newspapers were favourable. The *Angkatan Bersendjata*, reflecting the views of the Armed Forces, said: 'It is a good indication of closer relations between countries geographically pre-destined to be closer to each other.' Referring to the marines incident, the paper described it as a result of confrontation policy pursued by the Old Order and that the New Order had completely changed its confrontation policy into a good neighbour policy. The paper added: 'With magnanimity we want to forget the past. There is no need to cry over spilled milk.'

Sinar Harapan, representing the Christian views and one of the independent dailies, said: 'The door is open to put an end to the confrontation and to start a new page in relations between Indonesia and its closest neighbour to the north.' The paper said that Indonesia should also convince Singapore that from Indonesia there was no threat. It should also convince Singapore that the confrontation policy was something created by the Old Order which they had succeeded in overcoming.

Kompas, another leading newspaper, said: 'We consider the visit of Defence Minister Goh Keng Swee to Indonesia as a confirmation of the good neighbour policy and the regional orientation. The climax of this good relations has yet to come.

It is in the form of Prime Minister Lee Kuan Yew's visit to Indonesia and President Suharto's visit to Singapore. There is only the problem of timing left.' Meanwhile Ambassador Sunarso was replaced by General Rukmito.

I had crossed all hurdles and reached the last stage in the preparation for the Prime Minister's visit to Indonesia. President Suharto had made up his mind to invite Lee Kuan Yew. The question was only the timing.

13

The Prime Minister's Visit to Indonesia

Finally a time was fixed for the Prime Minister to visit Indonesia. It was from 25 May to 31 May 1973. I was really happy that the three years of effort I had put in was bearing fruit. I have finally succeeded in arranging for Lee Kuan Yew to see President Suharto. All the years of tension between Indonesia and Singapore are over. I felt very much relaxed.

I flew back to Singapore to make the necessary arrangements. What should Lee Kuan Yew do during his visit to Indonesia? Where shall he visit and whom shall he see? All these I had to know before a proper programme could be prepared. There were also some questions I wished to ask the Prime Minister. One of them was whether he would put flowers on the graves of the two marines when he walked past the graves of Indonesia's dead heroes who were buried at Kalibata. I asked the Minister for Foreign Affairs, Rajaratnam, whether he would get the answer for me. He said: 'You had better suggest that to him personally when you meet him.'

Then one day, the Prime Minister called me up for a chat. He asked me: 'How can I make Suharto happy? How can I befriend him?' I thought to myself that it was an opportunity for me to put the delicate question to him. I thus asked him frankly and bluntly: 'Do you want to be his real friend or just a cordial friend?' He replied: 'Of course, I want to be his real friend.' I said: 'Do not get angry with my proposal but I

Prime Minister Lee Kuan Yew playing golf with President Suharto during his visit in 1974

think this is the best way to make him forget the past and start afresh with you and be your real friend.' He said: 'Never mind, what is your proposal?' I told him that he should, whilst putting flowers in Kalibata, pass by the graves of the two Indonesian marines and also sprinkle some flowers. He was a little startled by my suggestion.

He said: 'What, is it necessary? Why should it be necessary?' I explained to him that the average Javanese believed in the existence of the soul. So long as the two souls that we had hanged were unhappy, it would be difficult for Suharto to have a clear conscience and it would be difficult for him to really befriend a person who was responsible for their deaths. The Javanese sometimes go to the graves to consult departed souls and souls are real to them. The Prime Minister listened for a while and said he needed time to think it over.

'I will let you know when the time comes,' he said. I knew of a top general in Indonesia who visited the grave of Gadja Mada, who was Prime Minister of Majapahit 500 years ago, to draw inspiration. Like the Chinese who visit the graves of their ancestors at Cheng Meng time, the Javanese also visit the graves of their ancestors from time to time. There are many ancestor worshippers among the Javanese in Indonesia.

In preparing for the Prime Minister's visit one small problem was that he had a habit of getting up late. That very morning, the SIA plane on normal schedule had to take off at about eight in the morning. The Prime Minister refused to charter a special plane because economically speaking, it would be a waste. He did not want to interfere with the SIA's schedule. So he had to get up early in the morning to catch the eight o'clock plane. After his arrival, we arranged for him to rest so that the courtesy call on Suharto would have to be in the afternoon.

On 25 May, Lee Kuan Yew's much heralded visit to Indonesia got off to a perfect start at Jakarta's Kemayoran Airport. Lee's party included his 18-year-old daughter Wei Ling, the Minister for Foreign Affairs, Rajaratnam, his Minister of State, Rahim Ishak, the President of the Development Bank Singapura, and Chairman of the Port Authority, Howe Yoon Chong, President of the National Trade Union Congress, Devan Nair (now President of Singapore), and Dr Phay Seng Huat, Chairman of the Public Services Commission.

A red-carpet welcoming ceremony in brilliant sunshine was awaiting the Prime Minister. A dark-suited President Suharto and the First Lady Ibu Tien walked to the tarmac just as the SIA Boeing 737 bringing the Prime Minister and his party touched down right on time at 9.10 a.m.

As the aircraft door opened, the President strode forward. At the foot of the aircraft, the two leaders shook hands and smiled broadly. A pretty Indonesian girl stepped up and garlanded Lee with orchids.

President Suharto introduced Lee Kuan Yew to his top aides who lined up along the red carpet. Then as the two leaders walked to a canopied dais, the military band struck up first Majulah Singapura and then the Indonesian national anthem, whilst a 19-gun salute boomed out at a distance.

Lee inspected a guard of honour mounted by men from Indonesia's four uniformed services — the army, the navy, the air force and the police.

After quick handshakes with local and foreign dignitaries on the tarmac, Lee and Suharto were driven off in the President's black limousine to Wisma Negara, the official palace for important guests.

Students carrying little flags of Indonesia and Singapore lined up from the airport to the Wisma. They waved as the motorcade drove by. They shouted 'welcome'. It was a sea of faces — young and old. They were all smiling and excited. Such a grand welcome was unprecedented in the history of Indonesia. The Indonesians really went out of their way to welcome the Prime Minister. Ibu Tien paid personal attention to the requirements of her guests at the Wisma. She put flowers and fruits in the rooms and made sure that the temperature of the room was suitable to the guests.

On arrival at the airport, Lee Kuan Yew told me that he would put flowers on the graves of the two marines. I immediately passed on the message to General Tjokropranolo, the President's Chief Security Officer, and I could see his face suddenly beaming with excitement. He immediately gave orders to get things prepared. And he went whispering to other Generals and Ministers at the airport.

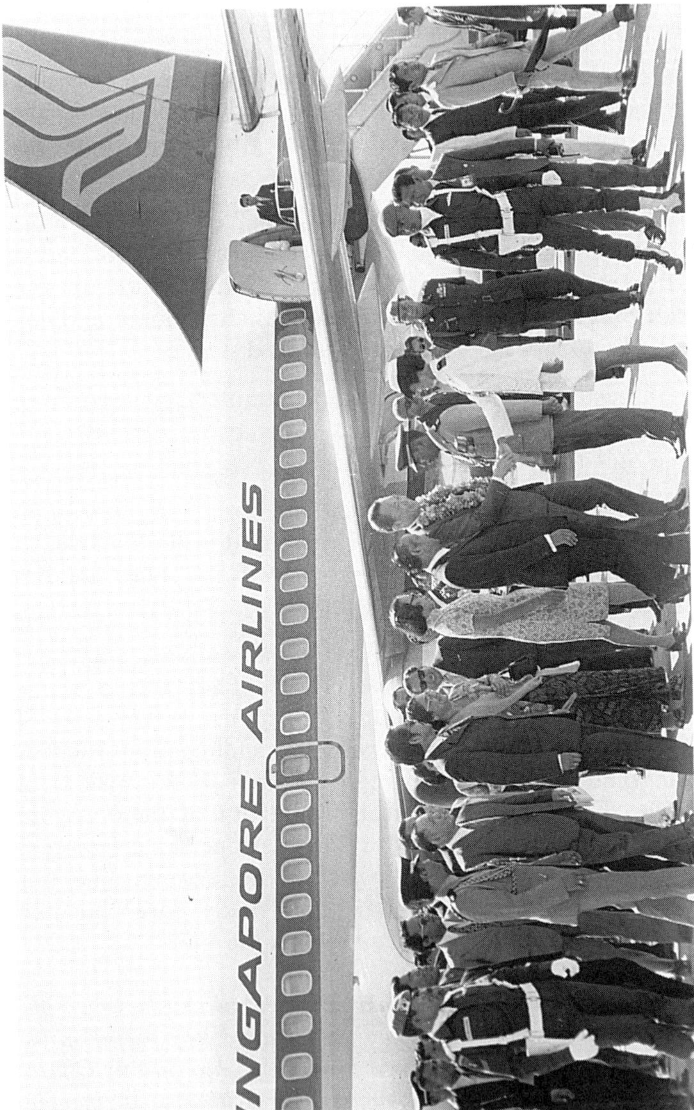

Prime Minister Lee Kuan Yew and his party was received by President Suharto at the airport

On the day of arrival, almost all Jakarta newspapers carried editorials welcoming Lee, but pointed out that relations between the two countries were far from perfect.

The Jakarta Times said: 'Prejudices between the countries remain, hampering progress towards development of friendship and cooperation.'

The Indonesian Observer said that although relations had improved recently, there was still a 'mutual feeling of mistrust.'

'Something is still missing in these relations to make them more cordial.'

Catholic daily *Kompas* said: 'What should be reached from this visit is not mainly to settle problems but to develop mutual confidence through more intensive personal acquaintances.'

Berita Buana said: 'It is clear that Singapore and Indonesia are interdependent on each other and cooperation between the two countries will bring positive results to South-East Asian stability.'

Kami said the urgent problem for Singapore and Indonesia was to overcome the psychological barrier and to realise economic cooperation for mutual benefit.

After the meeting, the leaders exchanged gifts. The Prime Minister gave the President a Singapore-made electronic calculator. He was presented a teakwood set of two chairs and a table — all hand-carved and polished. Mrs Lee presented Mrs Suharto with a Singapore-made carpet. Her hostess gave her a silver handbag and batik — both produced in Jogjakarta.

At night, the Prime Minister's first day in Indonesia was capped by a glittering black-tie state banquet given in his honour at the Istana by the President. At the pre-dinner cocktail, a bat suddenly flew into the hall, catching the eyes of all present and creating quite a furore. The bat made a dive round the hall and made its way out.

According to both Chinese and Javanese customs, a bat is a good omen. The Chinese character for bat (蝠) sounds very much like 'luck' and the appearance of 'fook' at such an occasion was a good omen. It augured well for the relations between the two countries. The Indonesian hosts were in a happy mood as they had been told that the Prime Minister would be putting flowers on the graves of the two marines.

The word passed round very quickly. The atmosphere was relaxed and both General Sumitro and General Ali Murtopo, in those days considered as the powerful right hand and left hand of Suharto, congratulated me for having done a 'good job'.

The banquet went off well. Lee Kuan Yew addressing the banquet said he found an identity of approach with Suharto on many major issues in the first talks he had with the Indonesian leader. Lee said he found the talks, lasting two hours, 'free of difficulties and differences of opinion.'

Lee said he was impressed to see the changes Jakarta had experienced compared to over a decade ago. Lee's last visit to Indonesia was 13 years ago.

He said: 'Although I was psychologically prepared to see a modern metropolis taking shape, I was nevertheless impressed by its physical transformation.

'However, I am even more impressed by the transformation in the outlook and politics of the Government of Indonesia under your leadership.

'The emphasis you have publicly placed on economic and social development has enhanced peace and stability for the whole region.

'In retrospect, perhaps it is as well that we had a few years to carefully and quickly reach the perception we have of each other.'

Addressing Suharto, Lee added:

'But it took us sometime to realise how determined you were to mobilise the energies of 120 million Indonesians and concentrate them into tapping the vast resources of over 3,000 major islands. But after the systematic dampening of politicking and refusal to be deflected from your constructive line of action, we realised that a profound and fundamental change in direction had taken place.

'It was a turning point in the long history of Indonesia, a turning point towards constructing and development, towards a better tomorrow for Indonesia.'

Lee continued: 'On the other hand, I hope that the last seven years may have enabled you and your Government to have a better understanding of what we are like in Singapore, that the making of a fast buck, the absence of scruples in the

Author had a chat with former Minister of Home Affairs in Indonesia

pursuit of wealth, associated with merchant adventurers, is a caricature which bears no resemblance to the establishment in Singapore, nor to the kind of society we have set out to build.'

Lee said if Singapore was not South-East Asian in its orientation and instinctive reflexes, Singapore would not have found such an identity of approach to many of the major issues that were discussed.

Lee ended: 'I believe that our discussions this afternoon have brought us closer and enabled us to have a better understanding of our respective thinkings on the common problems that face us in South-East Asia.'

Suharto, in reply, said Indonesia was delighted with the economic and social progress made in Singapore.

He said: 'Your leadership and the loyalty to Singaporeans are obviously one of the important keys which have brought about progress and welfare to the people of Singapore at the present stage.

'It is the resolve of the peoples in the region to jointly adjust their own future, to preserve peace and stability in the area, and not to allow this future to be determined by outside forces which often disregard and oppose the interests of the nations in this region.

'Such a new South-East Asia will certainly provide a positive contribution towards peace in Asia and in the world in general.'

Suharto underscored the building of closer ties between Singapore and Indonesia when he said: 'Geographically, our two countries are very close to each other. What we want to see more closely developed is the psychological ties, the friendship and brotherhood between the two neighbouring countries.'

The next morning, the wreath-laying ceremony was on at Kalibata Heroes cemetery. On arrival, solemn music was played, followed by the laying of the main wreath on the right side of the courtyard. After that, the Prime Minister was escorted to sprinkle flowers first on the Muslim generals, then the Christian generals who were victims of the 30 September 1965 'gestapu' coup. The graves of the two marines were less than 20 yards away from the Christian graves and the Prime Minister walked over and sprinkled flowers on them. When this was done, I noticed tears pouring out from the eyes of

Rukmito, Indonesian Ambassador to Singapore. He was apparently moved by the gesture. The other generals who accompanied the party were equally moved.

The next day, Indonesian newspapers praised Lee for the 'magnanimous gesture' in sprinkling flowers on the graves of the two marines and described him as 'a great man'. None of the newspapers described that act as an act of repentance on the part of the Prime Minister. That little gesture of his had won over many Indonesian hearts and was the key to the turning point of better relations between the two countries.

Late in the afternoon, Lee Kuan Yew went golfing with Suharto at the Rawamangun Golf Club, about 20 minutes from the city. Among those in the golf party were Admiral Sudomo, Naval Chief of Staff who was President of the Club, Rukmito and myself.

Before the golf game, the Governor of Jakarta, General Ali Sadikin, paid a courtesy call on Lee Kuan Yew at the Wisma. He gave Lee a silver 'kendi' (venerable jug), an equivalent of the Key to the City. 'Kendi' is an age-old Arabic custom. In ancient days, Arab households would place a kendi outside the house so that passers-by could drink from it.

Ali Sadikin, the man responsible for Jakarta's transformation, explained to Lee how he managed to improve the city.

Whilst Lee was playing golf, Mrs Lee had a separate programme within the palace grounds and was shown how Sumatrans held wedding ceremonies. Wei Ling went to the Indonesian Medical College and was warmly welcomed by the undergrads of the University.

On the same night, as Ambassador I gave a cocktail party at Hotel Indonesia, in order to enable the diplomatic corps and other dignitaries to meet the Prime Minister. It has often been said that ambassadors had only the duty to go to the airport to receive VVIPs and then to send them off again without any opportunity to meet their colleagues and the VVIPs. I wanted our Prime Minister to meet as many people as possible, particularly the diplomatic corps. That night, many ambassadors and journalists met the Prime Minister and had interesting conversations.

Meanwhile in Jakarta, Rajaratnam and Adam Malik, Foreign Minister of Indonesia, signed a border agreement at the Ministry of Foreign Affairs. The agreement provided for demarcation of the Straits of Singapore, and a boundary between the two countries roughly midway between the two shores. The treaty stated that it would strengthen bonds of friendship between the two countries.

On 27 May, Lee had a second meeting with Suharto for 90 minutes. After that, he had a press conference at the Wisma. Among other things, Lee said: 'The talk of psychological barriers arose from the problem of different systems we inherited. The Dutch ruled Indonesia for 300 years and the British were in Singapore for 150 years.

Lee said: 'And this leads us to misunderstand the moves and motives behind each act. I think the most important factor is the ability to reach to each other's inner thoughts as far as possible in a completely free exchange of views.'

'My own impression is that I am much more relaxed about the kind of thinking, the kind of projects, in terms of development and objectives which your President has proposed to me as those which are uppermost in his mind, namely the emphasis on stability which has been termed national and regional resilience, which is not very far in context from what we call ruggedness. In other words, taking things in our stride.'

After three days in Jakarta, the mission flew to Medan, the provincial capital of North Sumatra. There Governor Marah Halim gave the party a typical Sumatran welcome. Bersilat exponents in black, crouching on the tarmac of Medan's Polonia airport, went through their paces as local dignitaries were introduced to the Prime Minister. Flower girls carrying copper bowls sprinkled sweet-scented petals on the path of the party. Inside the small terminal building, Mr and Mrs Lee sat together on yellow cushioned handcarved chairs for the traditional welcome ceremony. Girls knelt to shower flowers around them to the accompaniment of Sumatran music.

A good number of local schools must have given the teachers and students a holiday for the occasion, for when the motorcade passed the streets — cool and shady because of the large number of tall trees — thousands of cheering schoolchildren in uniform standing three-deep waved their welcome with little plastic state flags of the two countries.

In the afternoon, Lee played golf at the Deli Golf Course for half an hour in heavy rain with Indonesian Foreign Minister

Prime Minister Lee Kuan Yew chatting with Foreign Minister, Adam Malik

Adam Malik. When we started off, the weather was fine. Then the rain came, we plodded on, soaked to the skin, but decided to call it off at the eighth hole. After changing into fresh clothes, Lee wrote in the club book: 'A beautiful course, a wonderful afternoon and a remarkable game abandoned at the 8th hole because of the rain — heavy rain. Must come to finish the round some day. Lee Kuan Yew.'

Before the reception given by Governor Marah Halim, Lee asked me: 'How to make the Governor happy?' I said: 'Put on the batik shirt which we bought in Jakarta. It should make him happy.' Then the Prime Minister, for the first time in his life, put on a batik. We went to our rooms, put on the batik and went downstairs. In the lift, we met Adam Malik who was in coat and tie. He saw us and was pleasantly surprised. He said: 'Wait, I have to go and change.' Down at the lobby, the officials of our mission were all in coat and tie. They saw us and were puzzled. It was too late to change and we went to the party as we were.

Governor Marah Halim who was also in batik was taken by surprise when he saw the Prime Minister in batik. He remarked: 'You have a nice batik.' Lee smiled. It was a gay relaxed party, quite typical of life in this town which gave no appearance at all of hustle and bustle. There are no high-rise buildings at all, and the townfolk travel about mainly by becak or bicycles. After a few drinks, Marah Halim presented a 12-foot long spear called 'tombak' to the Prime Minister. This 'tombak' was used in ancient days by warriors of the Batak tribe (one of the six ethnic groups in the province) together with a Batak battle-shield called 'taneng' and a band of steel called 'kalong' worn around the neck of tribesmen.

That night, we were entertained to some Batak dances and the Prime Minister was caught by surprise. He was asked to dance the Batak dance. It was a simple movement of just waving the hands in a flapping motion stamping one's feet. It was difficult for him to refuse. He stood up and did the dance. After that, he told Koh Peng Long, our Consul in Medan, that he would not go through such dances again. Peng Long took it that he did not want another occasion like this.

The next morning was supposed to be another ceremony to honour the Prime Minister as 'Rajah' of Batak at Prapat Town Hall. Koh Peng Long had told the organisers that the

Prime Minister would not attend such a function. I got up early in the morning and was having a stroll and admiring the panoramic view of Lake Toba. General Tjokropranolo, Chief Security Officer to President Suharto, came rushing to me angrily and excitedly. He said: 'Why did your Prime Minister refuse the honour given by the Prapat Batak community? This is going to create friction among the Bataks for he has accepted the high honour from another Batak community. It will create misunderstanding and there may be a fight between the two groups.'

I did not know that the Prime Minister had turned down the offer of the honour. I rushed to the residence of the Prime Minister. He was staying in the house where Sukarno was once detained during the revolution. It was a nice bungalow facing the Lake. He had just got up and was about to have breakfast. I asked whether it was true that he had turned down the offer of an honour by a Batak tribe. I explained to him the consequence of his turning down the offer. Then he said: 'All right, I will attend, but please do not ask me to dance.' I told him that that could be arranged.

We all attended the crowning ceremony of the Prime Minister as Rajah (Batak King) at the Prapat Town Hall. There a Batak Chief and an Indonesian official placed a cloth head-dress on the Prime Minister. It was the highest award that the Batak people of Lake Toba could offer. Soon after this came the climax of the ceremony when Lee was presented with the royal staff meant to show the bearer the right course to follow. The ceremony was simple and solemn. After that, every member of the mission danced except the Prime Minister. A crisis was averted.

It happened that the royal staff presented to the Prime Minister had been borrowed from someone and that person demanded it back. It came out in the newspapers and this embarrassed the governor. When Lee heard about it, he arranged for the royal staff to be returned to the owner. Meanwhile, Marah Halim, the governor, settled the matter with the owner by giving him a certain sum of money.

The mission toured the isle of Samosir, the largest island on Lake Toba, just off the mainland. The first time I visited Samosir, the protocol officer pointed at the island and said to me smilingly: 'The whole of Singapore can sink into that island.' He was trying to indicate how small Singapore was. The inhabitants — extroverts, warm and outspoken like most Bataks — live off the land, blessed by a pleasant climate most of the year. We were taken to the burial ground of Raja Sida Buta, the king of Samosir, who was said to have died 400 years ago. Our host related the story of the King's romance with Anteng Melila Senaga who was the loveliest maiden in Samosir. Her image was carved behind Sida Buta's coffin. We saw the dalang manipulating Si Gale Gale — a kind of puppet who did a Batak dance with the eyes rolling up and down. We also went to a site where the Bataks chopped human heads in ancient times. All along the way, villagers threw grains of rice into the air and chanted 'Horas, Horas' — a Batak exclamation which meant 'good day, welcome, long life and prosperity to you.'

At a press conference before the mission left for home, the Prime Minister was asked how he felt being made a Batak King. He said: 'It makes me feel older. When you collect honorary degrees and titles, it's a sign of old age which I think is sometimes a sobering thought.'

Back in Singapore, Lee announced that the Singapore Tourist Promotion Board (STPB) would send a mission to Lake Toba district in North Sumatra to see how it could help develop the tourist industry there. The STPB team would see how package tours for Singaporeans could be arranged using chartered flights for travel to Medan from Singapore and air-conditioned coaches to go from Medan to the Lake and resorts on its shores and on the isle of Samosir in the Lake.

These were subsequently done.

Mr Lee's visit to Indonesia took three years to prepare. But it was all over in seven days. The Prime Minister's visit can be considered a success in breaking down the so-called 'psychological barriers' between the two countries.

Then on 29 August 1974, it was President Suharto's turn to visit Singapore. The President's entourage included Adam Malik, the Foreign Minister, General Sukharmono, the Minister of State and State Secretary and their wives.

Singapore welcomed Suharto with a 21-gun salute and high military honours when they flew in for a three-day visit. The airport ceremony was one of the grandest seen in recent times with a 400-man military guard of honour and three bands from the military and police drawn up near the tarmac. The late President Sheares and the First Lady and the whole Cabinet led by Lee Kuan Yew were there to receive the guests.

As Suharto appeared at the door, the 21-gun salute fired by the Artillery regiment of Singapore Armed Forces boomed in the distance. Othman Wok, the Minister in attendance, Rukmito and myself, went up to the red carpet to receive the guests.

When Suharto left the airport in a Rolls Royce, 1,000 flag-waving school children cheered and hundreds of people lined the streets to welcome the party.

At the Istana, the Indonesian leader presented President Sheares with an autographed colour photograph of himself and Ibu Tien framed in sterling silver and a large wooden carving of mythological significance from Central Java. Ibu Tien's gift to Mrs Sheares was a solid gold jewel box finished in filigree work by master-craftsmen from Kendiri. President Sheares presented Suharto with a rosewood chest, engraved with the three Chinese characters: 'Happiness, longevity and prosperity.' Mrs Sheares presented Ibu Tien with a rosewood altar-shaped cabinet.

Suharto also presented Lee Kuan Yew with an elegant Indonesian wood-carving. Ibu Tien gave Mrs Lee a gold-threaded tray. Lee presented Suharto with a gold-plated Singapore-made camera and an electric flash. Mrs Lee presented Ibu Tien with a rosewood low buffet.

At the banquet given in honour of Suharto, President Sheares said: 'It was an accident that Asean came into being soon after Suharto's assumption of leadership in Indonesia. Today, after seven years, even sceptics had to concede that a real start had been made towards regional understanding; Asean had demonstrated a capacity for more than separate narrow national approaches in tackling the wider problems affecting the whole region.'

Suharto in reply said Indonesia could learn a lot from Singapore's success in industrialisation and economic development.

Suharto planted a Tembusu in the Jurong's Garden of Fame after visiting the Jurong industrial estate. He was impressed by Singapore's industrial expansion.

Prime Minister Lee Kuan Yew with President Suharto at the guard of honour in Jakarta

President Suharto and Prime Minister Lee Kuan Yew at the Rawamangun Golf Course, Jakarta

President Suharto toasting to Prime Minister Lee Kuan Yew during his visit to Indonesia

What's the joke? Adam Malik sharing a joke with the author at the latter's cocktail party in honour of Prime Minister Lee Kuan Yew

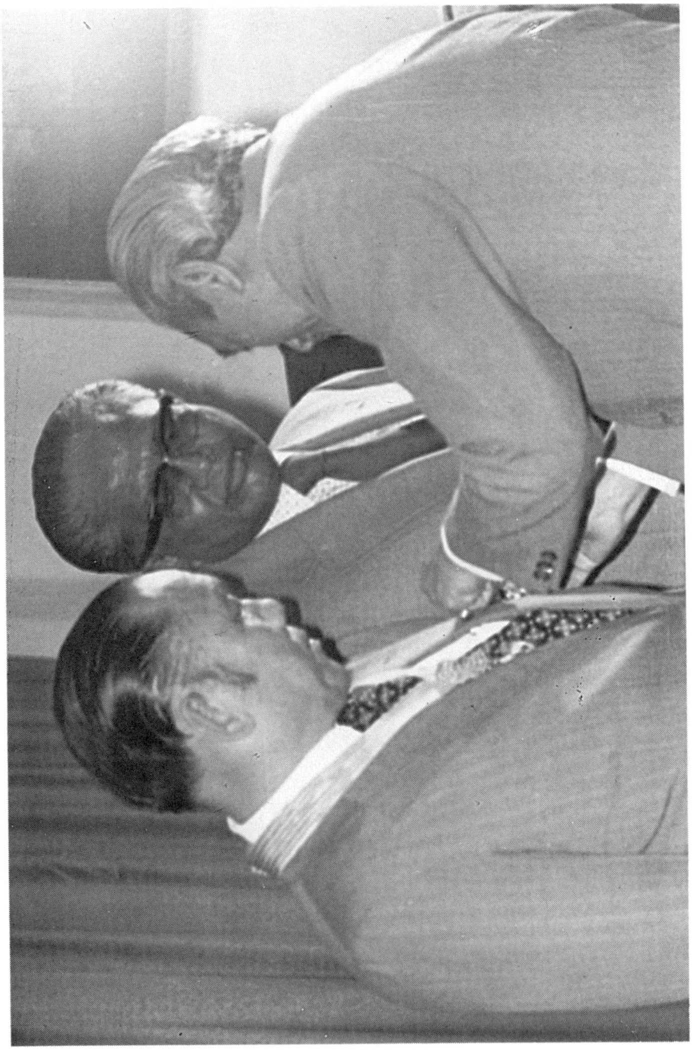

Adam Malik pinning the Bintang Jasa Utama (the First Class Meritorious Medal given by President Suharto) on the Chest of the author for the good work he has done in promoting the relations between Indonesia and Singapore

President Suharto saluting when the National Anthem was played at the Paya Lebar International Airport when he arrived in Singapore in 1974

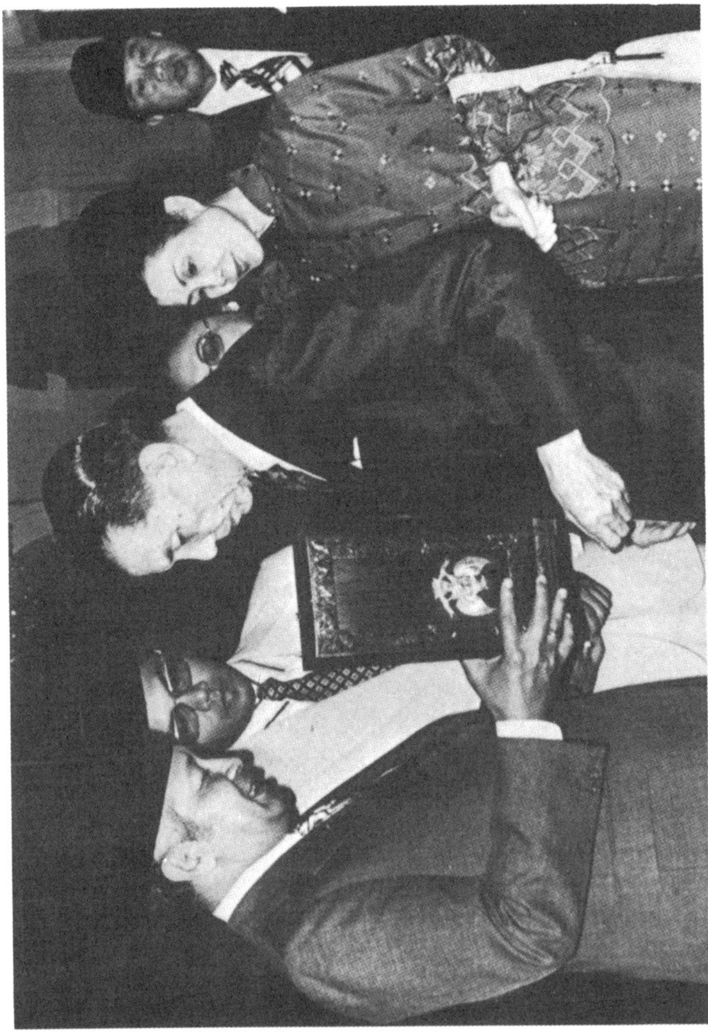

President Suharto presenting a gift to the late President Sheares when the former visited Singapore in 1974

Ibu Tien went to the Botanic Garden and had an orchid named after her. She picked the lemon-hued hybrid of Indonesian and Singapore parentage to bear her name. The orchid known as Dendrobium Tien Suharto is a cross between Dendrobium Noor Aisha, named after Singapore's former First Lady and Dendrobium Schulleri, a native of Indonesia's Irian Jaya.

Both the countries signed a basic agreement on economic and technical cooperation.

In Singapore, Suharto and Lee Kuan Yew had another round of discussions, this time on more specific matters. They came to a closer understanding after the visit.

When Suharto returned to Jakarta, he and the First Lady shook hands with each and every member of the diplomatic corps and others who were there to receive them. This took the diplomatic circles by surprise because it was the first time that he had done so. The Egyptian Ambassador to Indonesia commented that it was the first time he ever shook the hands of Suharto and the Ibu at the airport for he could not remember any other occasion during his 3½ years' posting in Jakarta. Similar comments were made by several other ambassadors. Reflecting back over the four years I had been in Jakarta, I could not remember Suharto ever shaking hands with the diplomatic corps either on departure or on arrival after his various overseas trips. It could be taken as a sign of overflowing happiness after the Singapore visit.

All the Indonesian leaders heaved a sigh of relief as relations between the two top leaders of the two neighbouring countries improved. The happiest person of all was Adam Malik who told me that after Suharto's private talks with the Prime Minister, he began to appreciate, for the first time, Singapore's position and her problems. He described the Kuan Yew–Suharto frank talk as most useful for it helped to clear up many doubts in Suharto's mind about Singapore.

Since then, the two leaders have met on other occasions and the relationship between the two countries has become stronger and friendlier.

By the end of 1974, I wrote to the Prime Minister and asked for permission to return home since I had accomplished my mission.

14

Cukong and the Anti-Tanaka Riots

The word 'cukong' is a new word in the Indonesian dictionary. It is a word coined by the Indonesians to describe a group of Chinese who provide the finance, establishment, business knowhow and enjoy all the business facilities such as licences and protection. The word has become popular but distasteful. It emerged after President Suharto came into power. The Chinese character 'cu' means 'master' or 'boss', and 'kong' can mean 'grandfather' or 'Godfather' or 'kongsi', a company. The cukong has many roles to play — financier, administrator, an escort, caretaker of household affairs and anything under the sun.

The cukong collaborates with licence holders who are indigenous Indonesians. Long before the 'new order', collaboration between experienced rich Chinese businessmen and inexperienced indigenous licence holders had been common. Many Chinese made unofficial arrangements with indigenous licence holders, the former providing capital, running the business and splitting the profit with the latter who held the licence.

When I first arrived in Indonesia in June 1970, the *Nusantara*, an Indonesian daily, was most vociferous in its attack on the cukong. It attacked the Pertamina and other business enterprises which had connections with cukongs. And in January 1971, it translated an article in the *Bangkok Post* which discussed in full the practice in Indonesia. According to that article, the cukong group consisting of more than 20 persons 'have wide holdings ranging from airlines and banks to flour mills, import-export companies, tourist corporations, restaurants, shipping companies, tin exporting concessions, rice milling plants, timber concessions . . . and a variety of others.' The article also said that cukongs had a steady and inside track to government contracts, investment credits and other funds and alleged that 90 percent of project aid money ended up in the hands of the cukongs. The article identified the generals who were connected with the cukongs.

The article shook Jakarta, and other newspapers picked up the story and went to town with them. Some Members of Parliament began to question the government on the matter. The government denied the charges. The editor of *Nusantara*, Dr Hafas, was prosecuted for his campaign against cukongism and later sentenced to two years' imprisonment pending appeal. The government's action against the anti-cukong campaign was interpreted by some foreign observers as a measure to 'reassure the Chinese that they could safely continue investing in Indonesia.'

The collaboration between Chinese businessmen and indigenous power holders had created resentment among some indigenous Indonesians, particularly the less successful businessmen. Foreign investments also became the target of criticism as they were seen to be more beneficial to non-indigenous businessmen because foreign investors preferred to work with Chinese businessmen rather than their indigenous counterparts for obvious reasons — the Chinese were generally better equipped in terms of business experience, capital and business knowhow.

The most striking example of this resentment occurred during the visit of Prime Minister Tanaka in January 1974 when a riot broke out causing enormous damage to private properties and injury to human lives. The anti-Tanaka demonstration by students went off quite smoothly on Tanaka's arrival. The students succeeded in jamming the traffic at the Halim airport. They could not get into the new Halim airport terminal for further demonstrations because of the clever military strategy of diverting the attention of the students to the new route and getting President Suharto' and his guests in and out of the airport by the old route. Tanaka came in hurriedly, got down the plane, shook hands with Cabinet Ministers and generals in the airport and was whisked away. There was no 19-gun salute nor inspection of a guard of honour.

As ambassadors were returning home from the airport, my car was the first car to leave the airport. As I was driving along the road, the student demonstrators had not dispersed. Suddenly, some of the students surrounded my car and one of them shouted: 'Tanaka, Tanaka'. They mistook me for Tanaka, and one of them asked me to get down. Fortunately, another student looked at the Merah Puteh flag with five stars and said: 'No, it is not the Japanese flag.' The students did not persist and I drove away. Anything could have happened in the chaos of a mass gathering. They could have pulled me out and beaten me up for nothing.

The following day, students started to burn cars at P.T. Astra International, a joint venture between the Japanese and local Chinese cukong William Chia Keng Liong brothers, backed by top generals. All the cars in the showroom, about 50 of them, were brought out and burnt. Then, the whole thing snowballed and people started to burn cars all over the city. Altogether 500 cars, predominantly Japanese-made, were burnt. A group of students moved to and fro at Imam Bondjol, the place where I lived. I was staying at home and I had a clear view of the whole incident. They attacked the President Hotel where the Japanese delegation was staying. They made an attempt at the Japanese Embassy which was on Thamrin Road, the grandest thoroughfare in Jakarta. They were pushed back by the military who fired into the air. They retreated to Imam Bondjol and went ahead again. It was a running battle. Then the whole demonstration went out of hand. The Senon Project, a shopping centre owned mostly by Chinese, and Chinese restaurants, notably the Prince Restaurant and the Sky Room, and famous massage parlours were burnt. The mob turned to looting. They went on a rampage until curfew was imposed from 6 p.m. I could hear the shouting, looting and the firing of pistol shots and machine-guns because the Prince Restaurant was only a stone's throw from my home.

When the firing subsided, a mob of students went along Imam Bondjol from house to house demanding that the residents lower the flag by half mast to mourn the occasion. From my first floor window, I saw them coming. I immediately instructed my butler Din to fold our flag. My neighbour, the Turkish Ambassador, refused to lower his flag and was having a prolonged argument with the students. Finally he had to give in. The next day, he had a heart attack. He has since passed away. When Adam Malik gave a press conference after the incident to Ambassadors and the diplomatic corps, he was asked why the students had asked the diplomatic corps to lower the flag which was contravening the immunity of the corps. Malik replied: 'Even I myself had to lower the flag.' The ambassadors laughed it off.

The students had taken to the street after Tanaka's arrival despite a stern warning issued through radio and television by General Panggabean jointly with General Sumitro that any further demonstration would be considered treason and would be dealt with severely. Later on, when the mob started their rampage, the Deputy Commander of Kopkamtib, General Mantek, issued warning after warning over the radio and TV that drastic action would be taken against law-breakers. But the armed soldiers could only manhandle the crowd and no firearms could be used. Apparently, they were ordered not to shoot. There were some clashes resulting in eight students and a number of soldiers being seriously injured.

Meanwhile, the state banquet for Tanaka was held at the Istana and both Suharto and Tanaka spoke, and their speeches were broadcast. The wreath-laying ceremony at Kalibata Cemetery was cancelled because of the continuing riots. Only at the Halim airport, the portraits of Mr and Mrs Tanaka, Suharto and Ibu Tien were displayed and in the rest of the city there were no portraits. On departure day, Tanaka with a smile of relief boarded a special JAL plane at 8.30 a.m. in the morning. He bowed 90 degrees to his host three times with a twitch on his face. The nightmare in Jakarta was over for him. Although there were no student demonstrators at Halim airport or anywhere in the city, Tanaka and party were taken to the airport by helicopters accompanied by President Suharto and his Army Chief of Staff. The authorities did not want to take any risk. Suharto and his Army Chief of Staff returned to Istana also by helicopter after sending off the guests.

It was a very quiet send-off. Again there was no 19-gun salute, no waving of flags or guard of honour for the guest.

Since the last evening, tension had died down in Jakarta. Student demonstrators returned to their campus after 1 p.m. when they realised that their movement had deteriorated into destructive vandalism by hooligans and looting by gangsters and the unemployed and had gone out of control. On their return to their campus, they issued a press statement condemning the acts of hooliganism, looting and burning of cars and properties.

The students' original aim was to demonstrate to Tanaka their anger and disapproval vis-a-vis Japan's underhand tactics of dealing with Indonesia. They were particularly unhappy with Japanese collaboration with Chinese businessmen. For some time, there had been widespread unhappiness with Japanese behaviour in Indonesia. They were seen crowding together, seldom mixing with local people. When the Japanese played golf, they always played among themselves and seldom with local Indonesians. You could easily recognise that the Japanese had gone ahead of you because they dragged their feet on the greens. When a ball hit you from behind before you had time to proceed, you knew they were Japanese. They ate together, slept together, visited places together and laughed and joked together without outsiders. They seemed to live in a world of their own, disregarding local conditions and unwilling to mix. The younger breed was even more arrogant, having no experience of World War Two. This had antagonised the Indonesians.

It was wrong timing for Tanaka to have visited South-East Asia. The climate in Indonesia was unsuitable for his visit. The then Japanese Ambassador, also Tanaka, was suffering from an illness and was not energetic enough to understand the grassroot problems. I think the Japanese Prime Minister was ill-advised to make the trip. The Ambassador died soon after his retirement.

Tanaka however had the opportunity to have a peep into the power struggle that was going on in Jakarta. He gave them an excuse to stage their second act of 'wayang play' of power politics.

The first act took place on 5 August 1974 in Bandung. The common plot was to pressurise President Suharto to get rid of the Aspris (his personal assistants) one of whom happened to be the Japanese lobby man. In Bandung, an anti-Chinese riot took place burning Chinese-owned cars and houses. When the first act was played, the schemers were still behind the scene. In this second act with Jakarta as the backdrop, some of the brains were exposed and cornered. Soon after the riots, a big swoop was on, resulting in the arrest of 250 people. Some of the leaders detained included Prof Serbani, a Senior Lecturer in the University of Indonesia and a top leader of the Parti Socialist Indonesia (PSI) who was believed to be one of the brains behind the student agitation. Another, a Dutch journalist, who had taken Indonesian citizenship, was also detained. He was Princen, one of those who switched over in favour of the Indonesian revolution during the Dutch action to regain their colony in the early 1950s.

In the melodrama of this power play, the most interesting figure was General Sumitro, who was then Commander of Kopkamtib (Operational Command for the restoration of Security and Order). For some time, with the support of the Bakin (the Government Intelligence Agency) he had been supplying information to President Suharto that the people were angry and hostile to the Aspri and that unless they were removed trouble would start. Suharto had been turning a deaf ear to such advice. In fact, when Suharto formed his first Government in 1967, he made a public statement that any of the Cabinet Ministers could be removed except the Aspris, who were personal assistants.

General Sumitro had in the past successfully and courageously defied Sukarno's orders and successfully smashed the communists when he was Panglima in Kalimantan (Borneo). Later, he gained the confidence of Suharto when he again succeeded in taming the communists in East Java, which incidentally also involved anti-Chinese measures. It was because of his courage and dynamic leadership that he was soon promoted as Deputy Commander of Kopkamtib, in charge of public order. When the students agitated against the Miniature Indonesia Project, he bravely curtailed the student movement but at the same time advised Suharto of the danger of the project.

Sumitro was intelligent, courageous and bold but appeared to lack wisdom. He failed to realise that Suharto was not a person who could be pressurised into doing things. Although Suharto listened to advice, he did not like his subordinates to dictate terms. In this instance, when things got out of control in Jakarta, Sumitro appeared before a large group of students ostensibly to pacify them. In his speech to the students, he asked them to trust him. When students asked him about the 'Tritura' meaning the three demands, he said he did not know and asked the students what they meant. The students spelt out — abolish Aspri, bring down prices and stop corruption. Incidentally, the Tritura slogan was also used in the 1966 students' agitation against Sukarno. At that time, it meant 1) ban the PKI, 2) down prices of foodstuff and 3) stop corruption.

Replying to the students, Sumitro said: 'You must trust me: let me take the responsibility of the Tritura. Now disperse and go home.' The students still did not disperse and Sumitro asked: 'Don't you still trust me?' Then opening the front of his jacket, he shouted: 'If you don't trust me, then kill me.' Almost stimultaneously, General Panggabean also spoke to some 5,000 students in another place. General Panggabean explained to the students that the government was sincere in wanting to cut down prices. He then asked the crowd whether they still trusted the government. They shouted 'yes'. He then asked the crowd whether they still had faith in Pak Harto (meaning Suharto). The reply was again 'yes'. It was interesting to compare the manner and statements made by the two leaders. One asked the crowd to have faith in President Suharto and the government and the other asked them to have faith in him — Pak Mitro. When Sumitro asked the students to have trust in him, he meant that they should trust him in settling matters with the President. It was not meant to challenge the President. But his words could be easily misconstrued.

Tanaka had gone all the way to spark off a riot which was smouldering for some time. He became the scapegoat. After the riots, Suharto dismissed General Sumitro, transferred his Bakin Chief, General Sutopo Yuwono, to the Netherlands as Ambassador and dissolved the Aspri. All in the Javanese style of compromise.

But the problem of cukongism remains the most delicate and intricate one, not easy to solve. The Chinese in Indonesia numbering about 3.5 million, are a heterogeneous and complex community. Despite the heterogeneous nature of the local Chinese community, most indigenous Indonesian leaders, with the exception of those affiliated to the communists and minor leftwing parties, perceive the Chinese as a homogeneous group which controls the Indonesian economy, resists assimilation and is loyal to an outside power, especially the People's Republic of China (PRC). President Suharto once described the Chinese as 3 percent controlling the 70 percent of the Indonesian economy. Dr Hafas, an anti-Chinese journalist of *Nusan-*

tara said to me once: 'There are still 250,000 overseas Chinese and another 750,000 stateless Chinese in Indonesia. These 250,000 Chinese control 70 percent of the money in circulation.'

In the 1971 general elections, the Golkar organised a dinner for the cukongs and raised RP100 million from it. The Golden Gate suspended business for two nights for the dinner. Big tycoons, bankers, traders, industrialists, shippers of all nationalities, both local and foreign, attended the dinner.

Before the dinner began, speeches were made by the Secretary-General of the Indonesian Chambers of Commerce Awaluddin Ghani, chairman of the Golkar Gen. Sokowati and Adam Malik, the Foreign Minister. Awaluddin, a prominent businessman, in his speech criticised Sukarno's regime for having ignored business circles and conspired only with the Communists and a handful of monopoly traders. He praised the Suharto Government for enabling 'national capitalists' to participate in the national reconstruction. Adam Malik appealed to national capitalists to join hands with the Golkar to reconstruct the country. He asked national capitalists not to be afraid of foreign capital and assured them that there would be no discrimination against them.

In this drive for funds, the 400,000 'becha' riders throughout Indonesia got a free shirt printed with the Golkar warangin symbol. Composers were employed to compose songs for Golkar. Long-playing records were made including the Golkar song and were distributed to all cukongs, embassies and various organisations. Plane-loads of entertainers went to outer regions to entertain the voters. Nearly in every nook and corner, you found the banyan tree symbol dominating the eyes.

At the dinner for ambassadors, Adam Malik explained that Golkar was not a political party, but a federation of all strata of Indonesian society including labourers, farmers, the professions, civil servants and the military.

The Golkar had won both the July 1971 and the 1977 elections and they expected to win in the 1982 general elections. In July 1971 the Golkar won 72 percent or 360 seats out of the 460 seats of Dewan Perwakilan Rakyat-Gotong Rojong (House of Representatives). The remaining 100 seats of DPR will be appointed by the President, 75 of whom would be from the Armed Forces and the other 25 from the functional groups.

(The whole 100 nominees were classified as functional group which comprises military and police personnel, teachers, lawyers, civil servants and other provincial groups.) Those 460 members of the DPR plus another 460 comprising representatives such as Governors of various provinces and members of the provincial and district councils, would make up the MPRS — Madjelis Permusjawaratan Rakyat Sementera (Provisional People's Consultative Assembly). The MPRS will elect the President and Vice-President and will meet once every year.

In 1977, the Golkar also won 70 percent of the 360 seats. The others contesting for seats were the PPP, the United Development Party — representing the Muslim parties — such as the N U Nahdatial Ulama (NU), the Partai Muslimin Indonesia (PMI), the Partai Serikat Islam Indonesia (PSII), the Pergerakan Tarbijah Islamijah (Perti) and the PDI (Indonesian Democratic Party), a combination of other non-Muslim parties such as the Partai Nasional Indonesia (PNI), the Partai Kristen Indonesia (Parkindo), the Partai Katolik, the Ikatan Penduling Kemerdekaan Indonesia (IPKI), and Proletarian Party (Murba).

The election system of Indonesia under the new order was a combination of the American presidential system and the Dutch and French systems of proportionate representation. The American system comes in when the President has full power to appoint his own Cabinet which will be responsible only to the President and not to the Parliament. The 360 members of the House of Representatives will be elected on the basis of proportionate representation according to the votes won by each political party. The three main groups — the Golkar, the PPP and PDI — will put up candidates for 26 electoral provinces on Nomination Day. The number of seats that will be allocated to each party will depend on the number of votes each group gets. Only political groups having a total membership of one million and able to fill in 100 candidates out of the 360 seats will be allowed to participate.

The cukongs have co-operated with the Golkar during the fund-raising campaigns.

How then did this misunderstanding between the Chinese and indigenous people come about? The tension between the indigenous Indonesians who are known as pribumi and the non-pribumi Chinese is a problem which will plague the government for some time.

Since Fah-hien, the Chinese Buddhist pilgrim, visited the island of Java in the year 414, the Chinese have been struggling for a living. The Chinese Government had always discouraged their citizens from going abroad. Section CCXXV of the 'Ta Tsing Leu Lee' of the Manchu dynasty said: 'All officers of government, soldiers and private citizens, who clandestinely proceed to sea to trade, or who remove to foreign islands for the purpose of inhabiting and cultivating the same, shall be punished according to the law against communicating with rebels and enemies and consequently suffer death by being beheaded.' The sons of the land of Confucius who left the graves of their ancestors are considered to be 'pu hsia', meaning 'lacking in filial duty.' But on the other hand, the Viceroy and Commissioner Tan said to Captain Dupong in May 1858 during the negotiations preceding the signing of the Tientsin treaties between America and China: 'When the Emperor rules over so many millions, what does he care for the few waifs that have drifted away to a foreign land. The Emperor's wealth is beyond computation. Why should he care for those of his subjects who have left their home, or for the sands they have scraped together.'

Fleeing from death, packed like sardines in a tin and suffering from hunger and exposure, they sailed in their dirty sailing tongkangs to the legendary rich and sunny South which they called 'Nanyang'. The emphasis placed in their value system on industriousness, frugality, self-reliance, venturesomeness and skill, together with some extraordinary adaptable and serviceable principles of social organisations, marked the immigrants out for economic success in a land of rich resources whose indigenous peoples were quite differently oriented.

The story of Chinese emigration is an alarming sad story, a story of misunderstanding, of destitutes and of refugees, a story which lasted for more than 1,500 years and still seems to last to the present day. From the seventeenth century to the twentieth, as the Dutch pressed ahead with their more systematic exploitation of the Indies economy, they needed the Chinese as the middlemen to deal with the indigenous people. Said Jan Pieterszoon Coen, the greatest of all Governors-General of the Dutch, who established the foundation of Dutch colonization: 'We need the Chinese to build this country. They are diligent and hardworking people of various trades and crafts and lovers of peace and honesty.' And so the number of Chinese increased since the 17th century, the people of 'various trades and crafts.' The Chinese were allotted a growing number of roles which the Dutch could not themselves fill. They were allowed to indulge in entrepreneurial occupations and they built up a comprehensive commercial and financial network extending from the major ports to the rural markets. The Dutch controlled the shipping and import-export trade and were fed by this network. In addition to being encouraged to take up commercial positions intermediate between the Dutch colonials and the indigenous population, the Chinese came in directly from 1860 to the 1930s as labourers on the plantations and in the mines producing commodities for western markets.

At one time, the Dutch became afraid of increasing Chinese power and influence and tried to curtail and minimise their various crafts and trades. In their attempt to defend their human rights and justice, a revolt against Dutch rule took place in 1740. This resulted in the most infamous Chinese murder in the first days of October 1740, the worst act of human violence by the Dutch, blackening Dutch Colonial History. Governor-General Valkenier killed hundreds of thousands of Chinese. The Kali (River) Tjiliwung turned red with blood and there was not a single Chinese anymore in Jakarta, then Batavia. Tanah Abang (which means 'Red Earth' in English), the name of a place, still stands as a black memory. Even Chinese outside Jakarta were sought to be killed. The Dutch Government offered 'two crown for every Chinese head'. The only comment from the Chinese Emperor was: 'It serves them right, these vagabonds running away from the country they belong to, leaving their parents' and ancestors' graves bare and naked in the sun without ceremonials.'

That was the first anti-Chinese riot started by the Dutch. After that the Dutch repented and made friends with the Chinese again. More and more Chinese left their home and sailed in their dirty tongkangs packed like sardines and came down south. They populated the long coastal areas of Java from Banten in the utmost West till Banjuwangi in the utmost East, where Chinese-like cities arose with the graceful Chinese roofs and the colourful artistic temples. Such were the old cities of Indramaju, Tjirebon, Tega, Pekalongan, Semarang, Djuwana, Rembang, Lasem, Tuban, Gresik, Pasuruan, Probolinggo and

Situbondo. Wherever they went, they brought along with them their culture, education, customs and traditions. They built schools and societies and they lived as a Chinese community with their loyalty to China.

For sometime I have been trying to find a metaphor to describe the Chinese and their relations vis-a-vis Indonesia, which has the richest natural resources in Asia. I think the cow and the milkman is suitable. Indonesia can be described as a fertile cow, rich in milk. When the Dutch conquered the land and owned the cow, the Chinese helped to milk it. For a short period, the Japanese wrestled away the ownership of the cow from the Dutch. There was not much milk then because the cow was sick. When Sukarno became the master of the cow, he was more concerned with glorifying the beauty of the cow and giving it a world image and had no time to nurse the cow and train his fellow countrymen in the art of milking. At the same time, he tried unsuccessfully to do away with the Chinese milkmen. When Suharto became the owner, he started intensively to milk the cow. As a result of the past performances and attitude of the Chinese cukongs, they now gained the reputation of not caring who owned the cow so long as they could milk it.

It was this attitude of the Chinese in the past as well as in the present that has created an under-current of tension between the indigenous Indonesians and the Chinese population. The Indonesian intelligentsia still remembers that before the Dutch came, most of the overseas and domestic trade had created a powerful and wealthy Indonesian middle class. With the influx of the industrious, thrifty, practical minded and flexible Chinese traders, this group of Javanese and Sumatran middle class gradually disappeared. The Dutch colonialists were more concerned with exploiting the natural resources of the country. It was never their policy to provide education or training for the pribumi. They brought with them a completely home-based administrative machinery. The Chinese regarded themselves as second class citizens but one class higher than the indigenous Indonesians. They helped the Dutch to exploit the country and the people. The seed of hatred had already taken root from those days.

During the Dutch East India Company days, many prominent Chinese were made Bupatis (district officers and village chiefs) or Regents for reasons of expediency, because of their economic power and efficiency. The efficient Chinese organised the link between the islands and the Northern Java Coast from where the agrarian produce had to be shipped to Holland. The Dutch found the pribumis incapable of filling this gap because of their easygoing habits. The Chinese made great profits out of such exploitations, and had antagonised the local population.

When the Indonesian revolution ousted the Dutch colonial masters from the country, the latter took with them the entire administrative infrastructure, from the Governors down to the ordinary clerks and typists, leaving behind not a skeleton staff to man the administrative machinery. Sukarno's nationalist anti-West fervour had brought with it drastic measures of nationalisation of all US and European dominated oil industry and the confiscation of Dutch estates. These measures frightened away all western capitalists. At that time, a defeated Japan was recuperating from the disastrous and humiliating surrender after the second world war. Thus, the Chinese became the only group of people in the country who had capital and business knowhow plus a deep understanding of the Indonesian character.

Sukarno was more interested in slogans and the revolution. He had no time to tap the natural resources of the country. He failed to utilise the Chinese capital and business knowhow to develop the country. Instead he took drastic measures to curtail their economic influence. It will be remembered that in 1957, Sukarno issued a decree banning all Chinese from retail business in the countryside.

I met Oei Tjoe Tat, a lawyer, and former Minister of State without portfolio attached to the Cabinet Presidium of Sukarno in December 1963, when he was released sometime in 1977 after serving 10 years in prison. Oei was the confidant of Sukarno and was arrested soon after the 1965 Gestapu Coup. According to Oei, Sukarno had curtailed the retail business of the Chinese in the countryside because of two reasons: Firstly, the pribumi had pressurised him to give them economic priority and he had to give way, and secondly it was for political reasons. The Muslim bodies who were worried that the Chinese would subvert the country through their retail shops throughout the country also pressurised him to close them down.

The policy was a failure because the pribumi who took over

the business could not run them. They did not believe in giving credit to their customers and the Chinese did. Soon their business flopped and the Chinese were allowed to run them again as warganegara of Indonesia.

During the Dutch regime, the Chinese were allowed to form organisations of a racial character. These organisations were not allowed to admit non-Chinese. The Dutch 'divide and rule' political maxim enabled them to rule Indonesia for three centuries. When the Japanese invaded Indonesia, they ordered the Chinese living in the villages and small towns to hang a name board in Chinese characters at the front of their houses to distinguish themselves from indigenous Indonesians in order to separate the one from the other.

When the Dutch were in power, an Indonesian-born Chinese Thio Thiam Tjong, the personal advisor of Governor-General Van Mook, took the initiative to form the Persatoean Tionghoa (PT) or Chinese union, with the purpose of unifying the ethnic Chinese in Indonesia. It was recognised by the Dutch and had been invited to send a delegation to the conference of the Dutch authority. It was also recognised by the Indonesian authorities of the early days when it was invited to Jogja for a meeting of minds, and represented in the Indonesian delegation to the Round Table Conference by one of its members. During those days, Chinese associations bearing Chinese names such as the Tiong Hoa Hwee Koan (THHK) were running Chinese schools such as Tiong Hoa Hak Tong and clubs, and the Tiong Hoa Siang Hwee representing the Chinese Chamber of Commerce, and Tiong Hoa Im Gak Hwee which was the Chinese music club and the Tiong Hoa Oen Tong Hwee, their sporting club. All these associations were exclusive to the Chinese.

After the Indonesian revolution, many Persatoean Tionghoa members were of the opinion that Chinese Indonesians needed an organisation not only to look after their interest but to guide them to fulfill their obligations to their adopted country. They felt that PT should be converted into a party in order to participate in nation-building. PT was transformed into Partai Demokratik Tionghoa Indonesia (PDTI) and Thio Thiam Tjong was elected Chairman. For three years, the party stagnated and could not make progress. It was never represented in the Parliament nor in the legislative body. It was discovered later that Thio, the Chairman who had a colonial background, having advised the former Governor-General, was the stumbling block. They went around looking for someone more suitable to be the Chairman, and they found an editor of several Indonesian dailies in East Java who was also minister without portfolio, a young man in his late thirties, Siauw Giok Tjaan to represent them. Siauw was regarded a leftist and had been gaoled three times by the Dutch and the Republic. He suggested that the party be transformed into an ordinary association with the main object of promoting democracy and to oppose racial discrimination and also that the organisation should open its membership to non-Chinese. The party was then dissolved and became the Badan Permusyawaratan Kewarganegaraan Indonesia (Baperki) or Council for Indonesian Citizenship.

According to the biography of Ang Siong Bie, 89, a Bandung-born Chinese who was the first treasurer of the Baperki, and who now resides in Canada, the Baperki opendoor policy was 'unprecedented in the history of Chinese associations in Indonesia.' Because of this ruling, it attracted the attention of Sukarno who gave it the strongest support. Baperki became popular among the Chinese but the pribumi had reservations about the organisation. Siauw, being a leftist, gained the support of only pro-Beijing organisations such as the PKI and leftwing organisations. The rightist and Muslim bodies shunned the Baperki.

The more important activity of Baperki was in the field of education. It set up Chinese schools throughout the archipelago, and in the early 1960s collected money to build a university. The university of Baperki opened its branches in Semarang and Surabaya. Ang's biography stated that 'in the heyday in the first half of 1965, the university had in Jakarta more than 6,000 students or about 10,000 taking in those from the branches.'

Never before in Indonesia had a university grown so swiftly. President Sukarno, enraptured by its speedy growth and early vigour, had given it a new name — Res Publika. Long before it was called Res Publika, it had opened wide its doors to the indigenous students, but only a few of them had ever entered, because indigenous students could easily get admission to the state universities.

It added: 'After the 1965 gestapu coup, the office of the Baperki was occupied by the army. In many places appeared posters alleging that Baperki was the patron of PKI and that Baperki was the financier of PKI. Luckily that was not true. Baperki had no money but many debts. PKI was building a four-storey building for its headquarters. Baperki could not afford to rent a modest house for its office, because the key-money was beyond its reach, therefore it had to borrow a space in the club house of Kiang Che Association. In its office the army might have found all the evidences, especially the annual financial reports, which exposed that financially Baperki was on the brink of bankruptcy.

'The Res Publika University was not opened again after the vacation. Many of its professors and lecturers did not turn up, many of its students were arrested or sought by the army. Its temporary main building in which was housed its faculty of dentistry was set on fire by some students of other private universities.

'Then, Baperki was outlawed. All members of the board of its central committee were blacklisted and their bank accounts were frozen. All its branches in many places throughout Indonesia met a similar fate. And many of its activists in different places were arrested and detained.'

The biography continued: 'The scourge of the Communists was not limited to arrests, confinement and torment, but developed into massacre of staggering proportion during several weeks in many regions outside the capital, particularly in East Java, Middle Java, Bali and some parts of Sumatra. How many people (ethnic Indonesians and Chinese) had been killed was only estimated, and estimates varied widely.

Mr Ang quoted John Hughes, 1967 winner of the Pulitzer Prize who wrote a special chapter 'Inquest on a massacre' in his book *Indonesian Upheaval* published in 1967. His conclusion was as follows:

'Thus, estimates of Indonesia's death toll range from a low 60,000 to a high 1,000,000 neither of which extremes is likely to be correct. Popular estimates have polarised around the 400,000 figure.

'It is indeed possible that something approaching half a million people were killed. If all these were communists, which they were not, it would still only mean that some 15 or 16 percent of the 3,000,000 party members claimed by Aidit (top leader of PKI) were executed.'

The genocide of pro-Beijing communists attracted strong protest and bitter criticism from Beijing Radio. In retort, Indonesian radio accused Beijing of instigating the coup. This radio duel was a prelude to an organised anti-China movement. The KAMI, the United Action of Indonesian students, was created, followed by the KAPI, the United Action of Indonesian Youths which staged anti-China demonstrations. The Chinese Trade Commission, the Chinese Military Attache and the Chinese Consulate-General were evicted from their residence. The KAMI and KAPI students broke into the Chinese Embassy ground and created a flag incident. The staff of the People's Republic of China went home to Beijing.

Soon after, the Jakarta Chinese associations Union was disbanded and its club house taken over by the army. All Chinese associations in Jakarta were disbanded and all Chinese schools closed. The authorities banned the *Sin Pao* — a pro-Beijing Chinese daily. And early in 1966 Res Publika University was taken over by the authorities which turned it into the Tri Sakti.

With the fall of Sukarno concluded the 20 years' 'Old Order' and it was replaced by the New Order of the Suharto regime. Under the New Order, there was a dissimulated authoritative order purporting that ethnic Chinese Indonesians ought to change their Chinese names into Indonesian. There was no government decree as such nor official proclamation. But there was an official announcement in the newspapers that the government had fixed a period in which the procedures of changing Chinese names would be made easy and that any Chinese who wished to avail themselves of the opportunity should do so.

Ang Siong Bie, in his biography, had this to say about the changing of names: 'Baperki, which ought to understand better the psychology of the ethnic Chinese Indonesians, believed that the integration of ethnic Chinese Indonesians into the Indonesian nation was more feasible and pragmatical. By integration was meant that they would remain a minority, would get the freedom to preserve their Chinese names, to live according to their culture, tradition and customs, so long as they would not be prejudicial to national interest; but they should be made through education, organisation, mass media and examples, useful, patriotic and loyal citizens who would be ready to sacrifice personal interest for the interest of the nation. But, this belief seemed incongruous with that of 'New Order' and had to be buried with Baperki itself.'

Since Baperki was banned, its central board committee members, one after another, were arrested, detained, interrogated and released, except Ang who was interrogated towards the end of 1966. And in December 1968, he left for Canada to join his son who had migrated there.

Ang, in the earlier part of the revolution, had helped people like the first Prime Minister Sutan Sjahrir, Amir Sjarifoedin and Mohd Natsir in their effort to stir up the masses throughout Indonesia to get interested in the revolution.

Siauw Giok Tjaan, 64, who was the Chief of Baperki, was made Minister without Portfolio for Peranakan Affairs in 1947 when he sided with the Indonesian nationalists. He was arrested and detained for 13 years by the Kopkamtib and released in 1978. Having settled down in Holland, he wrote a book called *Lima Jaman — perwujudan integrasi wajar* (Five generations — the situation of integration) published in 1981, in which he gave his view of the Chinese contribution to Indonesia and his view of Chinese integration into the Indonesian society. He felt that cukongism came about because the persons in power had not the experience to make use of the facilities that they had. He felt that the change of name would not change the nature of society and would only waste time and energy. He was against the type of assimilation process implemented by the present government.

Siauw was probably a member of the illegal PKI before World War Two. After the 1948 'MADIUN' affair, he was suspected to have been involved in the PKI rebellion and was imprisoned by the Indonesian authorities. He was soon released and became active again in Peranakan politics. His name was included in the Revolutionary Council of Col Utung when the 1965 Gestapu coup took place.

The only Baperki leader left in Indonesia who refused to be repatriated to Holland was Oei Tjoe Tat, 61, who was detained for 10 years and now lived in Jakarta after his release in 1977.

Oei was appointed Minister of State by Sukarno when in 1963 he went around the country doing propaganda for Baperki against anti-Chinese riots. Sukarno was attracted by his bravery and courage and offered him the post. He was a close confidant of Sukarno and accompanied the latter to Cairo, Beijing and many other conferences. I had an interview with Tjoe Tat who told me that during the confrontation against Malaysia, Sukarno sent him to various countries in South-East Asia to convince the Chinese that the confrontation was not aimed at the Chinese. Tjoe Tat in fact had made arrangements to see Lee Kuan Yew in Rome but something happened and the meeting did not materialise. Sukarno had asked Tjoe Tat to convey to Lee Kuan Yew that he had started the confrontation because he distrusted Tengku Abdul Rahman.

Tjoe Tat said he had gone to Penang and Kuala Lumpur under cover to carry out an assignment of Sukarno to see the reaction of the Chinese towards confrontation. He discovered that the Indonesian confrontationists had distributed pamphlets in Malaysia to explain that Indonesia had to confront Malaysia in order to save the Malays from Chinese domination. He returned to Jakarta and reported the matter to Sukarno. He told Sukarno that the pamphlets were distributed by helicopter by Indonesian confrontationists. Tjoe Tat was annoyed that Sukarno had on the one hand sent him to explain to the Chinese that confrontation was not aimed at them, but on the other hand allowed his men to distribute pamphlets contrary to his ideas. He questioned Sukarno about it. Sukarno was furious and flared up in a temper. He said: 'How dare you question my sincerity.'

Sukarno later made an investigation and discovered that one important member of his Cabinet was responsible for the pamphlets. He warned the person responsible that he would take drastic action against him if he did not cancel the pamphlets.

According to Tjoe Tat, he once asked Sukarno whether it was necessary to change names and Sukarno said: 'Why should you change your name. It was given by your father and you should respect your father.' He said Sukarno had always felt that the Chinese should be treated as one of the minorities.

Tjoe Tat was arrested only after Sukarno lost his power and was detained until 1977. He was put in the same cell as Subandrio and other PKI leaders. He was offered repatriation facilities to Holland but he refused. He said, 'When I was detained in the same cell as Subandrio, I felt that I was one of them. I am an Indonesian, I do not speak a word of Chinese and I am loyal to this country. I do not want to betray the lots of Chinese Indonesians who felt the same way as I do to Indonesia.

'They have kept me in as an Indonesian and I cannot leave the country for the sake of my own comfort. My roots are in Indonesia. My family have lived here for five generations.'

In Java the locally rooted Chinese community is known as Peranakan Tionghoa. They referred to the China-born Chinese as 'totok'. From the eighteenth to the early twentieth century Peranakan dominated the local Chinese communities. Immigration from China was moderate and assimilation to Peranakan society quite rapid. From the beginning of this century however, the number of immigrants rapidly increased, and the birth of the Republic of China brought about the rise of Chinese nationalism. The visit of Kang Yu Wei, the scholar of the late Ching Dynasty who advocated reformation in China, and other Chinese leaders encouraged the setting up of Chinese schools and Chinese associations. The Peranakans began to lose out in their effort to assimilate the Chinese. The Totoks preferred self-employment and were overwhelmingly found in entrepreneurial occupations. Peranakans showed a preference for professions and for clerical and staff positions in large enterprises.

During the decade from 1948 to 1958, the Chinese played foreign politics on Indonesian soil and it had become a great concern to the Indonesian authorities. There was a bitter struggle between Communist and Kuomintang. The Kuomintang associations bearing the colours of blue and white in their signboards clashed with the red and yellow pro-Communist associations. Pro-Taipeh and pro-Beijing newspapers fought it out in the open. This struggle permeated the whole of the Chinese community, from the schools down to the clubs. During the Sukarno regime, the pro-Beijing associations had an upper hand because Sukarno was flirting with the Jakarta-Peking axis and was friendly with the Chinese embassy.

Therefore the pro-Taipeh organisations were handicapped. In 1958, Taipeh aided the rebellion which broke out in Sumatra and the Celebes. This provoked the Indonesian authorities to crack down on the Kuomintang organisations. All Kuomintang organisations were banned and eventually schools and businesses with Kuomintang connections were closed. Then came the Gestapu Coup of 1965, when the Chinese Embassy was alleged to be involved with the PKI assassination of the seven generals, and the pro-Beijing associations including Baperki were closed and their leaders arrested and detained. The pro-Indonesian Chinese were few. Some fought along with the Indonesians against the Dutch and were not involved in foreign Chinese politics. But there were no associations to represent them.

After the 1965 coup, things changed. The Sukarno era of Baperki was over. I remember when I first visited Jakarta and Bandung in 1955 during the Afro-Asian conference in Bandung, there were still Chinese signboards everywhere. Chinese newspapers fought out their external wars within Indonesia and Chinese schools could be seen in every village. When I visited Indonesia again in 1960 to prepare for our Prime Minister's first visit, everything was still the same. But in 1970 when I was sent to Indonesia as Ambassador, there were no more Chinese signboards nor any Chinese associations or schools. Not only was the Chinese language considered 'harmful', but even Chinese religion and customs were regarded as undesirable. I was told that in 1967, a Presidential instruction stated that 'Chinese religion, beliefs and customs originated in their ancestral land and their various manifestations may generate unnatural influence on the psychology, mentality and morality of Indonesian citizens and therefore impede natural prosperity.' It was ordered that Chinese religion be observed only in family circles. But later in 1969, the government officially recognised two minority religions — Buddhism and Confucianism. Law No 5 of 1969 (UU No 5/1969) stipulated that these two religions and four others (Islam, Protestantism, Catholicism and Hindu-Bali) were officially recognised by the government. Since the Indonesian state ideology, the Pancasila, included 'Belief in God' as the first principle, every person in Indonesia was expected to have a religion of some kind.

The clearest manifestation of the New Order assimilation policy in the cultural field was the name-changing regulation issued in December 1966. Previously, a law (UU No 4/1964) had given all Indonesian citizens of foreign descent the opportunity to change their names to Indonesian (or Indonesian sounding) names. The applicant was required to obtain letters of recommendation from governors or local regents and local police chiefs. But the government did not publicise the law and did not actively encourage it. In December 1966, the Suharto government simplified the procedure in order to encourage name-changing among Indonesian citizens of foreign descent. They could simply submit their applications to the local authorities (usually governors, regents or mayors) to be registered. A low fee would be charged and the applications would be passed on to the Department of Justice. If no objections were raised by the local community in three months, the name would become legal. This regulation was effective from January 1967 to March 1968, but was later extended for an additional year because Indonesian citizens of Chinese origin who changed their names were fewer than expected. In August 1969, the Department of Justice announced that only 232,882 persons had changed their names.

In 1980, the Suharto Government further simplified its procedure for Chinese to be naturalised. He issued two decrees; the first known as the Presidential Instruction No 2/1980 was signed on 31 January 1980 and the second, the Presidential Decision No 13/1980, was signed on 11 February 1980.

Both decrees were only announced on 28 February 1980 in local newspapers. The government had played down the decrees due to their political sensitivity.

What are the meanings of these decrees?

To understand these decrees, some background information on the national status of ethnic Chinese is needed. It is estimated that there are three million ethnic Chinese in Indonesia, of whom 914,111 were PRC citizens, 122,013 were 'stateless' and 1,907 Taiwanese nationals. The first decree was aimed at those who were stateless and the second decree at the PRC citizens.

It is generally known that not all ethnic Chinese who are eligible for Indonesian citizenship possess citizenship certificates. The Presidential Instruction No 2/1980 aims at helping these people so that their national status will no longer be ambiguous. The Presidential Instruction No 2/1980 vested camats (sub-district heads) with power of issuing citizenship certificates. Prior to promulgation of this Instruction, this power was only given to the state courts. There are 270 state courts in Indonesia but there are 3,329 camats. With the transfer of power to camats, it is expected that the issuance of citizenship certificates will be accelerated.

According to the Presidential Instruction No 2/1980, the citizenship certificate issue should be settled before 17 August 1980. Approximately 100,000 Chinese Indonesians will be affected by this decree. This decree was quite controversial and some critics claimed that many might use this opportunity to become Indonesian citizens.

The second decree empowers the President to approve the applications for citizenship instead of the Cabinet which previously approved such citizenships under the 1958 Citizenship Act. This decree requires the applicant to declare a willingness to give up his original citizenship.

The most remarkable aspect of this second decree is the limited time given to Government bodies to process the application and the role played by the central Government. It is crucial to note that the decree stipulates that if necessary, a Team Gabungan (United Team) comprising of central Government officials from the Department of Justice, Home Affairs, Attorney's Office, Police and Bakin (intelligence) will be sent to the provinces to assist local authorities. Theoretically, an alien Chinese in Indonesia can be naturalised as an Indonesian citizen in less than three months.

The simplification of procedures for naturalisation of Chinese into Indonesian citizens is one of the steps the Suharto Government has taken to ensure that when Indonesia normalised relations with Beijing, the problems of the Chinese would be minimised. The authorities want to be sure that the Chinese are properly assimilated before embarking on normalising relations with Beijing.

What is meant by properly assimilated? This was what General Sumitro, one time strongman in Indonesia who was the Head of Kopkamtib, had to say when I had a game of golf with him in April 1971. 'I would like to see all Chinese in Indonesia forget their own culture and tradition and be assimilated completely into the Indonesian society. The Chinese should not continue to stick to their old customs and traditions or identify themselves with either Beijing or Taiwan.'

I think many Indonesians share his views and that was why the Indonesian authorities were taking steps to assimilate the Chinese.

Meanwhile, anti-Chinese riots continue to break out from time to time in Indonesia despite government measures to assimilate the Chinese. There is a superstitious belief in the Wall Street of Jakarta, known as Pintu Ketchil (Seow Nan Men), the centre of Chinese banking and trade, that anti-Chinese violence erupts in Indonesia once in eight years. Still fresh in the minds of most of the middle-aged and older generation Chinese are the incidents which took place at the interval of eight years since 1949. In 1949, many Chinese were murdered, their houses and cars burnt when the indigenous Indonesian went for them because many Chinese sided the Dutch colonials against the Indonesian revolution. Eight years later, in 1957, Sukarno took drastic action against the Chinese by banning the Chinese from all retail trade throughout the country. There were several unhappy incidents. In 1965, eight years later, a large number of Chinese were killed for their alleged involvement in the September 30 Gestapu Coup. The victims were mainly those Chinese who sympathised with the Baperki and the PKI and their affiliated unions and farmers' associations. In 1973, owing to the greedy manipulations of Chinese cukongs, riots broke out in Bandung and Jakarta. In December 1980, an anti-Chinese riot in Solo damaged 400 vehicles, 500 scooters and four houses were burnt. It was one of the most serious riots that ever occurred.

What is the cause of the frequent anti-Chinese riots in Indonesia? One of the fundamental reasons is the disparity of wealth between the indigenous Indonesians and the non-indigenous Indonesian Chinese. Although not all Chinese are rich and in fact the majority are poor, the bad image created by the minority cukongs could affect the well-being of the majority of innocent Chinese. Some of the cukongs have become too greedy. They do not confine their activities to exploiting the country's natural resources, but begin meddling with land grab which affects the livelihood of the common people. For example, in an attempt to get rich quick, a number of land speculators scrambled for land around Jakarta occupied by thousands of squatters. They used military power to evict the squatters forcefully.

Since these squatters do not hold land titles, they were paid the minimum compensation, hardly sufficient for them to find alternative accommodation. When they refused to vacate the land, soldiers in military uniforms arrived with bulldozers to tear down the houses. The cukongs either developed the vacated land into housing projects, reaping handsome profits, or sold them to developers at very high prices.

The trial of Robby Cahyadi, a young non-Chinese speaking Indonesian-born Chinese, who made a fortune by smuggling Mercedes Benz cars, became another useful weapon for the anti-Chinese elements to agitate and stir up anti-Chinese sentiments.

The cukongs may have changed their names into Indonesian names but this does not wipe out the prejudice against them. The Suharto regime is fully aware of the danger that anti-cukongism may lead to social unrest and economic chaos. Suharto's inner circle realises that any move to curtail the cukongs will lead to an exodus of Chinese capital from the country which will result in economic chaos affecting the smooth development of Repelita — Indonesia's development plans. Because of their capital, knowhow and the trust and confidence created abroad, even foreign investors from western countries and from Japan are beginning to have preference for Chinese cukongs as partners instead of pribumi entrepreneurs. They find that the Chinese cukongs not only have the capital, know-how and trustworthiness, but have powerful military connections. This has caused tremendous concern among the pribumi entrepreneurs. Unless this tendency is speedily checked, more and more pribumi entrepreneurs would be deprived of their chances of participating in the economic development of their country. The frustration could easily lead to an explosive situation which will be exploited by the extremists to stir up anti-Chinese violence.

It is against this background that the Suharto regime has encouraged the formation of the KADIN, the Indonesian Chamber of Commerce, comprising all indigenous Indonesian industrialists and traders with a view to promoting better understanding among them and to look after their welfare. The Kadin would try to consolidate the strength of pribumi entrepreneurs and would formulate schemes to help them.

A parliamentary committee has also recommended that the Parliament approves a large sum of money for the purpose of building up a pribumi middle class who will then be able to take over from the Chinese cukongs gradually. It would take some time to get a middle class built up.

The Suharto Government was sensitive to the resentments of the indigenous Indonesian businessmen. On several occasions, President Suharto himself appealed to the non-indigenous businessmen, meaning the Chinese, to seek indigenous partners so that the position of the latter would improve. He said all non-indigenous companies were obliged to sell 50 percent of their shares to the government which would then sell them to indigenous businessmen.

Celebrating the National Independence Day on 17 August 1972, Suharto made a speech and touched on the problems of pribumi and non-pribumi enterprises. He said the problem should be brought into the open and should not become a subject of secret discussion which would only sow the seed of tension. If the non-pribumi capital could be properly directed, the potentialities could become an asset. He said the problem should be seen in the right perspective, removing evil prejudice and rejecting racialist attitudes. The problem had its root from the disharmony in Indonesian society. It was an inheritance rooted decades ago. There was a small social class in a very strong economic position and controlling the greater part of Indonesia's economic position who has never played a big role in national economic life. It was a problem of social justice and it was from this basic point of view that the Government tried to solve the disharmony.

Suharto said the problem was how to develop a pattern of National Development that would broaden the involvement of all social forces and to redistribute the results of development in a more equitable way among the people. Taking this attitude did not mean that the Government would wipe out or kill the role of the economically strong group in the process of development.

He added: 'If the non-indigenous group has freely chosen Indonesia as their Fatherland and Nation, and if the indigenous group has accepted them as part of their own nation, then cooperation between the two groups is a necessity. The Government is thoroughly examining the policy, economic and legal instruments in order to bring harmony in this matter.' He suggested as an instance that the indigenous entrepreneurs or even any citizen should be given the opportunity to share the ownership of the enterprises owned by non-indigenous entrepreneurs by purchasing the company's shares on the stock exchange which was now in the process of creation.

After the anti-Tanaka riots, Suharto announced that the Government intended to deny medium term financial loans from state banks to non-indigenous Indonesians. On 22 January 1974, Suharto made a statement concerning policy directives for private investment. He reiterated that all foreign investment (with the exception of mining, banking and insurance operations) should be in the form of joint ventures.

'The national holding in joint-ventures shall be increased as fast as possible to a majority position of not less than 51 percent of the total holding . . . It is essential that within the national holding, there should be equality of interest between indigenous and non-indigenous Indonesians . . .

'Direct participation in new foreign joint ventures by non-indigenous Indonesian citizens will no longer be permitted. Participation is possible, however, by means of a corporate partnership between indigenous Indonesians and Indonesians from other ethnic groups which can then enter into an agreement for a joint venture with the foreign organisations.'

No time schedule was set to carry out this 'indigenization' of the enterprises.

Given the present economic situation in Indonesia where the development programme has been heavily dependent on foreign investment, the exclusion of non-indigenous capital would only jeopardize Indonesia's economic stability. If the exclusion law was applied only to the Chinese, it would still affect the economy since the Chinese play a key role in Western and Japanese enterprises. This is one of the paradoxes facing Indonesia. It wants to cut down its dependence on Chinese capital and knowhow but has to be careful in case the whole economy may be jeopardised.

On the cultural and social field, I see no turning back to the days of Baperki where the Chinese could be represented by a single body to fight for their interest. The assimilating process is fast making the Chinese forget their names, their culture and their own roots. The younger generation speaks only Indonesian and not even dialects. They are afraid to perform ancestor worship or to keep ancestral altars. They are afraid to celebrate the Lunar New Year. Some of them put on a moustache to look like Indonesians. In years to come, they will lose their roots.

The feeling of the Chinese in Indonesia was best described by an Indonesian-born Chinese who went back to China, took part in the 1911 revolution, got disillusioned and returned to Indonesia. He was Thung Liang Lee (deceased) who was secretary to Wang Chin Wei, one of the Chinese revolutionaries who collaborated with the Japanese during the occupation. Writing in March 1954 an article entitled 'The unreality of Chinese nationalism in Indonesia — an apologia and a reorientation', he said: 'The Chinese loath to assimilate themselves with the native population especially since owing to the Dutch colonial policy, assimilation did not mean equalization of rights with the Indonesians. They succumbed to the Dutch view of regarding the Indonesians as a somewhat inferior race; they inter-mixed but as a general rule, they did not legally inter-marry with the Indonesians. Racially, linguistically and psychologically, they are much closer to the latter than to any other group of the population, closer even than the China Chinese. But they not only persisted in their refusal to assimilate themselves with their natural brothers and sisters; they even refused to regard the country of their birth and upbringing as their own, true country . . . Yet, disregarding the facts of history and of ethnology, they tried to become as China-Chinese as possible.

'Chinese nationalism became an obsession which hampered their outlook and hindered their political advancement at every step. It enmeshed them in a mess of contradictions, causing friction and suspicion everywhere.'

Thung Liang Lee felt that the early immigrants prior to and during the early days of the East India Company were completely assimilated by the native population, which acquired a certain Chinese strain in their blood. He added: 'Some of the well-known Princely Houses and aristocratic families of Indonesia — like the Sultans of Palembang, Bantam, Ceribon — the regents of Tjiamis and Sumedang — have had Chinese ancestors and are proud to acknowledge the fact.'

Thung said: 'Lacking in historical perspective, unversed in international affairs, devoid of political realism, the 20th century Indonesian Chinese could only dream of a new China, which, once arisen to the position of a Great Power, would automatically secure for them the same privileged status which Japan had, as a special case, secured for their handful of nationals.

'China had become a panacea for all their woes and sufferings, real and imaginary. Thus they started a movement to repudiate the jus soli element in the Netherlands Indies National Law, and demanded the right for the Indonesian Chinese to owe political allegiance to the Chinese Republic. In this way they formally announced their intention of seeking redress of their grievances outside the framework of the existing political system. They were completely oblivious of the fact that what might be conceded as a special case to a handful of people, would be intolerable if applied to a considerable and unassimilable minority group amounting to over a million people. They could not realise that no country in the world could possibly tolerate even at the risk of provoking an international war, the formation of what in effect would be a state within a State.'

Commenting on the granting of citizenship to Chinese by the Indonesian authorities, Thung said: 'The grant by the Republic of Indonesia of the automatic warga negara status to all Sino-Indonesians was a measure of goodwill of an unprecedented nature. It was a declaration on the part of the Republic that we are wanted. It makes us all formally and legally Sino-Indonesians. It did not compel us, however, to accept the gift. But it put us in a far more favourable position than the Indo-European who had to make a special petition to acquire that status.

'The warga negara status must be made into a reality by a proper response on our part. And this response must consist in the realisation that our salvation depends on our realising the unreality of Chinese nationalism and our renouncing all political and sentimental ties with the country that in fact had never wanted us . . . .

'We must never again fall under the delusion of China being our Fatherland, of being our true own country which loves and protects us, and is therefore entitled to our allegiance and loyalty.

'Our true Fatherland is this country of Indonesia, the country of our mothers, our grandmothers, great-grandmothers, great-great-grandmothers. Our loyalty belongs to the Republic of Indonesia, and it must be one and undivided. Our efforts should be directed to making out of this archipelago the kind of commonwealth as we find in the United States of America — only without the racial discrimination that has become a blot on the American scene and a disgrace to modern civilization.

'A change of heart, more even than a reorientation of policy is required. For only with this change of heart can we devote our best efforts and energy to the construction of our new Fatherland, as statesmanship no less than self-interest demands. As the RI needs us, so do we need the RI. We require fair treatment and protection from the RI and the abolition of the last vestiges of the racial discrimination inherited from the old colonial regime. In return, we must give the RI not only our bodies, but also our souls.'

Thung was right when he said that 'our salvation depends on our realising the unreality of Chinese nationalism and our renouncing all political and sentimental ties with the country that in fact had never wanted us.'

Before and after the second world war when the heat of Nationalism was high, thousands of Indonesian Chinese went back to China for further studies or to serve the 'nation'. Some went back on their own, and others were repatriated. Nearly all of them were frustrated and disillusioned. During the cultural revolution, the Gang of Four treated all overseas Chinese as 'potential spies' or 'rightwing reactionaries' and they were severely persecuted. China had never wanted them. They escaped to Hong Kong and are stranded there, never allowed to return to their 'homeland' — Indonesia.

This is the tragedy of the Chinese overseas. The danger is that the tragedy may spill over to Singapore. Most Indonesian leaders saw Singapore as a Malay territory which was taken over by the non-Malays and later developed into a Chinese centre in the region. When Sukarno was still influential, Singapore was seen by Indonesia as a smuggling centre which was prosperous at the expense of Indonesia's economy. During the Indonesian regional rebellions (1957–58) Singapore was used by the rebels as a smuggling centre as well as a place from where they got their arms supplies. Considering Singapore as a threat to the Indonesian security, a powerful general, Djatikusumo, was sent to Singapore as the Ambassador to curb the activities of the rebels here.

When Singapore hanged the two Indonesian marines, the Chinese in Sorabaya, the headquarters of the Indonesian marines, became the first target of Indonesian rioters. The Indonesians generally find it difficult to distinguish between the Chinese in Indonesia and Singaporean Chinese. They thought they were the same. Their perception of the Chinese in Indonesia has blurred their view of the true nature of the Singaporean Chinese. They brought along their prejudices against the Chinese in Indonesia when they were dealing with the Singaporean Chinese.

Coming back to General Sumitro, who had become a friend of mine. Talking about the Chinese in Indonesia, he suddenly burst out with words such as the 'Lee Kuan Yew third China concept.' I immediately interrupted and said that there was no such thing as the 'Lee Kuan Yew third China concept' and I explained that Singapore leaders believed in the multi-racial society within the concept of a South-East Asian family of nations. He suggested that the topic of the Chinese in Indonesia could be discussed between Lee Kuan Yew and President Suharto. He said Lee Kuan Yew should come forward with some suggestions on how to solve the Chinese problems in Indonesia. I explained to him that the Chinese in Singapore regarded themselves as Singaporeans loyal to Singapore and that Prime Minister Lee Kuan Yew would not be in a position to speak on behalf of overseas Chinese in the region.

Subconsciously, people like Sumitro, a man who held high positions in the Indonesian Government, still harbour doubts about the Singapore Chinese and the role they will play. The Indonesian leaders perceive Singapore as a cultural and economic centre of the 'overseas Chinese' and hence create great problems for Indonesia in their efforts to assimilate the local Chinese and weaken the economic strength of the Chinese in Indonesia. A significant number of Indonesian Chinese students receive their education in Singapore. Indonesian Government officials considered this a problem because, in their view, these Indonesian Chinese received non-Indonesian education in Singapore and they would have problems in adapting themselves to the Indonesian population after their return to Indonesia. The Indonesian embassy here reveals that there are approximately 4,000 Indonesian Chinese students studying in Singapore. The Indonesian Government intended to apply rigid control over these students and prohibit students of Chinese descent from coming to Singapore to study in the future.

After 25 March 1973, when the Prime Minister visited Indonesia and after the return trip to Singapore of President Suharto in August 1974, there is better understanding between the leaders of the two countries. The frank talks between the two top leaders had helped to clear their doubts as to the motives and intentions of the two nations which are the bulwark of Asean. Prime Minister Lee Kuan Yew and President Suharto never at any time touched on the issue of the Chinese in Indonesia. Singapore consists of two million Singaporeans and no overseas Chinese. It is not the responsibility of Singapore to look after the Chinese in Indonesia or for that matter anywhere in this region.

The fact that Singapore has been willing to invest in Indonesia, to help Indonesia's economic development and to release trade figures between Singapore and Indonesia helped to eradicate many doubts existing in the minds of many Indonesian leaders. Apart from Singapore's friendly move, the international situation after the fall of South Vietnam, Cambodia and Laos to the Communists, also caused the Indonesian government to review its relationship with the neighbouring states. Asean has become increasingly important for the survival of non-Communist Asean states. This partly explains Indonesia's readiness to respond to Singapore's goodwill.

One important factor which has cleared Indonesia's doubts has been Singapore's assurance that Indonesia would be consulted on Singapore–PRC relations. The assurance has been repeated by Singapore leaders that it would only establish relations with the PRC after Jakarta normalises its relations with Beijing. This assurance, in fact, makes Indonesia trust Singapore, and feel that Singapore will not be used by the PRC as its fifth column.

The future good relationship between Singapore and Indonesia will depend to a large extent on one fundamental principle of not interfering in the internal affairs of each other. Singapore has respected the policy of the

Indonesian Government to assimilate its Chinese population and would not interfere with whatever they do with the Chinese population in their territories. On the other hand, Indonesia should also respect the various cultural and linguistic policies introduced by the Singapore Government vis-a-vis its population because of its special historial background. We believe that everyone must have cultural roots in order to blossom. This policy of tapping the roots should not be considered as something hindering the assimilation process of the Indonesian Chinese.

With this understanding, things should go well with the relations between Singapore and Indonesia.

15

Korea — Confucius' Dreamland

The Republic of Korea was the eighth country that I was accredited in my eleven years of diplomatic life. I covered Korea from Tokyo, flying there about once in three months. I had no office in Seoul, the capital of Korea when I first went there. Later, we appointed an Hononary Consul who is a Korean working as Agent for NOL. I had strongly pressed our government to open up an Embassy in Seoul, for Korea was fast becoming a country to be reckoned with in Asia. Its economy is progressing rapidly, making a GNP increase of more than 10 percent a year. In the Olympic games held in Seoul, Korea shock the world by obtaining many gold medals. It was after the Olympic games that Singapore sent a full-time Ambassador to Korea. The Korean people are dynamic and full of energy. Where they get their energy from? Is it racial or is it the influence of Confucianism. Whatever it may be, I have yet to come across a country so much influenced by Confucianism. Confucius would be happy, if he were still alive and happened to visit Korea.

I presented my credentials to President Chun Doo Hwan on 19th of October 1984. When he was at the height of his political power. The Ministry of Foreign Affairs protocol officer and a military attache came to my room at Lotte Hotel to brief me on the procedure.

At about 10.30 am, escorted by 10 outriders, the presidential car brought me to the Blue House — the Presidential Palace built in 1939 for the Japanese Governor General and which since has become the place where all Korean Presidents have stayed. The military band started to play martial music when I arrived. Wearing a tail-coat, I walked a few steps leading to the main gate accompanied by the chief of protocol. We stopped at a closed gate with a red carpet. One minute later, it opened up and at the end of the hall stood President Chun and his Foreign Minister Lee Won Kyung. I made a casual bow and proceeded towards them stopping about 3 feet in front of the President. The chief of protocol stepped forward and introduced me to the President. Then the another protocol officer came from behind and handed me my speech and I read it. The President replied in Korean but there was no live interpretation because a copy of his speech in English had been handed to me earlier.

The President had a brief conversation with me standing in the same position. He said he was pleased that Singapore had sent such a distinguished Minister to represent the country in Korea and he was happy that the Prime Minister had sent his most trusted man there.

When President Chun was at the height of his political power, he visited Japan in response to Prime Minister Nakasone's visit to Korea. That was the second time I met Chun. The first time was in Tokyo at a reception given by Emperor Hirohito. The second time was at the Blue House. I had to wait for several weeks before I could get a date to present my credentials because the Korean Foreign Ministry was busy preparing for Chun's visit to Japan. In his speech, Emperor Hirohito apologized for what Japan had done to Korea during her 25-year-old rule of Korea. Security was very tight during Chun's visit because of the 700,000 Koreans in Japan, nearly half of them were supporters of Kim Il-sung. Chun could have been assassinated by leftwing extremists. At home, Chun also faced protest from anti-Japanese students who were opposed to his visit.

When I was talking to President Chun, I could hardly foresee his future. I could not foresee that he would have to retreat to the Sorak mountains and lead a hermit life in disgrace after apologizing to the nation for his 'sins' as well as corruption and mismanagement of the country. The students wanted to put him to trial and have him executed.

The Blue House

Those who have occupied the Blue House never had had a good ending. The Blue House was built in 1939 for the Japanese Governor General who had to fled the country after the second world war. The first Korean President to occupy the Blue House was *Syngman Rhee*. The 70-year old prince (he was the descendant of the Yi Dynasty rulers of Korea for five centuries) entered politics in 1895, five years before Sir Winston Churchill. The people called him 'the Royal Rebel'. Steeped in fluent classical Chinese education, Rhee was greatly influenced by Confucianism. Yet, he eagerly grasped the libertarian Western ideas offered to him at the Seoul Methodist Mission School.

At 21 with reforms as his banner, he dashingly founded Korea's first daily newspaper and though already an Imperial Privy Councillor, led an anti-Japanese student demonstration.

Prison and torture were his reward. For six months, they cracked his sturdy body and then flung him behind bars for seven years. While in prison, he scribbled 'the spirit of Independence' and studied the works of Christ. This was his prelude to politics. He was alone and in darkness, while outside Korea embroiled itself in the Russo-Japanese war.

While in prison, the Japanese tortured him and had his hand maimed. The Japanese had caught him as a revolutionary leader and smashed his fingers in their steel clamps. He often blew those broken fingers whenever he was excited or worried.

Curiously enough, the war opened his prison doors. A nationalist government sent him to the United States on a vague diplomatic mission. There he met Theodore Roosevelt and at Princeton he earned his PhD. He also impressed a professor named Woodrow Wilson, who later became the US President. A new ideology solidified in his imagination: the ideology of self-determination.

While Rhee was slavishly worshipping Wilson in the US, Japan's military heel was ruthlessly tramping Korea into subservience. Rhee sailed home, flitting about mysteriously as a resistance organiser.

The threat of his life becomes lost in intrigues, in romantic cloak-and-dagger legends. It is said that he was once smuggled in (or out) in a coffin, and that he played cat and mouse with the Japanese secret police.

Then in March 1919, with the great Korean uprising bloodily crushed, his name reappeared solidly in history. Surviving Korea nationalists gathered in Shanghai in a brave but pathetic gesture of defiance, a 'Provisional Government of the Republic of Korea'. Its president was Syngman Rhee. And in that office, for the next 20 years, he was to remain the exiled president of a republic which had never known life and the head of a government which had never known office.

Rhee became the darling of Western liberals. His whole life was dedicated to his country's cause: his every movement, his every word appealed frantically to the feelings of the world.

In 1932, in Geneva (when vainly trying to slip Korea's case into a League of Nations debate) he met the Austrian woman Francesa Donnner whom he married at nearly 60 years old.

Then in 1945 when he was almost 70, Japan surrendered. In Seoul, American General Hodges dramatically introduced Syngman Rhee behind a screen to a vast meeting of Koreans. The crowd stared dumbfounded, then broke into a storm of applause. Their living legend was there. He was flesh and blood. He was the embodiment of a new Korea. In July 1948, at 73, Rhee was elected South Korea's first President. He moved into the Blue House. It was his moment of glory — his dream was fulfilled. Nothing lay in his way to one of the biggest and most successful political climax of all time.

In Korea, after 40 years of Japanese occupation, there were no resistance leaders ripe for promotion. There were no patriots as famous as Syngman Rhee. Rhee did not exactly lead his people to overthrow the Japanese rulers. He had joined them after the Japanese had left. He came from the American wilderness and he was then no more than a name to the Koreans, having been so long in exile. Rhee gained fame and power through historical circumstances. He was the Sun Yat-sen of Korea. Dr.Sun did not personally led the revolution to overthrow the Manchu dynasty. He was most of the time in exile and so was Syngman Rhee. The difference was that Dr.Sun Yat-sen died gloriously in his sleep and he was remembered as the father of New China, whilst Rhee held on to power far too long and had to be thrown out of the country.

It was the Americans who had put Rhee into power. Very few who knew Rhee's character had told the American General that unless the tempestuous quarrelsome and headstrong young man who had figured in independence Club activities in the late 1890's had changed for the better, he was scarcely the ideal father figure for a new and democratic republic. The Americans could not have been completely blind to the gamble. It was just that they had no one else to offer.

Syngman Rhee ruled the country for 12 years. He rigged the elections and became President for the fourth time at 84 following the presidential election which was marked throughout by outbreaks of violence and hooliganism. Rhee was irascible, dogmatic and dictatorial to the day he fled with his Austrian wife from a country that had decided to disown him.

The Syngman Rhee regime, backed by massive American and United Nations assistance, had a considerable record of its achievements. There were at least five times as many factories and plants in South Korea as there were 10 years ago. There were more than 60 universities and colleges as against eight in 1945 and these turned out over 20,000 graduates every year.

Rhee's achievements however, set no proud democratic fires alight in South Korea. By macabre coincidence, his opponents in previous elections all died suddenly. They were believed to be assassinated by him.

The methods adopted by Rhee's Liberal Party shocked Western observers. Intimidation and violence flared up before and during the polling. Two opposition campaigners and 60 voters were killed in rioting and bloody demonstrations by Rhee's supporters.

At 85, the formidable Rhee continued to bestride his tragically truncated country, calling for armed action against the Communist North and refusing to waver from his wretched vendetta against Japan and all things Japanese.

Then on 27 March 1960, Rhee offered to resign as half a million yelling rioters encircled the Blue House and dragged his statue through the streets, spitting on it and throwing stones. About 30 people were killed and 100 others wounded as police and troops hopelessly outnumbered clashed with crowds rampaging through the city.

In the National Assembly, Government and opposition members combined to, pass an all-party resolution demanding the 85-year-old President's resignation from all offices and declaring null and void the March 15 election, which had returned him to power.

Syngman Rhee flew to Honolulu where he died of a stroke at 90. President Park Chung Hee who took over the Blue House ordered deep mourning for Korea's first President. Although Rhee had ruled his people with strong armed tactics, nobody doubted the genuineness of his life-long ideal of a unified and independent Korea.

His body was flown back to Korea and a state official funeral was held for him.

The second President who stayed in the Blue House was Park Chung Hee. Park was a soldier-turned-politician who led a bloodless coup and toppled the civil government of US-educated Premier John M. Chang, who came to power after students uprising toppled the government of Syngman Rhee.

Park was the seventh son of a farmer, living near Taeger, Southeast of Seoul. After graduation from high school, he taught at a primary school for three years until 1940 when he entered the Manchukuo Military Academy.

After his graduation in 1942, he studied at the Japanese Imperial Military Academy and was a first lieutenant in the Japanese Army when the war ended. With Korea's liberation from Japan, he entered the new South Korea army and was commissioned captain in 1946. He won his first star during the 1950 – 1953 Korean war. By 1961, he was a major general and deputy Commander of South Korea's 2nd Army.

In 1961, he led the coup. As the head of a military junta, Park pushed through a series of drastic reforms aimed at cleaning up corruption and modernising the economy.

In 1963 when the nation returned to civil rule, he took off his uniform and won a hotly contested election to become President. His first five-year economic plan, launched in 1962, was a success.

Riding on the crest of his economic success, Park was re-elected to the Presidency in 1967 and 1971. But opposition to his rule was gradually mounting, both within South Korea and across the border in the north.

Angered by his decision to send 45,000 South Korean troops to fight on the American side in South Vietnam in 1966, North Korea began stepping up its border provocations. It reached a climax on January 21 1968 when 231 Communist commandos sneaked into Seoul and tried to storm the Blue House in an attempt to assassinate him.

In October 1972, Park proclaimed martial law, suspended the constitution, dissolved the Parliament and banned political activities. He promulgated a new constitutions which greatly strengthened the powers of the President at the expense of a new junta forming a weak Parliament, which enabled him to seek as many terms in office as he wished.

Late in 1973, opposition to his new ruling system mounted. Political dissidents, including college students and politicians, began demonstrating for the restoration of democracy.

Tragedy struck in August 1974, while Park and his wife were attending a public ceremony at the National Theatre in Seoul to celebrate Korea's liberation from Japanese colonial rule in 1945. A gunman tried to shoot Park but missed and killed his wife instead.

The first lady Madam Park, Yook Young Soo was the most loved lady in Korean postwar history. When she first moved into the Blue House after her husband was inaugurated, she told the press: 'I am determined the Blue House will not become my gilded cage.' Madam Park was humble and wore simple dresses as other Korean ladies. She liked to wear Korean fabric. She was always with her people despite the fact that she was staying in the Blue House. She once said: 'I must keep a personal contact with my people so that I can absorb and understand their problems. I must be the sounding board for their pleas.' When asked if the President sactioned such an undertaking, she said 'Yes, he feels it is my most important duty as his wife.'

'After all, he can't do it. His hours are filled with high level affairs of state, and we both believe it is the best way in which I can help the people.'

Madam Park spent all the time she had driving around in a jeep visiting farmers and labourers. She said it was easier when she was campaigning for the husband.

'Now, I cannot walk out of the Blue House and get into a jeep. I cannot go anywhere without aides, guards and press people accompanying me,' she said.

She, however, revealed that she did managed to sneak out alone undiscovered on Christmas eve. She laughingly told the press one day: 'Ever since I moved into the Blue House, I have been burdened by the worry of how to keep the door open between me and the people with whom I want to be with. There is a way, I must find it.'

Five years after his wife was shot dead, President Park who had ruled the country with an iron hand for 18 years was shot and killed by his intelligence Chief Kim Jae-kyu at the Blue House during a private dinner. Blood was again spilled at the Blue House. Park had used the Korean Central Intelligence Agency (KCIA) to keep his firm grip on the nation and had protected his authoritarian regime against political opponents. Ironically, he was shot dead by his KCIA Chief. KCIA, modelled on its American counterpart, was used by the Park administration to spy on thousands of South Korean citizens.

In perhaps one of its most controversial mission, the KCIA kidnapped opposition leader Kim Dae-Jung, Park's strongest opponent during the general elections, from a Tokyo hotel and dragged him back to Seoul, where he was kept under house arrest. Kim later fled to the United States.

Park's assassination occurred one week after the official visit of Prime Minister Lee Kuan Yew. It therefore came as a big shock to Lee and his colleagues. 'Under his dynamic leadership over the last 18 years, Korea has been transformed into a vigorous and thriving industrialised country,' said Mr S. Rajaratnam, the Foreign Minister, when he warned the big powers against exploiting the Korean tragedy. Prime Minister Lee was also impressed by Park's achievements.

When Park was assassinated, Korean GNP was four and a half times larger that it had been at the time of his inauguration. Per capita income had grown more than three times over the same period and exports, for many years the main source of GNP growth, were about 50 times larger than in 1962.

Park's success in engineering Korea' economic takeoff explained the political durability of his regime and enabled ordinary Koreans to tolerate a government which was authoritarian and corrupt.

Park's body was lying in state in the Blue House and was buried next to his wife at the National cemetery. It was the first time the Blue House had to house a corpse.

The third Korean leader to enter the Blue House was General Chun Doo Hwan, a 50-year-old former army general. When I presented credentials to him, he was already entering his fifth year of administration.

Korea went through a difficult period of soul-searching and adjustment to the post-Park era, characterised by political, social and economic instability. Out of this seemingly chaotic situation, there emerged a consensus that there must be a new constitution fitting the new political leadership. A more sophisticated citizenry was entering a new decade with vastly different problems and needs than those Korea had faced earlier in the 1970s. There was also agreement that in spite of the great success in development, there had been a number of negative side effects which needed immediate reform if Korea was to regain lost momentum and increase productivity.

During this period of transition, General Chun Doo Hwan emerged as the dominant leader of the nation, directing the reform, restoring order and setting new priorities for the government. In August 1980. Chun resigned from the Army and was elected President by the National Conference for Unification.

Ostensibly it was a carbon copy replacement for President Park Chung Hee, another army general who ruled from 1962 to 1979 and whose death in that year set off the period of political chaos which led to Chun's emergence, Korea's new leader in fact seems to be intent on doing things in his own way, which meant overturning the many institutions associated with his predecessor.

Chun's regime approach to common policy-making had resulted in a total, if temporary reversal of the basic priorities which governed economic policy from the early 1960s to late 1970s. In place of the personalised 'Park approach' to economic management, Chun has been trying to create a 'bottom-up' decision making process on the Japanese model and to decontrol the banking system.

The impressive thing about Chun's economic reform was the speed and decisiveness with which they have been implemented, especially when it came to dealing with opposition from inside the bureaucracy. If the Chun Government had stuck its neck out where economic policy was concerned, adventurous departures from the Park regimes' restrictive and authoritarian political postures would have been a good deal harder to identify.

The government had introduced a number of cosmetic measures (such as the lifting of a 34-year-old curfew which kept the nation's entire population off the streets from midnight till

4 am) with the evident purpose of creating the impression that Korea under President Chun was a marginally less regulated and regimented society than in Park's time.

Far more important than these domestic liberalization measures were a series of proposals for reunification with North Korea that were enveiled during the 12 months since Chun came to power. Whereas President Park maintained a low diplomatic profile vis-a-vis North Korea during most of his 17-year-rule, seldom proposing any more dramatic measures for the easing of north-south tension than a resumption of mail services or exchanges of information in divided families, Chun kicked off 1982 with the announcement to the South Korea National Assembly of an ambitious formula for peace talks which included proposals for setting up a National Council to discuss all possible ways of bringing the two halves of the country together.

The Chun's proposal differed from the initiative taken during the Park era in that they had been tested out on various sectors of South Korea public opinion before being publicly unveiled and were followed within a few days by a list of 20 specific projects designed to break the ice between Pyongyang and Seoul. These included such ideas as the construction of a sports stadium straddling the military demarcation line. What the initiative appears to demonstrate is that when Chun departs at the end of his 7-year term, he means to leave behind him a very different place from the emotionally-disturbed and economically troubled South Korea which he took over in 1981.

The question everybody was asking at the time when I arrived in Seoul was: 'Would Chun hold on to power after his term of office in 1988?'

I put this question to the then American Ambassador to Korea Professor Richard L Walker, who was a professor of Chinese studies. He did his PhD thesis on 'International relations during the Warring Period'. We discussed the issue in Mandarin for he was fluent in the language, having studied in China for many years.

Professor Richard said: 'I had a talk with Chun before he became President. I told him that President Park Chung Hee would go down in history as a good Korean patriot. What would he like to be remembered in history?' Professor Richard said that Chun was taken aback by his rather blunt question but replied that he would like to be remembered as the President who had handed power to the people peacefully after his term of office. Professor Richard also mentioned that President Chun had told President Reagan and the American cabinet the same thing about his preparedness to step down after his term. Chun would not name his successor too soon for fear that he (the successor) would became the target of attack by students.

Chun had kept his promise of handing power over to the people constitutionally and peacefully. He did not want to see a violent overthrow of the government. There was a presidential election after much bargaining between the Democratic Justice Party and the opposition. In the presidential election held on 17 December 1987, Roh Tae-woo, a former army general and a close confidant of Chun Doo Hwan, won the election and became President. I attended the inauguration ceremony of the installation of Roh Tae-woo as President. Chun held Roh's hands, welcoming him as his successor. I also attended a farewell party for Chun with many leaders praising him for his achievements. All went well and everybody thought that there was going to be a smooth handover of power constitutionally and that Chun was supposed to concentrate on a welfare committee with large funds collected for the training of Korean youngsters.

Unfortunately, protesting students and opposition parties rose up in a frenzy, demanding their pound of flesh from Chun, despite what he had done for the country.

The students called Chun a dictator and condemned him for using power for personal gain and self-aggrandisement. There was certainly abuse of power and corruption by his family relatives and administration officials, but he had largely wielded it to prevent anyone from upsetting his single-minded goal of turning South Korea into a strong economic force to be reckoned with. His younger brother Chun Kyong Hwan, 46, was arrested and had confessed in court that he had accepted thousands of dollars from businessman during his brother's 7-year term as President. He said he received 200 million won (S$562,600) from a South Korean businessman but that the money had gone to a *Saemaul* training programme. He confessed his sins and said:'I am sorry for the people and above all, I am heartsick because I have caused trouble for my brother. I should have lived within my means.'

The students never forgot Chun's role in the *Kwangju massacre* in 1980 when Chun ordered troops to fire on demonstrating students, resulting in at least 200 of them being killed. This single incident had marred the otherwise remarkable economic achievements of his administration.

Chun had to apologize to the nation over live television for corruption and abuses of power during his authoritarian rule on 24 November 1988. Downcast and at times on the verge of tears, Chun announced that he was giving up all his personal property to the state and was leaving the capital for a period of repentance in the countryside, a traditional form of atonement for disgrace officials.

Chun said, 'My dear people, I am really sorry. I am pained and ashamed of my past; I have no intention at all to make any excuse.'

The man to whom I had presented my credentials had absolute power when I met him, had his name dragged through the mud, his rural home set ablaze, his relatives arrested and gaoled. Thousands in the streets demanded that he and his wife be executed. He had to endure a crushing self-abasement, his dreams of a sedate retirement as his country's elder statesman was destroyed.

But his public apology, a script dictated by the government of his elected successor Roh Tae-woo, was the compromise that officials hoped would avoid the need to haul him through the courts.

Chun apologised for the forced dismissal of government officials and journalists when he took power; the death of opposition supporters who were sent to barsh re-education camps; and for corruption and embezzlement by some of his relatives and associates. He made a special apology for the bloody suppression in 1980 of an uprising by students and citizens in the southern city of Kwangju.

His property to be turned over to the state included his house in the capital, two golf club memberships and US$3.3 million (S$6.4 million) in cash. He also would have to return about US$20 million in political funds.

'I am ready to take whatever punishment our people want to hand over to me and I will wait for their judgement,' he said.

Millions of people crowded around television sets in shops and offices and in homes to witness Chun's apology.

Chun's searing humiliation was not enough for many members of the public who felt that it was too late and too little. A student leader said that the money Chun had promised to return was 'peanuts'. He said: 'Nobody believes Chun has no fortune abroad.'

Kim Dae-jung, a leader of the opposition 'Party for Peace and Democracy' and who was long considered the symbol of democratic resistance to Chun's iron regime, said he felt that the statement had 'failed to disclose the real facts concerning Chun and his family'.

Twenty minutes after making his statement, the ex-president left his home, which he had offered as repayment to the state, in a fashionable district of Western Seoul for his exile.

He sat stone-faced in his car while his wife Lee Soon Jia wept beside him. She had every reason to weep for she had always craved for glamour, power and a luxurious life. Unlike Madam Park Chung Hee who was loved and respected by the people, Lee Soon Jia was very much hated by many people. She was aloof, not easily approachable and had always put on airs wherever she went.

Lee was also forced to resign as chairwoman of a controversial welfare foundation the Sawsedae, an association to foster the new generation. It was Chun's intention to retire from the presidency and concentate on the activities of Sawsedae, to train young Koreans in the field of technology and to preserve Korean culture. Even this dream had disappeared.

Chun has left the Blue House for exile in an ice-bound temple deep in the mountains. Birds, a few Buddhist monks and hundreds of policemen (sent there to guard him against the students) were his companions. It was in Paekdam Temple, in the Sorak Mountains (where I once visited) along Korea's east coast.

Access is by a narrow road clinging to cliffs along a river gorge. There is an ancient Buddhist shrine in the temple compound and a few outbuildings.

Chun's room which he shares with his wife is small. It is furnished with two cushions, a table and a cupboard. The monks said that Chun and his wife ate rice and noodles and read by candlelight.

The police had recently lifted a blockade and reporters shivering in freezing winds gathered to have a glimpse of the former president.

Despite the fact that Chun was staying in a place off the beaten track, dissidents and students would not leave him alone. They had gone there eight times to stage demonstrations.

The Koreans are revengeful and unforgiving. Chun had done more for the Korean people and South Korea than most previous leaders. Despite his public apology to the nation, students still carry banners saying: 'We don't want apologies, we want to execute Chun.'

The Chun era is dying a painful death in South Korea. More painful than he deserves.

The fourth leader to moved into the Blue House was Roh Tae-woo, a former army general who won the presidential election by a margin of about two million votes. He won the presidential election because the two major opposition leaders Kim Dae-jung (who had contested against Park Chung Hee and was defeated and who went into exile) and Kim Young-sam (leader of Reunification Democratic Party) could not agree to join forces. The two Kims virtually delivered victory to the government candidate by their refusal to compromise.

It was the master stroke of Roh Tae-woo to grant amnesty to Kim Dae-jung to contest the presidential election that did the trick. Kim Dae-jung was banned from contesting the election because of a suspended 20-year prison sentence for sedition. He was under house arrest for 78 days before the amnesty. Perhaps Roh understood the Korean characteristic of 'no compromise' that he had allowed Kim Dae-jung to contest. He knew that if he allowed Kim Dae-jung to contest, the two Kims would fight it out and would split the votes of the opposition camp and that would give him a chance to win.

Kim Dae-jung had always believed that he had a larger support than Kim Young-sam from the crowd that attended his rallies. Dae-jung became so arrogant that he urged Young-sam to concede and withdraw his presidential bid. Young-sam naturally rejected his proposal.

In Korea, political factions are built around strong charismatic leaders rather than on the political ideologies of their leaders and these factions give unquestioning loyalty that overrides loyalty elsewhere. The roots of factionalism lie partly in Korea's traditional Confucianist system and its intolerance to opposing views or compromises.

Roh was a close associate of President Chun. He graduated from the IIth class of the Korean Military Academy — the class whose members led by Chun engineered the military coup of December 1979. The two men served together in South Vietnam and after Chun came to power, Roh headed the Defence Security Command, the army's political surveillance network.

He left the army in 1981 to serve as Sports Minister, Home Affairs Minister and chairman of the Seoul Olympics Organising committee before assuming his job as chairman of the ruling party.

Before the presidential election, Roh had asked me to arrange for a private meeting with Prime Minister Lee Kuan Yew when he visited Seoul in July 1986. Roh had always admired the way Singapore was run. He wanted to know why Singapore could be clean. He said to me once, 'Not only the streets of Singapore are clean, the government is also clean. How did Lee Kuan Yew do it?' The arrangement was made in a small Korean restaurant and I was also present. Roh mentioned that in the next few years, Korea would be in the watershed of history. He said if Korea could overcome the difficulty of deciding on a proper political system, its growth would then take off. Otherwise, he said Korea would be bogged down by political strife which would be detrimental to its economic development. Roh wanted to know the secret of Singapore's success. Prime Minister Lee spent some time explaining to Roh the importance of gathering enough like-minded talents who would be willing to work and secrifice personal gains. He stressed the importance of showing personal examples of political integrity and told him how it was done in Singapore. Lee advised Roh not to mimic the one-man-one-vote American system and that Korea should practise a system which could maintain some elements of Korean culture and its history.

I met Roh again when Prime Minister Lee visited Korea again after Roh became the President. Roh's soft spoken conversation style appealed to people, enabling him to befriend the people easily. He was humble and yet dignified. Before he became President, there was widespread speculation that he would succeed Chun and he was asked by the press about it. He said: 'My name in Korea 'Tae-woo' literally means a great fool. How can a fool run a great country like ours?'

Roh once said: 'I make much of organisation, or teamwork. I prefer a couple of ordinary men to geniuses. I prefer teamwork through harmony rather than the distinguished ability of a specific person.'

On his official visit to Seoul on 7 July 1988, Prime Minister Lee had another round of talk with Roh at the Blue House. He continued to ask many questions and tried to tap the experiences of Prime Minister Lee in running a country.

At the state banquet, Mr. Lee Kuan Yew described Roh's election as 'momentous events' to the credit of the people of Korea. Lee said: 'I hope the Korean people and their leaders will now have more time to work out their political destiny and to evolve institutions which are tailored to the character, culture and traditions of the Korean people.' He also said the successful conclusion of the Olympic games would be a great triumph for South Korea.

One week after Prime Minister Lee's visit to Korea, I went back to Seoul again, this time to say farewell because my term was up. I met President Roh Tae-woo once again at the Blue House. He bestowed on me the 'Meritorious Diplomatic Service Star' for my contribution towards promoting relations between the Republic of Korea and Singapore.

Roh's pragmatic leadership seems to be making headway in the Korean political scene. His approachable personality and willingness to compromise was bringing about better unity in Korean politics. According the newspaper reports, Roh was dissolving his own Democratic Justice Party to form a new political party to merge with two opposition parties led by Kim Young-sam and Kim Jong-pil, giving the ruling party a big majority in parliament. In this dramatic act, he had isolated Kim Dae-jung who would lead the only opposition party. This was yet another magic stroke of Roh, who is contemplating changing the Korean constitution in favour of a Prime Minister instead of a President more in line with the British and European constitution.

Koreans are by nature uncompromising. Roh's leadership may bring about a dramatic change in Korean political behaviour.

The Blue House had seen the rise and fall of three Korean leaders — Syngman Rhee had to flee the country after 12 years in

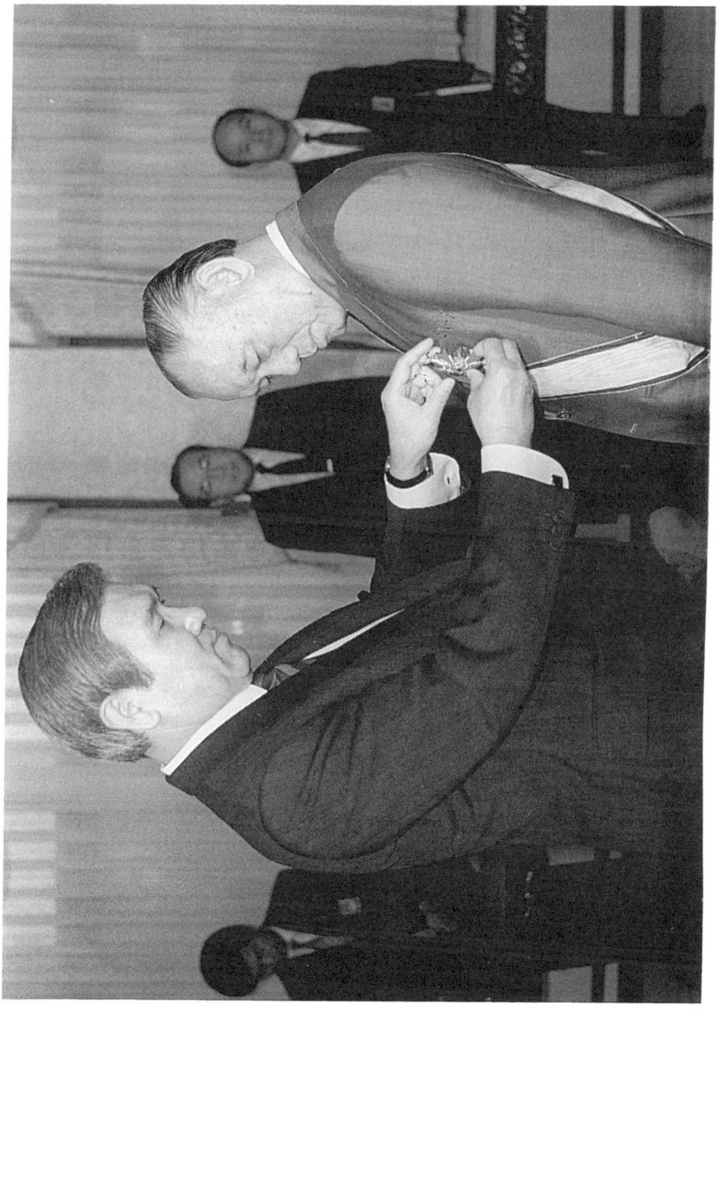

President Roh Tae-woo awarding Diplomatic Service order to the author

President Roh Tae-woo having a chat with the author at the Korea Presidential Palace

power, Park Chung Hee who had ruled the country for 18 years and was assassinated, followed by Chun Doo Hwan who had to apologize to the nation in disgrace before retreating to the Sorak Mountains for a hermitic life. What would happen to the new occupant of Blue House, nobody knew. But the future seemed brighter for Roh Tae-woo.

Anti-Bureaucratic Roots

The cause of the downfall of the Blue House occupants was the result of violent student demonstrations. The youngsters of Korea are hot-blooded and courageous. It is in the Korean blood. The patriotism of the Koreans is one which is written in blood. It is a patriotism like that of the woman who became a model wife by biting her finger and giving her blood to her parents. Koreans feel that they cannot love their country without shedding their own blood. It is a patriotism steeped in self-destruction, all for the common good and where the word 'desperateness' is the slogan. It is not a quiet patriotism but instead a noisy and at times, violent one.

Almost every leader faced violent student demonstrations ending in bloody clashes. It seems as if it is impossible for the citizen and the state to co-exist peacefully. Patriotism starts with the sacrifice of one self and the denial of one's happiness. It is the kind of patriotism for which one must foam at the mouth and harm bloodshot eyes. In Korea, to be both patriotic and alive is difficult.

Korean myths are unlike that of Greece and Rome which expressed thoughts on concepts of death, love and human destiny. Korean myths are generally not concerned with human life, but instead about the leaders and the founders of the nation. They are myths about politics and rulers.

However ignorant a farmer in Korea may be , he knows the stories of Admiral Yi Sun-shin who defeated the Japanese in the Imjin war of 1592, and the kiseng Nonkae who threw a Japanese general and herself over a cliff into the river in 1593 and of Saimdang, a famous scholar and of the 3,000 court ladies of Paekche who threw themselves over a cliff as a protest against the Silla conquest.

When I arrived in Seoul for the first time, I noticed the statue of Admiral Yi Sun-shin staring at me along the main street. All the statues in Korea are of people who fought and died for the country. This tradition of erecting statues and tablets continues until today. Examples are the tablets to those loyal spirits who were killed in the Korean war during the student revolt in 19 April, 1960.

This is quite different from the situation in the West. The English love the birthplace of Shakespeare more than they love the statue of Nelson. In Germany, the statues of Goeth and Shiller and the death mask of Beethoven are revered. One need not mention the statues or monuments in Paris.

The Korean spirit has been ruled by political patriots and heroes, while the Western tradition has been nurtured by cultural heroes, those who created culture and the arts.

The English used to say that they would prefer to give up the empire of India rather than lose Shakespeare. In Korea, the people have no spare time for this luxury. The reality of history creates in the Korean mind a desire to keep every inch of their land and try to live without disaster for one day rather than spend time on composing songs and writing flowery poetry. Korean poems do not express their emotions — they are odes to their rulers. The 'lover' who appears in poetry and song is not the usual lover, but instead the king of the country.

Koreans love to praise the dead rather than the living. Their philosophy that those living are all criminals while the dead are heroes. If Lee Chun had not died in the Hafae where he had gone to plead for Korean independence in 1919, and had instead lived to return to Korea, no one would have remembered his name. Miss Yu Kwan-sun of the independence movement, who was killed by the Japanese on 1 March, 1919, and the loyal official, Min Ch'ng Chong who killed himself in protest against the Japanese protectoral rights over Korea in 1905, would have suffered the same fate as Lee Chun.

The newspapers in Korea emphasize politics and politicians. Not many other countries give such importance to the political aspects of life as much as Korean newspapers. While a few words uttered by some small politicians appear in the headlines, a dissertation written by scholars who had spent tens of years in serious research receives only two of three lines in the newspaper's cultural column. Korea's tradition and history has been built on political consciousness and resistance.

When we visit Vienna, the very air we breathe is musical and even the silence sings; the names of stores and streets are named after famous musicians. Korea is different. There the air which we breathe is the air of demonstrations. In Seoul, there are many famous places connected with demonstrations. Take for instance, the March 1, 1919 demonstration — an area of Pagoda Park was the centre of the demonstration against the Japanese. The City Hall Plaza, on the other hand, was the centre of the April 19, 1960 student uprising. These places are monuments to history. In the Korean University campus, there are memorial statues to students who are killed during demonstrations rather than statues of musicians.

These are symbols of political tragedy in Korea. The Koreans suffer from a strong sense of insecurity and have always been afraid of foreign influence and domination. China's Tang rulers who wanted to dominate the Korean peninsular, decided to take advantage of the hostilities between the Three Kingdoms and pitted one against the other. They signed a treaty with Silla to help her conquer Packche and Kogurgyo.

In the 13th century, Mongol hordes invaded Korea. The devastating invasion by the Japanese armies under Hideyoshi began in 1592 in an unsuccessful attempt to conquer China through Korea. Without much resistance, Seoul fell within two weeks, while King Sonjo and his court fled north. Strangely enough, the tide of war from the sea created lasting fame for Korea. The Korean fleets with their superior mobility and fire power, inspired by the brilliant leadership of Admiral Yi Sun Shin, inflicted annihilating defeat on the large Japanese armada. The Japanese dreaded the fear of some onslaugther of the newly developed iron-clad vessels of Admiral Yi.

No sooner had the Japanese retreated than Korea found herself in another delicate position between the straggling Ming and Manchu powers of China. The Manchu armies invaded Korea twice, in 1627 and 1636, culminating in King Injo's surrender after a 44-day seize at South Fortress near Seoul..

Following these Manchu invasions Korea retreated into a stringent policy of isolationism and became known as the 'hermit' kingdom.

Perhaps one factor that reinforced the Korea's isolation was that Korea was 'off the beaten track' without sufficient natural resources to attract Western merchants.

In 1876, Korea reluctantly agreed to open her ports to Japan and in 1882 a treaty of friendship and commerce was signed between Korea and the United States. This was followed by similar treaties with Germany, Austria, Russia, Italy and France.

Unfortunately, Korea once again became the arena for a power struggle. This time Japan, China and Russia became prime competitors. Japan had won victory over China in 1895 and then over Russia in 1905. When Queen Min, the wife of King Kojong, was conveniently murdered in a Japanese plot in 1895, the strongest of the political figures was eliminated from the Korean scene. Japan now met no serious foreign objections to her eventual annexation of Korea, which was officially concluded in 1910. Thus, the dynasty ended with the abdication of King Sanjong, the 27th ruler of Yi, and Korea became a colony of Japan.

When Japan surrendered to the Allied Powers in 1945, most Korean took for granted that immediate independence of their country would be granted. However, national jubilation soon turned to disappointment as the country was divided at the 38th parallel. Then in June 1950, Korea suffered another setback with the Korean war and many lives were lost and the country became divided.

The average Korean had never really experienced peace and democracy. They only knew dictatorial rule and were suspicious of establishment. History has made them distrust any government.

It has often been said that the temperament of the Korean people is imbued with an anti-authoritarian consciousness. Over a long period of time, as I have explained earlier, Koreans were preconditioned to distrust anything initiated by the bureaucracy. This anti-authoritarian mentality was not confined to any specific social class; it was widespread among intellectuals, urban dwellers and rural people. No matter what the authorities did, the people were predisposed to opposition without considering whether it was good or bad, simply because it had been initiated by the bureaucracy. In other words, their anti-authoritarian inclination took precedence over any assessment of the memrits or demerits of a given issue.

The agonies and difficulties associated with modern Korean politics were rooted in the Korean people's disdain for authoritarianism. This anti-authoritarian attitude permeated not only the consciousness of the people but also their folk customs.

Why were the Korean people in the past inclined to oppose anything bureaucratic. Historian attribute this attitude to the fact that officials of Yi Dynasty Korea (1391-1910) and those who ruled during the Japanese colonial period (1910-1945) exploited people instead of protecting them. Hence, the bureaucracy came to symbolise terror rather than benevolence.

During the Yi dynasty, several ideological reform movements aimed at breaking down the barrier between the people and the bureaucracy were born. Unfortunately, these movements did not bear much fruit. With the advent of the Japanese colonial rule, which was far more brutal and oppressive than that of the Yi dynasty, the anti-authoritarian consciousness of the Korea people acquired greater intensity.

A compulsive drive for power has been one of the predominant and distinguishable phenomena in Korean bureaucracy and it seems to be largely affected by the authoritarian personality. Most bureaucrats in the past look to their superiors with a feeling of personal attachment and tend to identify themselves with them. On the other hand, they look to their subordinates in an essentially impersonal way, seeing them as 'working units' rather than people. They treat them impersonally, with no real or deep interest in them as persons.

It was this attitude of bureaucrats of the past centuries that cemented the ill-feelings of the Koreans towards anything bureaucratic and anything connected with the establishment.

The authoritarian attitude of the rulers have created in the Korean people a driving force and stamina to change society and to advance. This spirit is manifested in student demonstrations and the great desire to work. The society is a growing and dynamic one compared to the Japanese society which is already showing signs of decline because of affluence. The influence of Confucianism is still strong in Korea despite the fact that student demonstrations which were not encouraged by Confucius were prevalent.

Influence of Confucianism

The philosophy of Confucius entered Korea at nearly the same time as Buddhism and had a strong influence on social and government institutions. But it was not until the establishment of the Chosen Kingdom and its ousting of Buddhism from political influence in th late 14th century that Confucianism was elevated to the status of state cult, a position left vacant by the demise of Buddhism. Confucianism as an established state ideology existed up till early 20th century. Even today, family relationships, political attitudes, ways of problem solving and many other aspects of Korean life reveal the imprint of the Confucian tradition. As the unchallenged, uninterrupted sociopolitical ideology of historic Korea, Confucianism was the single greatest influence on the Korean political culture and provided the view of the universe in which Korean society and politics operated.

Confucian precepts represented by the Confucian classics were major objects of study by traditional Korean scholars and were valued for both their practical political wisdom and their philosophy of life in general. The 'formalities' of early Korean bureaucracy were based on Chinese Confucian models.

Confucianism became the official creed of the government. This development was an remarkable event in Korean history. Confucianism was the chief intellectual frame of thought throughout the entire Yi Dynasty. The observance of Ye, ritual and etiquette and ceremony had a significant impact both on the social conduct of the Korean people and on the development of the Korean politics and administration.

In a Confucian family, adults learn how to manage private affairs and to instruct others for the common good while the younger members learn to obey their parents and to play their proper roles in the kinship hierarchy. To this day, many aspects of Confucianism remain central to the Korean character. Today, Confucianism has 232 meeting places, 11,950 moral teachers and 786,955 adherests. A memorial ceremony in honour of Confucius and his diciples is held twice a year (in spring and fall) at Seoul's Songgyongwa Shrine.

Koreans pay great attention to death. Confucian funeral rites have been the most widely observed in Korea over a long period of time. When death is imminent, the whole family gathers. The house is cleaned, and the dying member is dressed in clean clothes. He is then put in a tidy room with his head toward the east. When a man is on his deathbed, his children and family must assemble around him and observe the death. If his children are not present to observe his death, they are considered unfilial.

At the onset of death, the body is covered with a cloth. According to tradition, the deceased is mourned for by loud wailing of his kins. This is called 'kok' or keening. At the same time, one of his male relatives my climb onto the roof to wave the dead person's coat and call his name three times for the soul to return. If it does not, then the finality of death must be accepted.

The family then goes into mourning wearing white clothes and begin preparing for the funeral by sending out obituary notices, preparing sacrificial food and building a coffin. The corpse is cleaned with perfumed water, changed into a shroud, and put into the coffin. The body is laid out strait and bound with hemp cloth in seven places. The top of the coffin is covered with red brocade, on which is written 'so-and-so's holy coffin' in white letterings.

Throughout the wake, the deceased's favourite dishes are placed before his casket. The descendants of the dead man dress in mourning clothes made of hemp cloth and sit on a straw mat outside the room where the coffin is placed. One of the long lasting customs is the large gathering of funeral guests. Even today, the size of such congregation is regarded as the ultimate greatness of the deceased.

The grave site is usually located on a hillside and the coffin is placed in the grave with a mound of earth about one-meter high over it. The selection of a tomb site is very important to the bereaved, because of the belief that the prosperity of the descendants depends upon whether an ancestral tomb is properly selected. Therefore, a geomancer is usually consulted before the site is chosen.

I attended the funeral of a friend's father in Seoul and witnessed the funeral ceremony which was typical of Confucius teaching. My friend made sure that he found a good grave site for it is an important obligation to one's ancestor. He believes that a good grave site would bring happiness and prosperity to the descendants.

Koreans also pay great attention to wedding ceremonies. In modern times, although many Korean young couples chose their own partners, a big percentage of them still tolerate arranged marriages by their parents or matchmakers. I attended a wedding ceremony in Seoul of a friend's son.

On that beautiful spring afternoon a refreshing breeze blew through the air. The inner court of the tile-roofed Korean-style house, open to the south, was filled with joyful conversation and festivity. In the background was an eightfold screen depicting several cranes flying over the pine trees against white clouds. A large tent was set up in the courtyard and a rush mat spread on the ground.

My friend came from a well-to-do family involved in business with Japan.

As the traditional Korean court music began, creating an atmosphere of solemnity, those gathered in the courtyard anticipated the start of the wedding. Standing in front of the screen was the officiator, a gray-haired scholarly gentleman wearing a white Korean coat and a traditional Korean top hat made of woven horsehair. More than a hundred friends and relatives of the couple engaged in small talk as they waited for the bridegroom to appear. At last, the groom entered the courtyard after walking down a path lined with blooming azaleas from a small hill in the backyard. He wore a blue full-length silk robe with a stiff embroidered belt, a magnificent black silk hat and a pair of black deerskin boots — the official costume of Yi Dynasty (1392 – 1910) courtiers. This attire was allowed only for wedding day because a marriage is regaded as the greatest event among the four life ceremonies — the celebration of one's coming of age, wedding funeral and sacrificial offering.

Walking behind the groom was a male attendant carrying a wooden wild goose called 'mokan' in Korean. As the groom and his attendant walked toward the courtyard, the bride sat patiently in a room waiting for the ceremony to start. She has looked forward to this day all her life.

"Now begin the rite of presenting the wild goose to the bride," said the officiator in a low but deep voice. Walking up the steps to the room where the bride sat, the groom knelt in front of the room and laid the mokan on a table. He then made two deep bows to his bride.

Offering the wild goose to the bride was equivalent to taking an oath that he would be faithful and true to her forever, just as the wild goose is faithful to its life-long mate. The two deep bows is a token of ultimate respect for his bride. There is a good reason for using a wild goose in the traditional Korean wedding

Seoul (Yonhap) — Four Mokchung (Buddhist monks), carrying Nojang's cane, enter as they drag Nojang (an old esteemed Buddhist monk) onto the open-air stage to the tune of taryong (a kind of ballad). This scene is the beginning of Act 4 - The Dance by Nojang, of the Pongsan Talchum or mask-dance drama, Korea's No. 17 Important Intangible Cultural Asset

Seoul (Yonhap)—A group of small hand-drum players twirl paper streamers from their hats as they perform nongak, Korea's traditional farmers' music and dance, in the Korean Folk Village. As the performers dance, they execute syncopated rhythms on their percussion instruments, in accordance with the instructions from the troupe leader standing in the middle

ceremony. The wild goose (or mandarin duck) symbolises extreme devotion to one's mate for a lifetime.

The bride had to stand motionless on the west side of a nuptial table, displaying no emotions, while the groom positioned himself on the east side of the table, facing his bride. According to the Korean custom, the west side is the position of honour and the groom should give this place of honour to his precious wife-to-be.

The nuptial table in the courtyard was laden with jujubes, chestnuts, dried persimmons and red beans. A potted dwarf pine tree and a dwarf bamboo tree were also displayed to symbolize the couples' mutual fidelity. The pine was chosen because it is always green and the bamboo because it always grows straight. A pair of red and blue candles were also conspicuous and laid on the other two smaller tables were a rooster wrapped with red silk and a hen covered with blue silk.

The officiator then solemnly announced the rite of exchanging bows. Before making their formal bows, the couple had to wash their hands — the groom first followed by his bride. Attendants accompanying the couple would hand them towels to dry their hands.

Soon it was time for the newly-wed couple to offer wine to each other in a gesture signifying for better or for worse. After offering three times, the officiator solemnly pronounced the couple to be officially married.

The food we ate included 'Kimchi', a must for most Korean meals and which made Korean food famous. 'Kimchi' is a spicy and fiery type of Korean salad with pickles; a mixture of vegetables, chillies and tree roots. Unlike the Chinese and Japanese vegetables, 'Kimchi' is heavily dressed with spices and condiments — chilli, pepper, garlic, shrimps, oysters, razor clams and even fresh fruits. Westerners who have tasted 'Kimchi' would never forget its tingling hot flavour. In Korea, 'Kimchi' is propared before the temperature falls to the freezing point. In late November or early December, most housewives are busy preparing bulk amounts of 'Kimchi' for storage over the winter months. Any trip to Korea would be incomplete without a taste of 'Kimchi'.

For newly weds the ideal place for honeymoon is the Cheju Island, about an hour's flight to the south of Seoul. This is the largest and most famous island in Korea. It was once chosen as one of the ten unspoiled tourist paradises in the world by

'Newsweek'. This 'Island of the Gods'(as it is frequently called) has much to offer for tourists. Its exotic scenery is quite different from the peninsula in that it has a sunny, subtropical climate, a unique lifestyle and as attractive cultural heritage. When Prime Minister Lee visited Korea in July 1988, he made a trip to Cheju. Known over the years as a place of exile for those facing political persecution during the 'Chosen' Dynasty, Cheju developed a sort of 'exile' culture. Visitors can almost sense the feeling of exile when they visit the island. The market is perhaps the most lively and delightful place in the village. Tourists can sample traditional Cheju food in honey restaurants, drink rice wine in a wayside tavern and enjoy amusing traditional folk plays in the performance yard.

The beauty of Cheju is that there is not a single industrial plant in the island. The air is extremely clean and refreshing. All over the island, there are lots of fruit trees (mandarin oranges, pineapples) grown in 'hot' houses. The people speak a dialect which is not easily understood by the average Korean. We went to a waterfall where the water falls directly into the sea. This was the first of its kind I had ever seen. A short distance from this waterfall is a small bungalow where the late President Syngman Rhee had stayed. It has since been turned into a honeymoon hotel. We went to a seaside resort with a chain of seafood restaurants.

We went into a famous restaurant owned by a Korean poet. Outside the restaurant was a poster which read:'Japanese are not welcome'. The restaurant was well-known for driving away Japanese tourists. As the owner had passed away, his children are less anti-Japanese and now-a-days some Japanese are seen in the restaurant. The owner was also a well known calligrapher. His calligraphic scrolls were displayed all over the restaurant. The strokes were quite professional. I remember one poem which he wrote: 'Korea appears to be male-oriented, in reality, female concepts and values are practised, according to an American professor who had spent more than 20 years in Korea.' Korean husbands, according to him, enjoy the very rare right of second, third, fourth and sixth (not often but not too rarely) wives at a time. Foreigners often see English language newspapers showing an amicable relationship between wife and concubines, and get the impression that in Korea, wife and concubines cooperate to keep their husband happy. But in actual fact this is not so. Korean husbands are in fact the most henpecked in the world.

In Seoul, there is a club for henpecked husbands. It is not widely known but it has over a thousand members. They go there whenever they were pecked by their 'hens' to share their miserable stories. The chairman of the club is a very dignified cabinet minister and vice-chairman is a retired three-star general of the ROK Army Forces who is well known as one of the most daring commander during the Korean war.

This peculiar attribute of Korean husbands seems to be part of the Korean heritage. It seems that the ninth king, King Songjong of the Yi Dynasty, had an unusual sense of humor. One afternoon, he summoned all his cabinet ministers and made them assemble in the courtyard, where two poles each with a flag were planted. One flag was green and the other was white. Presently, the king appeared.

'Listen' he said without a trace of humour on his most dignified face, which was rather unusual for him. 'I want to know who is the bravest among you. Give me your word of honour. The person who can swear that he is really unafraid of his wife can walk to green flag and those who are afraid of your wives are to sit under the white flag.' There was a moment of hushed whispers and commotion. Then, they proceeded one followed by another, to the victorious white flag. There was one, however, who seemed to hesitate, perplexed and at a loss as to what to do. Then he moved slowly to the green flag. The King appeared to be satisfied and called to the solitary man under the green flag.

'Tell me, young man, how come you're not afraid of your wife,' he asked.

'It is not that I'm not afraid of my wife, your Majesty,' he answered, 'but I have been ordered by my wife not to join the crowd under any circumstances.' The King nodded approvingly.

Koreans are by nature rather superstitious. The unknown has always fascinated and perplexed them. While many turn to religion in an effort to deal with the great mysteries of life, others resort to occult practices such as fortune telling. The strong impact of modernization and the higher level of education among Koreans have undoubtedly contributed to the erosion of superstition. Nevertheless, fortune telling (or chom in Korean) is still practiced widely throughout Korea. Unlike other forms of occult, fortune telling has been relatively unaffected by the winds of modernization and Westernization. In fact, it seems to have become more fiercely entrenched in recent years. Ironically enough, it has been gaining popularity among young women, who until recently brushed it off as mere superstition.

Fortune telling was introduced into Korea via China some 2,000 years ago during the early ancient 'Three Kingdoms' Period. It coincided with the importation of Chinese letters and Confucianism, which have had enormous influence over the Korean way of life.

Oriental fortune telling, including the Korean version, is based primarily on two Chinese classics — 'I-Ching' and the 'Maisans' (the book of Probabilities). Through I-Ching, one of the five principal philosophical classics of China, one can supposedly determine a man's fate by studying the principle of yin and yang. The 'Maisans' deals more specifically with one's future destiny.

The professional fortune teller (or Chomjangi in Korean) performs a variety of services — choosing an auspicious date for a ceremony (such as wedding or naming a new-born), giving advice to job-seekers, matching one's 'kunghap' (horoscope of one's birth) against that of a prospective spouse, predicting whether a youth can pass a college entrance examination and much more.

It is difficult to determine exactly how many professional 'Chomjangi' reside in Seoul, but a city government tally estimates the figure to be about 4,000. There may be as many as 80,000 in Korean, according to a report compiled by the Ministry of Culture and Information.

Another fortune teller in Seoul says that in addition to panic-stricken parents with college bound children, he gives advices to businessmen facing slumps or on the brink of bankrupcy, candidates for seats in the National Assembly, ladies scheduled to be married soon and others facing great difficulties.

Korea's taboo language and folk beliefs are deeply rooted in the structure of the consciousness and social structure of the Korean people. They continue to govern the lives of Koreans in this time of highly developed science and technology.

Most Westerners feel ill at ease with numbers 13 and 666. For Koreans, the unlucky number is four, which they associate with death because the Chinese characters for four and death have the same pronunciation. Most elevataors in high-rise buildings in South Korea skip the fourth floor, stopping instead at the third and fifth floors.

A Korean who plans to get married soon would not attend others' weddings. It would also be impossible to get him to attend a funeral service. It is taboo for Koreans to do that. A bridegrooms's laughter on the wedding day is also a taboo as it portends that the couple's first child will be a girl. So bridegrooms who long for sons have to hold back their laughter on this day.

A university institute in Seoul reported recently that Korea has some 500 taboos that have been handed down orally. It took 25 years and required more than 2,000 man-days to collect them, according to the report.

'Don't slip out of the house to drink in the night or you will come across a 'Tokkaebi'(Korean ghost) on your way to the tavern.' This warning against excessive drinking reflects the wit and insight inherent in Korean taboos.

Korea is a country of Kim, Lee and Park. A stone thrown from a hill in Seoul would hit either a Kim, Lee or Park. According to a census conducted by the Economic Planning Board, there were 274 family names in Korea and those with the names of Kim, Lee and Park accounted for 45 percent of the total Korean population, estimated to be 340,420,000 as at November 1985.

Koreans who go by the family name of Kim numbered 8.76 million or 21.7 percent of the nation's total population, those using Lee accounted for 5.98 million or 14.8 percent, and those using Park made up 3.43 million or 8.5 percent.

Chinese style surnames were first used by royal families during the ancient Koryo Dynasty (918 – 1392) and became popular in the mid-eleventh century during the Chosen Dynasty (1392 – 1910).

Chinese characters were used in Korea as early as the first century BC. Then in the 'Three Kingdoms' period, according to an historical record, a Paekchean named Wang In went to Japan taking many Chinese books with him. This leads us to believe that Chinese culture and characters had achieved considerable popularity in the Korea of the 'Samban' period and during the 'Three Kingdoms' period. The use of Chinese characters entered a new era during the Silla period because Silla's unification was achieved with the armed support of Tang China and contacts between the two countries were frequent.

The pioneers in the use of Chinese characters in Korea have always been the aristocrats and the scholars in Chinese learning;

A scene of the royal procession during the enthronement of an emperor in the Yi Dynasty

the common people merely followed. The reason for such a strong influence of Chinese characters on the Korean language is among others, due to the general historical fact that the language of highly civilized people always flows down and it is common for the privileged of any society to boast of their ability to speak foreign languages.

Korean scholars and intellectuals had been using Chinese characters until 1446 when the 4th king of the Yi Dynasty, King Sejong instituted Hangul-the Korean alphabets in order to meet the need for letters to rightly record the spoken words of the time and in particular to lessen the inconveniences suffered by people who used the Chinese characters which were hard for the common people to understand. He collected many materials, aided by a group of young scholars and perfected a new system of letter forms and its expressive rules.

Chinese characters had long been abolished officially. All the Chinese characters which had filled nearly every signboard in Korea suddenly disappeared one day in the early 1970s. And all the official papers have been written exclusively in Hangul for a good many years. But the fact remained that the problem had given rise to a number of renewed discussions every now and then among Korean scholars, professors, writers and journalists. Finally a new wave of discussion rose in the wake of a proposal which was made to the government jointly by 20 organisations associated with language in favour of the revival of the Chinese characters in Korean education.

The proposal pointed out that the history of the Chinese characters was much longer than Hangul, that more than 50 percent of Korean language are derived from Chinese letters and that Korea could never do without them in many fields of their writing.

The problem of whether Chinese characters should be abolished or not created a chaotic factor in Korean life. Every once in a while it has become a grave political issue and a periodical national fever.

In 1970, Korea decided to phase all the Chinese characters out of middle and high school texts and Koreans believe that the problem of Hanmun was finally and definitely solved. In early 1980, the Ministry of Education surprised Koreans by announcing that it had at last 'finalised the problem' with a selection of 1,800 basic Chinese characters to be taught in middle and high schools and that they should be taught right away. This has remained so until today.

In South Korean newspapers, one can find a mixture of Hangul and Chinese characters. The Koreans find it difficult to do away with them. In North Korea, however, all newspapers have done away with Hanmun. It is ironicaly that a country closer to Communist China should decide to do away with Hanmun whereas in anti-Communist South Korea Hanmun still survives. Koreans often say that their culture is more ancient and more superior than the Japanese. This explains why only a small minority of the Koreans residing in Japan, about 700,000, have taken up Japanese citizenship.

One thing which the Japanese have admitted was that they have learned from the Koreans the art of making pottery especially the satsema and bluish-green type.

When the Japanese army under the command of Hideyoshi, invaded Korea in 1592, the Japanese envied the porcelain and other earthenware products made by the dexterous korean artisans, and they took many pieces of ceramic artwork back to Japan for use in their tea ceremonies. The Japanese kidnapped over 80 Korean ceramic experts and shipped them to Kyushu. The captive Koreans later developed a new ceramic tradition in Kyushu.

I met the 14th descendant of 'Chin Ju-kan' who was then 63 years old, in Kagoshima when I was Ambassador to Japan. The first 'Chin Ju-kan' was kidnapped to Japan and has since been making pottery. I visited his pottery plant in Kagoshima as well as his home. We became friends. He was tall grew a beard, and was married a Japanese, although both his father and grandfather had Korean wives. In those days, Japanese had banned Japanese-korean intermarriages. Chin told me that in the old days, Japanese were jealous of Koreans' skill in pottery making and often smashed their kilns in order to prevent them from producing pottery. Some of them were even beaten.

Chin said his ancestors were luckier because the Japanese samurai in Shimazu after hearing about the Japanese atrocities against Korean ceramists, strictly ordered the Japanese to keep away from the village where Korean potters lived. He also bestowed on the Koreans samurai status in order to protect them. In

1666, Korean kilns begun to spread throughout Japan bringing in money for the villages.

Chin who graduated from Waseda University became the secretary of former Prime Minister Hidoshi Ashida. He later gave up his job to carry on his ancestor's profession because he loved pottery.

When I visited his home, I had a glimpse of his family ceramic collection. One of them, made by his grandfather, captured my attention. It was a huge satsema vase, much taller than myself and it was superly crafted. He told me that the vase was specially made as a wedding gift for Tokugawa's last prince and as a dowry for the princess. During the war, the vase was given away to Italy as compensation. When Chin visited Italy, he saw the vase, fell in love with it and persuaded the Italians to sell back to him. It was at a time when the communists were burning antiques and they sold to him for Y180 million. He had to borrow from the bank and it took him a long time to settle the debt.

'It is worthwhile. It is a valuable heirloom to the Chin family.' he said.

I noticed another interesting piece also produced by his grandfather. It was the figure of 'Chong Kwei'(ghost catcher) stepping on the head of a European devil. I could not help laughing when I saw that piece.

Chin often visit Korea in search of his roots.

Another reason why the Koreans feel more superior to the Japanese is that they believe it was through Korea that Japan got Buddhism and the Chinese characters (Kanji).

According to Korean record during the reign of the Emperor Kimmei (540 – 571AD) Syssonsg-nyong of Paekche sent to the Japanese emperor an image of Shaka Butse in gold and copper, several flags and umbrellas and a number of volume of 'sutras'. The King of Paekche was also recorded to have sent a laudatory memoriabilia concerning the teachings of Buddha. It is said that over centuries Paekche had been the chief 'cultural connection' between the island archipelago and the continents progressive civilization. Paekche wanted Japan as a military ally against her domestic enemies — Silla and Koryo. When a new ruler came to the throne in Japan, Paekche sent over 200 holy books, along with a meditation monk, a nun and a reciter of mantras plus a maker of Buddhist images and a temple architect to Japan. There were as yet few if any native craftsman in Japan who understood the basic of how to construct a Buddhist temple. Thus the wholesale importation of advisors from Paekche was made and they became the brains behind the operation.

Panmumjom – the Dividing Line

Another important place I visited was Panmumjom, the place where the Armistice Agreement was signed to settle the bloody Korean war. We had to get special permission to visit the place. There is an average of 60,000 tourists a year visiting the south side of Panmumjom and about 12,000 tourists visiting the north side.

The Korean conflict was never terminated by a peace treaty. The battle was stopped by an Armistice Agreement but no political accord had been reached. The United Nations Command and the Republic of Korea continue to guard against renewed aggression along the 151 mile frontier that marked the line contact with north Korea and Chinese forces over four decades.

In Korea, World War II ended with Soviet forces accepting the surrender of all Japanese troops north of the 38th parallel and United States forces accepting the surrender in the south. The pledge expressed at the Cairo Conference and in the Potsdam Declaration promised that Korea in due course shall become free and independent. However, the surrender arrangement was exploited by the Communist to create an artificial barrier along the 38th parallel, dividing a country which has been unified for almost 2,000 years.

The Korean Armistice Agreement is primary a military document; an agreement between the two sides to end the military conflict. However, it does contain a recommendation for convening a political conference within three months to discuss the unification of Korea and the withdrawal of all foreign troops. Such a conference was held in Geneva in 1954, nine months after the truce was signed but failed. Another attempt was made to bring about re-unification between 1971 and 1973 through a political dialogue between North and South Korea, but the dialogue also failed. In 1980, another attempt was made to resume a political dialogue between North and South. Today, no mutually acceptable solution has been reached and Korea remains divided.

The Military Armistice Commission is the principle agency established to supervise implementation of the truce terms. The meetings are held in the Joint Security Area. The south side of the military demarcation line was blocked by a big tree. Two United Nation Command officers tried to chop off the big tree and were brutally chopped to death by North Koreans with an axe. The axe is still being exhibited by the North Koreans in their museum across the other side of Panmumjom. Later, the Americans had to despatch military force to chop off the tree.

We also visited a tunnel dugged by the North Koreans right into southern territories. They had the intention to dig a tunnel to house about 10,000 troops. The tunnel was discovered after a North Korean surveyor in charge of the project defected to the south. The tunnel is now a show piece of North Korean ambition.

As of December 1982, the United Nation Command has documented over 73,000 separate North Korean violations of the agreement.

What will happen to the reunification of North and South Korea? President Roh said last year that he would abandon the policy of "confrontation" and would try to help North Korea keep away from isolation. He even appealed to the United States to be more friendly towards North Korea.

Although Roh could not point any signs of North Korean eagerness to end a largely self-imposed isolation, he seemed confident that Kim Il Sung's regime in Pyongyang would be affected by recent changes in Eastern Europe and Soviet Union and the gradual death of Communism.

It was Stalin who installed Kim Il Sung in 1945. Stalin equipped the North; as forces with tanks that enabled them to invade South Korea in 1950 and overrun nearly all of it in few weeks. It has now been confirmed that Russians flew many of North Korea's aircraft in that war. When the Americans and others came to the rescue of the South, it was Mao who saved the North's regime from utter disaster by sending in a huge Chinese army. So China's influence was dominant in Pyongyang for some years after the 1950 – 53 war.

The rift between the Soviet Union and China in the 1960s far from weakening Kim's position, permitted him to exploit his big neighbours rivalry. He had drawn money and equipment from both of them for the armed forces that he has always maintained at a size greater than that of South Korea, while refusing to tow either the Soviet or Chinese line.

Ever since the choice of South Korea as the site for the 1988 Olympics, North Korea had been demanding a share of the games. Last year, after turning down the offer of a few minor events, it called for a boycott; but only Cuba responded to the call. The Soviet Union and China have readily accepted invitations to send teams to Seoul in September.

Would Kim now feel obliged to grasp Roh' outstretched hand, if only because an emergence from isolation would make North Korea less of the odd-man-out in comparison with China and the Soviet Union.

This is clearly what Roh hopes for. But, just as clearly, Kim fears that the whole framework of his hermit kingdom will collapse if he lets even a gentle wind from the outside blow into his kingdom.

The real question would be whether the Kim's resistance would now be overcome by other people in North Korea, his son Kim Jong Il among them perhaps. Some people at the top must now see the need to follow the Soviet Union and China in starting to change with the times.

16

Japan — Myth and Reality

Forty six years ago, when I was doing my morning bowing to Emperor Hirohito at the little village of Butterworth, I did not in my wildest dreams believe that I would one day see the Emperor face to face as Singapore's Ambassador to Japan. When I presented my credentials to the Emperor, I had a good look at the man who once controlled almost the whole of Asia and who was regarded as God to millions of Japanese who could not raise their heads to see him.

For several decades, Emperor Hirohito was 'God' to most Japanese. He was the 124th descendant of Japan's first Emperor Jimmu, who was believed to have descended from the supreme heavenly divinity, the Sun Goddess Amaterasu-omikami. After the war, the 'God' image became a myth. Hirohito came down from the heavenly palace and shook hands with the ordinary people in order to inspire them to work hard to rebuild the nation. He was after all a human being. The Japanese worked so hard that within 40 years of their defeat, they became an economic giant.

The Emperor saw his nation conquering almost the whole of Asia; he saw the nation fall to pieces as a defeated nation and he witnessed the nation rising again to be a great economic giant having so much influence over the world's economy. He would go down in history as one of the dynamic figures in Japanese history.

One year after my arrival in Tokyo, I was invited to a special luncheon hosted by Emperor Hirohito at the Imperial Palace. It is a custom in Japan for every Ambassador and his wife to lunch

Time to board the Imperial horse cart and present credentials to Emperor Hirohito

The royal carriage used to bring author to the Royal Palace to present credentials

once with the Emperor. The Imperial Palace also invites Ambassadors to duck netting parties, comorant fishing outings in Gifu and acrobatic performances by specially trained Imperial horses in the Imperial gardens.

The lunch was also attended by Prince Hitachi, Princess Hitachi, Gaimusho Vice-Minister and a number of Imperial protocol officers. All of us wore morning coats. The lunch was rather formal. No speeches were made but the Emperor, old and frail, was in a mood to talk. I talked to the Emperor for ten minutes. There was an interpreter.

As usual the Emperor always asked about whether we had gotten used to the Japanese weather to start off the conversation and whether we liked Japan. I took the opportunity to ask the Emperor, which period of his 60-years reign he liked best. He pondered for while and said: 'It was 1921 when I visited Singapore on my way to Europe. I went to the Botanic Garden, it was beautiful.' I said: 'Oh, I was not born yet.' He laughed loudly and asked: 'How are the rubber trees in Singapore?' I explained to the Emperor that in Singapore there were very few rubber trees and that rubber trees were found in Malaya. He said he saw some rubber trees in the Singapore Garden. It must have given him the wrong impression that Singapore had many rubber trees.

I told the Emperor that he must be very proud of the Japanese people who had recovered from the ruins of war and made Japan into an economic giant within 40 years. He smiled and said: 'Yes, I am proud of my people.' The Emperor then asked what I thought was the world's economic situation. I said the best thing was for richer countries to help poorer countries and if they did so there would be lesser chances of war. He said: 'You are right. This is the way it should be. The rich must help the poor.'

The protocol officer told me that they had to rush through the lunch and finish it early because the Emperor usually takes a nap in the afternoon.

Later on in my four-year stay in Japan, when I talked about my special lunch appointment with the Emperor, the Japanese especially the older generation could not believe their ears. In Japan, not many Japanese have the opportunity to have lunch with their Emperor. My lunch appointment with the Emperor made the older generation of Japanese respect me more.

However, when I met leaders and members of the Japan

Socialist Party or people from Okinawa, I never talked about my lunch with the Emperor. Till today, the JSP and Communist Party never salute to the Hinomaru (Japanese National Flag) nor would they sing Kimigayo (Japanese National Anthem). They feel that Japan should have a new national flag and a new national anthem. When Crown Prince and Crown Princess visited Okinawa in October 1987, at Naha, the capital of Okinawa, a man hauled down the Hinomaru flag and burnt it. Before giving himself up, this man held a press conference and condemned the Hinomaru and Kimigayo as 'bloody history and sins'. He said the hoisting of the Hinomaru and singing of the Kimigayo had led to a mass suicide at Chibichirigama, Yomitan in 1945, after the United States armed forces landed on the main island of Okinawa.

The Crown Prince read out a message by the Emperor expressing 'deep sadness and pain' over the World War II fighting that claimed the lives of 200,000 Okinawas. The Emperor was supposed to attend the National Athletic Meet but could not go because he had just recovered from an operation.

Okinawa was the scene of the final and bloodiest World War II battle in the Pacific. About 100,000 civilians of Okinawa, 100,000 Japanese soldiers and 13,000 US troops were killed in the fighting. Okinawa was the only place in Japan where World War II battles were fought on Japanese soil. It was under US occupation for 27 years. Residents of Okinawa were still bitter over the fighting there and believed that the Emperor was responsible for the war.

Not only in Okinawa, but everywhere in Japan, many students refused to sing Kimigayo. For centuries, the Japanese had an emperor and a centre of loyalty. Now, the youngsters do not respect the Emperor.

Immediately after the Second World War, the Japan Communist Party had advocated that the role of the Emperor be abolished, but this proposal was very unpopular. At the same time, two powerful Allies wanted to prosecute or hang the Emperor. They were Great Britain and the Soviet Union, a rare case for these two to team together. The British had not come to terms with Japan's victories between late 1941 and early 1942, which undermined the empire of India. The British wanted a scapegoat. But, MacArthur refused to do so after having met the Emperor. The Emperor took personal responsibility for all military and political actions taken during the war and was ready to be punished. That impressed MacArthur.

Had MacArthur taken the decision to put the Emperor on trial and hang him, history would have been different for Japan. Japan has had one straight line of emperors from the first to the 124th and the Japanese are so used to having a centre of loyalty, following the good example of the emperor. Without a emperor they would be lost like a ship without a radar.

For 46 years the Japanese have rallied to Hirohito's last wartime command. The miracle they created was the work of real people — the shopowners, farmers, housewives, blue-collar workers, salarymen and dedicated elites — who paid full measure for renewed greatness with years of self-denial and toil. Seen from today the brilliance of their achievements obscures the depth of their defeat. In the blink of an eye, historically speaking, the Japanese built one of the world 'mightiest' economies and the nation rose like the mythical phoenix from its own ashes.

The Roppongi Chancery

Unlike my assignment in Egypt when I had to suffer a great deal of inconveniences and had to stay in the Cairo Hilton Hotel for several months before I acquired a residence, my trip to Tokyo was a comfortable one. My Chancery and residence was situated in Roppongi (six plants or trees — incidentally, either my predecessor or the original owner had planted six trees in the compound) and was the centre of entertainment for youngsters. There were hundreds of bars, restaurants, nightclubs, mahjong parlours and mysterious places for the young and old to squander away their money. On Saturday nights, the roads were jammed with people of all varieties in various fashions. Telephone numbers with juicy pictures filled all the empty spaces of telephone booths and there were pedlers selling all sorts of artistic works and souvenirs.

The Chancery is a respectable ten-storey building with modern design and a separate entrance for the Ambassador's residence. Unlike Cairo where I had to take a drive for 15 minutes to reach the Chancery from home, in Tokyo I walked through the corridor from my residence to my office. The Ambassador's dining hall was impressive and whenever I threw a dinner for my guests, they were always impressed. The function room could take in about

700 people and at every National Day, more than 700 guests attended my national day party.

The Singapore Embassy is the envy of most diplomats because not many countries could afford to own their own embassies. This was the good work and contribution of my predecessor Wee Mong Cheng, who had the forsight to purchase the property after much persuasion with our treasury officials.

In Tokyo, several African embassies had to close down because they could not afford to pay the ever increasing rent for their embassies. The first to close down was the Uganda Embassy and the Ambassador Ernest Obitre-gama and three of his staff were recalled. The Ambassador announced before he left for home that the embassy had to close because of financial reasons and not for diplomatic reasons. The prices of land and rent increased 97.4 percent during 1987 in the areas where embassies were situated. The Liberal Democratic Party (LDP) and some trading companies have suggested that the Government build an Embassy Building' to house those countries which could not afford to rent premises. They feel that the Government should not sit idly and see financially handicapped foreign embassies close down one after another.

As a result of soaring land prices, a number of foreign embassies were either selling their vacant lands within their embassies or offering to multi-national companies the opportunity to develop their vacant space into multi-storey housing projects that would gain profit for the countries concerned. The Australian Embassy announced over the television that it was selling part of their vacant land within the compound of the Ambassador's residence. The Canadian and Thai embassies were also negotiating with multi-nationals to develop their vacant space.

Tokyo has a huge diplomatic community. It has 120 embassies — the biggest one, and the American Embassy has more than 100 staff members. Life for an Ambassador of a small country like Singapore with less than half a dozen staff was really hectic. Every three days, there was a national day celebration and as usual it was discourtous not to attend a national day function. There were other receptions given by other Ambassadors of friendly countries and the never ending parties of the ruling LDP, multi-national companies, and cultural organizations. Not a single evening was without a party or reception. In the day, the Ambassador had to receive guests from all walks of life, answer questions from the Ministry of Foreign Affairs, Singapore and to write weekly reports on the political, economic and cultural happenings in Japan.

Among the Asean countries the Singapore embassy had the least staff. The Thai Embassy had 50 staff, Indonesia 40 and Malaysia 30 staff.

Fortunately in Japan, there are no strict rules for diplomatic corp. to follow. In Cairo and Jakarta, an Ambassador had to return the call when an Ambassador called on him. In Tokyo, most Ambassadors do not return calls. In many cases, newly arrived Ambassadors did not even call on their seniors. The problem was that the Dean of the Diplomatic Corp, the Ambassador from the Ivory Coast, who had stayed on for nearly 20 years did not care very much for the welfare of his diplomatic colleagues. During my four-year stay in Tokyo, he had not called a single meeting of Ambassador to discuss common problems. During his 20-year stay, he did not take the trouble to learn even spoken Japanese.

For Asean countries, the six ambassadors meet once a month by rotation in one another's residence to discuss common problems and have dinner together. Because of our unity and the strategic position of Asean in the eyes of the Japanese, the Asean Committee has become the envy of many countries in the diplomatic corp. Prime Minister Nakasone was particularly good in his public and human relations with Ambassadors of Asean countries. On my first birthday when I arrived in Tokyo, I received a roasted turkey specially sent with a covering note from Prime Minister Nakasone to congratulate my birthday. When Takeshita took over, however, this human touch was lost. I later learnt that Nakasone made this gestures only to Asean Ambassadors and the Ambassador of the United States.

Japan paid special attention to Asean Ambassadors because Asean is the hinterland of Japan from where she derives her natural resources. Asean is also an important investment target for Japan. For this reason, the Asean Committee exerts certain amount of influence with the Gaimusho (Japan Ministry of Foreign Affairs). Two years ago when I was the chairman of ACT, we jointly protested to Gaimusho because the former Minister for Foreign Affairs Sakurauchi was about to leave for Phnom Phen. We thought that if Sakurauchi were to go to the Cambodian capital, it would be misconstrued that Japan had recognised the

Asean ambassadors in Japan in 1985

Author gave a one-man exhibition in Ginza, Tokyo in 1986

Heng Samrin regime. Foreign Minister Kuranari called us up and we represented our protest. Later, Sakurauchi cancelled his trip to Phnom Phen.

In the four years and two months I worked in Japan, I took a keen interest in studying the Japanese society. I mixed a lot with Japanese politicians, the leaders from the various factions and studied the complicated system of Japanese politics. I also made friends with the chairmen and presidents of the leading Japanese multi-nationals and tried to find out the administrative systems of multi-nationals and the spirit behind the companies. I also worked closely with the bureaucrats who controlled the various ministries. Being interested in culture, I got in touch with the cultural world — artists, calligraphers, musicians, writers and journalists.

I have always believed that to understand a country, it is important to understand the culture of the people.

During my stay in Japan, the thing uppermost on my mind was: What made the defeated Japanese race turn defeat into success, achieve the economic miracle and become the strongest economic giant. My observation of Japanese society has given me a clue to the secrets of their success.

Group Consciousness

One of Japan's most prominent national characteristics is the individual's sense of the group. At every level of society the Japanese have a very strong sense of who is on the inside and who is not. The group draws firm boundaries between 'us' and 'them'. Group ties can be so close that members feel collective responsibility for each other's actions. Loyalty to the group and a willingness to submit to its demands are thus key virtues in Japanese society. It is the values of the group, rather than abstract principles, that serve as morality for many Japanese.

The land-intensive method of producing rice involved back-breaking and never-ending labour and plenty of willing hands. Going it alone was out of the question, so villagers were compelled to get along with their neighbours. Individual farmers could survive the uncertainties of the weather, meet the heavy burden of the samurais or daimyo's taxes and deal with other emergencies only if they submerged themselves into a group, and put the welfare of the community before their individual desires.

A sense of the village's vulnerability to unpredictable outside forces was prevalent.

This sense of group commitment grew in the Japanese psyche because they isolated themselves from the outside world for nearly 300 years during the Tokugawa Shogunate. Tokugawa banned all contacts with foreigners (except for a few Dutch traders in Nagasaki's small island of Nishima) on penalty of death when they found the spread of Christianity threatening the Japanese way of life. They outlawed Christianity as a religion and coined the slogan "Expel the Barbarians".

After 300 years of isolation, the Japanese discovered that they were after all weak and backward when Commodore Perry and his black ships bombarded Japan. After the Meiji Restoration, the Japanese began to embrace all the material and scientific advances and popularised the slogan: "Forget the East, learn from the West". Although they became modernised, they were never Westernised. The sense of group commitment remained in the Japanese character.

It is this spirit of group commitment that made the Japanese work for a company for their whole lives. They climbed from the bottom of the ladder, devoting their whole energy and time for the interest and benefit of the company. Very few got to the top. Even the very few who got to the top and became chairmen or presidents still remained "salarymen". When they retire, they get a large sum in gratuities, but they are by no means rich. After retirement, they stay in small houses some two hours away from Tokyo by shinkansen — "bullet train" for their cars would have been withdrawn and they have to leave the company supplied houses.

It is this spirit of sacrifice, I think, that makes Japan overcome her difficulties and turned into an economic miracle. In Asian and European societies, everybody is for himself. Every employee thinks of becoming rich whereas in the Japanese society, every member of the company works hard so that the company can become the No.1 company in Japan and better in the world.

Groups come in all varieties in Japan, but most Japanese seem to focus their lives on one central group. This is usually a work group, such as a university department, a faction within a political party, a subsection in the office, or a unit in a factory. Japanese who are not part of a tight group at work may become active in one of Japan's new religions or join a local consumer union or political association. The members of this group are a person's nakama, or buddies and can easily become more important to him than his family. The group affiliation is more important than the individual's profession. The values of the group become the individual's values, and a large part of his leisure time is spent in the company of colleagues and other group members. It is among nakama that they are formed and thrive, and without regular doses of contact they wither.

The most extreme form of surrogate family group identity is found in underworld gangs, whose members pride themselves on being the only modern Japanese to keep alive the spirit of samurai. Crime bosses are called *Oyabun* (parent figure) and their henchmen are *Kobun* (child figure). Kobun are supposed to be ready to lay down their lives for their Oyabun or to mutilate themselves in atonement for any violation of the code of loyalty.

When former Prime Minister Tanaka was investigated for suspected involvement in the Lockheed affair, his chauffeur commited suicide rather than admit to investigators where he had driven the boss on certain crucial days.

The Pacific war was the most terrifying manifestation of Japan's sense of destiny and the ability of its people to band together against the outside. The nation was one great underworld gang, with the Emperor as its Oyabun. Millions of Kobun died for their Oyabun, and none so proudly or with a greater sense of fulfilment as the kamikaze pilots.

Comformity

The second element in the Japanese character is conformity and predictability in the behaviour of its members. From childhood, Japanese are told to conform. They are taught that people will laugh at them if they behave unacceptably. In the classrooms, they seldom stick their necks out for fear that "the nail that sticks out will be pounded down" as the proverb says. At home and in school, Japanese children are taught to fit in rather than stand out, and the habits of intellectual submission that they learn as students follow them into adulthood.

Whenever I went out with Japanese friends for lunch or tea, invariably, the subordinates will order the same dish or drinks as their superiors. They follow the superiors.

Japanese do not believe in elitism. There are no blue-eyed boys. They do not believe in prima-donnas. Their universities have no "honours degree". Nobody gets a helicopter promotion. Every university graduate, whether a genius or a mediocre-starts from the bottom of the ladder when he joins a company. They get the same pay and promotion for at least ten years. The slighest individualistic tendency is frowned upon.

When you meet a Japanese, the first thing he asks from you is a 'meishi' (namecard). When he receives your name card, the first thing he does is to see what company you belong to, not your position. If you belong to a top multi-national such as Mitsubishi or Mitsu, even if you are a small manager, he will respect you. If you are the Managing Director of a small and unknown company, you get less respect. This is so because the Japanese care more for the strength of the group than for your individual position or talent.

Many Japanese find such conformity comforting because it eliminates the nerve racking necessity or making choices. Japanese generally do not like to make decisions. They prefer to follow the crowd or conform to group decisions.

Samurai Spirit

Another important factor in the Japanese character is the spirit of Bushido or commonly known as the "samurai spirit". Before World War II, almost every Japanese read Hagakure, the bible for every Japanese. Hagakure, written by Taishiro Tsunetomo in the late 17th century after Tokugawa Ieyassu had seized control over all of Japan following the turmoil of civil war. Hagakure offers a panorama of do's and don'ts for samurai's. It teaches the guiding concept "to die" as the very basis of the samurai's life. It is the philosophy of death. Basically, this philosophy applies to the samurai's ethic of shame.

"When confronted with two alternatives, life or death" the hagakure stresses that one should choose death without hesitation. According to Yamamoto Tsunetomo, the man who initiated the philosophy," one's unflincing mind to dive into possible death saves one from shame".

Hagakure teaches one to polish up, through everyday training, his mental attitude for the time of crucial need. The samurai's main duty is to serve his Lord. At the slighest fault or misconduct of the retainer (the samurai), the Lord could order him to commit seppaku or hara-kiri (slashing one's stomach with a knife and having one's head chopped off, or be stripped of his stipend or starve to death).

Tsunetomo perceives this world as "empty, uncertain and floating — contrary to the Confucian stand of existentialism. His philosophy is that man should live his life doing whatever he likes to do, and the greatest misfortune of a man of action is to fail to die after closing the final chapter of his accomplishments.

In Japan, it is not uncommon to find two loving couples jointly committing suicide at the height to their romance. They fear that if they drag on with the romance, something sour might happen and that would destroy the beauty of love.

The leaders and many other revolutionary samurais who triggered the Meiji Restoration of 1868 were considered heroes who underwent the "resolved action bordering on insanity thereby answering the call of Hagakure."

It was this spirit of Bushido that inspired the Japanese to conquer China, to bomb Pearl Harbour and to march southwards into south east Asia. It was this spirit that brought about the miraculous economic recovery from the ashes of defeat of conquered Japan into a triumphant economic giant.

It is the same spirit that is driving the Japanese to conquer the world economically. Every Japanese worker would like to see his company achieve world pre-eminence, and collectively for Japan to become the world's most important economic power. The devotion of the Japanese workers and salarymen to their enterprises they work for spring from this spirit of samurai. They have an intense pride in seeing Japan triumph over other nations particularly the Western countries in economic competition. Behind every Japanese mind is the determination to take revenge against the United States for dropping the atom bomb in Hiroshima and Nagasaki. They want to show to the world that Japanese race is a race to be reckoned with.

Attitude Towards Work

The other important ingredient in Japan's success is the Japanese attitude towards work. The individual worker brings to his job a set of attitudes and expectations that make him the perfect company man. The cliche about the Japanese being workaholics has caught on for a reason. The Japanese probably love their companies more and work harder at their jobs than any other people on earth.

There is an established tradition among Japanese, be they ordinary workers, cooks, sweepers, or managers, to find ways and means to improve on their jobs. This perfectionist tendency is found in every profession. They do this as a matter of habit and not inspired by any material motives.

In recent years for instance, the Toyota Motor Company's 48,000 employees came up with more than a million formal suggestions to improve quality or lower costs. This is an average of 27 suggestions per employee. The management accepted most of the suggestions and saved millions of dollars.

It is this natural habit of every Japanese to improve on their work that enables Japan to develop the "state of the art" technology on the shop floor. In no other country can production engineers so quickly take the very latest technological breakthroughs and build them into inexpensive consumer products. No one can seriously compete with Japanese manufacturers of quartz watches, electronic cameras, stereos, video equipments or pocket calculators. Although the basic technology for all these products came from the West, in some other areas Japanese technicians are already catching up.

I used to watch a Japanese doing his work. If it is in a restaurant, you would find the cook preparing the food with complete devotion as if to make sure that his customers will enjoy the things he cooks. Underneath the pyramid-shaped white cap, his eyes follow the food he is holding with full concentration. It is not easy for him to stand before his customers with the white cap, for he has served at least five years behind the kitchen cutting vegetables and sweeping the floor before reaching his present position. He is prepared to be a cook throughout his whole time, hoping that one day when he has saved enough money, he can open his own restaurant.

I saw the chauffeur of an Ambassador dusting his car as seriously as a samurai carrying a sword. In every lift in department stores, the lift girls bow at you and say "Ohayo gozaimas". For a salesgirl, she would say "Arigato Gozaimas" even if you go away emptyhanded.

It is this work attitude that makes progress possible in Japan.

Myth and Reality

I have dealt with some of the characteristics of the Japanese that were responsible for the rapid recovery of Japan's economy, and which made them turn defeat into victory. I shall now give my impressions of the peculiar features of the Japanese which foreigners, especially Westerners, find difficult to understand. I find that the Japanese character has two sides or double faces. I use myth and reality to describe it.

Everything in Japan is between myth and reality. Japan is a rich country, yet the majority of its people are not rich. In other words, Japan's richness is a myth and the reality is that most people are poor.

Japanese maintain two faces; one a face for the ordinary people who are considered an outsider and is known as "tatemae". When he meets a stranger or anyone who is not close to him, he puts on the tatemae face, a face that is respectable, polite, cool and yet not revealing any feelings. To hide one's feelings is a virtue in Japanese culture. The Japanese have mastered the Confucius doctrine of not showing happiness or anger in one's face. But when he meets a true friend, someone he can trust and who understands him, he shows the other side of his face which is known as "honne" — the true self. He then pours out his feelings, grievances or happiness without any restraint.

It is not easy to get a Japanese to show you his "honne" face. It takes time especially for a foreigner to understand the real feelings of his Japanese friends. Westerners more often than not see only the tatemae faces of Japanese because they are hidden behind the cool faces. In my four years in Japan, I must admit that I have not seen many "honne" faces. One must spend a great deal of time with your Japanese friends in favourite bars or nightclubs drinking together before they can open up and take you as a friend.

The "tatemae" face is a myth and the "honne" face a reality.

Japanese politeness is well-known. This is one of the things I enjoyed most living in Japan. Wherever you go, restaurants, departmental stores, post offices, theatres, you meet smiling polite faces. The Japanese bow to you, say polite words. When I see Japanese bowing to one another endlessly, I think of the ants. They behave like ants. It has become part of Japanese culture to be polite. They need no courtesy campaigns.

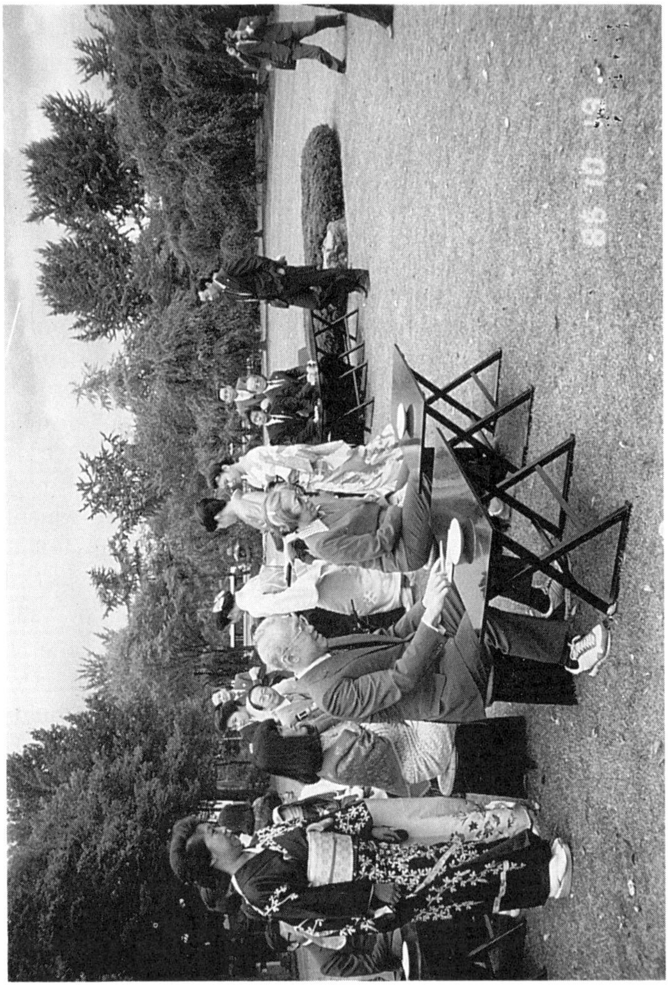

In 1986 Prime Minister Lee Kuan Yew and Mrs Lee visited Japan and enjoyed a tea ceremony in Tokyo

But, I find Japanese bowing and smiling rather superficial. It is only skin-deep. Nobody knows what goes on behind the smiling faces and bowing. It is just listening to the Japanese saying "Hai, hai"(Yes, Yes). When Japanese say "hai" they do not mean "yes"(in the sense they have agreed) just "I hear you". They bow to you as a matter of courtesy. You see the smile and the bowing, but not the sincerity of the heart.

How can one imagine that a bowing race like the Japanese could have been so cruel during the Second World War. The atrocities committed in China and Southeast Asia were committed by the same polite people.

They are a people with two faces: politeness from Confucius teaching and brutality from the spirit of samurai.

Japanese love cherry blossom. When cherry blossoms appear in spring, Japanese gather together and have a picnic under cherry blossom trees. They drink sake and bring their food and cakes with them. They sing and celebrate the rare occasion. Cherry blossoms are shortlived. They last at most ten days and then are gone.

The shortlived cherry blossoms have a great impact on the Japanese psyche. Life is short and one must make the best use of it. They also believe that the souls of their departed visit them every year around the cherry blossoms trees and share with them their enjoyment. Although cherry blossoms are beautiful, they have a special significance for the Japanese and they relate cherry blossoms with their dead. Therefore, do not say "you look as beautiful as cherry blossoms". The Japanese will not be too happy with your compliments.

It is because of this cherry blossoms pysche that the Japanese like to be forgetful. At the end of the year, the Japanese have a special party called the "Forget the year" party. Nearly every company, ministry and social organizations celebrate the "Forget the year" occasion. The purpose of the party is to enable all members attending the party to forget what happened during the whole year. The Japanese like to forget the past and start anew with the New Year. If one keeps remembering the past, one would be burdened by the past and would not get on with their work for tomorrow.

I was invited to such functions almost every year. In one occasion, the host asked me to make a speech. Being frank as usual,

I said that the Japanese are so forgetful that they have forgotten what they did during the Nanking massacre, unlike the Chinese who are forever remembering the past. They would dig up a corpse and cane it for 30 days in order to punish the dead. The Japanese normally forget and forgive what a person has done when he is dead. They never talk bad about a dead person.

Although the Japanese are forgetful, they do not forget the old. They respect someone who is older than themselves. Seniority in the company as well as seniority in Japanese politics are based on age and experience.

Japanese like to wear new shoes, new clothings, drive new cars and appreciate anything new. Most Japanese do not keep their cars for more than three years. Every year, they must have new clothing. They also like sashimi, and sushi and fresh meat and eat them raw. They particularly like Fugu, a type of fish with bloated stomach which is the most poisonous. A special license is required before Fugu can be sold.

Japanese like modern inventions and admire the West for their modern scientific technology. But, the Japanese have an unusual capacity to retain traditions which are old and useful. The Japanese are good copiers. They derived their cultural inspiration from China. They imported Chinese culture in large quantities since the Tang dynasty. Traditional cultures that once flourished in China but have long disappeared from Chinese soil can still be found in Japan.

For instance, when I attended a music function at the Imperial Palace a few years ago, I listened for the first time to Tang music played during the Tang dynasty. This brand of slow moving Tang music has been modified by the Japanese and have become the "Ga music" of the Japanese Imperial Palace.

The costumes which charming ladies used to wear during the Sung dynasty have long disappeared in the Chinese mainland. Today, Japanese ladies still wear them and walk in the streets of Tokyo, and especially so in smaller cities in Japan. The Japanese call this type of traditional costume "kimono". It has become an important part of Japanese culture. It is a custom for every Japanese lady who has reached the age of 21 to possess at least one set of "kimono" and to wear it when the wedding bells ring.

Sumo wrestling was performed in Xian as early as the Han dynasty. One can see Sumo wrestling carved on the walls in many parts of China. This sport became the popular sport for emperors in various dynasties until the Ching dynasty. But after the Ching dynasty, it disappeared. Today, one can see Sumo only in Japan. It has become a national sport for Japan and most Japanese believe that they invented the Sumo.

Japanese therefore have a two-faced character. They like new things and yet retain old traditions.

The Japanese are practical and pragmamtic people. They have the capacity to absorb new culture, digest them and mould them into their own culture. They throw out what is useless and retain what is good. This is the genius of the Japanese mind.

For instance, the Japanese copied a great deal of Chinese culture. They learn Buddhism and Confucianism from China. They sent their scholars to China since the Tang dynasty to study Buddhism. China was well-known for their eunuchs who played an important role in Chinese politics. In Japanese history, no eunuchs existed in any period.

Chinese ladies bound their feet during the Ching dynasty. The Japanese have not copied this ugly aspect of Chinese culture.

In China, the monks were not allowed to get married. They had to undergo stringent rules against sex. The Japanese do not follow the Chinese rules on sex. Japanese monks are allowed to take wives. I have seen many Japanese monks marrying beautiful ladies. Some even keep concubines.

Another pragmatic Japanese approach to solving family drawbacks is to take in a son-in-law and make him take the father-in-law's surname. Many rich and powerful Japanese in the political arena and business circles happen to have no son. They overcome their difficulties of inheritance by taking in bright son-in-laws. Kakuei Tanaka, the former Prime Minister, was one of those who had no son and took in a son-in-law. Although this practise originated from China, it is not commonly practised in China.

The Japanese are not religious people. Neither are they ideological people. There is an anecdote about the Japanese that goes something like this: A Japanese is baptized in the Christian tradition, married according to Shinto ritual, and buried as a Buddhist. The reason for this religious activity while alive, the story goes, is to cover all the options for the after life. Religious observance in Japan is indeed rich and varied, thanks to a healthy interchange between different religious traditions. People who go to Buddhist temples are just as likely to visit Shinto shrines, whilst Christian churches, though small in number, are not without their congregations.

Most Japanese claim no religion for themselves. No specific day is set aside for rest and worship as in many Western countries. But when trouble arises, Japan calls upon the gods.

Although Japanese are the most modernised nation in Asia, they are superstitious. When a new building is being inaugurated, they would invite the Shinto priest to bless the building. Atop the Mitsukoshi Department Store in Ginza is an O-inari shrine, the shrine of the fox — the favoured deity of merchant. Many buildings have O-inari shrines somewhere in the building.

Few Japanese will admit religious beliefs, but there are 81,357 Shinto shrines and 75,466 Buddhist temples recognized by the government in Japan. These figures do not include the myriad jizo-sama guardians and tiny shrines that dot the roadsides. Major railway companies require management to visit the founder's mausoleum; large advertising agencies make pilgrimages to Naritasan Shinshoki temple near Tokyo's international airport to ensure good business, and the kannushi priest is called upon to exorcise evil and pray for good luck at every new construction site. As one Japanese businessman put it,"it can't do any harm, and it just might do some good."

Of all Japan's so-called new religious, the Soka Gakkai (Value creating society) has the highest profile. With 17 million registered followers and vast riches resting in banks throughout the nation, Soka Gakkai perhaps commands more economic, political and social influence than any religious organization in Japan. I know the boss of this giant organization personally. His name is Daisaku Ikeda, a man just over 60 and regarded by most followers as divine. In recent years, Ikeda has increasingly involved himself in international activities, holding meetings with leading figures all over the world including our Prime Minister Lee Kuan Yew.

Soka Gakkai runs a political party indirectly called the Komeito which has 59 members of the Lower House and 27 seats in the Upper House. Komeito is the only political party in Japan with roots in a religious organization. In an obvious move to separate religion from politics, the party became an independent organization in 1970 although over 90 percent of its current representatives in the Diet are Soka Gakkai members.

I was invited by Ikeda to have dinner at Soka Gakkai headquarters and without prior notice, he bestowed on me the honourable title of Honourary Doctorate by the Institute of Eastern Philosophy for my contribution to the research of Eastern Philosophy.

For members of the Nichiren Buddhism, the formula is quite simple. Just remember the words: "Nammyoho Rengakyo" and repeat it a hundred times and the Goddess of Mercy (the God for this religion) will come to his or her help. This easy method of getting god's assistance drew many people into the religion and many claim that their prayers were answered in times of trouble.

In Singapore, there is a Soka Gakkai branch which runs the Nichiren Buddhist organisation, and which has about 10,000 members. Every year, this organization puts up a gigantic show of acrobatics at our National Day parade.

Japanese believe in the existence of soul. They believe that death is not the end of a person. The soul leaves behind and must be pacified. Japanese even erect monuments for their enemies when they perish. They put one to commemorate the Mongolian invaders who were drown off Japan sea.

Unlike the ancient Egyptians, the Japanese feel no need to preserve the body through mummification, nor do they share the Christian belief in the resurrection of the body at the Last Judgement. The Japanese believe that after death the body is simply reabsorbed into nature.

All heroes of Japan have a special place in the Yasukuni shrine in the centre of Tokyo. This includes the soul of Tojo, the Prime Minister of the war-time cabinet, who was tried and hanged for his crime in leading Japan into the second World War. Prime Minister Nakasone made an official visit to Yasukuni shrine and this spark off strong protest from China and Korea and other religious leaders who were non-Shintoist. Nakasone in later years had to give up going to the shrine.

Japanese are the least ideological. Japanese politics are based on personal loyalty. They trust their 'Oyabun' and leave everything to their leader. The Liberal Democratic Party is in fact a myth. There is no such thing as LDP. The party comprises of five factions led by five individual leaders. When I first arrived, there were the Tanaka faction, the Suzuki faction, the Fukuda faction, the Nakasone faction and the Komoto faction. The LDP does not have a specific ideology. The five leaders may have different political views. Each faction go to town to collect their own political funds. Anyone who wants to go into politics must first of all get the support of the leader of a faction because he needs his financial support. To run for elections, a candidate would need to be attached to a faction and he would need at least $2 million (Singapore dollars). This can only be supplied by the factional leader. The fund which he gets from the party is too small to fight an election.

Japanese minds are more money-oriented, project-oriented and materialistic. They are more down-to-earth. They care very little about what type of Socialism or what type of ideology would suit Japan. They are more attuned to problem solving than bickering over ideology.

Japanese Dreams

In Japan, if you were to ask any Japanese what hopes they have for their children, their answer would be to send them to Tokyo University or one of the prestigious universities. The parents would choose the best kindergarten and then whichever primary or middle schools that would promise to send their children to Todai or Wasada and Kiow Universities. They would go to Juku schools where special extra lessons would be taught. The students crammed their brains and energies towards one objective: to reach Tokyo University. In Japan, all students are scared of the "Examination Hell". There is virtually no time for any of them to have extra-curricula activities. Those who got into Tokyo University have their whole future planned for them. They would be employed by either Government departments or by the multinationals. The Government and the multi-nationals co-operate with the University for the supply of their best brains.

What do the students do when they get into Tokyo University? For four years, most of them have fun. They do whatever they like — playing guitar, swimming, golf (if they can afford), sing or whatever hobbies and games they like. They seldom study. It is like a long holiday for them. Lecturers and professors do not care whether they attend classes or not. They believe that at this period it is important for the students to spend their time doing whatever they like so that their minds would be free. Just as well they do not spend their time on studies, for their training begins when they join the government or multi-nationals. Unlike the universities in the United States where they train students professionally at university level, the students in Japan are trained by multi-nationals when they are recruited.

Everyone begins from the bottom irrespective of their results in school. The multi-nationals go for the University the students belong to and not for their results. The Universities decide the status and not the students results. There is no honours degree. The Japanese do not believe in "elitism" and in fact discourage elitism.

Everyone goes through the mill and nobody is promoted in the helicopter fashion like Singapore. For at least ten years, all graduates are treated equally and get the same salary. When they reach middle age, if they perform well, they would be promoted to higher positions. Those who are found useful are gathered near the window to read newspapers and idle. This group is called "madogiwazoku"(the tribe belonging to idling near the window).

To a certain extent, the high status of the Tokyo University is a myth. In reality, the students do not study much when they get into the university.

Power and Status

The Japanese like status more than money. Politicians in Japan struggle hard in order to become at least a Cabinet Minister if not the Prime Minister. Once he becomes a Cabinet Minister, then he has made it for he has attained his target in life. Even if the Cabinet seat is warmed for only one day, he would be remembered in history that he has been a Cabinet Minister. In my assignment in Japan for slightly more than four years, there has been two changes of Prime Minister, three changes of Foreign Ministers and many changes for other ministries.

It is not important whether the Prime Minister has real power. Everyone knows that the present Prime Minister Kaifu is a puppet Prime Minister because he belongs to the smallest faction in the LDP. His word do not carry much weight. It is the largest LDP faction — the Takeshita faction, or a combination of other strong factions that control the policy of the government. But it does not matter the least. For the Japanese, the status symbol is the position one holds. It is the ambition of every Japanese to be either the chairman or president of a multi-national, a vice-minister of a ministry if he is a civil servant (vice-minister is equivalent to

Japan's former Prime Minister Takashita met Asian ambassadors in his office on December 1987

Permanent Secretary in Singapore) or an Ambassador. Although the chairman or president may be just "salaryman" earning his wages, he carries the status recognised by society and is well respected.

Another myth in Japan concerns the status of women. When we view the Tokyo televisions, we often come across stories of husbands beating up their wives like they beat animals. The stories give the impression that Japan is a society of male chauvinists and that women do not matter in their social structure. When we are invited to dinners or receptions, invariably the wives of guests are not included. Women are supposed to look after the homes. When we invite Japanese guests, their wives will only attend when we insist that they attend. This gives the impression that women are inferior to men in the Japanese society. This is a myth. In actual fact, all women in Japan hold the purse of their husbands. They are the Finance Ministers at home. Nearly all Japanese husbands hand their monthly salary to their wives and ask for their pocket money every morning or once a week or month from their wives when they go for work. The wife take care of everything at home: rent for the home, public utility charges, money for children's education, food and everything connected with the running of the household. The husband is free from such burdens and can concentrate on his work. This system has been coined "Kaka Tenka"(the world of the women). The "Kaka Tenka" is a system which fits in with the division of labour and has a stabilising effect on society, for the wives do not have to worry that their husbands would fool around outside their homes.

When I meet my Japanese friends, I often ask the question "Do you give all your salary to your wife?" Invariably, the answer is "Yes". Even chairmen and presidents of multi-nationals say "Yes" when I ask that question. But, the husbands have a common secret: they do not hand over their bonuses or whatever money they earn beyond their salaries.

Another myth is that civil servants would be stranded when they leave their jobs. This is not the case in Japan which has a well-known system of "Amakudari" (descend from heaven). When they are vice-ministers in a ministry, they do favours for certain multi-nationals connected with their work and do not ask for favours in return. When they retire these multi-nationals would invite them to sit in the board of directors or make them advisors with a 'fat' pay. This is considered as jobs fallen from heaven.

The Japanese always return a favour when someone gives them one. To them, this is tradition and not bribery.

Wealth Disappears After Three Generations

In Japan, it is difficult to distinguish between the rich and the poor. In the streets of Tokyo, almost everyone wears a suit. It is very hard to know whether they are rich or poor.

There are few who inherited wealth from their parents. They are rich and powerful, but they do not throw their weight around and do not show off. Thus the difference between the rich and poor are not so glaring. Such rich people usually live inconspicuously and thus do not create envy in the eyes of the poor.

In many cases, those who have inherited immense wealth from their forefathers lose them after three generations. The inheritance tax in Japan is very heavy — it goes up to something like 80 to 85 percent. When someone dies, the government would take away 80 to 85 percent of his wealth in terms of inheritance tax.

I had a friend who was a professor. All his life he had worked in the University and did not care very much for his father's wealth. His father owns a multi-storey building in Ginza — the golden shoe of Japan with the highest land price. When his father died, he inherited the building and the government asked him to pay a huge size of inheritance tax. He just could not do it and he commited suicide by jumping off from the highest floor of his building.

In Chinese families, wealth normally disappears after three generations because their descendants squander away the wealth in a life of luxury. In the case of Japan, the government is the beneficiary of such wealth.

Japan's is one of the rich countries which distributes wealth fairly equally.

Rich Country But Poor People

Although there is a fair distribution of wealth, the rich are in the small minority. The country is rich, an economic giant which is buying up the best parts of America and elsewhere. But the lifestyle of the average Japanese is not an enviable one. An average worker leaves his home early in the morning in a packed train or shinskansen after a rushed breakfast. Some of them had to be literally pushed into the trains by specially hired students who do the job of pushing people into the trains. Being a workaholic he returns home late at night. If he returns home too early, he might surprise his wife who may ask him:"Why so early? Have you been sacked?" or "Have you become a madogiwazoku?" The wives of most Japanese are fearful that their husbands would come home early. They are afraid to lost face if their neighbours think that their husbands are useless at their places of work. So, when a Japanese finishes his work early, he would frequent the bars, or play mahjong at the inumerable mahjong shops in Tokyo or play "pachinko". Pachinko is a unique form of entertainment. It is a pinball machine with ball bearings flashing past the eyes at a rate of more than one a second. It is a form of gamble and when he wins, he gets a prize which can be exchanged for money unofficially.

The average salarymen experience very little family life and have not much time for exercises, not to mention to develop his other latent talents such as music, painting or writing.

Even after a lifetime of work, he could hardly save enough money to buy a humble flat. The company provides him with lodging when he is a bachelor, but when he gets married he has to move out and is expected to look after his own housing. As land prices soar, there is no hope of a salaryman owning a flat, not to mention a house which may be two hours away from Tokyo. The average living quarters in Japan is far below the desired standard. To purchase this type of inferior Japanese house, the average Japanese family must spend 6.3 times their annual income, while the average America or European family can acquire a better house at a price about three times their annual income. That is why Westerners refer to the quarters the Japanese live in as "rabbit hutches".

The Japanese Government is not responsible for the housing of her people. It is the companies that look after the housing problem.

In 1983, only 57.9 percent of Japanese houses had flush toilets, compared to 98 percent of American homes, 98.9 percent of British homes and 79.1 percent of Italian residences who had already installed flush toilets in early 1970s.

I once met the advisor of Ajinomoto, a 70-year-old Japanese

who has climbed to the top position of the company and who loves antiques. He was introduced to me by a famous Chinese painter "Fan Zhen". One day, Fan Zhen suddenly asked me whether I would like to visit the home of this Japanese gentleman to see his collection of antique paintings and calligraphy. Of course I was interested, for it is a rare occasion for a foreigner to visit the homes of Japanese. The Japanese advisor was taken by surprise when Fan Zhen told him that I was interested to visit his home. He hesitated for a while before agreeing. But, late at night, I received a telephone call from his secretary informing me that the advisor was not ready to receive me because I was an Ambassador. He thought that his house was too small to invite an Ambassador. His secretary said the antique calligraphy could be specially arranged to be brought to my embassy for my appreciation.

The next day, the advisor brought his most precious antique calligraphy to the embassy for me to view. I took an calligraphy expert who was employed by the Beijing Museum of Forbidden City for ten years to view the calligraphy. My expert friend told him blantly that his antique calligraphy were imitations and he was down-hearted. He never invited me again to see his other collections since then.

This incident struck me that most Japanese must be living in poor condition. If the advisor of a respectable company would not dare invite me to his house, then one can imagine the miserable condition of the ordinary salarymen.

In my four years in Japan, I had only twice been invited to Japanese homes. The first was the holiday resort of the late Takahashi, owner of Japan's biggest ball bearing company, a multi-millionaire who runs a company in Singapore and another in Thailand. He owns a villa in Karuisawa, the famous holiday resort for rich people in the mountains. He took my family in a helicopter to his home and we stayed for one night. It was easily the grandest villa in Japan. He used to invite Prime Minister Nakasone to stay in the resort. Takahashi, unfortunately passed away because of illness at the age of 60.

Another invitation came from the president of Kajima, Japan's biggest construction company with investments throughout the world. It was Kajima which built the Singapore Embassy. It was customary for Kajima to arrange for an Asean golf game with

Asean Ambassadors and after the game to dine in his luxurious home near our Embassy in Ronponggi.

An official of the Gaimusho who was stationed in Singapore when I was the Minister of State for Foreign Affairs was a close friend of mine. He asked me for a painting and I gave him one. He promised to take me to his home to view the painting, but till the time I left Tokyo, he had not kept his promise. Probably he thought his house was too small and shy away from keeping his promise.

I have visited the homes of many Chinese artists from China and they were really miserable.

The high food prices in Japan are exorbitant despite the high appreciation of the yen. You can buy Thai rice or American rice ten times cheaper than Japanese rice. However you still have to buy Japanese rice because Thai rice and American rice are not available in Japan. There are of course cheaper places to eat and the salarymen often frequent such places.

Comparing the areas of parks in major capital cities, Tokyo's lack of green space is astonishing. It had 2.1 square meters per one citizen in 1984, while Paris had 12.3 and Bonn 37.4 in the same year. London had square meters in 1976, Washington D.C. had 45.7 in the same year.

Living in Tokyo for sometime gives one a crammed feeling. The air in the morning is not that clean because of pollution. I really pity youngsters because of the lack of recreation centres and entertainment facilities. As there are no community centres like those in Singapore where residents can go for their recreation, educational training and entertainment, the Japanese youngsters in Tokyo have only one place of outlet — the Harazuku, a place closed to traffic on Sundays. Youngsters of all types gather there to express their feelings. They play guitar, dance or do all sorts of games just to let off 'steam'.

To play tennis or swim in Tokyo would cost a lot of money beyond the reach of the average Japanese youngsters.

Generally speaking, the quality of life of the average Japanese is inferior to that of Singaporeans in terms of housing, recreation and entertainment facilities. They may get a higher salary and their GNP may be higher, but life in Japan especially in Tokyo is not that rosy.

Pachinko and Entertainment

As a result of the lack of entertainment facilities, most Japanese spend their leisure hours on Pachinko. I have yet to meet anyone in Japan who had not played pachinko. I did not ask the Emperor whether he had played the game, but I suppose he could be the only person in Japan who had not played pachinko.

In Tokyo and in every city of Japan, you would not miss a pachinko parlor. Such parlors are always crammed with devotees who sit there for hours watching ball bearings flash past their eyes. Pachinko parlors are filled with dirty smoke for Japanese are not only habitual pachinko devotees but seasoned smokers. A Tokyo University professor who is a Shakespeare expert once said "If Shakepeare was alive in Japan today, I am sure he would love pachinko."

"Pachinko is life as well as drama, sometimes tragedy and sometimes comedy. That is what Shakespeare is all about".

The game is also big business and parlor owners make hugh sums of money — the equivalent of 3 percent of Japan's total gross national product is spent on pachinko. Grateful owners reciprocate by awarding selected players the pachinko culture award.

One year the winners included the leader of the Japan Socialist Party, Takako Doi, an enthusiastic player.

This is how the game is played. A player first buys a box of ball bearings and feeds them into the machine (the name pachinko is said to have been derived from the sound of the balls ricocheting about). The aim is to direct the stream of balls through a maze of nails into selected slots. The machine disgorges a load of ball bearings into the successful player's tray and these can be exchanged for a variety of prizes. The open secret is that players can choose cash as well, even though the law bans pachinko gambling for money. A band of professionals even manage to make a living off the game.

"Most people come here because they want to get their money back,''said a pro who also runs a pachinko school in Tokyo. "I think more than 80 percent of the players are losing money."

The number of machines in Japan has almost doubled since 1981 to well over 3 million and the gross income of the 14,000 garish, neon-clad pachinko parlor last year came to 10 trillion yen or about US$75 billion. Most pachinko parlors are owned by

Koreans or Chinese. According to a US magazine, the richest man in Japan is a pachinko owner.

Out of curiosity, I once visited a Pachinko parlor and betted one thousand yen. I lost it in no time.

Pachinko first appeared in Japan before World War II and in the last decade or so the game has become an important source of tax revenue for the government.

Apart from playing pachinko, Japanese like to frequent bars. They have their favourite bars. After dinner, they always end up in bars, from one bar to another. The richer ones visit nightclubs with floorshows of nudist performances. In Shinjuku, there are places of sex shows where the spectators are invited to perform if they wish.

Geisha houses are meant for the really rich. Such entertainment has somehow lost its flavour as less and less modern girls want to be Geisha girls. Japanese businessmen and politicians like to forget themselves in front of geisha girls because these girls can entertain them with soothing conversations and can sing and dance. They can confide in geisha girls who are trained to keep secret. Since one Geisha girl had exposed Prime Minister Ono, the reputation of geisha girls have declined.

The Japanese are very fond of playing mahjong and there are hundreds of mahjong shops for them to choose. They often play mahjong in specific shops. It is common for businessmen to play mahjong with government officials or politicians. Invariably, the businessmen would lose. This is a nice way to grease the palm. In Japan, they have invented a mahjong table which could automatically arrange the mahjong pieces without reshufling. The Japanese have a slightly different way of playing mahjong. They do not carry flowers like the Chinese mahjong.

Golf is a favourite game for well-to-do Japanese. It is very expensive to play golf in Japan. In Tokyo, one has to travel one or two hours by car to the golf club, play for four hours and return in three hours because of heavy traffic. This would mean putting aside the whole day for golf. To join a golf club would be beyond the means of average salarymen. The most respectable golf club, the Kogane, has a membership fee over $2 million (Singapore dollars). Therefore, Japanese are crazy about golf when they are sent abroad because it is so cheap to play golf compared to their home ground.

As Ambassador, particularly when I am a member of the Singapore Island Club, I had the privilege of playing in Tokyo's most prestigious golf clubs because they have reciprocal arrangements with SICC. But, in Tokyo, even if you become a member, you still have to pay green fees for playing, except that green fees for members are lower.

Japan's Power Elite

Who rules Japan? Who has the power to decide for the nation and control the destiny of the 100 million Japanese? I ask this question when I sat foot in Japan just as when I sat foot in Indonesia. In Indonesia, I discovered that President Suharto was the strongest figure, surrounded by a number of generals and civilian advisers who controlled the destiny of the nation. In Japan, I could not find my answer because power is defused. Japan is controlled by a power elite — the politicians, the bureaucrats and the businessmen — who decide on policies and determine the course of actions for Japan and its fate. No single section of the power elite can decide on policies of the nation without consulting the other sections. That is why Japanese decision takes a long time to materialise. In Japan this consultation is called "nemasasi". Everything in Japan is decided by "nemasasi" — a sort of concensus which must reached before a final decision is reached.

An intriguing characteristic of the relationship among the three groups constituting Japan's power elite is that: 1) Politicians are more powerful than bureaucrats 2) Bureaucrats are more powerful than businessmen, but 3) Businessmen are more powerful than politicians because the ruling party needs their financial support. The three groups form an endless circle within the decision-making process.

The politicians who control the government budget has an upperhand over the bureaucrats and can decide what funds to spend for their constituencies. When Tanaka was Finance Minister, he made the treasury spend a large sum of money to build a sinkansan to his constituency in Niigata which became a white elephant.

Bureaucrats however, can create problems for politicians by delaying action and sticking to rules. The bureaucrats in Japan often say that they are the masters of the soil for politicians can come and go but they will stay. They have control over the businessmen because they have to depend on their guidances in business projects and policies.

The businessmen always think they are "king makers" because they provide the political funds to ministers and their political party.

The power elite in Japan has one thing in common and that is to protect Japan's interest. Japan is able to recover so quickly from the World War II defeat into an economically strong nation because the best brains of the country emerge as the power elite in the three groups.

If this balance of power continues in Japan, all is well. The danger is that if the neo-nationalist rightwing which aspires to make Japan a major political and economic power should take over control of the country, then nobody can guarantee that history would not repeat itself especially when Japan has already become the strongest military power in Asia. There are indications by some rightwing ministers like Fujio, the former Minister of Education who felt that the Japanese had the right to write their history books according to what they think is correct and based on historical facts.

Young Japanese today do not know what actually happen in the Second World War. Japanese textbooks do not tell them the truth that Japanese had committed atrocities. As they grow up, they may feel so arrogant that they are a superior race in Asia and may think they have the right to rule more inferior people. When one does not learn the mistakes of history, one may be tempted to repeat the same mistakes.

Epilogue

It has been nine years since I terminated my service as an Ambassador, and fifteen years since I first became an Ambassador. Many things have happened since then. Most of the leaders I have met in the host countries I was accredited to have passed away. The list includes Nasser, the former President of the United Arab Republic, the 'Lion' of the Arab World who died when he was 52. He was too young to die. Ayub Khan, former President of Pakistan, also died a few years after I had presented credentials to him in 1968. He never expected that his country would be split into two — Pakistan and Bangladesh. Haile Selassie, the 'Conquering Lion of Judah', 'the King of Kings' and 'the Elect of God', was deposed by a group of pro-Communist young blood. He was 83. Nobody would believe that this only monarch in the world wielding absolute power over his rich empire of Ethiopia for 54 years would die a miserable death in a humble three-room mud hut in an army barrack. Then again, Tito, the great military hero of Yugoslavia, the leader of the non-aligned movement, died peacefully in Ljubljana when he was 88. Never did he envisage that after his death, Yugoslavia — his dream land could turn into a living hell.

I do not know what has become of the former President Charles Helou of Lebanon, who promised to come to Singapore whether as President or as a private citizen. I have great sympathy for his country which was once a heaven but is now hell. I remember the beautiful days I spent in Hotel Phoenecia, easily the most elegant and ultra-modern hotel in the Middle East. It is now in ruins and peace is still a long way off in Beirut.

I arrived at Jakarta just in time to witness the death of Sukarno, who had ruled Indonesia for 17 years with words and slogans. I spent 4½ years in Indonesia, seeing quite a bit of the Suharto regime.

All that has happened has become history. It is often said that one must write history from a distance. Nine years is a distance long enough to reflect on what one has done.

It is easier to write the history of those leaders who have passed away, particularly when the situations in the countries concerned have changed. But it is most difficult to write the history of those who are still alive, particularly those who are still in power.

I have tried my very best to be impartial when I write about the leaders, dead or alive.

Having been an Ambassador of a small country, I had the advantage of having the acquaintance of many leaders at one time. Between June 1968 and June 1970, I was Ambassador and High Commissioner for five countries — Egypt, Pakistan, Yugoslavia, Ethiopia and Lebanon — all at the same time. I had an office in Cairo with only three on my staff and operated from there. It was a big diplomatic empire stretching across two continents and three oceans. I had no office in any of the other countries and had to stay in hotels when I was out of Cairo. I met different leaders and different peoples, heard different languages and saw different beliefs and customs and experienced different political systems at work. It really enriched my knowledge and experience.

A few names are still stuck in my mind. My good friend in Cairo, the Indian Ambassador Apa Pant, the Yogi and philosopher, has retired in Poona, still healthy and strong because of his Yoga exercises. The Cambodian colleague in Cairo, Sarin Chlak, whom I met again in Dar-es-Salam for the non-aligned meeting, became, for a short while, the exiled Foreign Minister of Prince Sihanouk. When he returned to Cambodia after the Khmer Rouge took over Cambodia, he mysteriously disappeared. Nobody knows whether he is dead or alive. My good friend, the former Chief of Asian Desk, Ramzy, has retired from diplomatic service and is living quietly in Cairo.

The many Indonesian personalities I have mentioned in this book — the former Vice-Presidents, Ministers and Generals — those in power and those who are not in power are still old friends of mine. I will never forget the help and assistance they gave me during my stay in Indonesia.

After ten years of absence from the diplomatic circle, I returned to the field as Ambassador to Japan and Korea (1984–1988) and retired in July 1988. A great deal of changes have taken place in both countries.

I saw two Prime Ministers — Nakasome and Takashita and three foreign ministers — Shintaro Abe, Kuranari and Uno. They have all been helpful to me. I saw the ups and down of Japanese politicians. My assignment gave me an opportunity to study the Japanese political system and Japanese power play.

Emperor Hirohito whom I met on several occasions have passed away. The fact that no single Japanese had committed Lara-kini signifies the end of the samurai spirit. How long will Japan's prosperity last without the samurai spirit?

I enjoyed my stay in Japan because she is a technologically advanced and well organised country and have good relations with Singapore. Unlike my assignments in Cairo and Jakarta where I had special tasks to fulfil, my post to Japan was more easy-going. It was a pleasant assignment with enriching experiences. Culturally and in terms of productivity, there is a lot that Singapore can learn from Japan. Similarly, I think the Japanese can also learn a lot from Singapore in the system of political campaigning and in the way of cleaner politics.

In Korea, a lot of changes have also taken place. When I presented credentials to President Chun Do-Hwa, least did I foresee that he would be forced to step down in disgrace and exiled himself to a lonely mountain. His successor Roh Tae-Woo, another military man was luckier when he managed to hand over power peacefully to a non-military civilian leader Kim Yaung-San, who is now the President. Kim is the first non-military leader to reside in the Blue House and I hear he is gaining popular support because of his anti-corruption campaign and his determination to clean up the government and to enforce clean politics.

Can the Kim Yaung-San regime change the altitude of the Korean students who have been traditionally anti-bureaucratic? Only time will tell.

Index